Hybridizing Mission

American Society of Missiology
Monograph Series

Chair of Series Editorial Committee, James R. Krabill

The ASM Monograph Series provides a forum for publishing quality dissertations and studies in the field of missiology. Collaborating with Pickwick Publications—a division of Wipf and Stock Publishers of Eugene, Oregon—the American Society of Missiology selects high quality dissertations and other monographic studies that offer research materials in mission studies for scholars, mission and church leaders, and the academic community at large. The ASM seeks scholarly work for publication in the series that throws light on issues confronting Christian world mission in its cultural, social, historical, biblical, and theological dimensions.

Missiology is an academic field that brings together scholars whose professional training ranges from doctoral-level preparation in areas such as Scripture, history and sociology of religions, anthropology, theology, international relations, interreligious interchange, mission history, inculturation, and church law. The American Society of Missiology, which sponsors this series, is an ecumenical body drawing members from Independent and Ecumenical Protestant, Catholic, Orthodox, and other traditions. Members of the ASM are united by their commitment to reflect on and do scholarly work relating to both mission history and the present-day mission of the church. The ASM Monograph Series aims to publish works of exceptional merit on specialized topics, with particular attention given to work by younger scholars, the dissemination and publication of which is difficult under the economic pressures of standard publishing models.

Persons seeking information about the ASM or the guidelines for having their dissertations considered for publication in the ASM Monograph Series should consult the Society's website—www.asmweb.org.

Members of the ASM Monograph Committee who approved this book are:

Roger Schroeder, Professor of Intercultural Studies and Ministry, Catholic Theological Union

Sue Russell, Professor of Mission and Contextual Studies, Asbury Theological Seminary

RECENTLY PUBLISHED IN THE ASM MONOGRAPH SERIES

Yohan Hong, *A Theological Understanding of Power for Poverty Alleviation in the Philippines: With Special Reference to US-Based Filipino Protestants in Texas*

Jinna Sil Lo Jin, *Ignored: A Practical Theology Inquiry of Korean-Speaking Young Adults in a Transnational Congregational Context*

"As Asian, African, and South American churches send more missionaries into the world, the cultural landscape for missionaries becomes more complex and the challenge of negotiating cultural differences more multilayered. Lee has conducted a careful ethnographic research project to explore the challenges and tensions within multicultural mission teams in a limited-access country. . . . There is much to learn here, and much work yet to do before multicultural mission teams are as effective as Christian missionaries should be."

—Michael A. Rynkiewich, Asbury Theological Seminary, retired

"Peter T. Lee challenges outmoded anthropological concepts ingrained in mission-agency thinking and underlying much missionary training. *Hybridizing Mission* reminds us that 'people are not "something" or "someone" to be scrutinized,' helping us move beyond current fashions of 'shallow multiculturalism or an increasingly ethnicized hybridism.' Important reading as we consider the complex mixtures of ideas and settings global messengers of Jesus face."

—David Greenlee, Operation Mobilization

"Peter Lee ingeniously weaves the theory of cultural hybridization into the narratives of the missionaries' lived experiences in the field among the local people and with their multicultural teams. Lee also provided an exceptional literature review from leading scholars on cultural hybridity that will help readers further understand the concept. This is a must-read for missiologists and missionaries as globalization accelerates cultural mixing. Cultural hybridity is among us and within us."

—Juliet Lee Uytanlet, Asia Graduate School of Theology

"As mission becomes increasingly multinational and intercultural, Christian workers from around the world mix with each other as well as the people in the ministry context, and the complexities multiply. Drawing on current global trending, Peter Lee uses data from North Africa to develop the concept of 'diasporic habitus' to highlight the impact of complex social contexts which create hybridizing experiences. Such blending energizes all who occupy the missional space. I affirm this conceptualization."

—R. Daniel Shaw, Fuller Graduate School of Mission & Theology

"In a world of rapid globalization, cultural hybridization, and internationalization of mission teams, fresh approaches are needed to understand the dynamics of cross-cultural kingdom work. In exemplary manner, Peter Lee's work does just that, demonstrating how new models can be applied in examining intercultural social processes and personal changes experienced by international Christian workers."

—Craig Ott, Trinity Evangelical Divinity School

"In *Hybridizing Mission*, Peter Lee brings his hybridized self to scrutinize and apply a cultural-hybridity lens to multicultural ministry teams in a third space of a North African country. He breaks fresh ground and develops new insights that are highly pertinent for the emerging realities of polycentric diasporic Christianity of the twenty-first century. A timely and substantial contribution to global missiology."

—Sam George, Wheaton College

"Hybridizing Mission brings deep sensitivity and a disciplined eye to the nuanced and complex textures of the human beings engaged in mission in a particular North African context. Pushing beyond our facile reliance on essentialism to understand difference, Lee significantly advances hybridity theory in this well-researched volume on the complex interactions of a multicultural mission team in a Muslim context."

—Hunter Farrell, Pittsburgh Theological Seminary

Hybridizing Mission

Intercultural Social Dynamics among Christian Workers
on Multicultural Teams in North Africa

PETER T. LEE

FOREWORD BY
TITE TIÉNOU

American Society of Missiology Scholarly Monograph Series 60

☙PICKWICK *Publications* · Eugene, Oregon

HYBRIDIZING MISSION
Intercultural Social Dynamics among Christian Workers
on Multicultural Teams in North Africa

American Society of Missiology Scholarly Monograph Series 60

Pickwick Publications
An Imprint of Wipf and Stock Publishers
199 W. 8th Ave., Suite 3
Eugene, OR 97401

www.wipfandstock.com

PAPERBACK ISBN: 978-1-6667-3774-5
HARDCOVER ISBN: 978-1-6667-9752-7
EBOOK ISBN: 978-1-6667-9753-4

Cataloguing-in-Publication data:

Names: Lee, Peter T., author. | Tiénou, Tite, foreword.

Title: Hybridizing Mission : Intercultural Social Dynamics among Christian Workers on Multicultural Teams in North Africa / by Peter T. Lee ; foreword by Tite Tiénou.

Description: Eugene, OR: Pickwick Publications, 2022 | American Society of Missiology Scholarly Monograph Series 60 | Includes bibliographical references and index.

Identifiers: ISBN 978-1-6667-3774-5 (paperback) | ISBN 978-1-6667-9752-7 (hardcover) | ISBN 978-1-6667-9753-4 (ebook)

Subjects: LCSH: Missions—Anthropological aspects. | Intercultural communication—Religious aspects—Christianity. | Multiculturalism.

Classification: BV2063 L44 2022 (print) | LCC BV2063 (ebook)

09/26/22

To Ji Hye "Elena" Lee

Contents

List of Figures and Tables

FIGURES

TABLES

Foreword

THE STUDY AND PRACTICE of Christian mission necessarily touch on all dimensions of human life. Since humans have always existed as culturally rooted beings, one of the perennial issues requiring the ongoing attention of mission scholars and practitioners is the cultural dimension of human life. In the contemporary world, Christians engaged in God's work must attend to the issue of culture with awareness of the current realities of people's lived experiences. Around the world numerous individuals experience lives of cultural fluidity and complexity. Consider, for example, the case of Abdulrazak Gurnah, the 2021 winner of the Nobel Prize for Literature. A 1968 immigrant to the United Kingdom, born in 1948 in Zanzibar before Zanzibar joined independent Tanganyika in 1964 to form the United Republic of Tanzania, is Gurnah Zanzibari, Tanzanian, African, English or British? Not surprisingly, the Nobel Prize winner recoils from being identified by any of these qualifiers. As you read *Hybridizing Mission: Intercultural Social Dynamics among Christian Workers on Multicultural Teams in North Africa,* you will notice similarities in disposition between Peter Lee and Abdularazak Gurnah. In light of their own lived experiences, Lee and Gurnah want their readers to move beyond the misunderstandings resulting from the potential stereotyping of individuals based on their ethnic, national or cultural identifications. Lee and Gurnah provide these readers with approaches for understanding a culturally diversified world.

Readers of *Hybridizing Mission* will detect in the text, here and there, the author's dissatisfaction with the lack of attention to the lived experiences of contemporary international Christian workers and his frustration with the oversimplified framework of what he refers to as "an essentialized view of cultures." So, in this work, taking "cultural diversity and intercultural contacts" as givens, Lee seeks "to understand the nature of intercultural social processes and their influence" on Christian workers by using the "conceptual framework" of "cultural hybridization theories." His

exploration focuses on the empirical reality of complex sociocultural processes in specific lived experiences of Christian workers. This is the reason
he wants the readers to know that "[t]he conceptual focus of this study is
on dynamic sociocultural processes of *hybridization* rather than on a static
notion implicit in the noun form *hybridity*." Lee's choice of hybridization
as a concept that helps address the ongoing processes of today's complex
cultural phenomena engages the ambiguous and opaque idea of hybridity
without all the entanglements of the scholarly debates pertaining to it. Indeed, many people feel and know the effects of cultural hybridization before
they have a vocabulary for it. Understood as a process, hybridity should
cause us to pay more attention to the reality and complexity of cultures, especially in a "world . . . haunted by the spectre of difference vanishing" with
"fears that everything will become uniform."[1] Regardless of one's opinion
concerning fears of cultural homogeneity, human cultural differences do
not disappear; they are reconfigured, and they thrive through what Jean-
Loup Amselle calls processes of "branchements" or "connections."[2] These
processes occur in the everyday life of individuals.

Lee offers hybridity and hybridization as useful concepts for students
and practitioners of Christian mission to attend to the rich and complex
lived experiences of people. Agreeing with scholars who contend that
"complex cultural phenomena, such as cultural hybridity, must be studied
in context and at multiple levels," in this work, Lee devotes his attention to
an empirical analysis of the intercultural experiences in the everyday life of
a particular group of international Christian workers. The author indicates
that he conducted this inquiry by availing himself of the "analytical and interpretive potential of cultural hybridity concept for missiological research."
He submits that one characteristic of the contributions of his work lies in it
"pioneer[ing] using cultural hybridization theories in missiological research
by adopting them in its conceptual framework and experimenting with
them in an empirical study to understand complex sociocultural processes."
In making this assertion, Lee does not claim to have produced the first
missiological work taking on board the notion of hybridity. He does note
the existence of a "growing number of missiologists [who] express interest in the hybridity concept as a tool to study phenomena of globalization,
migration and diaspora communities." But, based on his assessment of the
literature, he contends that "for the most part, missiology has only recently
begun to engage the concept of cultural hybridity" and that "current missiological discourses are not well informed about recent scholarly discussions

1. Bayart, *Illusion of Cultural Identity*, 6.
2. Amselle, *Branchements*.

on cultural hybridity." Readers need not agree with Lee's evaluation of the state of missiological engagement with issues related to hybridity in order to gain insights from this work, a ground-breaking contribution to mission research and practice.

Readers will find an aspect of this contribution in chapter seven, a chapter where Lee builds on the work of Ien Ang, David Parker, Stuart Hall and Pierre Bourdieu to advance "diasporic habitus as a notion that explains the lived realities of [the] international Christian workers." *Diasporic habitus*, as Lee defines it, is "a system of internalized dispositions and schemes acquired by those who live *meaningfully* in a country or culture different from their own." This "system of internalized dispositions" shapes the everyday complex social and cultural realities of all individuals living with hybridization. Lee's idea of diasporic habitus provides scholars and practitioners of Christian mission with a conceptual framework for restoring and understanding the richness and depth of the lived experiences of people.

Hybridizing Mission exhibits the type of mission scholarship envisioned in this remark made by Andrew Walls: "Research to be of practical value must be thorough."[3] This thorough work deserves your careful attention.

Tite Tiénou

Research Professor, Theology of Mission and Dean Emeritus
Trinity Evangelical Divinity School, Deerfield, Illinois

References

Amselle, Jean-Loup. *Branchements: Anthropologie de l'universalité des cultures.* Paris: Flammarion, 2001.

Bayart, Jean-François. *The Illusion of Cultural Identity.* Translated by Steven Rendall, Janet Roitman et al. Chicago: University Of Chicago Press, 2005.

Walls, A. F. "Some Recent Literature on Missionary Studies." *Evangelical Quarterly* 42 (1970) 213–29.

---

3. Walls, "Some Recent Literature on Missionary Studies," 223.

Acknowledgments

As I COMPLETE THIS work, I look back to about a decade ago when this journey began. I was staying at a guesthouse in a rural area in Southern Europe to spend some time with God in solitude. As I reflected upon my life and confronted my fears about my future, I heard a still, small voice from God nudging me to trust him and pursue further missiological training. I felt assured that he'd never leave me alone on this journey. This book is evidence of his faithfulness. He sent wonderful people who provided me with timely words of wisdom, affirmation, and practical help. I regret that I can only mention some of them here. I'm eternally grateful to all these friends who left an imprint on my life during this decade-long pursuit.

First, I want to thank Tite Tiénou for walking with me throughout this journey. He was empathetic and identified with me immediately. His wisdom, so liberally dispensed, sustained me throughout my studies, especially at those crucial junctures. When I was submerged and drowning in self-doubts, he helped me come up to the surface and breathe again by reminding me why I *must* do this study. He personifies the best kind of *diasporic habitus* to inhabit as a Christian leader. My use of the term owes to his penetrating insight on the topic.

I'm also grateful to Michael Rynkiewich. His gracious answers to my questions often calmed my nerves in times of anxiety during my field research and data analysis. From theoretical non-sense to tedious technical details, he entertained all my musings and raised profound questions that took my thinking to another level. I cannot imagine a better conversational partner for this study than "Dr. Mike."

I thank Craig Ott for having been my steady skipper in the rough waters of doctoral studies. I've benefited greatly by being on the receiving end of his sensitive pastoral care, incisive scholarship, and decisive leadership.

I also want to mention several others who helped me get to this point. Bob Priest challenged me with his dedication to empirical research in missiology. His inspiration lives on in this study. Harold Netland has been an exemplary model of a scholar-teacher. His gentleness, humility, and uncompromising scholarship displayed in his classrooms and my interactions with him continue to gain my utmost respect. Joy K. C. Tong, with her indefatigable spirit as a social researcher, had a profound influence on my approach to field research, especially when things did not seem to go well. She didn't just teach me research methods; she passed on the spirit of a true researcher. Peter Cha has not only been a teacher but a caring big brother to me. His genuine how are you's and listening ears always encourage my heart. Sam George gave his time and wise advice so freely during the early stage of my doctoral research. His invitation to share my thoughts in writing and speaking produced much fruit in my growth as a missiologist.

I am thankful to my research participants and many international Christian workers who helped me in this study. They were far more than my research subjects. They provided many cups of coffee and tea, delicious meals, rides to and from train stations and airports, and comfortable places to rest my weary soul. They allowed me to enter their daily lives, shared their joy and excitement, and trusted me with their hurts and pains. Their lives continually inspired and challenged me throughout this project; their stories often turned my coding sessions into times of thanksgiving, joyful laughter, and tearful intercession. They helped me grow as a Christian worker and a missiological researcher through it all.

I want to thank my colleagues in Operation Mobilization, who taught me about the life lived out in mission, and my fellow PhD students in the Intercultural Studies program at Trinity Evangelical Divinity School, who were my soundboard and support group. I also thank all my ministry partners who believed in me, saw my studies as the continuation of my ministry in North Africa, and offered their unwavering support.

My father, Elder Young Hui Lee, who recently entered his eternal rest, and my mother, Reverend Soo Hoon Lee, have been the best parents an "ICW" son could ever have. Where would I be today without their prayers and unchanging love and support? My three children, Joshua, Michael, and Kristin, have brought and continue to bring so much delight into my life. It would be an understatement to say that I am grateful to my wife, Ji Hye. She not only "gets" me but accepts me as I am and continues to pour her love unconditionally upon me. She is "Elena," my bright, shining light. Without her sacrifice and support, I could not have done this work.

I give all glory, honor, and praise to Jesus Christ, who is *malik al-muluk* and *rab al-arbab* and yet chose to be with those in the margin. Because of him, even I, formerly a marginalized *neither-nor* immigrant teenager, could have become a *both-and* minister of the gospel who strives to be all things to all people for the sake of his kingdom. May his name be praised in all places throughout all eternity, Amen.

Abbreviations

ICW   International Christian Worker
IMO   International Mission Organization
ISP   Intercultural Social Process
MCT   Multicultural Team
MSA   Modern Standard Arabic
NAC   North African Country (the country of field research site)

1

Introduction

THIS STUDY EXPLORES INTERCULTURAL social dynamics among international Christian workers (ICWs) who work as part of multicultural teams
(MCTs) in a North African country (NAC).[1] It seeks to better understand the
nature of intercultural social processes and their influence on these Christian
workers. Findings from this study would contribute to the theory and practice of intercultural missions. This study is a qualitative inquiry that utilizes
ethnographic methods to gather and analyze data. It incorporates cultural
hybridization theories in its conceptual framework to interpret the research
findings and synthesize those interpretations into coherent concepts. The
field research was conducted in NAC, where religious freedom and religious
diversity among its national population were limited by law. Purposive sampling was used to recruit and select forty-nine participants who were identified as ICWs. The data was collected using in-person interviews, participant
observation, and relevant documents shared by some participants. The rest
of this chapter provides an overview of this research.

BACKGROUND

Christian mission during the last few decades can be characterized by
its increasing global nature and cultural diversity. According to recent
reports, there are more national Christian workers, foreign missionaries,
and international missionary sending agencies today than ever before.

1. In this study, the phrase "international Christian worker" will be used as much as
possible, in place of the traditional term, "missionary" to avoid misunderstandings and
negative connotations associated with the term in the context of North Africa. In fact,
"worker" is the term preferred by most foreign missionaries in North Africa.

These numbers are predicted to grow for next few decades.[2] We witnessed the accelerated globalization of missions during the past half a century. As more workers from younger churches in the Global South joined missionary movements started by older churches in the Global North, many mission organizations, both old and new, grew in the breadth of countries and cultures represented amongst their constituting members. As these organizations served globally, "multicultural teams" (MCTs) became an important practice in carrying out their ministries.

Despite the relevance of multicultural teams in global missions, little is known about experiences within multicultural teams, particularly how one's experience in another culture is affected by living and working closely with culturally diverse people and vice versa. There is a notable lack of empirical research on international Christian workers (ICWs) who serve alongside cultural Other. As they enter and live in a new cultural context, Christian workers' social experiences are influenced by relationships with colleagues from other cultural contexts. Although these lived experiences are missiologically relevant, missiologists have rarely studied them in depth. When we consider the complexity of intercultural life and the potential of international migration for the global missionary movement, current international Christian workers in multicultural teams who hail from many national, cultural, and/or ethnic backgrounds deserve more careful attention from missiologists.[3]

In today's globalizing world, international Christian workers can be seen as a unique kind of migrants with "transnational religious connections."[4] Paul Hiebert recognizes the importance of their role as "transcultural mediators" in rapidly changing societies.[5] ICWs leave their home culture and move to another. While living in a new cultural context, many of them establish new patterns of living. Even as they adapt culturally to the new locale, ICWs maintain strong social ties with their family members, friends, supporters, and churches in their sending country. They are often financially supported by them. They keep up with the latest news and trends back "home." In many cases, they work with virtual teams that are only mobile devices away from instant communication and collaboration, no matter where they are based. As they travel to other countries to visit their supporters, participate in conferences, take vacations, or

2. Zurlo et al., "Christianity 2019," 97; Johnson et al., "Christianity 2018," 25.

3. See Walls, "Mission and Migration"; Walls, *Crossing Cultural Frontiers*; George, "Diaspora"; Wan, *Diaspora Missiology*; Hanciles, "Migration and Mission"; Hanciles, *Beyond Christendom*.

4. Wuthnow and Offutt, "Transnational Religious Connections."

5. Hiebert, "Missionary as Mediator," 301; Hiebert, *Gospel in Human Contexts*, 188.

conduct their mission work, developing a capacity to "snap in and out" of cultures becomes necessary.[6]

In his assessment of American "missionary cosmopolitans" from the past, historian Joseph Hollinger notes that they went to other cultures intending to change people there; they were instead changed by the people they encountered, returning with a different outlook of the world and becoming contributors toward social changes in their home society.[7] What might be involved in these changes that happen to international Christian workers if that is the case? What do these changes do to their way of life? Could these changes be better understood using the lens of cultural hybridization? This research aims to seek answers to these questions.

STATEMENT OF PURPOSE

The purpose of this study is to explore the nature, contributing factors, and outcomes of intercultural social processes in the lived experiences of international Christian workers that work with multicultural teams of international mission organizations (IMOs) in a country in North Africa. This study focuses on how their intercultural social experiences in their multicultural teams and the local context respectively and collectively influence the social and cultural change processes at a micro, individual level.

RESEARCH QUESTIONS

The research questions (RQs) for this study are as follows:

1. How does living in the North African country mediate the intercultural social experiences of international Christian workers who are part of a multicultural team?

2. How does working with a multicultural team mediate their intercultural social experiences?

3. What are the outcomes of their intercultural social experiences in NAC while working with a multicultural team?

The final form of these research questions was not reached until the later stage of this study; these RQs were revised many times throughout the analysis stage in this research. As an exploratory study of an empirically

---

6. A veteran international Christian worker who had served in four very different cultural contexts once described developing her intercultural adjustment skills to me as "snapping in and out of" different cultures. This provides a picture of what is required of today's international Christian workers.

7. Hollinger, *Protestants Abroad*.

little-known phenomenon, this research was undertaken with caution to avoid "answering the wrong question."[8] While the main research concern remained the same throughout, the research questions and methods were further refined as the study progressed.

RESEARCHER REFLEXIVITY

This section briefly describes some of the personal advantages and disadvantages identified and reflected upon by the researcher. Since many of my personal traits and tendencies could either help or impede this study, I had to consider them carefully. As a person well-adapted to both "Western" and "non-Western" social contexts, I naturally tend to function as a bridge person in culturally complex settings. My knowledge of the research population and the research site was certainly an asset to this research. However, my familiarity could also have been a liability as it could have created blind spots and interfered in the analytical process.

Additionally, in studying international Christian workers of MCTs of IMOs other than my own, I might have introduced another bias into the study. I might have glossed over the differences or exaggerated the similarities between the IMOs of my participants and my own IMO, or vice versa. My prior understanding of the local context from my past living experiences in NAC could have also hidden important patterns from my view.

I had immigrated to the US at the age of fourteen and experienced marginalization as a minority person. I tend to be skeptical of the majority group in many social contexts I enter, and I can become suspicious of those who have power and privilege in some situations. I can also be critical of ICWs who lack cultural awareness. As an Asian American who worked in an organization shaped predominantly by a "Western" cultural and historical framework, I have sometimes been misunderstood and unfairly stereotyped based on my ethnicity. Some of these incidents were harmless, whereas others were hurtful. For better or worse, these experiences would have influenced my thinking and motivations for this research.

Court helpfully writes, "Qualitative researchers collect and analyze data through the lens of who they are. Their research journey involves both utilizing and seeing beyond their experiences, knowledge bases and values in order to arrive at understanding of the lives of the research participants."[9] Throughout this project, I tried both to utilize and to see beyond my prior knowledge, continually thinking about my relationships with the participants. I practiced "nearing" and "distancing" myself mentally and

8. Maxwell, *Qualitative Research Design*, 73.

9. Court, *Qualitative Research*, x.

emotionally from them in order to gain a perspective of both an insider and an outsider. Court notes, "Reflexivity is, by definition, two-directional, with cause and effect affecting one another. We could see researcher reflectivity as an essential aspect of research reflexivity. When researchers reflect critically on their work they change the practice of research, which then conducts itself (as it were) differently."[10] The nature of social research may be that the researchers are never the same after the research is completed as they get involved in the lives of the participants. While there is no way around the researcher's personal biases in qualitative research, being aware of these factors allowed me to use caution and discernment in making decisions throughout this project.

During the fieldwork, it became apparent that I already had a large amount of insider knowledge as someone who had lived in NAC and worked with a multicultural team for over a decade as an international Christian worker. I understood, perhaps better than many of the research participants, the dynamics of the NAC local settings, social norms, the local languages, MCTs' functions, and operations of IMOs. I had much prior experience working with both Westerners and non-Westerners and leading an MCT. How did these affect my research? It perhaps gave me an advantage in terms of efficiency in data collection and analysis. I could use my knowledge to skip the obvious and probe less apparent topics in interviews. I could make meanings out of the participant data more quickly. However, it might have made me less sensitive to something new or odd. There was a risk of mistaking the odd for the ordinary. However, it was helpful that I had left NAC and lived in the United States for several years before returning to conduct field research in NAC.

I noticed changes and newness in the field, but I was not a stranger; I was familiar with many local matters. The four years of removal from the setting seemed to have allowed me a more distanced view as an observer, while the ten years of having lived in NAC in the past provided me with a keen understanding of the participants and their experiences. It also helped me gain access to the research population. The researcher reflexivity was something I continually monitored and reflected on during the entire course of the project.

In the end, I conducted this research not as a distant, disinterested observer but as an active participant in the social drama among the ICWs of MCTs. I was not just a researcher to my participants. To some of them, I was a fellow ICW with a track record of leading an MCT in NAC for many years. To others, I was a former colleague with whom they had closely worked.

10. Court, *Qualitative Research*, 11.

Still, to some others, I was a trusted friend. Naturally, my collection, analysis, and interpretation of the data involved active engagement in the participants' lives, not only during the fieldwork but also for months and years before and after the fieldwork through my relationships with them. While my background helped me gain access to people and information, it also created an opening for potential biases. To mitigate this risk, I constantly reminded myself of these potential pitfalls throughout the project. I also devoted enough time during the fieldwork and the analytical process for self-reflection. Writing these down in personal memos and research memos was an important part of practicing researcher reflexivity.

RATIONALE FOR RESEARCH

My research concern was conceived while working with multicultural teams (MCT) of an international mission organization (IMO) in the research location for over a decade. Seeing complicated intercultural issues unfolding in MCTs in NAC without satisfactory answers led me on a pursuit to seek a deeper understanding of foundational issues and empirical phenomena in MCTs. I undertook this study with what some may call an insider-outsider approach.[11] While I was able to utilize my prior knowledge and experience as someone who was part of the research population in the past, I was also able to maintain some analytical distance from the participants as someone who had lived outside NAC for several years at the time of fieldwork.[12]

As previously mentioned, there is a lack of missiological literature addressing complex cultural factors in the lives of ICWs. There are historiographical studies of past missionary figures. Empirical studies of various ethnic and religious groups are published with regularity. Mission practices that are known to be effective are quickly circulated. There are even some studies conducted on children and families of missionaries.[13] The literature on missionary care addresses the emotional and psychological issues in international Christian workers.[14] However, none of these address what adult ICWs experience as they enter, live, and minister in a new cultural context. For some reason, contemporary international Christian workers and their intercultural experiences are seldom studied empirically.

11. See O'Reilly, *Ethnographic Methods*, 98.

12. If someone else had conducted this research a decade ago, I would have been an ideal participant.

13. See Pollock et al., *Third Culture Kids 3rd Edition*; Baker and Priest, *Missionary Family*.

14. O'Donnell, *Global Member Care Vol 1*; O'Donnell, *Doing Member Care Well*; O'Donnell and O'Donnell, *Global Member Care*.

It is odd that contemporary ICWs, who might become the topic of some future historical studies, are not given due attention. This is unfortunate since empirical studies of today's international Christian workers could yield the fruit of understanding how persons who live interculturally are shaped by intercultural social relations. Studies of ICWs could inform missiology by shedding new light on the processes of acculturation, cultural adaptation, transnationalism, and identity negotiations among those persons engaged in intercultural missions.

Additionally, little is known about multicultural ministry teams. There have been several doctoral dissertations during the past decade written on some aspects of multicultural mission teams.[15] There are a few books,[16] articles, and book chapters[17] published on the topic that mainly deal with leadership, management, communication, or working relationships within these teams. While helpful, they do not necessarily address what international Christian workers experience in their intercultural interactions on these teams. Moreover, most of these studies rely on management literature that usually utilizes an essentialized view of cultures, namely, works by Hofstede,[18] Trompenaars,[19] and GLOBE.[20] At best, this line of management thinking on culture is questionable and represents a view no longer supported by most cultural anthropologists. It is also increasingly criticized by scholars within the management field itself for its misrepresentation and over-generalization of culture and problematic cultural constructs called "national dimensions of culture."[21]

15. E.g., Green, "Cultural Theory Training"; Kim, "Perceptions of Working Relationships"; Hong, "Leadership and Followership."

16. E.g., Roembke, *Building Credible Multicultural Teams*; Silzer, *Biblical Multicultural Teams*; Hibbert and Hibbert, *Leading Multicultural Teams*.

17. E.g., Cho and Greenlee, "Avoiding Pitfalls"; Moreau and Snodderly, *Reflecting God's Glory Together*; Hibbert and Hibbert, "Managing Conflict in a Multicultural Team."

18. Hofstede, *Culture's Consequences*; Hofstede et al., *Cultures and Organizations*.

19. Trompenaars and Hampden-Turner, *Riding Waves of Culture*.

20. House et al., *Culture, Leadership, and Organizations*.

21. See Brewer and Venaik, "Globe Practices and Values"; Brewer and Venaik, "Individualism—Collectivism"; Brewer and Venaik, "Misuse of National Dimensions"; Brewer and Venaik, "Ecological Fallacy"; Fellows and Liu, "Use and Misuse of the Concept of Culture"; Hermans and Kempen, "Moving Cultures"; Kuper, *Culture*; McSweeney, "Hofstede's Model of National Cultural Differences and Their Consequences"; McSweeney, "Cultural Diversity within Nations"; McSweeney, "Dynamic Diversity"; McSweeney, "Ecological Mono-Deterministic Fallacy"; McSweeney, "Hall, Hofstede, Huntington, Trompenaars, GLOBE: Common Foundations, Common Flaws"; McSweeney, "Globe, Hofstede, Huntington, Trompenaars: Common Foundations, Common Flaws"; McSweeney et al., "Claiming Too Much, Delivering Too Little"; Messner,

International Christian workers on multicultural teams face unique challenges of cultural adjustments. They work with multinational, multicultural Christian organizations that operate globally and live in changing cultures in their ministry contexts. They maintain social ties with those who sent them from their home country, which also goes through cultural changes. How do social and cultural processes in these three distinct cultural settings—home country, the multicultural team, and NAC—affect the international Christian worker? How do ICWs perceive and interpret these changes? How do they respond to shifts that seem to be happening everywhere, including where they currently live and from where they were sent?

As they go on with their life and ministry, these ICWs in NAC need to negotiate social relations in the local context of NAC and within their multicultural teams. These international Christian workers are living at the intersection of multiple cultural flows. However, the typical discourse on multicultural teams is based on anecdotal understandings, essentialist perspectives of culture, cultural differentiation using suspect models, and somewhat superficial appeals to "unity in diversity." While today's global missionary movement faces challenges in communication, leadership, and teamwork, these are usually issues on the surface. At a deeper level, issues of power, inequality, ethnocentrism, and prejudice can be found. Traces of "Orientalism"[22] and "Occidentalism"[23] flare-up in unexpected places, deepening the divide. Many of these underlying issues are present within microcosms of multicultural teams of international mission organizations today.[24]

Selecting these international Christian workers of MCTs as research subjects may also help me focus on the processual and dynamic sociocultural realities rather than fixed traits of a bounded ethnic group. They can provide data on the realities of mobility and fluidity of religiously motivated transnational migrants rather than a territorialized cultural construct. This may be the kind of research mode needed to study complex cultural flows in globalization, migration, and diaspora, as promoted by scholars such as Arjun Appadurai.[25] "Cultures" or cultural elements are not isolated from

---

"Misconstruction of Hofstede"; Midgley et al., "Diversity and Unity of the Global Mosaic"; Nathan, "Non-Essentialist Model of Culture"; Ortner, *Anthropology and Social Theory*; Shweder, "Moral Maps, 'First World' Conceits, and the New Evangelists"; Touburg, "National Habitus"; Tung and Verbeke, "Beyond Hofstede and GLOBE"; Venaik and Brewer, "Critical Issues in Hofstede"; Venaik and Brewer, "Common Threads"; Venaik and Brewer, "National Culture Dimensions."

22. Said, *Orientalism*.

23. Buruma and Margalit, *Occidentalism*.

24. See Lee, "Toward a Third Space."

25. Appadurai, *Modernity at Large*; Appadurai, "Globalization and Research

lived experiences; they are deeply embedded in the lives of people. Therefore, they can only be explored in everyday events, experiences, emotions,
thoughts, words, behaviors, and social interactions. These can be drawn
from ICWs' personal experiences through interviews and observations of
their interactions with one another.

This study seeks to understand what these Christian workers experience and how culture(s) and people(s) are shaped as they move through
complex intercultural social processes. Insights from this study can help
build healthy communities of Christ among these ICWs and their MCTs
so that they can live out "togetherness-in-difference"[26] as a crucial facet in
this globalizing world.

CONTRIBUTION

This study contributes to filling a knowledge gap in both mission practices
and missiological research. There has not been a study that inquired of
international Christian workers on multicultural teams about their intercultural social processes and how these experiences affect changes in their
perspective and sociality. Moreover, international mission organizations
and their multicultural personnel have been given insufficient attention
in missiology.[27]

Thus, the missiological significance of this study lies in the following
four points. First, it contributes to the discussion of how to approach cultural
diversity in the global missionary movement. Second, it addresses the cultural issues arising out of the mobile and transnational aspects of Christian mission. Third, it pioneers using cultural hybridization theories in missiological
research by adopting them in its conceptual framework and experimenting with them in an empirical study to understand complex sociocultural
processes. Fourth, it explores the analytical and interpretive potential of the
cultural hybridity concept for future missiological research.

DEFINITION OF TERMS USED

The following are the definitions of terms that are used in this book. *International mission organization* (IMO) refers to a large independent,
non-denominational Christian mission agency, organization, or society
with a presence in many countries around the world. It generally carries

Imagination."

26. Ang, "Together-In-Difference."

27. Although, as I have previously mentioned, there are several recent doctoral dissertations that looked at some aspects of multicultural mission teams, much of this field
of study is left underexplored.

out mission work by recruiting, resourcing, and ministering in multiple nations. It would typically have hundreds or even thousands of staff workers with various citizenships around the world.

A *multicultural team (MCT)* loosely refers to a team of international Christian workers composed of members from two or more countries or cultural backgrounds.

Cultural hybridity is a concept that generally refers to "the production of things composed of elements of different or incongruous kind."[28] *Cultural hybridization* is defined as "sociocultural processes in which discrete structures or practices, previously existing in a separate form, are combined to generate new structures, objects, and practices."[29]

North Africa will refer to a generic region in the northwestern part of the African continent and arbitrarily include Morocco, Algeria, and Tunisia. The North African country where the field research was conducted will be referred to as NAC.

While I recognize that the terms "West" and "Western" are problematic for a number of reasons, it is difficult to escape from them. They are deeply embedded in categories and languages in use. The fact that there are no suitable alternatives makes it even harder to abandon these words. Thus, primarily for convenience, I will use "the West" or "Western" (in a quotation mark or without where appropriate) to generally refer to the region, people, cultures, and history linked to "the historically Christian West"[30] and "non-Western" to refer to the rest of the world. While these terms are increasingly becoming awkward to use in academic research, they highlight the fact that the entanglement of such words in people's consciousness is part of this study's broader background.

The term *intercultural social* is used repeatedly throughout this study. Rather than using "cultural and social" or "sociocultural," I chose this phrase to refer to both the intercultural and social aspects of the participants' lived experiences. The intercultural and the social are seen as intricately interwoven in the study.

International Christian worker (ICW) is used throughout this project to refer to the research participants. While these participants are known as Christians in the local communities where they live and work, they are not identified by local people as "missionaries." The participants do not use this term to refer to themselves in their ministry context because this could cause misunderstandings and stereotypes among the local people, who

28. Ang, *On Not Speaking Chinese*, 194.
29. García Canclini, "Introduction: Hybrid Cultures," xxv.
30. Hollinger, *Protestants Abroad*, 1.

often connect missionaries with Western imperialism. Thus, I will refrain from using the term "missionaries" as much as possible and refer to them as international Christian workers or ICWs instead.

ORGANIZATION OF THE BOOK

Many qualitative studies are organized in six chapters, with each chapter corresponding to the following contents—introduction, precedent literature, research methods, findings and analyses, interpretation and synthesis, and conclusion.[31] The first three chapters of this book follow the standard structure of qualitative research writing mentioned above. However, I deviate from the standard format from chapter 4 by presenting findings from data analysis not in a single chapter but by organizing them and developing them into three thematic chapters from chapter 4 through chapter 6. In chapter 7, this work returns to the standard format and provides further analysis, interpretation of findings, and conceptual synthesis of insights uncovered by the study. Chapter 8 will bring the entire work to a proper conclusion.

In this introductory chapter, I have described an overview of this book. I provided the background and context for this study. The research purpose and research questions (RQs) were unambiguously stated. I reflected on the researcher's impact on the research and researcher reflexivity. The rationale for this research emphasized why this research was needed, and potential contributions were mentioned. Also, the terms that were to be repeatedly used throughout this study were defined. In the next chapter, I will provide a critical summary of precedent literature relevant to this study—this literature review aids in developing the conceptual framework for this research. Cultural hybridity and hybridization theories are the focus of this literature review.

---

31. Refer to Bloomberg and Volpe, *Completing Your Qualitative Dissertation*, 2019.

2

Literature Review

THIS CHAPTER IS A critical summary of precedent literature relevant to this research. It examines scholarly works written on the subject of cultural hybridity with special attention given to its theories, development, and significant debates. This review is intended to establish the general conceptual framework and theoretical trajectory of this study. Since there is substantial literature on this topic in multiple academic disciplines, focused attention will be given to major works that fall under the general categories of cultural anthropology, cultural studies, and postcolonial theory. I will begin with the background of the concept of cultural hybridity by reviewing the development of several core concepts of cultural hybridity. I will also go over key terms used by a leading scholar Homi Bhabha and trace the scholarly debates that have unfolded around five major claims against cultural hybridity theories. I will finish this chapter with a brief examination of the current state of cultural hybridity theories, recent empirical research, and the place of cultural hybridity within the field of missiology.

Cultural hybridity has been a prominent topic in humanities and social sciences during the past few decades, especially the 1990s and 2000s. Its discussion has raised questions about cultures, boundaries, and personhood in complex ebbs and flows of what many would call globalization. Since the 1970s, the concept of "culture," which social scientists once took for granted, has undergone a significant reconfiguration. This "reflexive turn" has significantly altered how social researchers conduct ethnographic fieldwork. It has changed research practices in cultural anthropology, and subsequently, other social and human science disciplines.[1] The

---

1. O'Reilly, *Ethnographic Methods.*

notion of cultural hybridity, which is inseparable from the idea of culture, may present a fertile ground for research for missiologists who seek to understand the relationship between Christian mission, cultures, and the notion of "person in mission"[2] amid seemingly volatile and unpredictable consequences of the oft-mentioned trio of globalization, migration, and urbanization phenomena.

DEVELOPMENT OF CULTURAL HYBRIDITY THEORY

The idea of cultural hybridity generally refers to "the production of things composed of elements of different or incongruous kind."[3] This simple description hides its conceptual ambiguity.[4] The notion of hybridity is also controversial; many scholars have heavily contested it in academic discussions.[5] Its portrayal is paradoxical; it is viewed as powerful and subversive while also seen as ordinary and pervasive.[6] Before going any further on discussing the concept, it would be helpful to note its broader background. Three theoretical streams should be considered as the backdrop of the development of cultural hybridity theories.

Conceptual Background

First, recent discussions on cultural hybridity have primarily been produced in the field of colonial discourse analysis, also called postcolonial studies.[7] Leading scholars who are given credit for theorizing cultural hybridity, such as Homi K. Bhabha, Paul Gilroy, and Stuart Hall, are linked to postcolonial studies. Edward Said and Gayatri Chakravorti Spivak, though their works were not usually seen as directly contributing to the theories, made an important contribution by their incisive critique of the continuing Western colonial framework and helped create a theoretically rich ground in which cultural hybridity theories could arise.[8]

2. Rynkiewich, "Person in Mission."

3. Ang, *On Not Speaking Chinese*, 194.

4. Izenberg, *Identity*, 332; Burke, *Cultural Hybridity*, 54; Hutnyk, "Hybridity," 87; Kraidy, *Cultural Logic of Globalization*, 2–3.

5. Kraidy, *Cultural Logic of Globalization*, 2–3.

6. Ang, *On Not Speaking Chinese*, 200; Ang, "Together-In-Difference," 150; Burke, *Cultural Hybridity*, 112; Said, *Culture and Imperialism*, 15; Werbner, "Dialectics of Cultural Hybridity," 1997, 1; Nederveen Pieterse, *Globalization and Culture*, 2015, 123–24.

7. Young, *Colonial Desire*; Axford, *Theories of Globalization*; Kraidy, *Cultural Logic of Globalization*.

8. Young, *Colonial Desire*; Burke, *Cultural Hybridity*; Huddart, *Homi K. Bhabha*; Moore-Gilbert, *Postcolonial Theory*; Werbner and Modood, *Debating Cultural Hybridity*.

Second, it is essential to note that cultural hybridity is deeply intertwined with elements of the French poststructural schools. Bhabha,[9] arguably the most distinguished theorist of cultural hybridity, develops his ideas while frequently citing, interacting with, and building on works by Jacques Derrida,[10] and also to some degree, Michel Foucault.[11] In her now-famous essay, Spivak[12] sharply criticizes Foucault[13] and Deleuze and Guattari[14] for their failure to recognize contradictions in their own works. She suggests that in discussing as complex a topic as colonial history and power relations, it would be naïve to subscribe to a notion that only emphasizes lived experiences of marginalized colonial subjects without sufficiently paying attention to the intellectual framework that shapes the entire historical landscape. Thus Spivak admonishes these theorists for their failure to grasp a Eurocentric colonial framework—in which their scholarship is situated—that silences the marginalized.[15] It leads to her emphatic conclusion: "The subaltern cannot speak."[16]

However, she maintains that Derrida[17] provides a line of thought that may further decolonize the intellectual framework and incorporates Derrida's ideas in her own analysis.[18] Ultimately, her pioneering work provides a backdrop for Bhabha's development of hybridity and mimicry concepts. In Bhabha and others' writings, it is not difficult to notice this kind of poststructuralist proclivity to challenge and de-center dominant discourses that maintain essentialist ideologies.

Thirdly, the emergence of cultural hybridity concepts coincides, perhaps not coincidently, with a significant shift in social and cultural anthropology, which took place during the 1980s through the 1990s. In what is sometimes referred to as "the reflexive turn," social and cultural anthropologists began to question how ethnographic research was conducted and critique how their accounts were written from positioned

9. Bhabha, *Location of Culture*.

10. E.g., Derrida, *Of Grammatology*; Derrida, *Writing and Difference*; Derrida, *Dissemination*.

11. E.g., Foucault, *Order of Things*; Foucault, *Archaeology of Knowledge*; Foucault, *Power/Knowledge*.

12. Spivak, "Can the Subaltern Speak?"

13. E.g., Foucault, *Madness and Civilization*; Foucault, *Language, Counter-Memory, Practice*; Foucault, *Power/Knowledge*.

14. Deleuze and Guattari, *Anti-Oedipus*.

15. Spivak, "Can the Subaltern Speak?," 275.

16. Spivak, "Can the Subaltern Speak?," 308.

17. E.g., Derrida, *Of Grammatology*; Derrida, *Margins of Philosophy*.

18. Spivak, "Can the Subaltern Speak?"

views.[19] Talal Asad was one of the first anthropologists to argue for a need to consider power relations and positionality in field research and analysis.[20] Since then, numerous scholars have written on the reflexive nature of ethnographic accounts and the need for revising the popular notion of culture. As a result, the discipline of anthropology has not been the same ever since. There are many notable works by anthropologists that both reflect and inspire this shifted view.[21] These works point toward a significant transition that occurred in social sciences. It seems that this shift has influenced cultural hybridity theories and vice versa. Many of these anthropologists would likely find among leading scholars of cultural hybridity some of their more eager conversation partners.

Contributions Made by Homi K. Bhabha

Since Homi Bhabha's influence on the notion of cultural hybridity is foundational to subsequent discussions in this study, he would merit a separate, albeit brief, treatment in this section. The prominence of the cultural hybridity concept in academic disciplines in humanities could be traced back to Bhabha's groundbreaking essays.[22] His seminal book, *The Location of Culture,* is perhaps the single most important work on cultural hybridity from postcolonial perspectives.[23] In this compilation of twelve essays, Bhabha develops several key concepts of cultural hybridity: mimicry, ambivalence, liminality, and the Third Space.[24] He proposes that the most important and relevant cultural innovations take place in the liminal space between cultures. Bhabha frequently engages Frantz Fanon, Edward Said, Derrida, and Foucault in presenting his view.

19. O'Reilly, *Ethnographic Methods*, 212–13.

20. Asad, *Anthropology and Colonial Encounter.*

21. E.g., Clifford and Marcus, *Writing Culture*; Clifford, *Predicament of Culture*; Marcus and Fischer, *Anthropology as Cultural Critique*; Marcus, *Ethnography through Thick*; Appadurai, *Modernity at Large*; Fox, *Recapturing Anthropology*; Featherstone, *Undoing Culture*; Hannerz, *Cultural Complexity*; Hannerz, *Transnational Connections*; Kuper, *Culture*; Baumann, *Contesting Culture*; Baumann, *Multicultural Riddle*; Ortner, *Fate of "Culture"*; Ortner, *Anthropology and Social Theory*; Abu-Lughod, "Writing Against Culture"; Gupta and Ferguson, "Beyond 'Culture.'"

22. Burke, *Cultural Hybridity*; Dirlik, "Postcolonial Aura"; Hutnyk, "Hybridity"; Kraidy, "Hybridity in Cultural Globalization"; Kraidy, *Cultural Logic of Globalization*; Papastergiadis, "Tracing Hybridity in Theory"; Werbner, "Dialectics of Cultural Hybridity," 1997; Yúdice, "Translator's Introduction"; Young, *Colonial Desire.*

23. Huddart, *Homi K. Bhabha.*

24. Bhabha, *Location of Culture.*

According to Bhabha, culture's creative powers are not confined within essentialized "cultures" or "nation-states."[25] Instead, they are located, or even thrive, in ambivalent interstitial spaces where cultural hybridity emerges. Bhabha criticizes the past colonialism, its continuing hegemony in the present, and the failure of critical theory to recognize the significance of the ambivalent, in-between positions of colonial subjects and minorities living in Western societies.[26] He observes that colonial subjects' marginalized status activates their "subaltern agency" and thwarts domination by the colonizer.[27]

Despite many criticisms he has received, various academic disciplines recognize Bhabha's contributions to critical theory.[28] He deserves credit for formulating a perspective that calls out the remnants of old colonial essentialist claims still found in social sciences.[29] He conceptualized hybridity as a "counter-hegemonic move,"[30] removing the notion from its nineteenth-century racial concepts and placing it in the modern cultural and political realms.[31] However, Bhabha's most significant contribution might be that he challenged and further expanded Edward Said and Frantz Fanon's vision by focusing not so much on the colonizer[32] or the colonized[33] but articulating the ambivalent relationship between the two.[34] It should be noted that Albert Memmi, a contemporary of Frantz Fanon, also explored the complex relationship between the colonizer and the colonized.[35] While Bhabha builds on Fanon and Said's writing, he curiously omits Memmi in his work on cultural hybridity. As the rest of this literature review will show, Bhabha's enormous influence is evident in the works of other critical scholars.

25. Bhabha, *Location of Culture*.

26. Bhabha, *Location of Culture*.

27. Bhabha, *Location of Culture*, 265.

28. Bhabha's book, *Location of Culture* may be responsible for opening a flood gate of new analyses of culture, society, and politics within critical scholarship. According to Google Scholar, the book has been cited well over 59,000 times in published literature as of August 2021.

29. Papastergiadis, "Tracing Hybridity in Theory," 262.

30. Venn, "Narrating the Postcolonial," 262.

31. Kraidy, "Hybridity in Cultural Globalization," 319.

32. Said, *Orientalism*; *Culture and Imperialism*.

33. Fanon, *Wretched*; Fanon, *Black Skin, White Masks*.

34. Moore-Gilbert, *Postcolonial Theory*, 114–16; Young, *Colonial Desire*, 161.

35. Memmi, *Colonizer and the Colonized*.

KEY IDEAS OF CULTURAL HYBRIDITY

In discussions of cultural hybridity, several important themes emerge. It would be beneficial to investigate them. These are the cultural process of hybridization, problematizing boundaries, and several terms that frequently appear in cultural hybridity discussions. These would help gauge the wide-ranging but interconnected sub-themes linked to cultural hybridity theories.

Cultural Process of Hybridization

While Homi Bhabha presents perhaps the most mature theory of hybridity, it may be Néstor García Canclini who proposes the most convincing analysis of the *cultural process of hybridization*.[36] His seminal text, *Hybrid Cultures: Strategies for Entering and Leaving Modernity*, is a systematic study of cultural hybridization processes and is considered foundational to the field of cultural studies in Latin American contexts.[37] García Canclini defines *hybridization* as "sociocultural processes in which discrete structures or practices, previously existing in a separate form, are combined to generate new structures, objects, and practices."[38] He is quick to qualify "discrete structures" as not indicating any existing pure condition but only prior hybridization. He then admits the immediate difficulty of describing so many different phenomena with a single word. This is why it would be important to look at how scholars describe these sociocultural processes using various terms.

García Canclini argues that the focus in studies of culture should be on dynamic cultural processes of hybridization rather than static notions of hybridity.[39] He contends that in modern societies, politics of nation-building has hidden these on-going cultural processes as governments and politicians invoke "imagined communities"[40] based on shared culture and history.[41] In the more recent context of increasing movement of people, mass media, and free-flowing market capital, once-concealed transnational routes of cultural hybridization are reappearing, making these processes more visible.[42] The goal of studying these processes then, he argues, should be making the world more understandable and thus co-habitable

36. García Canclini, "State of War"; García Canclini, *Consumers and Citizens*; García Canclini, *Hybrid Cultures*; García Canclini, "Introduction: Hybrid Cultures."

37. Kraidy, "Hybridity in Cultural Globalization," 320.

38. García Canclini, "Introduction: Hybrid Cultures," xxv.

39. García Canclini, "State of War," 43.

40. Anderson, *Imagined Communities*.

41. García Canclini, "State of War," 44–45.

42. García Canclini, "State of War," 47.

amid differences.[43] He points out that most cross-cultural theories make quick comparisons and contrasts without carefully considering "the *unequal* ways in which groups appropriate, combine, and transform elements from several societies."[44] In other words, an inadequate understanding of these unequal sociocultural processes, not a lack of awareness of concrete cultural differences, might be the culprit that obscures our view of social realities in the world. He also writes:

> The *descriptive* contribution to the notion of hybridization can acquire *explanatory* power if we situate it within structural relationships of causality or correlation, and it can also operate as a *hermeneutic* resource when it alludes to relationships of meaning. In order to fulfil these last two functions, it is necessary to articulate hybridization with other concepts, such as modernity/ modernization/modernism, social integration/segregation, difference/inequality and reconversion.[45]

Here, García Canclini seems to suggest that studying processes of hybridization could provide interpretive tools for social worlds if researchers use them to explore the relationship between social structure and agency. He views that analyzing hybridization processes in conjunction with other significant social theories could also be fruitful. His statement alludes to the potential benefits of studying processes of hybridization.

Other scholars seem to affirm García Canclini's perspective. Paul Gilroy eloquently observes a darker side of how these processes play out in the history and aftermath of "the black Atlantic system" alongside the current global flows.[46] Lila Abu-Lughod illuminates the cultural, social, religious, and political landscape in Egypt; she observes how globalizing flows intermingle around a seemingly innocent task of national television programming.[47] Ulf Hannerz's description of cultural flows and processes of "creolization" largely concurs with García Canclini's theory of hybridization processes.[48] In exploring continuity and boundary of identity, Alberto Melucci insists the static and essential notion of identity be abandoned.[49] Instead, we are to examine "the dynamic processes of identification" or

43. García Canclini, "Introduction: Hybrid Cultures."
44. García Canclini, *Consumers and Citizens*, 90–91.
45. García Canclini, "State of War," 41–42.
46. Gilroy, "Route Work."
47. Abu-Lughod, "Objects of Soap Opera."
48. Hannerz, *Cultural Complexity*; Hannerz, *Transnational Connections*.
49. Melucci, "Identity and Difference."

"the processes by which individuals construct their identities."[50] While warning against "groupism"[51] of the Chinese diaspora communities, Ien Ang presses for "more processual and flexible understandings of identity, ethnicity and nation."[52] Gerd Baumann considers two main discourses of the culture concept in globalization discussions and argues that we need to validate both the dominant discourse of reified cultures and the demotic discourse of negotiating cultural identity to develop successful multiethnic alliances.[53] Baumann uses a language of negotiation and renegotiation that mediates the process of culture-making. This aligns with the kind of hybridization process proposed by García Canclini as a robust paradigm to develop public policies for Latin American states.[54]

Jan Nederveen Pieterse, a globalization scholar who contributed to discussions of cultural hybridization, argues that globalization and its impact on cultures can best be explained as processes of cultural hybridization that produce global *mélange*—or a mixture—cultures.[55] He sees hybridization as "a *cross-category* process" that mixes cultural elements that are perceived to be separate.[56] For him, the views such as the "clash of civilizations" thesis by Samuel Huntington misconstrue the reality of continual, ongoing interactions between cultures.[57] Similarly to García Canclini's view, he argues that while hybridization processes have always been active throughout history, they are often hidden from sight by dominant groups. He contends that the on-going intercultural mixing in the current globalization illustrates that all cultures are hybrid cultures, and all cultures are always going through processes of hybridization.[58] His perspective challenges the essentialist view of culture widely held and promoted at the popular level.

Challenging Existing Boundaries

Scholars generally agree that the significance of cultural hybridity is in its capacity to challenge boundaries.[59] Nederveen Pieterse writes, "The

50. Melucci, "Identity and Difference," 64.
51. Brubaker, "Ethnicity without Groups," August 2002.
52. Ang, "Beyond Chinese Groupism," 1194.
53. Baumann, "Dominant and Demotic Discourses," 222.
54. García Canclini, "Introduction: Hybrid Cultures."
55. Nederveen Pieterse, *Globalization and Culture*, 2015, 67.
56. Nederveen Pieterse, *Globalization and Culture*, 2015, 81.
57. Huntington, *Clash of Civilizations.*
58. Nederveen Pieterse, *Globalization and Culture*, 2015, 91.
59. Axford, *Theories of Globalization*, 104.

importance of hybridity is that it problematizes boundaries."[60] Indeed, hybridity is often conceptualized relative to existing boundaries. Nederveen Pieterse is especially critical of the persistence of essentialized boundaries in academia.[61] For him, cultural hybridity is necessary because of the assumption of cultural purity and fixed boundaries.[62] Concurring with this view, Ien Ang provides a representative summary of many scholars when she states, "As a concept, hybridity belongs to the space of the frontier, the border, the contact zone. As such, hybridity always implies a blurring or at least a problematizing of boundaries, and as a result, an unsettling of identities."[63] Perhaps this blurring, unsettling nature of cultural hybridity makes the majority group in society or those in a dominant position uncomfortable with the concept.

Ulf Hannerz uses the term "creolization" to denote cultural mixing and borrowing processes.[64] He deems the concept helpful in interpreting the interactions between the center and the periphery of cultural production. He recognizes the volatility in the boundary zone and rightly presumes the unpredictable results of these interactions.[65] In articulating the boundary concept, Bhabha sees boundaries as the places where both cultural translations and misappropriations emerge.[66] He assigns the significance of the content of cultures as only secondary to their boundaries. He muses, "For it is by living on the borderline of history and language, on the limits of race and gender, that we are in a position to translate the differences between them into a kind of solidarity."[67] He seems to privilege the boundaries as the site of interactions and transactions between powerful cultural forces.

Meanwhile, García Canclini declares that "all cultures are border cultures."[68] According to George Yúdice, who translated much of García Canclini's original works from Spanish to English, García Canclini's significant contribution to the discussion on Latin American cultural studies is his proposal that "in late modernity all identities straddle borders, whether geopolitical, cultural, or epistemological."[69] He pays special attention to

60. Nederveen Pieterse, "Hybridity, So What?," 220.

61. Nederveen Pieterse, *Globalization and Culture*, 2015, 100.

62. Nederveen Pieterse, *Globalization and Culture*, 2015, 108.

63. Ang, *On Not Speaking Chinese*, 16.

64. Hannerz, *Transnational Connections*, 68.

65. Hannerz, *Cultural Complexity*, 266.

66. Bhabha, "Cultural Diversity," 155; Bhabha, "In Between Cultures," 107–9.

67. Bhabha, *Location of Culture*, 244.

68. García Canclini, *Hybrid Cultures*, 261.

69. Yúdice, "Translator's Introduction," xi.

interactions at cultural borders and suggests that identities are best viewed as "processes of *negotiation*" at these borders.[70] When he shifts his discussions of cultural hybridity, as he frequently does, onto political implications in Latin America, he seeks to understand how borderline interactions unfold and potentially prevent conflicts. He argues for the necessity of a taxonomy of interpretive categories to explain hybridization as it occurs in diverse contexts.[71] For García Canclini, a theory of cultural hybridization presents an upside potential for reducing intergroup tensions. This is a critical point when considering how essentialized categories are frequently invoked to build symbolic ethnic boundaries that perpetuate various conflicts.[72] Nederveen Pieterse also contends that this is where hybridization comes in—to resist racializing ideologies, celebrate the crossing of boundaries, and dismiss claims of purity by giving salience to ambiguous borderlines.[73] However, he is realistic when he anticipates some boundaries to fade away naturally while others persist and new ones appear as hybridization processes continue their course.[74]

Seeing a surge of nationalist movements in Australia and elsewhere, Ien Ang advocates for taking the hybridity concept beyond theories into practices in daily lives.[75] She reflects on both Stuart Hall's influential writing and the political situation—the troublesome rise of nationalist movements—in Australia at the end of the twentieth century. She writes that these movements can largely be attributed to White Australians' fear of losing their place in *their country*, similar to recent happenings in the United States and parts of Western Europe. Ang suggests a way forward for cosmopolitan, multicultural, and global intellectuals like herself.[76] She hints that they can do more in their own life settings than just writing critical essays and scholarly analyses, such as intentionally sharing and interacting with "Other" about their daily lives or merely doing life as a part of a local community. She writes:

> What such mundane local interactions can contribute to, I believe, is the incremental and dialogic construction of lived identities which slowly dissolve the boundaries between the

70. García Canclini, *Consumers and Citizens*, 96.

71. García Canclini, "State of War," 44.

72. Hall, "New Ethnicities," 255.

73. Nederveen Pieterse, *Globalization and Culture*, 2015, 57.

74. Nederveen Pieterse, *Globalization and Culture*, 2015, 125.

75. Ang, "Identity Blues"; Ang, *On Not Speaking Chinese*; Ang, "Together-In-Difference."

76. Ang, "Identity Blues."

past and the future, between 'where we come from' and 'what we might become,' between being and becoming: being is enhanced by becoming, and becoming is never possible without a solid grounding in being. As subjects from multiple backgrounds negotiate their coexistence and mutual interconnection, the contradictory necessity and impossibility of identities is played out in the messiness of everyday life, as the global and the local interpenetrate each other.[77]

She maintains that these micro-level human interactions at cultural boundaries can go a long way in engendering positive social changes in societies marred by divisions along imaginary borders of race, ethnicity, and culture. Ang also uses Chinese diaspora communities in the cosmopolitan city of Sydney as an example of how cultural hybridization occurs among diverse people with Chinese heritage.[78] She shows how ambiguous and messy is the boundary between the Chinese and the non-Chinese. It is in this context of blurry ethnic, cultural boundaries that Ang emphasizes hybridity as a crucial concept that "foregrounds complicated entanglement rather than identity, togetherness-in-difference rather than separateness and virtual apartheid."[79] She challenges clear-cut identity markers often imposed on different members of a society for political motives. To tackle these issues, she calls for empirical research that utilizes the cultural hybridity concept and investigates the social phenomena at these imaginary cultural borders.[80]

Hybridity as Agency

Many proponents of the cultural hybridity concept share an optimistic view of its potential for agency. In fact, at the heart of Bhabha's concept of hybridity is his anticipation of agency. In words that perhaps best summarize his substantial work on hybridity, he states, "My contention, elaborated in my writings on postcolonial discourse in terms of mimicry, hybridity, sly civility, is that this liminal moment of identification—eluding resemblance—produces a subversive strategy of subaltern agency that negotiates its own authority . . . ."[81] He sees hybridity's potential for agency, which becomes more salient at the margin, the periphery, and the in-between

---

77. Ang, "Identity Blues," 11.

78. Ang, "Together-In-Difference"; Ang, "Beyond Chinese Groupism."

79. Ang, "Together-In-Difference," 141.

80. Ang, "Together-In-Difference," 148.

81. Bhabha, *Location of Culture*, 265.

space of ambivalence if it does not seek its own authority.[82] Out of Bhabha's political imagination emerges a paradoxical notion of cultural hybridity that defies its prior understandings. He underscores the marginalized position in which hybridity is often found; if it possesses any authority, power, or hegemonic claim, it can no longer create a space for negotiating unequal powers and thus loses its agency. This is a crucial point in Bhabha's conception of hybridity missed by many of his critics. Bhabha does not describe hybridity as generating powerful movements, whether political, social, or cultural. He maintains that hybridity is salient as long as it remains frail; it is prophetic so long as it is peripheral.

For Ien Ang, the importance of hybridity theory lies in its potential to inform analyses of complex social phenomena.[83] While hybridity is not the answer to all contemporary social questions, it is a useful "heuristic device" that undermines fixed identities and interrogates essentialized boundaries.[84]

Among theorists of cultural hybridity, it is perhaps García Canclini who expresses more interest than anyone in hybridity's political potential. Writing with the politically turbulent Latin American contexts in mind, he is not satisfied with a descriptive function of hybridity; it is the explanatory and interpretive potential of hybridity that appeals to him. His goal is to find a way forward not only in social research but also in public policies; he is hopeful that Latin American nations can benefit from agency of hybridization regarding power, inequality, and group conflicts.[85]

It would also be important to note the limits of cultural hybridity in its transgressive agency. Pnina Werbner, a British urban anthropologist, is concerned that hybridity, in some situations such as minority diaspora communities in the West, may be harmful to the very people for whom hybrid phenomena are invoked.[86] Using Bakhtin's[87] distinction of intentional, conscious hybridity from organic, unconscious hybridity, she observes that the organic, unconscious type of cultural hybridity tends not to upset existing social orders.[88] However, intentional, inorganic hybridity could become a source of further conflict and marginalization of minority groups, writes Werbner.[89] As an example of the risk of inorganic hybridity, she presents

---

82. Bhabha, "Culture's In-Between," 58.

83. Ang, "Together-In-Difference," 141, 146.

84. Ang, "Together-In-Difference," 149–53.

85. García Canclini, "Introduction: Hybrid Cultures," xxx.

86. Werbner, "Limits of Cultural Hybridity."

87. Bakhtin, *Dialogic Imagination*.

88. Werbner, "Dialectics of Cultural Hybridity," 5.

89. Werbner, "Limits of Cultural Hybridity."

the case of how Muslims in Great Britain were further marginalized after the controversy surrounding the Rushdie affair.

The novel *The Satanic Verses* by Salman Rushdie is a creative autobiographical literary fiction that deals with the diasporic dilemma of plural and changing identities.[90] The author is known to have written it with no ill intention toward Islam or any other religion.[91] Indeed, Rushdie's articulation of the idea of hybridizing realities in a diasporic exile is recognized as a point of inspiration and empathy by Bhabha.[92] Nevertheless, Rushdie's novel caused such severe reactions by Muslims worldwide, including British Muslims, that an unintended consequence of the controversy was a demotion of Muslims' social standing in Great Britain. The Muslim reaction to Rushdie led to the public perception that Muslims were intolerant and backward, further increasing discrimination against Muslims in Britain.[93] She warns that hybridity tends to "play dangerously on the boundary and can thus become a source of offense," which negates the intended goal of elevating those in the margin of society by maligning their agency.[94] She observes:

> Whether cultural hybridity is generative and fertilizing depends on how its varied audiences interpret it. For some, multiculturalism, cultural borrowings and mixings, constitute an attack on their felt subjectivity. In a world in which local people feel their culture to be under threat from globalizing Western cultural forces or from incoming stranger migrants, interruptive hybridity may be experienced not as revitalizing and fun, but as threatening a prior social order and morality.[95]

This perceptive comment is a warning against those who promote cultural hybridity as a new trope for convenient multiculturalism or naïvely believe that there is only upside potential for cultural hybridity. Similarly, Ien Ang is concerned that "the rhetoric of hybridity can easily be put to political abuse if it is coopted in a discourse of easy multicultural and multiracial harmony," and believes that "we cannot escape the predicament of hybridity as a real, powerful and pervasive force in a world in which complicated entanglement is the order of the day."[96] Therefore, as a possible remedy against abuses and potentially offensive misuses of hybridity that cause cultural conflicts,

90. See Rushdie, *Satanic Verses.*

91. Kakutani, "'Satanic Verses.'"

92. Bhabha, *Location of Culture.*

93. Werbner, "Limits of Cultural Hybridity."

94. Werbner, "Limits of Cultural Hybridity," 138.

95. Werbner, "Limits of Cultural Hybridity," 150.

96. Ang, "Together-In-Difference," 150.

Werbner calls for an anthropological theory of hybridity. Such a theory would show that intercultural encounters are "always contextual and sited" no matter where these contacts may occur.[97]

The Third Space: Bhabha's Integrating Theme

Certain words repeatedly appear in Bhabha's work on hybridity.[98] Terms such as ambivalence, enunciation, mimicry, and the Third Space are used somewhat fluidly in theorizing hybridity. He uses these interconnected— and conceptually integrating—terms to depict intercultural relations in postcolonial realities. Although Bhabha is known to have theorized cultural hybridity, it may be more accurate to say that he conceptualizes *the Third Space* integrating all these other notions, including hybridity.

Ambivalence is used to indicate "a continual fluctuation between wanting one thing and its opposite" or "simultaneous attraction toward and repulsion from an object, person or action."[99] Both Bhabha[100] and Werbner[101] give Mikhail Bakhtin credit for developing a socio-linguistic theory of hybridity that led to the conception of ambivalence as a critical characteristic of cultural hybridity. As previously mentioned, Bakhtin developed the theory of organic (unconscious and unintentional) and inorganic (conscious and intentional) linguistic hybrids.[102] He showed how two antithetical movements could take place at the same time when one uttered an intentional hybrid language. He wrote:

> [T]he novelistic hybrid is not only double-voiced and double-accented (as in rhetoric) but is also double-languaged; for in it there are not only (and not even so much) two individual consciousnesses, two voices, two accents, as there are two socio-linguistic consciousnesses, two epochs, that, true, are not here unconsciously mixed (as in an organic hybrid), but that come together and consciously fight it out on the territory of the utterance.[103]

Bhabha takes this idea further and describes the moment of "doubled utterance" as an opening of "a space of negotiation where power is unequal

97. Werbner, "Limits of Cultural Hybridity," 150.

98. Bhabha, *Location of Culture*.

99. Young, *Colonial Desire*, 161.

100. Bhabha, "Culture's In-Between."

101. Werbner, "Dialectics of Cultural Hybridity," 1997.

102. Bakhtin, *Dialogic Imagination*.

103. Bakhtin, *Dialogic Imagination*, 360.

but its articulation may be equivocal."[104] When a language is intentionally, consciously uttered, or enunciated, it necessarily involves both the language spoken and intended by the speaker and the language heard and interpreted by the listener, which are not necessarily the same. Bhabha seems to argue that between the speaker and the listener is the space in which utterance has dual meanings embedded in the exchange. He ingeniously takes this linguistic idea and applies it to intercultural transactions during the colonial era between those who had power and those who did not. Bhabha writes that cultures and cultural differences are expressed, or uttered, by acts of cultural *enunciation*; these acts create an ambivalent space that confuses and potentially neutralizes the preexisting essentialized hierarchies.[105] He states, "The enunciation of cultural difference problematizes the binary division of past and present, tradition and modernity, at the level of cultural representation and its authoritative address."[106]

Bhabha shows that those with power and privilege are faced with *ambivalence*, which ironically appears where differentiation is taking place; the concept of ambivalence manifests itself in paradoxical situations such as the colonial India or migrants living in "the West" where cultures are *enunciated* in the cultural contact zones.[107] Bhabha suggests that there is a need to recognize the subverting potential in the margins of cultures.[108] In the liminal space, both the strong and the weak take on equivocal positions of power. The weak gains power, while the strong loses it. This is a paradoxical nature of hybridity conditions in a global society.

Another word frequently invoked by Bhabha is *mimicry*. The word typically means an act of imitating or copying.[109] But he adopts this term as a descriptor for colonial experiences. He writes:

> [T]he discourse of mimicry is constructed around an *ambivalence*; in order to be effective, mimicry must continually produce its slippage, its excess, its difference. The authority of that mode of colonial discourse that I have called mimicry is therefore stricken by an indeterminacy: mimicry emerges as the representation of a difference that is itself a process of disavowal. Mimicry is, thus the sign of a double articulation; a complex

104. Bhabha, "Culture's In-Between," 58.
105. Bhabha, "Cultural Diversity," 157; "Foreword," xiii.
106. Bhabha, *Location of Culture*, 51.
107. Bhabha, *Location of Culture*, 50–51.
108. Bhabha, "Foreword."
109. "Mimicry, n."

strategy of reform, regulation and discipline, which 'appropriates' the Other as it visualizes power.[110]

Here, Bhabha argues for the subversive potential of "organic hybridity" inadvertently created by colonial powers when they forced their image upon their colonial subjects. While not intentional, this replica of colonial powers produces something that might appear to be a copy but something else in reality—a "slippage"—that defies the colonial authority; it enables agency for the colonized in what he describes as "the Third Space" of cultures. Bhabha explains that those with power may impose fixed identities on "Other," but they can do so only by making direct contact with "Other," which would inevitably result in mimicry.[111] He sees this as a process that turns the table and subverts the viciousness of colonial domination—the more the colonial powers dominate colonial subjects, the more the "slippage"; the more the "slippage," the more exposed the falsehood of fixed, imposed identities.

Bhabha also uses "the Third Space" to characterize the nature of hybridity.[112] Representing "the space across and between boundaries," the Third Space is used in conjunction with terms such as liminality, interstice, and in-between-ness.[113] Bhabha writes:

> It is significant that the productive capacities of this Third Space have a colonial or postcolonial provenance. For a willingness to descend into that alien territory—where I have led you—may reveal that the theoretical recognition of the split-space of enunciation may open the way to conceptualizing an *inter*national culture, based not on the exoticism of multiculturalism or the *diversity* of cultures, but on the inscription and articulation of culture's *hybridity*. To that end we should remember that it is the 'inter'—the cutting edge of translation and negotiation, the *inbetween* space—that carries the burden of the meaning of culture.[114]

Bhabha sees that cultural hybridity can make up for the shortcomings of the idea of cultural "diversity" often invoked in multiculturalism. For him, diving into "that alien territory" of *the Third Space* opens the possibility of prevailing over ethnic conflicts, identity politics, and flaws of multiculturalist policies. In the quoted statement above, Bhabha reveals where he

110. Bhabha, *Location of Culture*, 122.
111. Bhabha, *Location of Culture*, 159.
112. Rutherford, "Third Space: Interview with Homi Bhabha," 211.
113. Nederveen Pieterse, "Hybridity, So What?," 239.
114. Bhabha, *Location of Culture*, 56.

believes the location of cultural production lies—the *inbetween* space of cultures. For Bhabha, precise assessment of social realities becomes possible only in this liminal space since any other notion, he contends, can lead to mistaking cultural differences as unsolvable puzzles.[115] He suggests that this "in between space" informs the contemporary debate between "communitarians" who put forth the homogeneous identity and "cosmopolitans" who seek multicultural identity.[116] While he uses vague language to describe the Third Space concept, he appears to imply that any communication, conversation, translation, or interpretation between "Self" and "Other" can only happen in this Third Space of cultures.[117] For Bhabha, cultures must be enunciated in the Third Space. The colonizer and the colonized, the powerful and the powerless, meet to create ambivalent relations exemplified in the cultural slippage of mimicry. These can result in a powerful form of cultural production, subversion of fixity and hierarchy, and newness produced by cultural processes of hybridization.

DEBATES ON CULTURAL HYBRIDITY

Due to its contemporary currency, it may be easy to forget that the notion of cultural hybridity had to endure heavy resistance within academia.[118] There have been some sharp criticisms of the concept. These can be summarized as "allegations of theoretical uselessness," "suspicion toward the high priests of hybridity," and "the charge that hybridity rhetoric embraces the logic of transnational capitalism."[119] John Hutnyk adds the problematic biological and racialized roots of hybridity to this list, while Barrie Axford alludes to its ironic essentialist tendency.[120] These five claims against cultural hybridity will be reviewed in this section, along with responses by leading theorists of hybridity. These debates were essential not only for the development of the theories but also for the proliferation of the concept and its applications in various academic fields. As this concept is now being given attention by more missiologists, a review of these past debates may preemptively address some of the similar issues arising or being repeated in mission studies.

115. Bhabha, *Location of Culture*, 232.

116. Bhabha, "Unpacking My Library Again," 204.

117. Bhabha, "Cultural Diversity," 156–57.

118. Burke, *Cultural Hybridity*.

119. Kraidy, *Cultural Logic of Globalization*, 66.

120. Hutnyk, "Hybridity Saves?," 39; Axford, *Theories of Globalization*, 104–5.

Hybridity's Roots in Biology and Old Racial Theories

One of the most common criticisms against cultural hybridity theories is the question of validity based on its origin in biology—hybrid refers to the off-spring of two different plants or animals—and its adaptation in the nineteenth century's racial theories.[121] The critics point out that hybridity was formerly used as a biological concept and thought to be harmful to society. The fact that it has now returned to serve as a contemporary cultural theory should raise suspicions of its persisting connotations of infertility and racism.[122] Jonathan Friedman argues that the notion of hybridity contains remnants of "the same racial language that it seeks to criticize."[123] The critics' claims become more nuanced when they begin to suspect a conceptual link between hybridity and the assumed purity for its anterior elements before hybridizing.[124] They question the concept's seemingly bizarre nature of "difference and sameness in an apparently impossible simultaneity."[125] They wonder if the attention given by hybridity perspectives to the racial issues is actually masking the critical issues of class and gender inequality.[126]

While he admits the apparent limitations of the term highlighted by these critics, García Canclini suggests that hybridity as a concept does not need to remain in the realm of biology and its negative racist history. Mentioning Karl Marx's *reproduction* (from biology to political theory) and Pierre Bourdieu's cultural *capital* and linguistic *markets* (from economics to social and linguistic theories), he argues that a concept in one discipline can successfully be adopted into another as long as the notion maintains "theoretical consistency" and "explanatory power."[127] He maintains that the most important question should not be whether a concept originates from another discipline or not but whether it is capable of explaining something which was previously not clearly understood.[128] In hybridity, he sees such a concept with a potential for producing innovative intercultural theories and

---

121. Lewellen, *Anthropology of Globalization*, 99; Young, *Colonial Desire*, 6; Hutnyk, "Hybridity Saves?," 39; Friedman, "Hybridization of Roots," 234; García Canclini, "Introduction: Hybrid Cultures," xxvi.

122. Young, *Colonial Desire*, 6; García Canclini, "Introduction: Hybrid Cultures," xxiv–xxv.

123. Friedman, "Hybridization of Roots," 235.

124. Hutnyk, "Hybridity," 81.

125. Young, *Colonial Desire*, 26–27.

126. Papastergiadis, "Tracing Hybridity in Theory," 258.

127. García Canclini, "Introduction: Hybrid Cultures," xxiv.

128. García Canclini, "Introduction: Hybrid Cultures," xxvi–xxvii.

practices.[129] While it is not clear whether the old racialized connotation has completely been removed from the notion of hybridity, new conceptions and applications of hybridity in social sciences and cultural studies appear to distance themselves from the past history of hybridity by focusing on the cultural and social phenomena on the ground.

Misuse of Hybridity

Critics point out that a wide variety of theoretical misuses of hybridity make the concept highly problematic.[130] These critiques may primarily be the results of what Kraidy calls "strong divergences on the meaning and implications of hybridity."[131] Werbner rightly describes this as "an elusive paradox" and maintains a difficulty inherent in the hybridity concept to adequately address and reconcile its interruptive power with its routine and universal nature.[132]

Jonathan Friedman, one of the most ardent critics of hybridity, makes no small claim when he asserts that the notion of hybridity results from a confusion of the category of culture with the category of ethnicity.[133] While he notes García Canclini's prominence in Latin American studies, Friedman points out that García Canclini presumes a hybridity condition even before engaging in the fieldwork.[134] He disapproves of García Canclini for his focus on artists and cultural elites in Tijuana, Mexico, instead of choosing to look at the hybrid identities of migrants from rural areas. Friedman does not deny the concept of hybridity.[135] What bothers him is García Canclini's inattention to the positional difference between the researcher and the subject. He argues that García Canclini's conclusions about cultural elites, who may be similar to the scholar himself, cannot be generalized to migratory workers in Tijuana who may drastically be different from an elite scholar like him. Friedman faults García Canclini for his generalized assumption that hybridity is salient in every socio-cultural group in Tijuana, although his research methods only allow for examining a small social segment. It is not hard to see that understanding any form of hybridity would require careful consideration of the

---

129. García Canclini, "Introduction: Hybrid Cultures," xxvii.

130. Hutnyk, "Hybridity"; Hutnyk, "Adorno at Womad"; Kraidy, "Hybridity in Cultural Globalization"; Kraidy, *Cultural Logic of Globalization*; van der Veer, "Enigma of Arrival."

131. Kraidy, "Hybridity in Cultural Globalization," 321.

132. Werbner, "Dialectics of Cultural Hybridity," 1997, 1.

133. Friedman, "Hybridization of Roots," 253.

134. Friedman, "Hybridization of Roots," 250.

135. Friedman, "Hybridization of Roots."

particularity of specific social contexts, as suggested by Friedman.[136] While it is not clear in these discussions whether García Canclini was indeed so unaware of these issues highlighted, Friedman suggests that hybridity must be understood in context and must not be viewed as a do-it-all solution to all matters related to globalization and culture.

John Hutnyk calls hybridity "a usefully slippery category" mobilized to explain almost any cultural phenomenon of the day.[137] He directly charges Bhabha for abusing the term.[138] Although he sees the benefit of hybridity in exposing boundary maintenance that differentiates and excludes minorities, Marxist scholar Hutnyk does not think that hybridity discussions are going far enough.[139] Though not entirely rejecting the notion, he advises researchers to look for "what it achieves, what contexts its use might obscure, and what it leaves aside."[140]

Peter van der Veer has a different concern. He points out that scholars such as Bhabha and Spivak rely heavily on literary texts to analyze sociocultural phenomena.[141] While not entirely dismissing the value of literature for social analysis, van der Veer argues that such analysis must go beyond the text to connect to the particular context in which the literary work is located. Friedman also doubts that hybridity theories fully reflect lived realities since their core ideas are largely drawn from literary works.[142] One wonders, however, if literature would be so severely limited and limiting as a tool for sociocultural analysis as both Friedman and van der Veer insist. Historian Gerald Izenberg points out that the concept of identity, another highly ambiguous term often invoked in sociocultural analysis, was first explored in European literary works produced between the World Wars.[143] The modern concept of identity was first developed in the field of literature before philosophers, and eventually, social scientists adopted it. It shows that social scientists should not dismiss literature too quickly.

It is true, however, that the loaded nature of the hybridity concept tends to obscure the view of cultural processes taking place throughout history. Anthropologist Emiko Ohnuki-Tierney, who recognizes both ubiquity and misuse of hybridity, pleads scholars to discontinue the use of the trope. She

---

136. Friedman, "Global Crises," 85.
137. Hutnyk, "Hybridity," 79–80.
138. Hutnyk, "Hybridity," 81.
139. Hutnyk, "Adorno at Womad," 122.
140. Hutnyk, "Hybridity," 83.
141. van der Veer, "Enigma of Arrival," 103.
142. Friedman, "Global Crises," 78.
143. Izenberg, *Identity*.

fears that it might lead their research away from the historical analysis necessary to understand culture more accurately.[144] Such a plea, however, has been seen before in social sciences. There was a call by cultural anthropologists to discontinue the use of the notion of *culture* as traditionally rendered in the past.[145] There was also an appeal to discard the trope *identity* altogether in social research.[146] These examples illustrate both the disputed and celebrated nature of these terms. Perhaps this plea by an anthropologist to abandon *hybridity* also shows its peril and appeal for social sciences.

An Imagined World for New Cosmopolitan Elites?

The harshest criticism of leading theorists of cultural hybridity may be the accusation that they imagine a world that can only be indulged by a few influential diasporic intellectual figures like themselves.[147] Aijaz Ahmad, who is skeptical of postcolonial scholars in general and Bhabha in particular, writes about Bhabha with almost condescending phrases such as "a very modern, very affluent, very uprooted kind of intellectual"[148] and "the migrant (postcolonial) intellectual."[149] Similarly, Arif Dirlik refers to prominent postcolonial scholars as "Third World intellectuals who have arrived in First World academe" and accuses their theoretical work as "an expression not so much of agony over identity, as it often appears, but of newfound power."[150] Though Hutnyk recognizes these scholars for breaking new theoretical ground, he also sarcastically calls them "High-profile intellectual names on the elite conference circuit"[151] and "the institutionalized social theory equivalent of household names."[152]

While these acid comments resemble unfounded personal attacks rather than scholarly debates, they represent strong sentiments among the critics who protest that hybridity proponents speak from an elevated position of power and privilege and that their prominence enables them

144. Ohnuki-Tierney, "Always Discontinuous/Continuous," 190.

145. E.g., Abu-Lughod, "Writing Against Culture"; Ortner, *Fate of "Culture"*; Trouillot, "Adieu, Culture"; Agar, "Culture," June 2006; Agar, *Culture*, 2019; Kuper, *Culture*.

146. E.g., Brubaker and Cooper, "Beyond 'Identity.'"

147. Kraidy, "Hybridity in Cultural Globalization," 322.

148. Ahmad, *In Theory*, 68.

149. Ahmad, "Politics of Literary Postcoloniality," 13.

150. Dirlik, "Postcolonial Aura," 339.

151. Hutnyk, "Hybridity," 98.

152. Hutnyk, "Adorno at Womad," 118.

to obliterate existing views at will.[153] This claim is ironic since intrinsic to hybridity theory is its penchant for challenging systemic powers and essentialized hierarchies. These critics also argue that these scholars' theories are highly abstract and conceptually untenable, and their conception of the world is far removed from the reality perceived by the mass. These criticisms against hybridity theorists seem to extend to hybridity theories themselves. For example, van der Veer calls for a critical examination of the notion of hybridity developed in cultural studies.[154] He explicitly calls out Bhabha's work when he writes, "What I find striking about these statements [by Bhabha] is that they seem to invoke the traditional romantic trope of the 'self-made individual' who invents here a notion of almost total innovation, of new subject-formation in 'in-between' sites, inhabited by migrants as pioneer settlers."[155]

Friedman also raises a series of questions about Nederveen Pieterse's[156] claim that hybridity is normative in the contemporary world and suggests that it indicates the formation of a new elite group with an ideological dominance.[157] In a sharp criticism of Stuart Hall, Friedman questions Hall of "an implicit agenda" which he explains, almost comically, as a scheme of "First you colonized Me and I was dispersed and became transnational, and now I take on the identity that was bestowed upon me and use it as a weapon against essentializing discourses that were the core of the colonial era."[158] Friedman seems to be unconvinced by Hall, if not amused. However, elsewhere, Friedman shares a more sympathetic view of these well-known diasporic scholars when he observes:

> The global, cultural hybrid, elite sphere is occupied by individuals who share a very different kind of experience of the world, connected to international politics, academia, the media and the arts. Their careers, especially if they were born in the Third World and live in the First, are thoroughly cosmopolitan, but not . . . in a modernist sense. Rather, they are defined in cultural terms, in terms of the combination of differences, often quite reflexively.[159]

153. Lee and Harold, "Potential or Threat?: Adopting Cultural Hybridity as a Concept for Diaspora Missiology," 9.

154. van der Veer, "Enigma of Arrival," 102.

155. van der Veer, "Enigma of Arrival," 95.

156. Nederveen Pieterse, "Globalisation as Hybridisation."

157. Friedman, "Hybridization of Roots," 235–36.

158. Friedman, "Hybridization of Roots," 243.

159. Friedman, "Global Crises," 84.

To be sure, Friedman sees how pervasive hybrid conditions are and recognizes the complexity of the contemporary world.[160] What seems to trouble him, though, is the descriptive and normative use of the concept by these scholars. He builds an argument against Hall, Nederveen Pieterse, and García Canclini that they are responsible for conceptualizing hybridity as an objective notion and generalizing it to the entire world.[161] Moreover, he warns leading intellectuals of the hybridity theory about the risk of falling into a pit of arrogance and cultural disconnect when he states:

> In the global circuits of high culture, intellectual culture, media elites and diplomatic cores, there is a global identity, a cosmopolitan identity constructed on the basis of a multicultural world. It is a self-identified hybrid identity encompassing the cultural plurality of the world on which it is totally dependent for its self-definition. But as this is an all-encompassing identity it must define other people's realities for them. Hybridity becomes truth and national, local, ethnic and other restricted identities become backward, red-neck and nationalist. Global becomes equivalent to cosmopolitan and then to urban and hybrid.[162]

To these criticisms, Nederveen Pieterse responds in the strongest terms.[163] Calling these attacks innuendos, he admonishes critics for speculating on the motives of the hybridity theorists rather than engaging in more constructive discussions about crucial issues at hand. Reacting to Friedman,[164] Nederveen Pieterse perhaps goes a bit too far in comparing the critic's distaste for cosmopolitanism to Hitler's Nazi ideology.[165] While his response to Friedman overstates, it underlines that these criticisms are not analytical in nature but ideological. Dismissing these critiques as insensible, he states that such attacks do not help advance scholarship.[166]

One important point that this particular debate reveals is how biographical factors are involved in hybridity discourses. While critics made their attacks appear unnecessarily personal, these claims against so-called "migrant intellectuals" also show a connection between social location, identity, ideology, and scholarship. Many leading postcolonial scholars trace

160. Friedman, "Hybridization of Roots," 251.

161. Friedman, "Hybridization of Roots."

162. Friedman, "Hybridization of Roots," 254.

163. Nederveen Pieterse, "Hybridity, So What?"; Nederveen Pieterse, *Globalization and Culture*, 2015.

164. Friedman, "Hybridization of Roots."

165. Nederveen Pieterse, "Hybridity, So What?," 228.

166. Nederveen Pieterse, "Hybridity, So What?," 228–29.

their roots to former colonies and have immigrant experiences in the West. They represent cosmopolitan, border-crossing, and multicultural intellectuals.[167] For example, Bhabha was born in India to a Parsi family, educated at Oxford, and now occupies a prominent academic post at Harvard University.[168] Edward Said was born to a Palestinian Protestant family, grew up in Egypt, was educated at Princeton and Harvard and taught at Columbia University.[169] Stuart Hall was born in Jamaica, studied, lived, and taught for decades in England.[170] Ien Ang was born in Indonesia to a Chinese diaspora family, educated in the Netherlands, and currently teaches in Australia.[171] Jan Nederveen Pieterse traces his ancestry to the Dutch and Indonesian; he has taught many years in the US.[172] These prolific scholars' biographical data demonstrate that one's personal experiences may have the potential to both inform and misinform scholarship.

A Powerful Hegemony Colluding with Capitalism?

There is a claim that cultural hybridity creates a new hegemony in collusion with global capitalism. Those who make this claim accuse postcolonial intellectuals of their role in building a new cosmopolitan power that co-opts hybridity into becoming a framework for capitalist globalization, creating new hybrid cultural markets, and legitimizing the global capitalist agenda.[173] Van der Veer observes how urban consumerism quickly absorbs new hybrid forms of religion and culture and even thrives in them. He states, "From this perspective, the hybridity celebrated in Cultural Studies has little revolutionary potential, since it is part of the discourse of bourgeois capitalism and modernity which it claims to displace."[174] He implies that postcolonial scholars themselves might be a part of the problem. They act as the very bourgeois capitalist elites whom they claim to supplant and, in the process, lose significant political potential. Friedman portrays hybridity as "a positioned representation of reality" that "clearly harbours hegemonic intentions" and falsely generalizes the particular.[175]

167. Burke, *Cultural Hybridity*, 3.

168. "Homi K. Bhabha."

169. "Edward Said."

170. "Stuart Hall (Cultural Theorist)."

171. "Ien Ang."

172. "Jan Nederveen Pieterse."

173. Ahmad, "Politics of Literary Postcoloniality," 12; Kraidy, "Hybridity in Cultural Globalization," 22–23; Hutnyk, "Hybridity," 79.

174. van der Veer, "Enigma of Arrival," 104.

175. Friedman, "Hybridization of Roots," 237.

Dirlik comments that hybridity theorists fail to attend to the actual power inequality within existing structures by ignoring social and political location, including their own.[176] He maintains that postcolonial scholars' hybridity is contradictory so long as they remain in prominent positions within elite academic institutions in the West.[177] Indeed, inadequate dealing with subalternity, power, and inequality in global relations has been pointed out by both critics and proponents alike as a critical gap in cultural hybridity studies.[178] Hutnyk also charges that the hybridity discourse hides disparities in political, social, and economic powers.[179] He is not sure if cultural hybridity is any different from the old hegemony; he sees the same pattern of hierarchy repeated by the type of transnationalism advocated by postcolonial scholars.[180] According to Dirlik, though postcolonial discourses, including hybridity discussions, address relevant and valid issues of our day, they often turn these real issues too abstract and subjective, thereby missing the opportunity to deal with contemporary forms of hegemony and persistence of totalizing structures.[181]

In response to these claims, Stuart Hall writes with an indignant tone as he rebukes Dirlik's comments as "such stunning (and one is obliged to say, banal) reductionism, a functionalism of a kind which one thought had disappeared from scholarly debate as a serious explanation of *anything*, that it reads like a echo from a distant, primeval era."[182] However, Friedman uses this rebuff by Hall as evidence of the hegemony. In defense of Dirlik's argument and critique of Hall, he writes:

> this discourse is one that has identified with the cosmopolitan space of the global system and has vied for a hegemonic position within that space. This is not functionalism but, on the contrary, a hypothesis about competition within the highest echelons of the system. It is about factions of the elite and about the formation of intellectual hegemony. Hall's style of presentation does much to verify such an hypothesis.[183]

---

176. Dirlik, "Postcolonial Aura," 342.

177. Dirlik, "Postcolonial Aura," 343.

178. Axford, *Theories of Globalization*, 105; Hutnyk, "Hybridity Saves?," 40.

179. Hutnyk, "Hybridity Saves?," 41.

180. Hutnyk, "Adorno at Woman," 118.

181. Dirlik, "Postcolonial Aura," 355–56.

182. Hall, "When Was the Post-Colonial," 259.

183. Friedman, "Hybridization of Roots," 245.

Friedman insists that he also finds a hegemonic attitude in Bhabha's patronizing comments against those who do not agree with his framework.[184]

This is another hotly debated aspect of the cultural hybridity discussions. Although inconclusive, the ambiguity of cultural hybridity leaves much to be desired in how it addresses issues of hegemony, power, and capitalist agenda. Bhabha appears to privilege hybridity and leaves the door open for criticism from many angles.[185] One could argue, however, that the potential of hybridity explored by Bhabha and others is more nuanced and far-sighted than given credit by these critics. Indeed, Bhabha, who has remained silent for almost two decades about these criticisms, has a concise but firm response.[186] It will be discussed later.

Another Form of Essentialism?

Among social theories, cultural hybridity is often invoked as an antidote against essentialism.[187] Ironically, it is also criticized for advancing another kind of essentialism.[188] As Peter Burke notes, the term "essentialism" has become a weapon of choice in attacking an opponent in today's scholarly debates.[189] Hybridity is not immune from such attacks. Referring to some conceptions of cultural hybridity as "an insufficiently self-reflective construal of culture," Nikolas Kompridis, a Canadian philosopher and political theorist, perceptively argues that the notion tends to overemphasize the fluid, borderless nature of culture, further clouds our understanding of culture, and ends up essentializing the very idea of hybridity recruited to fight against essentialist views.[190] While he finds helpful elements in the hybridity concept, he is critical of the excessive anti-essentialist line of thinking prevalent in hybridity discourses. He warns, "When we unreflectively subscribe to *essentialist anti-essentialism*, when we allow our talk of 'construction' to

---

184. Friedman, "Global Crises," 78–79.

185. Bhabha, "Culture's In-Between"; Bhabha, "Unpacking My Library Again"; Bhabha, *Location of Culture*; Bhabha, "Cultural Diversity"; Bhabha, "In Between Cultures"; Bhabha, "Foreword."

186. Bhabha, "Foreword."

187. Bhabha, "Culture's In-Between"; Bhabha, *Location of Culture*; Nederveen Pieterse, "Globalisation as Hybridisation"; Nederveen Pieterse, "Hybridity, So What?"; Nederveen Pieterse, *Globalization and Culture*, 2015; Axford, *Theories of Globalization*; Kompridis, "Normativizing Hybridity/Neutralizing Culture"; Werbner, "Dialectics of Cultural Hybridity," 1997.

188. Axford, *Theories of Globalization*, 104–5.

189. Burke, *Cultural Hybridity*, 1.

190. Kompridis, "Normativizing Hybridity/Neutralizing Culture," 319.

distort its object, we come uncomfortably close to a position which fictionalizes culture and identity, turning into a mere 'construction.'"[191]

Robert Young also provides a persuasive critique of an essentializing tendency within the hybridity concept and postcolonial scholarship in general.[192] He wonders if the past notions of culture have been wrongly accused of being more essentialist than they were. He states:

> The question is whether the old essentializing categories of cultural identity, or of race, were really so essentialized, or have been retrospectively constructed as more fixed than they were. When we look at the texts of racial theory, we find that they are in fact contradictory, disruptive and already deconstructed. Hybridity here is a key term in that wherever it emerges it suggests the impossibility of essentialism. If so, then in deconstructing such essentialist notions of race today we may rather be repeating the past than distancing ourselves from it or providing a critique of it.[193]

Young raises a legitimate question for hybridity theories. He warns that the same errors made in cultural and racial theories in the past can be repeated today in the so-called cutting edge scholarship.

Though he seems to be generalizing what he deems as weaknesses of hybridity theories to an extreme, Friedman's contention that hybridity can potentially form another essentialized identity should be noted.[194] His claim that hybridity's essentializing tendency is epitomized in its elite proponents might still be a bit too harsh. However, he astutely argues that hybridity is conceptualized, just as the notion of ethnic purity or racism, "on the same essentialised and fundamentally objectified notion of culture."[195] He questions hybridity's capacity to create "anything other than new categories of the same type"[196] and concludes, "Hybridity is founded on the metaphor of purity. The notion of pure hybridity is a self-contradiction."[197] Although most cultural hybridity theorists would perhaps disagree with Friedman's assessment and Friedman might have overstated it, it is still a critical insight that must not be ignored.

191. Kompridis, "Normativizing Hybridity/Neutralizing Culture," 324; emphasis was added.

192. Young, *Colonial Desire*.

193. Young, *Colonial Desire*, 27.

194. Friedman, "Global Crises," 78–79.

195. Friedman, "Global Crises," 82.

196. Friedman, "Global Crises," 83.

197. Friedman, "Global Crises," 82–83.

These arguments by critics and the inherent ambiguity of the hybrid-ity concept raise questions about its trustworthiness as an interpretive tool. On the other hand, Bhabha, García Canclini, and Nederveen Pieterse make strong cases for hybridity's explanatory power and agency.[198] How does one break out of such a theoretical impasse? As Hutnyk suggests, we may need "a more radical analysis"—not necessarily a Marxist one that he advocates but perhaps using innovative empirical research methods that go beyond meta-theories—to get to the bottom of these issues.[199]

CURRENT STATUS OF CULTURAL HYBRIDITY

While there is vast literature available on conceptual discussions of cultural hybridity, empirical literature remains rather thin. This poses a challenge to any attempt to study the phenomenon empirically. A key to such a study might be using hybridity as an interpretive framework rather than making it the object of the study. This may help us better understand social phenom-ena embedded in complex intercultural situations.

General Acceptance of Cultural Hybridity Theory

As it was seen in the prior section, a fierce debate on cultural hybridity in-volving scholars in anthropology, cultural studies, and postcolonial theory ensued from the mid-1990s through the mid-2000s. There have not been any further active discussions after this period. Cultural hybridity theory has gained a large following and is adopted in numerous fields, including theology.[200] Despite some of the weaknesses and limits mentioned earlier, arguing against hybridity may no longer be tenable to producing construc-tive discussions. Nederveen Pieterse writes that hybridity is now taken for granted and accepted as the norm.[201] More recent discussions do not focus so much on whether hybridity is useful or not but instead on investigating variations and nuances of hybridizing phenomena.

Some studies in social sciences have embraced cultural hybridity per-spectives in their research framework. An extensive, growing list of such projects can be compiled from diverse contexts and disciplines. Such a list

---

198. See Bhabha, *Location of Culture*; Bhabha, "Foreword"; García Canclini, *Hybrid Cultures*; García Canclini, *Consumers and Citizens*; García Canclini, "Introduction: Hybrid Cultures"; Nederveen Pieterse, "Hybridity, So What?"; Nederveen Pieterse, *Globalization and Culture*, 2020.

199. Hutnyk, "Hybridity," 99.

200. Cf. Joh, *Heart of the Cross*; Keller et al., *Postcolonial Theologies*.

201. Nederveen Pieterse, *Globalization and Culture*, 2015, x.

may include studies of globalization and essentialized culture of the San people in Namibia,[202] the subaltern agency and positionality in a complicated socio-political situation in Egypt,[203] the cultural production of arts in the border town in Mexico,[204] cultural realities of Chinese immigrants in Australia,[205] expressions in the cinema of the Caribbean region and its relation to the diaspora,[206] historical and cultural processes of hybridization in China,[207] the diaspora in Francophone islands of Mauritius and La Réunion,[208] Turkish women in Germany and their liminal experiences,[209] changing black cultural politics in Great Britain,[210] the place of Muslims and their religion in France,[211] identity and intercultural competencies of 1.5-generation Chinese migrants in New Zealand.[212] This partial, small sample represents an increasing number of studies that adopt the hybridity concept. It shows the salience of the concept for social research today.

Debating Cultural Hybridity, the edited volume by Werbner and Modood, was republished in 2015 with a new foreword by none other than the preeminent scholar of hybridity, Homi K. Bhabha.[213] In the new foreword, Bhabha, who has long been silent on the topic, provides a concise and yet sharp analytical jab at both proponents and critics of the concept.[214] In just five pages, Bhabha writes a brief commentary on the current state of hybridity discussions. Such revisit by a pioneering erudite, no matter how brief, is a welcome sign for scholars who study a theoretical concept as contested as cultural hybridity.

The fourth revised edition of the book, *Globalization and Culture* by Nederveen Pieterse, has recently been published.[215] In the previous edition, he had updated nearly every chapter and added a new chapter curiously

---

202. Sylvain, "Disorderly Development."

203. Abu-Lughod, "Objects of Soap Opera."

204. García Canclini, *Hybrid Cultures.*

205. Ang, "Together-In-Difference"; Ang, "Beyond Chinese Groupism"; Liu, *Hybridity and Cultural Home.*

206. Hall, "Cultural Identity and Diaspora."

207. Nederveen Pieterse, *Globalization and Culture*, 2015.

208. Prabhu, *Hybridity.*

209. Ewing, "Between Cinema."

210. Hall, "New Ethnicities."

211. Laroussi, *Postcolonial Counterpoint.*

212. Wang and Collins, "Becoming Cosmopolitan?"

213. Werbner and Modood, *Debating Cultural Hybridity.*

214. Bhabha, "Foreword."

215. Nederveen Pieterse, *Globalization and Culture*, 2020.

titled "Hybrid China."[216] In the new 2020 edition, Nederveen Pieterse adds two more chapters—a brand new one at the end titled "Populism, Globalization, and Culture," which addresses the recent phenomena of nationalism and right-wing populist politics in many countries and a new first chapter titled, "What Is Culture?" which seems essential for a background to his discussions on populism.[217] These new chapters illustrate the continued relevance of cultural hybridity theories into the current decade.

In 2005, García Canclini's seminal *Hybrid Cultures* was republished with a new introduction by the author.[218] Notably, the latest editions of these three influential texts include newly written sections by these leading scholars. They respond to some of the criticisms they received since their prior publications and share their own recent reflections. These new commentaries by the leading voices of cultural hybridity theories provide a sense of closure to the prior debates and signal launching points for new discussions in sociocultural research.

In his new foreword to *Debating Cultural Hybridity*, Bhabha responds, albeit indirectly, to some of his sharpest critics, including those who contributed chapters to this very volume.[219] He suggests that some of these criticisms may stem from a misreading of his works. He gently rebukes the hijacking of the hybridity concept by some in a direction he did not intend. Bhabha clarifies that he never meant hybridity to be a do-it-all meta-narrative.[220] He regrets that the concept has become a tool for so-called "globalisers" of capitalism and their hegemonic intentions rather than remaining as alterity and a liminal voice between powerful societal forces. Bhabha disapproves of the proliferating diversity talks—the diversity rate, the number of cultures represented in a group, etc. In his mind, this sort of superficial diversity only produces problems which we began with, such as the challenges to social cohesion, integration of migrants, and peaceable multicultural cohabitation, rather than providing a way forward. Bhabha perceptively observes, "*The claims of global hybridity rest increasingly on the scale of diversity, not on the diversity of scale.*"[221] In other words, cultural hybridity theories were to highlight the diversity of sources of power and agency coming from unexpected places. Instead, they have been turned into yet another toolkit of hegemony in some contexts. He reiterates a less

216. Nederveen Pieterse, *Globalization and Culture*, 2015.
217. Nederveen Pieterse, *Globalization and Culture*, 2020.
218. García Canclini, "Introduction: Hybrid Cultures."
219. Bhabha, "Foreword."
220. Bhabha, "Foreword," x.
221. Bhabha, "Foreword," xi; emphasis Bhabha's.

celebrated thesis of his hybridity theory—the potential of cultural hybridity is attained if it remains in the liminal, in-between spaces of today's social and cultural structures.[222]

In his introduction to the latest edition, García Canclini helpfully provides his maturing thoughts and clarifies his prior writing on hybridization.[223] Again emphasizing hybridization as the object of inquiry, not hybridity, he advocates for moving the analysis beyond descriptive when he writes:

> Precisely as we move from the descriptive character of the notion of hybridization—as a fusion of discrete structures—toward developing the concept as an explanatory resource, we are able to indicate in which cases the mixes can be productive, and when they generate conflicts owing to something that remains incompatible or irreconcilable in the practices brought together.[224]

Although he advocates for the notion of hybridization as an analytical tool to interpret the sociocultural realities in the world, he is clear about its limitations and weaknesses. He presents a nuanced perspective that sees cultural hybridization as a social reality, a social analysis tool, and a paradigm for developing new public policies in Latin America.

Methods of Hybridity Research

Since hybridity theories have not been used much in social research, the empirical literature is somewhat limited. Some scholars have proposed ways to do empirical research using cultural hybridity—or postcolonial theories in general—in the research framework. Nederveen Pieterse helpfully suggests that fruitful research would select forms of hybridity "that illuminate the variety, spread, depth, and meaning of hybridity, or shed light on history, past or future."[225] As he points out, since not every instance of hybridization may be worth studying, researchers need to discern which cases might be most useful. García Canclini suggests that focusing on the *intersections* of cultures may produce the most fruitful research.[226] Similarly, Appadurai recommends that researchers look for ethnographic projects that can be undertaken in multiple locations throughout the world,

---

222. Bhabha, "Foreword," xiii.
223. García Canclini, "Introduction: Hybrid Cultures."
224. García Canclini, "Introduction: Hybrid Cultures," xxviii.
225. Nederveen Pieterse, *Globalization and Culture*, 2015, x.
226. García Canclini, *Consumers and Citizens*, 12.

considering the fractal state of global flows.[227] While Young sees the potential of postcolonial scholarship to write "critical ethnography of the West," it is regrettable that this insight has rarely been translated into empirical research of Western societies.[228]

There is a consensus among scholars that complex cultural phenomena, such as cultural hybridity, must be studied in context and at multiple levels. For example, Kraidy believes that hybridity research needs to be grounded in particular contexts and "operationalized" in case studies.[229] García Canclini stresses the need to have an interdisciplinary approach in studying cultural hybridization in its specific situation.[230] Inda and Rosaldo call for "a concrete attentiveness to human agency, to the practices of everyday life . . . to how subjects mediate the processes of globalization," while Ohnuki-Tierney asserts the need for *microanalysis* of individuals who go through social processes in their historical context.[231]

Appadurai explains five types of global flows that have become more pronounced under accelerated globalization.[232] These are *ethnoscapes* (flows of people), *mediascapes* (flows of media), *financescapes* (flows of capital), *ideoscapes* (flows of ideologies), and *technoscapes* (flows of technology).[233] Appadurai uses this scheme of five "-scapes" to provide a robust framework for studying globalization. He suggests that we pay special attention to "process geographies" that reflect today's mobile nature of people and consider multiple motions and flows within the social organization of the world.[234] These suggestions are certainly easier said than done. Designing a research project that can successfully integrate the hybridity concept with a salient empirical approach would be an on-going challenge for researchers.

Philipp Stockhammer, a German archaeologist who utilizes hybridity in his interdisciplinary approach to studying historical material cultures, provides a helpful paradigm of using the hybridity concept in empirical research. He suggests three dimensions or levels of studying hybridity. The first dimension is to focus on "the construction and perception of hybridity—and purity as its opposite—by different individuals or groups." The second is to see

227. Appadurai, "Putting Hierarchy in Its Place," 46.

228. Young, *Colonial Desire*, 163.

229. Kraidy, *Cultural Logic of Globalization*, vi, viii.

230. García Canclini, *Hybrid Cultures*, 3.

231. Inda and Rosaldo, "Tracking Global Flows," 7; Ohnuki-Tierney, "Always Discontinuous/Continuous," 185, 190.

232. Appadurai, *Modernity at Large*.

233. One wonders whether "viruscape" (flows of virus) should perhaps be added to the list in light of the current, powerfully disruptive COVID-19 pandemic.

234. Appadurai, "Globalization and Research Imagination," 232.

"hybridity as a metaphor for a scientific approach that aims at analyzing and deconstructing asymmetric power relations that result from assumptions of cultural purity." The third is to study "hybridity as the basis of a methodological approach for the analysis of transcultural encounters."[235]

The main approach taken throughout this project would be similar to Stockhammer's third approach, which uses hybridity as an analytical tool. This study sees cultural hybridity as an interpretive lens through which experiences of cultural intersections and intercultural exchanges are analyzed. Fruitful studies of hybridity would not dwell only on its constructiveness; they would analyze and deconstruct power relations based on essentialized boundaries or utilize hybridity as a means of interpreting intercultural social negotiations. These suggestions for further research provide helpful guidelines for conducting empirical field research that incorporates the cultural hybridity concept.

Cultural Hybridity and Missiology

A survey of missiological literature reveals that, for the most part, missiology has only recently begun to engage the concept of cultural hybridity. Considering the prominence of cultural hybridity in social sciences and cultural studies today, this lack of engagement by missiology with the concept is somewhat surprising. It may indicate discomfort among mission scholars, particularly evangelicals, with postcolonial studies. It is also alarming as it hints that current missiological discourses are not well informed about recent scholarly discussions on cultural hybridity.

Robert J. Schreiter is one of the first missiologists, if not the first, to converse with Bhabha's theory in a discussion of globalization and theology.[236] Pointing out that cultures "constantly borrow and reconfigure themselves through new knowledge and practices," Schreiter maintains that the hybridity concept can contribute to mission studies by providing a path to gain a better understanding of religion, especially the ongoing development of migrant faiths in Europe and their relation with the next generations of Europeans.[237]

Some missiologists have argued for moving missiological discourse from a static and bounded notion of culture to understanding culture as dynamic and fluid; others have contributed by challenging the essentialized notion of cultures and ethnicities, especially concerning representation and

235. Stockhammer, "Questioning Hybridity," 2.

236. Schreiter, New Catholicity.

237. Schreiter, "Cosmopolitanism," 31.

identity.[238] Though they do not directly engage the postcolonial theories, they have contributed to engendering an openness toward the contemporary scholarship in social and human sciences.

More recently, some missiologists have begun to include the notion of cultural hybridity in their writing. For example, Danny Hsu proposes that the hybridity concept can provide a helpful analytical tool in understanding and interpreting cultural changes in contemporary Chinese society.[239] R. Daniel Shaw calls for missiologists to look at hybridity as a metaphor for deconstructing traditional ways of rigid, mostly negative views of religious syncretism.[240] He calls for recognizing some seemingly non-Christian spiritual practices as "manifestations of hybridity" rather than outright syncretism.[241] Shaw and Burrows expand this view more fully in their edited volume, *Traditional Ritual as Christian Worship*.[242] Through select case studies written by mission scholars and practitioners from around the world, they argue that orthodox Christianity is hybrid in nature, and Christians must allow room for traditional rituals of other cultures and religions to be adapted and transformed as new indigenous forms of Christian worship.

In her ethnographic study of "Tsinoys" in the Philippines, missiologist Juliet Lee Uytanlet juxtaposes the concept of hybridity and homogeneity and investigates the nuances and variations of ethnic identities constructed by the Chinese in the Philippines.[243] Hers is one of the few empirical studies, or perhaps the only study, in missiology to date that has utilized a cultural hybridity perspective in its research framework.

A growing number of missiologists express interest in the hybridity concept as a tool to study phenomena of globalization, migration, and diaspora communities.[244] Their works touch on the basic premise of hybridity

238. E.g., Rynkiewich, "World in My Parish"; "Person in Mission"; "Corporate Metaphors"; "Postmodern Anthropology for Mission"; *Soul, Self, and Society*; "Mission in the Present"; "'Do Not Remember'"; "Challenge of Teaching Mission in an Increasingly Mobile and Complex World"; Howell, "Globalization, Ethnicity, and Authenticity"; Howell, *Christianity in Local Context*; Howell, "Multiculturalism, Immigration and Church"; Howell and Zehner, *Power and Identity*; Flanders, *About Face*; Christofferson, *Negotiating Identity*; Adeney, "Why Cultures Matter"; Hiebert, "Evaluation of Church Growth"; Tiénou, "Reflections on Michael Rynkiewich."

239. Hsu, "Searching for Meaning."

240. Shaw, "Beyond Syncretism."

241. Shaw, "Beyond Syncretism." 16.

242. Shaw and Burrows, *Traditional Ritual As Christian Worship*.

243. Uytanlet, *Hybrid Tsinoys*.

244. See Mallon, *Traditioning Disciples*; Howell, "Multiculturalism, Immigration and Church"; Wan, *Diaspora Missiology*; Yip, "Contour of Post-Postmodern Missiology"; Ott, "Globalization and Contextualization"; Tira and Yamamori, *Scattered and*

and make a conscious effort to incorporate the language of hybridity. There are now missiological conferences that focus on cultural hybridity.[245] These show an increasing awareness among mission scholars of the potential benefit of the concept of cultural hybridity.

Considering how cultural hybridity theories in mainstream academia have been utilized as a paradigm for understanding globalization, migration, and multicultural societies for some time, missiology, which is only now beginning to explore them in this way, has much to catch up. Complex cultural phenomena in the contemporary global scene are likely to continue to challenge conceptual boundaries and methodological limits of missiology in the coming years. The notions of cultural hybridity and the cultural process of hybridization remain underexplored in missiology. In moving forward, the hybridity concept may present a viable interpretive framework for mission scholars in understanding conceptually and empirically challenging sociocultural phenomena.

SUMMARY AND CONCLUSION

From its birth in postcolonial studies through its conceptual development and controversial debates, the notion of cultural hybridity has had a substantial influence on multiple disciplines in humanities and social sciences. Despite concerns raised in the past, it has become a significant concept utilized for social and cultural analysis in various academic disciplines. While the growing literature on cultural hybridity testifies its prominence, it also raises concerns about misuse. Its increasing usage in framing research for various contexts seems to solidify its standing among social theories. Although it is widely recognized as powerful and pervasive, cultural hybridity's analytical potential may not have been fully realized, and its possibilities for agency barely explored. In concepts of cultural hybridity and hybridization, mission scholars may find a useful paradigm for missiological research.

In this study, cultural hybridity theories—specifically, a processual theory of cultural hybridization—inform the entire research process. From the conceptual framework and research design to fieldwork and data analysis, all aspects of the research process have been conducted with an understanding that processes of hybridization are normative, pervasive, and active in intercultural relations. The conceptual focus of this study is

---

Gathered; Nehrbass, *God's Image and Cultures*.

245. The Lausanne Consultation on the theme "Hybridity, Diaspora, and Missio Dei: Exploring New Horizons" was held in June 2018 in the Philippines. The theme for the annual meeting of American Society of Missiology in June 2021 was "Hybridity in Mission: Mixed and Multiple Identities in the *Missio Dei*."

on dynamic sociocultural processes of *hybridization* rather than a static notion implicit in the noun form, *hybridity*. The idea of the Third Space, as an integrative sub-concept of cultural hybridity, is incorporated in observations of intercultural relationships in the life contexts of the participants and analyzing their social experiences.

There are certain risks in using an abstract theory with few prior empirical studies as the conceptual framework for a qualitative research project. I attempted to mitigate these risks by adopting an approach referred to by Jackson and Mazzei as "thinking *with* theory."[246] I use cultural hybridization theories to "think *with* . . . data" and "use data to think *with*" cultural hybridization theories to gain insights and understandings.[247] Foucault writes, "Theory does not express, translate, or serve to apply practice: it is practice."[248] This study, therefore, will not necessarily dichotomize theory and practice. In fact, there is something to be gained by a certain level of ambiguity.

I also give due consideration to human agency, especially in challenging existing categories and respond to structural constraints. International Christian workers (ICWs) illustrate it through the creative strategies they adopt in the host society in the North African country (NAC) and within their multicultural teams (MCTs). I take the major arguments in the hybridity debates seriously. These must be considered as stark warnings to missiological researchers who want to consider the concept in their studies. Finally, it needs to be stated clearly here that cultural hybridity is not necessarily considered an object of this study; instead, it is a sociocultural hermeneutic framework used for analysis and interpretation of lived realities.

246. Jackson and Mazzei, *Thinking with Theory in Qualitative Research*; Jackson and Mazzei, "Thinking With Theory: A New Analytic for Qualitative Inquiry."

247. Jackson and Mazzei, *Thinking with Theory in Qualitative Research*, vii.

248. Foucault, *Language, Counter-Memory, Practice*, 208.

3

Research Methods

THIS STUDY UTILIZED QUALITATIVE research methods to explore intercultural social dynamics among international Christian workers (ICWs) who worked with multicultural teams (MCTs) in a North African country (NAC). The focus of this study was on producing rich descriptions, learning through an inductive-iterative process of analysis, and synthesizing meaningful, cohesive, and plausible interpretations of the participants' lived experiences.[1] While this study is not a traditional ethnography, various ethnographic research methods were central to the data collection and analysis.[2] This chapter describes in detail the research methods employed in this study.

OVERVIEW

Qualitative research methods and ethnographic methods have a large overlap; distinctions between them are not always clear.[3] Therefore, for categorizing purposes, this study may be described as a qualitative inquiry with ethnographic features. As such, data collection and analysis were most critical to the research results. Data collection was mainly achieved by interviews with individuals and married couples, a group interview, participant observation of team meetings, and observing social interactions by the participants. I collected recent newsletters of several participants

1. See Merriam and Tisdell, *Qualitative Research*, 3–21.

2. See O'Reilly, *Ethnographic Methods*; Spradley, *Ethnographic Interview*; Weiss, *Learning from Strangers*; Emerson, Fretz, and Shaw, *Writing Ethnographic Fieldnotes*.

3. Merriam and Tisdell, *Qualitative Research*; Hammersley and Atkinson, *Ethnography*.

and intercultural training materials from three different mission organizations. I also captured some of the relevant and publicly available information on the websites of mission organizations of which the participants were members. The design and nature of this study make the researcher the primary research instrument.[4]

The process of data collection was divided into three phases. In the first phase, I conducted an initial field study in NAC for a week and had a total of nine interviews with seven individuals and two married couples. I also had a group interview with a multicultural team composed of five international Christian workers.[5] During this phase, I contacted other potential participants and secured future interviews. I also collected personal newsletters from some of the participants.

The second phase began after I returned from the initial field study trip. I transcribed some of the initial interviews and began to think more deeply about the data. Based on my experiences from the first phase, I adjusted the interview questions and revised the research questions (RQs). I reviewed the training materials and newsletters of the participants that I had collected. I also viewed the websites of the mission organizations to which some of the participants belonged. I continued researching relevant literature to aid in thinking about the data and interpreting their meanings.

The third phase involved a field study of three weeks, during which I conducted interviews with thirteen individuals and thirteen married couples. Due to the logistical difficulty of enlisting teams, no more group interviews were conducted. Throughout fieldwork, I modified the research methods, adapting to the situation and needs of the moment.

Since I was exploring the complex lived realities of a group of people in a unique intercultural, multicultural context with few similar empirical examples while using an abstract concept as the framework, I needed to design the research in "a more loosely structured, emergent, inductively grounded approach for gathering data."[6] It means that the conceptual framework was often revisited, and the research questions went through multiple revisions. I exercised a high degree of flexibility in carrying out this research. As I realized that my original research design was unnecessarily rigid, I changed the methods on the ground during fieldwork. This research began with basic qualitative research methods involving mostly personal interviews. Then it shifted more toward classic ethnographic methods of observation, participant observation, and writing of fieldnotes as it progressed.

4. Maxwell, *Qualitative Research Design*, 88.
5. Refer to O'Reilly, *Ethnographic Methods*, 132–37.
6. Miles et al., *Qualitative Data Analysis*, 2014, 19.

One of the challenges in this study was the difficulty of pinning down the research questions. My RQs evolved throughout the study. According to Gibbs, the flexibility of qualitative research allows research questions to be decided late in the study "if the original questions make little sense in the light of the perspectives of those . . . studied."[7] RQs were indeed decided late in the research as they were refined and reformulated repeatedly.[8] After thinking deeply about what the data seemed to indicate, I settled on the RQs toward the end of the coding work.

The rest of this chapter will provide more details of the research methods used in this study. The next section describes the research location, including why the actual site is not made public. Then I explain the research population and the participant selection process. After describing the data collection methods, I devote a significant portion of this chapter to explaining the process of data analysis, which was a very complicated endeavor but also the heart of this project. I will then discuss the issues of the trustworthiness of this study, translation, delimitation, and limitation of this project. I close this chapter with a summary and conclusion section.

RESEARCH CONTEXT

The field study took place in a region in North Africa. It would be helpful to consider both the geographical context of the region in North Africa and the multicultural teams of international mission organizations (IMOs) as the research context. This study builds on the idea, "An effective study of culture focuses on the intersections."[9] The research location in North Africa has been an intersection of many cultural flows throughout its history with influences from Arab Muslims, indigenous Berbers, the Africa continent, and Western Europe. Multicultural teams are intercultural social groups in which Christian workers with various cultural backgrounds and nationalities work together. These teams provide the context for micro-level intersections of cultural flows. A research context in which various cultural currents intersect at multiple levels would be an ideal setting to learn about intercultural social processes and how they occur among individuals and groups. Thus, this study was conducted with participants who had lived in these two different levels of cultural intersections.

7. Gibbs, *Analyzing Qualitative Data*, 4.

8. Miles et al., *Qualitative Data Analysis*, 2014, 25.

9. García Canclini, *Consumers and Citizens*, 12.

North African Country (NAC)

The country where the fieldwork was conducted is located in the North Africa region.[10] Due to the sensitive nature of visible Christian presence in a region with limited religious freedom and potential risks to the research participants' safety and long-term security, the research site will not be disclosed in this study. I intentionally keep the research site vague by using ambiguous language or providing local descriptions that are generalized to the entire region of North Africa. Throughout the study, the research location will be referred to as NAC, indicating a North African country.[11]

The state religion of NAC is Islam. There is a relative religious homogeneity throughout North Africa. When this region gained independence from the French colonial rule during the 1950s and 1960s, over 95 percent of its population was reportedly Sunni Muslim of the Malekite rite.[12] According to Willis, the people of the *Maghreb*—Algeria, Morocco, and Tunisia—maintain "an Arab and Islamic identity."[13] Islamist movements have been active and gaining strengths during the past half-century.[14] As attested by recent ethnographic studies conducted in the region, Islam has an unmistakable influence in all spheres of society as it is deeply embedded in everyday life. Some researchers also find that people in the region continuously negotiate their social, ethnic, cultural, political, and religious status; they reshape their identity in the confines of religious and political establishments and globalizing forces that flow in and out of the region.[15] It is essential to note that NAC and its people are not sitting still in the past but continually adapting and changing, just like the rest of the world.

Women's rights and gender relations are complicated issues in the larger Arab Muslim world to which NAC belongs. Moroccan Sociologist Fatima Mernissi writes about her experience of once hearing a Muslim man recite to her a *Hadith*, which states, "Those who entrust their affairs to a

10. In this study, the term North Africa will be used to indicate the northwestern corner of the continent that includes Morocco, Algeria, and Tunisia. These three countries have much in common as Arabic, French, and Berber languages are widely used, they were under the French colonial rule, and are situated off the Mediterranean Sea.

11. For an overview of the region, refer to Michael J. Willis's *Politics and Power in the Maghreb*. It provides a helpful summary of the modern history and recent situation of these three countries.

12. Willis, *Politics and Power in the Maghreb*, 203.

13. Willis, *Politics and Power in the Maghreb*, 199–200.

14. Willis, *Politics and Power in the Maghreb*, 155.

15. See McDougall and Scheele, *Saharan Frontiers*; Scheele, *Village Matters*; Holmes-Eber, *Daughters of Tunis*; Newcomb, *Everyday Life in Morocco*; Hafez and Slyomovics, *Anthropology of the MENA*.

woman will never know prosperity!" Upon this encounter, she decides to research the sayings of Prophet Mohammed, which shapes what she calls "a tradition of misogyny" within Islam against women.[16] She concludes that her contemporary Muslim men's view of women was based on an old image of slave women from the eighth and ninth centuries.[17] Whether this view from the 1980s still holds today is not clear.

Nonetheless, her observation sheds light on women's traditional social place and modern gender relations in the Arab Muslim world. It has direct implications for international Christian workers who serve in majority Muslim societies such as NAC. These issues are not, however, as one-sided or straightforward as they are often portrayed in the media.[18] Some variations and nuances need to be incorporated in our understanding of these issues, not underestimating the agency of Muslim women.

Multicultural Teams (MCTs) of International Mission Organizations (IMOs)

It might appear more logical to think of a multicultural team as a unit of analysis than a research context. At the beginning of this study, I considered a multi-case study of multicultural teams of international Christian workers. However, I decided instead to study the intercultural social experiences of individual Christian workers who were members of these multicultural teams for two reasons. First, defining the boundaries of these teams was difficult. A case is usually defined as "a phenomenon of some sort occurring in a bounded context."[19] Multicultural teams in NAC are part of larger transnational mission organizations that span the globe. Making an MCT as a case or a unit of analysis creates a need to investigate its larger global organization. It could make the project more daunting by expanding its scope and moving the research away from exploring intercultural social experiences of its members, which is the main interest of this project. Secondly, access to these teams did not look promising as I heard a report from a trusted contact person in NAC that there were only a few functioning MCTs within NAC at the beginning point in the research. Working with individual Christian workers as the research cases instead of teams would solve these two issues and turn MCTs into the context in which the research participants socialized and worked.

16. Mernissi, *Veil And The Male Elite*, 49–81.

17. Mernissi, *Veil And The Male Elite*, 194–95.

18. See Hine, "Negotiating from the Margins"; Abu-Lughod, *Muslim Women Need Saving?*

19. Miles et al., *Qualitative Data Analysis*, 2020, 24.

Most international mission organizations (IMOs) structured to operate multicultural teams in their mission fields are part of new mission movements that arose out of the Western church after World War II.[20] These mission organizations rediscovered the concept and value of missionary teams and organized their ministry structures around mission teams.[21] Meanwhile, the rise of a world Christianity and the church in the majority world meant that the center of gravity of world Christianity had shifted from the Global North to the Global South.[22] In her reflection on today's global mission, Dana Robert writes, "today's convert might very well be tomorrow's missionary."[23] Rather, one could say that yesterday's converts have become today's missionaries. Many international mission organizations actively recruit and send out Christian workers from countries that only received missionaries not too long ago. Forming multicultural teams with globally recruited Christian workers has become a norm for many of these mission organizations.

Why Multicultural Teams (MCTs) in a North African Country (NAC)

The selection of NAC as the field research site is appropriate for this study for several reasons. I lived in NAC for over ten years and went through cultural adaptation in the local context as an ICW. For most of that period, I led an MCT and worked with teammates with various cultural backgrounds. As a qualitative inquiry that utilized the researcher as the primary instrument, familiarity with the research context and the research population was advantageous to gaining insights into the lived experiences of these Christian workers. It was found especially helpful since there were constraints on time and budget for fieldwork. My contacts around the country allowed me to tap into their network of international Christian workers in several different cities in the country. Due to my personal history and the long-term presence of my mission organization in the country, I enjoyed some built-in credibility with the research population. It made the location more convenient to recruit participants for this research. While caution is required in studying people well known to the researcher, it can also help obtain rich data not easily accessed by outsiders. Abu-Lughod's field study of the human rights of

20. Pierson, *Dynamics of Christian Mission*, 323.

21. Pocock, Van Rheenen, and McConnell, *Changing Face of Missions*, 262–63.

22. Jenkins, *Next Christendom*.

23. Robert, *Christian Mission*, 177.

Muslim women in Egypt is a good example.[24] It shows that this way of doing research has advantages in developing "thick description."[25]

This North African country presents a unique context for Christian mission. It is a cultural intersection of largely three cultural streams—Western European, Arab-Middle Eastern, and Continental African. It experiences the usual ebbs and flows of globalization as a developing nation. NAC is predominantly Muslim, with Islam as the national religion. Proselytism is prohibited by law. There is no officially recognized Christian church for its citizens. National believers are scattered and relatively few. Unlike some other Arab nations, there is no nationally established, official Christian church organization that can accommodate foreign international Christian workers under its wings. Officially, Christian workers are not able to enter the country on a religious visa. They do not usually identify themselves as "missionaries" and maintain a low profile. Without the umbrella of existing religious structure in which ICWs often settle in other countries, the context of NAC forces them to engage the majority people of the land who live in a very different "plausibility structure"[26] as self-identified Muslims.

In this setting, most ICWs in MCTs are tasked with adapting to their multicultural team members and concurrently to the local people in a context of restricted religious climate. Such a setting could engender rich and diverse intercultural social engagement. It makes this particular place an ideal location for studying cultural processes of hybridization.

RESEARCH POPULATION AND SELECTION OF PARTICIPANTS

The purposive sampling method was used for selecting participants in this study. An ideal participant would be an international Christian worker (ICW) who was serving with a multicultural team (MCT) of an international mission organization (IMO) that operated globally and who had spent at least two years in NAC. Seven participants who had lived in NAC for two years or less ended up being included in the sample. When recruiting research participants, it was not clear whether I would find enough participants due to a declining number of ICWs who worked with multicultural teams in NAC. I decided to interview these less-experienced workers for two reasons. First, in case I did not find enough participants and needed more data, I could use their interviews as part of the data; secondly, I thought that more-recently-arrived ICWs could recall more vividly their recent experiences of adaptation and adjustment to NAC and

---

24. Abu-Lughod, *Muslim Women Need Saving?*

25. Geertz, *Interpretation of Cultures.*

26. Berger, *Sacred Canopy.*

their team. Ideally, my participants would also be part of an MCT with five or more team members who had at least two nationalities or two cultural backgrounds. This MCT would regularly meet for spiritual input, fellowship, and mutual encouragement.

These guidelines for participant selection were used to ensure a sufficient level of sociocultural dynamics in the participants' lives, making this study more trustworthy. I contacted members of multicultural teams whom I had known in the past or those Christian workers who might know such persons to enlist their help for recruiting study participants. I recruited six participants through the "snowball sampling" method.[27] Among the participants, fifteen were ICWs I knew personally, and twenty-eight were introduced to me by someone I knew before. Even when I did not know the participants well, having a trusted mutual friend helped me gain access to these ICWs and build rapport with them during the interview.

Issues of Security and Privacy

One of the critical elements in this study was protecting the privacy and security of the research participants. There were several issues involved: the risk of compromising their local ministries, the risk of compromising their identity and thus potentially their long-term stay in this country, and team protocols that prohibited the participants from sharing sensitive information related to their team or organization. ICWs would rarely reveal sensitive internal information to those outside their teams. Also, their privacy took on a new meaning in the context of this research because the sharing of sensitive personal information could have ramifications for their relationships with others, especially team members. Their teammates might identify who the participants were and what they said concerning their team relations. Even with aliases, other people on their teams might recognize them if they read this work.

In light of these risks, I put in place and maintained strict security and privacy protocols throughout this project to protect the participants' identities. A decision was made early in the research design that the name of the country, city, and area where the participants resided would not be revealed. Thus, I use generic names such as "City A" and "Town C" for geographic locations. To refer to the country where the fieldwork was conducted, "NAC" is used. The generic name indicates that it is a North African country. Pseudonyms are used for all participants. For two of the participants, more than one aliases were used to make it more difficult for others to guess who the participants are. Only minimal personal details pertinent to the research

27. O'Reilly, *Ethnographic Methods*, 44; Patton, *Qualitative Research and Evaluation*, 298–99; Merriam and Tisdell, *Qualitative Research*, 98.

and presentation of findings are shared in this book. In some cases, a person's citizenship, ethnicity, or first language was changed or anonymized so long as the same meaning could be retained.

Another challenge in presenting this study was figuring out how to describe and explain intercultural social phenomena being observed more vividly—thus providing enough details to communicate the research findings clearly—without revealing information that could give away the identities of my participants. I continued to wrestle with this issue for the duration of the research. Some of the details were necessary to provide support for my arguments. These very details might also give away who this person was, if not to the reader, then to some of the other participants and their team members. Their interviews included sensitive information, including comments about their teams, organizations, team members, and leaders. These were, at times, critical or negative. Some of the interview content also indicated their identity as Christian "missionaries" and their membership in particular international mission organizations. All these factors were carefully considered in this project, especially for presenting the research.

Figure 1. Citizenship of the Forty-Nine Participants, by Continent

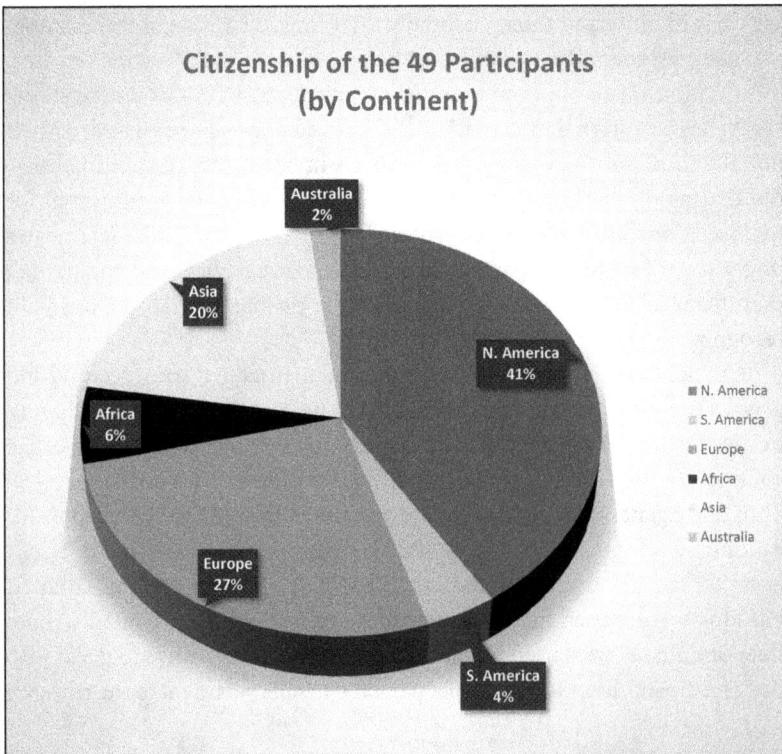

Citizenship of the 49 Participants (by Continent)

Australia 2%
Asia 20%
N. America 41%
Africa 6%
Europe 27%
S. America 4%

■ N. America
▨ S. America
▨ Europe
■ Africa
Asia
▨ Australia

Profile of Research Participants

A total of forty-nine international Christian workers were interviewed for this research. Forty-seven of them were part of eleven different MCTs of seven IMOs. These teams were working in six different cities and towns in NAC. Two of the participants were part of two different same-culture teams, one Korean and another "Anglo American."[28] There were thirteen different passport countries in all six continents among the participants. There was a great diversity among them in gender, age, education level, racial categories, languages, and occupational or professional platforms in NAC.

These forty-nine participants were interviewed in three different formats: twenty individual interviews, fifteen married couples' interviews, and one group interview with an MCT of five ICWs. Among these, thirty-five participants were interviewed in English, and fourteen of them were interviewed in Korean. Among those interviewed in English, nineteen were native English speakers, fourteen were speakers of English as a second language, and two were speakers of English as a third language or beyond.

In Table 1, the overall profile of the research participants is included. More than 60 percent of the participants were women; 75 percent were married. The participants' average age was forty-two, and the average number of years lived in NAC was just under eight years. More than 70 percent had a college and/or graduate degree. Nearly half (twenty-three out of forty-nine) of the research participants were involved in a business, and about a quarter of them worked with NGOs. For more details of the research sample, please refer to Appendix C.

Table 1. Profile of Research Participants

Gender		Marital Status	
Male	Female	Single	Married
19	30	12	37

---

28. A term such as "Anglo American" gives the impression that it is an essentialized group. There is certainly a great deal of cultural diversity among so-called Anglo Americans. The same thing can be said of Koreans. They may not be as monocultural as we would think. Unfortunately, for lack of a better way to describe people, I find it virtually impossible to stay clear of such terms.

Age				
20-29	30-39	40-49	50-59	60+
6	17	15	9	2

Highest Level of Education Completed				
High School	Some University or Vocational School	Bachelor's	Master's	Doctorate
3	10	19	13	4

Number of Years in NAC				
20+ yrs	10–19 yrs	5–9 yrs	2–4 yrs	2- years
4	13	4	19	7

Occupation/Professional Platform in NAC				
Business	Teaching	NGO	Student	Retired
23	2	12	10	2

Number of Participants per Interview Language	
English	Korean
35	14

Language Profile of the Thirty-Five Participants Who Were Interviewed in English		
Native English Speakers	Speakers of English as 2nd Language	Speakers of English as 3rd language or beyond
19	14	2

I recognize the problem of some of the racial, ethnic, and cultural categories used in this study. While these categories are diffuse, contested, and ambiguous, their popular use cannot be ignored or glossed over in social research. There are no better alternatives to use in place of these categories. More importantly, the research participants often used these terms. Some participants showed an awareness of the fluid nature of culture, ethnicity, and race while still reverting to use the popular, essentialized rendering of these categories. The participants tended to describe cultural differences at varying levels of hierarchy, such as sub-cultures within a nation, nations, continents, a mixture of generalized racial or ethnic categories, etc. For this study, precise definitions of racial, ethnic, and cultural categories will not be pursued. Instead, the participants' words and categories in their everyday life will be retained since language expressions from their lived experiences are likely to shed light on the ideas deeply embedded in their consciousness and embodied in their everyday life.

DATA COLLECTION

The fieldwork began in May 2018. I visited the research location for one week to implement and complete the first phase of the research. During the second phase, from mid-May through the end of August 2018, I worked on transcribing the initial interviews, doing initial coding and data analysis, and adjusting research methods. The third phase commenced in September 2018. I visited research sites in NAC for a second fieldwork visit for three and a half weeks and completed the rest of the data collection.

Interviews

The primary mode of data collection was personal interviews with twenty individuals and fifteen married couples. One of these interviewees participated in both an individual interview and a married couple interview with the spouse. Thus the total number of participants for this research was forty-nine. Participants were recruited from the pool of ICWs who worked with MCTs in NAC. While I used prepared interview guides to facilitate the interview process, the actual interview questions and discussions were adjusted as needed. This allowed for flexibility and spontaneity, accommodating the participants' needs. Except for one married couple who did not want to be recorded, all interviews were recorded using two digital audio recording devices. Twenty-four interviews—fourteen individual interviews, nine married couples interviews, and one group interview—were conducted in English. Twelve interviews—eight individual interviews and four married couples interviews—were conducted in the Korean language. These interviews lasted anywhere between an hour to three hours. Interviews with married couples tended to last longer than interviews with individuals.

I attempted to collect "rich data" through a series of questioning that probed their lived experiences.[29] The participants did not passively provide vague information; most of them actively collaborated to explore and construct plausible realities based on their own lived experiences. Inevitably, thought activities of recollecting and analytical processing were involved. Rather than an objective view of reality, which is impossible to attain, the realities perceived and constructed by these workers were, when analyzed carefully, credible and valuable sources for gaining an understanding of how these intercultural social processes occur in the lives of these ICWs.

In addition to interviews with individuals and married couples, a group interview was conducted during the first phase of the field research. Five ICWs, who were also interviewed individually, participated in this group interview. The purpose of this group interview was to enhance the understanding gained from personal interviews. Rich data were generated by interactive discussions and even conflicting views through a creative group process.[30] The group interview questions were adopted from the individual interview questions and adjusted to engender open discussions in an active forum among participants.

Although the format of this group interview was similar to a focus group, there were some differences. A typical focus group would have as participants those who are strangers to one another. But this group interview was with members of a multicultural team in the context of their regular practice of team meetings.[31] Interviewing "a naturally occurring group" is a well-established practice in ethnographic research.[32] This group interview session had qualities of a focus group in which an active forum among participants generated additional data for understanding interactive group dynamics.[33] It is, however, more fitting to call it an ethnographic group interview conducted with "people whom the ethnographer has established a relationship, over time, in settings in which . . . the ethnographer has become familiar."[34]

29. Merriam and Tisdell, *Qualitative Research*, 108–9; Maxwell, *Qualitative Research Design*, 126; Miles et al., *Qualitative Data Analysis*, 2014, 4.

30. O'Reilly, *Ethnographic Methods*, 134–38.

31. Merriam and Tisdell, *Qualitative Research*, 114.

32. O'Reilly, *Ethnographic Methods*, 134–38.

33. Saldaña and Omasta, *Qualitative Research*, 93–94.

34. O'Reilly, *Ethnographic Methods*, 137.

Due to the uncertainty of the participants' availability, interviews had to be conducted in whichever available form and shape whenever opportunities presented themselves. This group interview was such a case where a team of five people became available for a group session during their weekly team meeting. Four of the participants had already been interviewed individually before the group interview. One remaining participant was interviewed after the group interview.

These in-depth interviews with individuals, couples, and a team probed personal accounts of ICW's while working with multicultural teams and living in NAC. Interview questions investigated how intercultural social dynamics were unfolding, how they affected the participants' self-understanding, lifestyle, and ministry, and how multicultural team experiences might have mediated these processes.[35]

Participant Observation

Interviews conducted in this study were supplemented by my participation and/or observation in team meetings, other gatherings of MCTs, informal interactions between those who fit the research population, even those who did not directly participate in this study, and the physical surroundings. Abu-Lughod reminds us, "The first principle of ethnography . . . is to listen and watch."[36] Ethnographic emphases in this qualitative inquiry entailed careful listening and observing. The research participants were both "informants" to whom I listened and "actors" whom I observed in their natural settings.[37]

Much of the participant observations took place naturally while spending time with the participants over meals, car rides, visiting a local NAC friend together, or spending a night in their homes, often without a clear distinction between participation and observation. For example, I engaged in active observation while conducting personal interviews or having informal meetings with participants. In some situations, I joined the participants in their normal daily activities in work and family life. According to O'Reilly, there is a tension between participating and observing, between the strange and the familiar.[38] No researcher can engage in just one activity at a time. During my fieldwork, participation and observation tended to happen simultaneously. Observations, ideas, and personal reflections that resulted from participant observations were jotted down in quick,

35. The interview topic guides can be found in Appendix B.
36. Abu-Lughod, *Muslim Women Need Saving?*, 8.
37. Spradley, *Ethnographic Interview*, 32–33.
38. O'Reilly, *Ethnographic Methods*, 112.

short-hand notes on a small pocket notebook I carried around and were later typed in full fieldnotes whenever I found time.

Documents

As secondary sources of data, I collected newsletters from five married couples and three single women. A review of these Christian workers' newsletters provided insights into how they communicated about their life and ministry in NAC to their friends, family, and supporters back in their sending country. I also collected training materials of three different international mission organizations, of which thirty-eight of the forty-nine participants were members. These were materials used in training for intercultural adaptation and multicultural teamwork for these workers. I also visited the websites of all seven international mission organizations (IMOs) of the participants, observing the content and design of these websites and recording my thoughts in researcher memos.

DATA ANALYSIS

Analyzing the entire corpus of the collected data was the most challenging part of this research; it was also the most rewarding. Scholars point out that the data analysis section in many qualitative research reports often remains too vague for readers to understand how the researcher came up with the findings.[39] It is a mistake for qualitative researchers to reduce the entire data analysis process to a catchphrase, "themes emerged."[40] While there is a place for such language, data analysis is too complicated and messy to describe with only a simplistic phrase. This section attempts to go beyond the cliché by making data analysis methods more transparent and less mysterious. While it would not be possible to describe all the details of the long and grueling process of analyzing data, I will share the key details of how I went from the raw data to the research findings and then from these findings to further analysis and interpretations.

The large volume and complexity of the collected qualitative data for this study required an analytical process that was multi-layered and evolving. Saldaña helpfully describes my experiences in analyzing data throughout this study when he writes, "Answers to research problems emerge sometimes from systematic and persistent work, sometimes through long

39. Maxwell, *Qualitative Research Design*, 105; Humble and Radina, *Moving beyond "Themes Emerged,"* xix; Dickie, "Data Analysis," 49–50.

40. Humble and Radina, *Moving Beyond "Themes Emerged."*

inward reflection, and sometimes through serendipitous discovery."[41] A creative process of qualitative data analysis resulted in the consolidation of data into meaningful and significant categories. The themes and concepts described in chapters 4 through 7 are the results of a consolidating process that required all my cognitive resources. Through this process, a vast amount of information was condensed and categorized. I then interwove them, with an array of fresh ideas about intercultural social processes and personal changes in ICWs, into a conceptual synthesis. The most critical faculty needed for my data analysis was thinking continually about the participants and their lived realities beyond the surface of qualitative data collected. No method or tool can substitute for deep thinking. As Robert E. Stake writes, "Good research is not about good methods as much as it is about good thinking."[42] Rigorous analytical methods used in this research were a major part of my thinking process.

On-going Analytical Process

While I spent much time coding the collected data, its analysis did not occur only during this period; it was an on-going process throughout fieldwork, transcribing interviews, doing a formal analysis, and writing up this project. It would be difficult to separate data collection and data analysis.[43] In a sense, some of the analyses began during my own past life in NAC, long before this research was designed and implemented. Even if biased and positioned as they may be, my experiences proved to be rich resources that enabled me to reflect, compare, and analyze what I observed and heard throughout the study. While at the research location, I recorded my observations and reflections in fieldnotes. I wrote separate researcher memos to preserve my thoughts, feelings, impressions, ideas, and questions on the data, their meaning and significance, their connection to existing theories and concepts, and possible interpretation of the patterns and categories being constructed in my mind. Quick note-taking in a pocket notebook and taking pictures with a smartphone were some of the concrete methods used to capture moments and to help me remember details of my observations and thoughts.

Due to time constraints in the field, interviews were not transcribed immediately, but only after returning home. Taking two separate field research trips helped with analysis as there was a four-month period between the first and the second field research trip, which allowed me to transcribe some of

41. Saldaña, *Thinking Qualitatively*, 186.

42. Stake, *Art of Case Study*, 19.

43. Gibbs, *Analyzing Qualitative Data*, 4.

the initial interviews, make some observations and analysis of the initial data, and make necessary adjustments in my data collection methods for the second trip. During the first research trip, ten interviews, including a group interview, with eleven participants were conducted; the second trip included twenty-six interviews with a total of thirty-eight participants.

All interviews were transcribed verbatim. I transcribed some of the interviews myself, but most interviews were transcribed by professional transcribing services.[44] The transcribing work was itself an essential part of the analytical process. I listened and re-listened to all interviews that I had conducted, reliving those moments of honest and sometimes vulnerable conversations with my interlocutors. While I was listening to the interviews, I corrected any errors in the transcripts and made revisions. I became more familiar with the data during the transcription process. As I was revising transcripts, I raised questions, noted interesting parts, and had some serendipitous moments of discovery. After I finished reviewing and revising the transcripts, I began to code the data.

I read newsletters collected from five married couples and three singles among the participants. These documents showed how these Christian workers communicated to their supporters in their sending countries about their ministry, local adaptation, and their growing understanding of cultures. Rather than coding these documents, I referred to the content as background information on these participants. Additionally, I viewed websites of seven different IMOs, of which my participants were members, to obtain information about these global entities. I also reviewed intercultural training materials used by three of these mission organizations.

I learned the importance of writing analytic memos early in the research process.[45] In one of my memos written during a coding session, I wrote, "So far I have written seventy-four memos from the beginning of this study, and I suspect it will be 150–200 memos by the time I finish. These recordings of thoughts, reflections, questions, and feelings are important for the writing-up process. They also provide credibility as . . . legitimate audit trail." I proved to be correct in my prediction since I had written over 160 researcher memos throughout this study.

---

44. Commercial online transcribing services, Rev.com and Temi.com were used for transcribing interviews conducted in English. For interviews done in Korean, I used four different professional transcribers.

45. See Miles et al., *Qualitative Data Analysis*, 2014, 95–99; Saldaña, *Coding Manual*, 2016, 44–54.

Managing and Organizing the Data

With a large amount of data gathered, management and organization of the data were a critical part of this research. I installed NVivo 12 on my laptop computer and used it for these tasks. I recorded and saved all interview transcripts, fieldnotes, and researcher memos as Microsoft Word files. I imported all these files into an NVivo file. Then I coded all of the imported interview transcripts and fieldnotes using the NVivo software. Coding sessions were accompanied by the writing of researcher memos, in which I wrote down various thoughts, feelings, and reflections related to the activities and experiences for the day. They helped me develop my analyses of the data and retain new ideas about the relationship between coded materials. These memos were recorded and saved within the same Nvivo file throughout the project. This file was backed up daily to a secure online cloud storage location and a separate backup directory on the laptop. The data was handled with care throughout the research process, ensuring their electronic and physical security. The laptop was password-protected to prevent anyone from gaining access to the data in case it was lost or stolen.

NVivo 12 software was utilized for organizing, sorting, recording, and analyzing the entire corpus of data for the duration of this research. I found it to be a powerful and sophisticated research tool that could handle a massive amount of qualitative data generated during this research. In performing data analysis for this study, I used the organizing and recording tools available in NVivo 12 to assist in my analytic thinking process. The wide variety of data management and visualization tools—namely, hyperlinks and text search tools—helped me think about my research topic and the data in ways that would have been difficult to do without the software.

However, it should be noted that it is only a tool. It cannot be substituted for the researcher's analytical thinking that connects the data, ideas, theories, and personal intuitions. The researcher generates codes from reading transcripts; NVivo does not create meaning; it only records what the researcher makes it record. Although the automatic coding function can code the data to a degree, NVivo or any other computer-assisted qualitative data analysis software (CAQDAS) should not be seen as some magical tool that spits out a code after another. Just as Microsoft Word does not write any research paper for the researcher, NVivo does not analyze the data. The researcher does. Breakthroughs in artificial intelligence technology might change the future of qualitative data analysis. For now, the most meaningful part of the analyzing work—deep thinking—remains entirely the researcher's. In fact, the researcher is the most critical research instrument in a qualitative inquiry.

Inductive, Deductive, and Abductive Reasoning

Data analysis in this study involved both inductive and deductive reasoning.[46] After collecting, transcribing, and organizing the qualitative data, I began to code. I looked for patterns and common qualities that could be found between different cases in an inductive mode of analysis. As I determined different terms for different codes through initially coding several transcripts and fieldnotes, I grouped them together and constructed categories that seemed to explain the content. As I continued to code new transcripts, I looked for evidence for these categories in a deductive mode of analysis. Sometimes, these categories remained unchanged; other times, discarded. In many cases, these categories went through a continuous process of consolidation, separation, and revision. The process was iterative, going back and forth between inductive and deductive reasoning modes to create meaning and develop themes from the data.

For example, some of the codes that resulted from coding the first interview transcript were *I am homeless, losing home, being unfairly labeled,* and *essentializing cultures. I am homeless* and *losing home* became important codes that contributed to understanding a sense of loss among several participants of their cultural belonging. It resulted in constructing a major category called *cultural homelessness,* described in detail in chapter 6. *Being unfairly labeled* was a code assigned for a story told by a participant. It was later discarded from the list of codes. Still, it led to a further reflection of what this participant experienced, especially the person's emotional and relational aspect, producing a more robust analysis. *Essentializing culture* became a significant code that signaled a crucial finding in this research. This code from the first transcript recurred in many other places in the dataset. I determined that this could be interpreted as a response by the participants to vast cultural and personal differences experienced in their multicultural teams. In the end, I developed this code into a category that was described in detail in chapter 5.

The analytical process also included a third type of reasoning that Svend Brinkmann refers to as the "abductive approach."[47] Abduction can be an effective form of reasoning "in situations of breakdown, surprise, bewilderment, or wonder."[48] It is not a dataset or an extant theory that guides abductive reasoning, but "astonishment, mystery, and breakdowns in one's understanding" since abduction is about "breakdown research

---

46. Merriam and Tisdell, *Qualitative Research,* 17.

47. Brinkmann, "Doing Without Data"; Brinkmann and Kvale, *InterViews,* 224–25.

48. Brinkmann, "Doing Without Data," 722.

that operates from the researcher's own life."[49] This research was deeply connected to my personal experiences in NAC as an ICW working with an MCT. It is influenced by my existing relationships with former colleagues and some puzzling social phenomena that I had observed among them. It was perhaps natural that I used an abductive approach without being aware of it. It should be pointed out that these three modes of reasoning were not mutually exclusive but were often integrated into the data analysis process in this research.

Coding Methods

Before coding the data, I developed a specific coding plan to handle a large amount of data and accommodate this study's loose, exploratory nature. The literature on qualitative data analysis agrees that coding is a discovery process requiring an open mind.[50] As I studied coding methods, I learned that the way qualitative methodologists presented coding varied greatly, from simple[51] to complicated[52] to somewhere in between.[53] Among these, Saldaña's coding methodology proved quite helpful in providing several concrete methods directly applicable to this study.[54]

Saldaña suggests that many researchers make the common mistake of coding the raw data into descriptive codes that only show the data content.[55] It is difficult to make meaning out of people's lived experiences when codes provide only basic descriptions. To take the analysis from a basic descriptive level to a more analytical, conceptual level, I came up with a systematic coding strategy early in the coding phase. I began the coding activity with a couple of exemplary transcripts and fieldnotes as I tested different coding methods and produced experimental codes. I initially used three grounded theory coding methods called *In Vivo Coding*, *Process (or*

49. Brinkmann, "Doing Without Data," 722–23.

50. O'Reilly, *Ethnographic Methods*; Merriam and Tisdell, *Qualitative Research*; Gibbs, *Analyzing Qualitative Data*; Miles et al., *Qualitative Data Analysis*, 2020; Humble and Radina, *Moving beyond "Themes Emerged"*; Court, *Qualitative Research*; Miles, Huberman, and Saldaña, *Qualitative Data Analysis*, 2014; Saldaña, *Coding Manual*, 2013; Saldaña, *Thinking Qualitatively*; Saldaña, *Coding Manual*, 2016; Emerson et al., *Writing Ethnographic Fieldnotes*; Charmaz, *Constructing Grounded Theory*; Bazeley and Jackson, *Data Analysis with NVivo*; Jackson and Bazeley, *Data Analysis with NVivo*.

51. E.g., O'Reilly, *Ethnographic Methods*; Merriam and Tisdell, *Qualitative Research*.

52. E.g., Saldaña, *Coding Manual*, 2016; Charmaz, *Constructing Grounded Theory*; Miles et al., *Qualitative Data Analysis*, 2014.

53. E.g., Court, *Qualitative Research*; Gibbs, *Analyzing Qualitative Data*.

54. Saldaña, *Coding Manual*, 2016.

55. Saldaña, *Coding Manual*, 76–78.

Action) Coding, and *Initial (or Open) Coding*.[56] *In Vivo Coding* is a method that takes an exact word or phrase from the data to form a code.[57] *Process Coding* produces codes in gerund forms (-ing words) to show action and process.[58] *Initial Coding* stays close to the data and creates provisional codes that are revised, combined, or dropped later.[59]

As coding progressed, I used *Process Coding* as the primary method and *In Vivo Coding* as the secondary. I also included *Descriptive Coding*, which simply describes the content and *Versus Coding*, which contrasted two opposite attitudes or emotions.[60] Using a mixture of these methods to code the first five documents, I accumulated over 260 codes, which were too many. I kept coding a few more interview transcripts and fieldnotes before making adjustments to these codes. Meanwhile, I continued to reflect on these coding sessions and recorded my thoughts in researcher memos. In the end, the initial coding phase generated more than 420 codes. During this early stage of coding, I tried to stay close to the data and produce descriptive codes since this was an exploratory phase in which various ideas needed to be expressed, recorded, and considered before consolidating them into more conceptual and analytical codes or categories.

Codes and groups of codes underwent continual revision throughout the coding process until the entire dataset was coded. Then codes were refined, groups of codes were reviewed, and some were combined to form larger categories. These activities led to the creation of a three-level hierarchical code structure that reflected my initial data analysis. The categories and codes became loose building blocks for further analyses of comparing the data between different cases, looking at patterns, and interacting further with existing literature.

An additional coding method needs to be mentioned. I utilized *Dramaturgical Coding* to engender a deeper understanding of social situations with tension or conflict reported by the participants.[61] *Dramaturgical Coding* helps analyze social life by using the theatre imagery as a metaphor for examining people's motives and actions.[62] Erving Goffman is credited

---

56. See Saldaña, *Coding Manual*, 2016.

57. Saldaña, *Coding Manual*, 105–10.

58. Charmaz et al., "Evolving Grounded Theory"; Saldaña, *Coding Manual*, 2016, 110–15.

59. Charmaz, *Constructing Grounded Theory*, 116–18.

60. See Saldaña, *Coding Manual*, 2013.

61. See Saldaña, *Coding Manual*, 2016, 145–50; Charmaz, *Constructing Grounded Theory*, 273–77; Miles et al., *Qualitative Data Analysis*, 2020, 68–69.

62. Charmaz, *Constructing Grounded Theory*, 273.

for its core ideas.[63] Goffman thought that there were two essential parts to individuals' social conduct: "the individual as character performed" and "the individual as performer."[64] As actors, humans create impressions on the audience by playing their parts; as characters in a drama, they also play particular character attributes that they appear to possess.[65] *Dramaturgical Coding* derives an understanding from this stage performance aspect of social life, helping the researcher examine people's actions and the motives behind them and bringing the hidden elements of social life to the foreground.[66] I used *Dramaturgical Coding* on seventeen participant stories that were imbued with tension and conflict. Details of this coding method can be found in Appendix E. I incorporate some of the results of this analytical method in chapters 4, 5, and 6, adding dramaturgical interpretations of some of the richest data in this study.

From Coding to Further Analysis

It took me about four months to work through a total of thirty-six interview transcripts created with forty-nine individuals (twenty interviews with individuals, fifteen interviews with married couples, and one group interview), which were about 1,600 double-spaced pages of texts. I also coded forty-one fieldnotes written during the research trip, which were about sixty double-spaced pages in length. In the three-level code structure that I had created, the top and mid-level codes became useful for constructing conceptual categories that went beyond descriptives. There were six top-level categories. Among these, I decided to select three as my core categories to be explored further. These three categories ended up becoming the three major themes described respectively in chapters 4, 5, and 6.

The first theme describes the intercultural social experiences of ICWs in NAC. It analyzes their initial experiences, on-going social life and negotiation of social norms, and how they navigated their social context in the setting. The second theme relates to their intercultural social experiences in their MCTs. It relates to their initial experiences, the inner workings of their teams, on-going social relationships, and their strategies for navigating their organizational life. The third theme addresses personal changes experienced by the participants.

63. Saldaña, *Coding Manual*, 2016; Charmaz, *Constructing Grounded Theory*.

64. Goffman, *Presentation of Self*, 253.

65. Goffman, *Presentation of Self*, 17.

66. Charmaz, *Constructing Grounded Theory*, 273–74.

According to Gibbs, one of the most challenging aspects of data analysis for inexperienced qualitative researchers is interpreting the data.[67] He points out that many end up interpreting their data based on their initial impressions and fail to go beyond the surface level of analysis. He states that recognition of categories and patterns should not be the end goal of analysis. He contends that the researcher needs to find causality for the phenomenon being described by answering the question, "Why do these kinds of people tend to do or say these kinds of things in these situations?"[68]

To advance the analysis from a descriptive level to a conceptual level, I focused on the relationship between the three main themes selected and the sub-categories constructed under each. In so doing, I saw several analytic possibilities. Among them, I chose three analytic categories that seemed to provide the most salient interpretations of the phenomenon of intercultural social processes being studied. Firstly, thinking about the relationship between ICWs' social experiences in NAC and their social experiences in MCT yielded the notion that these two experiences mediate each other. Intercultural social processes represented by these two kinds of experiences are indeed inseparable. These two processes are interwoven and braided, and they help our interlocutors construct "cultures." Secondly, focusing on the relationship between overall intercultural social experiences of ICWs and their personal changes indicates that the participants displayed qualities and behaviors best explained by the concept of "diasporic habitus."[69] Thirdly, some of the categories constructed in chapter 5 suggest that the research participants used two contradicting views of culture to cope with cultural differences and diversities in their midst.

From Analysis to Writing Up

Once all the raw data were coded and sorted by categories and themes, I began to write up the content for the chapters that corresponded to the main themes of this research. The writing work itself was an intense analytical process since I had to re-read and think through the categorized materials and determine which ones among the raw data best represented each idea being generated. To produce descriptive narratives for each theme and category, I selected and further reduced the amount of coded data that were sorted into each. This entire process led me to make mental connections between the categories generated and the conceptual framework of this study, helping me draw meanings out of the data.

67. Gibbs, *Analyzing Qualitative Data*, 186.

68. Gibbs, *Analyzing Qualitative Data*, 109.

69. Parker, "Chinese Takeaway"; Ang, "Inhabiting the Diasporic Habitus."

As I was writing up the narratives for the major themes, I discovered that the data organized under the codes I had settled on were too diverse for me to write a coherent segment on each code. It became apparent that I needed to split these codes further into smaller sub-codes in order to represent the coherence of the data without losing their nuance. So, I ended up splitting some of the codes I had previously lumped together. This process of splitting and lumping codes from the sorted dataset took additional months. It taught me a lesson that qualitative data analysis never ends; it is an on-going iterative process from the beginning of the study to the end of writing the final draft of the report.

This experience merits the question: why do we make a mental separation between data analysis and other aspects of a qualitative research project? It seems that the analytical process has been the undercurrent through everything I had done in this study, from the conception of the research problem and research design to data collection, coding, and the write-up. What Saldaña refers to as "thinking qualitatively" seems to be the same as thinking and analyzing continually.[70] Indeed, data analysis has been an iterative process from the beginning till the end of this study. It may be more accurate to say that the *formal* data analysis stage began with data collection and intensified during coding while the entire research was a continual analytic process.

As I was writing up some of the participant narratives by describing and explaining them, I realized that some of these would include not only the participants' words but also my interpretation of them. The reader might notice that the narratives sometimes converge in a single voice and, other times, diverge into two—the participant's voice and the researcher's voice. During analysis, I used both my personal knowledge of the participants' lived experiences and their MCT-NAC context as well as the data directly obtained from the participants. While this might have influenced the descriptive analysis in this study, I decided that the benefits of personally knowing some of the participants and their contexts would outweigh the potential disadvantage of introducing personal biases, which are, in any case, not avoidable in social research.

Informal Pilot Study

In early 2018, during the research design phase, I conducted an informal pilot study with five persons who were similar to the actual research participants.[71] The primary purpose of the pilot study was to refine my research

70. Saldaña, *Thinking Qualitatively*.
71. Refer to Appendix D for a full report of the pilot study.

questions and interview protocols.[72] This pilot study helped examine and refine the overall design of this study.[73]

I conducted semi-structured individual interviews with five career international Christian workers who had recently returned to the US. Each interview was about thirty minutes in length. I asked them questions about their cultural upbringing, their initial cultural adjustments after arriving in their field of service, what role their team played in their cultural adaptation, any personal changes that were noticeable to them due to these intercultural experiences, and where they currently found their "cultural home."[74]

There were several findings that further clarified how to go about conducting this research. First, the participants perceived and recognized a process of cultural change in them and the factors that influenced it. As this kind of cultural and social change was at the heart of the proposed research, this provided some assurance for the chosen research methods. Second, participants showed a decent capacity to reflect and articulate their intercultural experiences. Third, this pilot study reinforced my decision to focus on the dynamic process of hybridization, not a static notion of hybridity.[75] This distinction was maintained throughout the research. Lastly, I recognized a need to pay close attention to three different kinds of interactions taking place—between the international Christian worker and the MCT, between the international Christian worker and the local context, and between the MCT and the local context—and their mediating effects on the international Christian worker's social experiences. These findings were incorporated into the overall research design.

TRUSTWORTHINESS OF RESEARCH

This study's trustworthiness is supported by the rigor in the research design, data collection, and data analysis methods.[76] Focusing on the emic view and sustaining long-term contact with many participants were advantages for this project.[77] It was also designed to produce a "thick description" of

---

72. Yin, *Qualitative Research from Start*, 35.

73. Locke, Spirduso, and Silverman, *Proposals That Work*, 76.

74. Vivero and Jenkins, "Existential Hazards"; Hoersting and Jenkins, "No Place to Call"; Liu, *Hybridity and Cultural Home*.

75. García Canclini, "State of War," 43.

76. Merriam and Tisdell, *Qualitative Research*, 238–39.

77. O'Reilly, *Ethnographic Methods*, 226–27.

nuanced and complex lived experiences.[78] It presents rich, detailed descriptions of the context, the participants, and research findings.[79]

This research incorporated triangulation by "collecting information from a diverse range of individuals and settings, using a variety of methods."[80] As explained throughout this chapter, I used various data collection methods, including three different formats for interviews and participant observation. I collected personal newsletters and information on the websites of international mission organizations. I also obtained and reviewed intercultural training materials used in some of these organizations.

A sufficient level of diversity among my participants ensures the richness of the collected data. As shown in the participant profile in Figure 1 and Appendix C, the research sample included many different nationalities. Many of the participants were fluent in languages other than English and had membership in eleven multicultural teams of seven different mission organizations. They were male and female, single and married, and from a wide range of age groups, education levels, and experiences in NAC. The participants also lived in six different cities and towns in NAC.

Credibility of this research was strengthened by respondent validation.[81] During the summer of 2019, I had face-to-face meetings with four of my participants when they visited my area in the US and received their feedback on my preliminary findings. I was able to discuss with them the main themes generated through my analysis. They affirmed this study's main findings and added some thoughts as to why ICWs went through personal changes.

As an extra measure, I included interviews with two international Christian workers who were part of a culturally-homogeneous team. Since this was not a comparison study, ICWs of same-culture teams were not part of the primary research sample. However, I compared how they articulated their intercultural social experiences and those of the participants and noted the differences.

TRANSLATION AND USE OF DUAL LANGUAGE

Language is a critical aspect of qualitative interviews.[82] I conducted a total of thirty-six interviews—twenty individual interviews, fifteen interviews with

78. Geertz, *Interpretation of Cultures.*

79. Merriam and Tisdell, *Qualitative Research*, 257.

80. Maxwell, *Qualitative Research Design*, 128.

81. See Merriam and Tisdell, *Qualitative Research*, 246; Hammersley and Atkinson, *Ethnography*, 181–83.

82. Flick, *Managing Quality in Research*, 17.

married couples together, and one group interview. Among these, twenty-five interviews were conducted in the English language (thirteen individuals, eleven married couples, and one group); eleven interviews were done in the Korean language (seven individual interviews and four interviews with married couples). One participant was interviewed twice, once individually and once with the spouse. Among those interviewed in English, there were nineteen native speakers and sixteen speakers of English speakers as a second language or beyond. Three participants had limited proficiency in English. Fortunately, they were interviewed with their spouses who had a higher level of English proficiency and helped with the expression and translation of words or phrases in their own language.

Moreover, I, the researcher, have a bilingual ability, being at the fluency level of an educated native speaker in both English and Korean. All interviews conducted in the Korean language were transcribed verbatim, and the transcripts were coded and analyzed directly from Korean without being translated into English. My ability to work with both languages at a high level allowed me to manage the data in this way, saving time. In most cases, Korean transcripts were coded into English words and phrases. Some codes were initially in Korean but later were consolidated into codes in English.

DELIMITATION AND LIMITATION

This study is delimited to international Christian workers who served with multicultural teams of international mission organizations in NAC. Two ICWs who worked with monocultural teams were interviewed, although they were not part of the primary research population, to increase the study's trustworthiness. Since it was not the focus of this study, I did not attempt to investigate the ministry aspects in the participants' lives. However, the things related to their ministries were still discussed since the primary reason for these ICWs workers residing and working in NAC was their Christian faith and a sense of calling in Christian mission. Focusing on their intercultural social experiences meant that their way of life, including how they ministered as Christian workers, was also probed.

This study is limited by the very nature of qualitative methods. Bloomberg and Volpe write, "Generalizability is not the goal of qualitative research; rather, the focus is on transferability—that is, the ability to apply findings in similar contexts or settings."[83] As a qualitative inquiry, this study seeks transferability or "naturalistic generalization," which is achieved by exploring particular contexts and discovering new patterns, insights, and understandings of human life that can lead to understanding other contexts.[84]

---

83. Bloomberg and Volpe, *Completing Your Qualitative Dissertation*, 2016, 12.

84. Court, *Qualitative Research*, 32.

Nonetheless, this study's findings should be seen as applying only to the research population at the research location. If anyone attempts to relate insights from this study to another context, they should do so cautiously with a clear understanding of the limits in this research.

SUMMARY AND CONCLUSION

In this chapter, I provided the details of the research methods utilized in this study. This was a qualitative inquiry using ethnographic methods for data collection and analysis. A total of forty-nine international Christian workers (ICWs) who worked in a North African country (NAC) participated in this study, helping to explore and produce an understanding of their experiences of intercultural social life. The research sample was highly diverse, with various diversities present among them, such as nationalities, spoken languages, age, and years lived in NAC. Traditions, customs, and limited religious freedom in NAC put restrictions on how ICWs could live, work, and conduct themselves socially. The research participants' security and privacy were taken seriously throughout this project, ensuring their safety and longevity in the place of their service. The overlapping research contexts of NAC and MCTs of international mission organizations (IMOs) were also described. These contexts provide a research setting in which various cultural flows intersect the participants' lives.

Data collection involved interviewing individuals, married couples, and a multicultural team (MCT). It also included participant observation, personal newsletters of participants, and intercultural training materials from three IMOs. I also reviewed the websites of seven IMOs of which my participants were members. I organized and analyzed the dataset by using NVivo 12 computer software. Data analysis was the heart of this project; it was both an ongoing process from the beginning to the end of this research and a formal work using various coding and analyzing methods. Analyzing a large amount of complex data was challenging but also rewarding. To be transparent about the research process, I included some details of how data analysis was done. Also, a summary of the pilot study is included.

I utilized various means to ensure the trustworthiness and credibility of this study. Both English and Korean were used during the data collection stage, but the analysis was mainly performed in English. While this study is limited by the nature of qualitative research, exploring people's lived realities at the intersection of multiple cultural flows might help produce an understanding that may be transferable to other settings. The next three chapters will discuss the three major themes developed in this research through the data analysis.

4

Intercultural Social Experiences in a North African Country (NAC)

THE PURPOSE OF THIS study was to explore the nature, contributing factors, and outcomes of intercultural social experiences of international Christian workers (ICWs) who served with multicultural teams (MCTs) of international mission organizations (IMOs) in a North African country (NAC). This study focuses on how their lived experiences in their surrounding sociocultural context *and* within their MCTs influence intercultural social processes at the individual level that result in personal changes in them. This is the first of three chapters that will present findings from coding, sorting, and analyzing the collected data.

The focus of this chapter is on the lived experiences in NAC by the research participants. It addresses the first research question, "How does living in the research location in NAC mediate intercultural social experiences of Christian workers who serve with multicultural teams (MCTs)?" This chapter is organized by presentations of four categories drawn from the data. These are the participants' initial experiences in their local NAC context, their on-going social life in this context, negotiating social norms with the local people, and their strategies for navigating the NAC context. It addresses the nature of and factors related to living and working in the context of NAC. Presenting the data in this way may explain how local contextual factors influenced intercultural social experiences of ICWs, and how these experiences contributed toward resulting personal changes.

INITIAL EXPERIENCES IN LOCAL SETTING

When asked about their initial adjustments to life in their local setting, many participants recalled their experiences of first days and weeks in detail. Some shared their first impressions—both positive and negative—of their initial local surrounding. Others talked about their experiences of learning the local social norms. Some of them described what made them feel welcomed by local people. A majority of them talked about the challenges they had faced during their initial adaptation, such as the stress of adapting to an entirely new environment, communication difficulties, and some unpleasant experiences with the local people.

First Impressions of the Local Setting

The majority of those who talked about their initial impressions of NAC were very positive. Their initial impressions far exceeded their expectations. Most frequently mentioned were warm and friendly welcome by the local people, their hospitality, and the ease of building friendships with those they encountered. Melissa, who grew up in North America, said, "I guess I . . . was just very surprised at how warm and . . . the culture is just so much more about talking with each other and bumping shoulders." Myungsook was impressed with the warmth of people that she felt NAC was like heaven. Philip, a dad who arrived with small children, commented, "It's really a children-friendly culture." He and his wife recalled that there was a bit of discomfort on their part when local people out on the street tried to kiss their young children, but once they realized that it was a gesture of friendliness, they felt welcomed in their new country.

Some younger women came to the country with concerns of harassment from men on the streets but were surprised by how safe and comfortable they felt. Ashley said, "I expected a lot of physical harassment. And there hasn't been, which has just been lovely." Melissa also said, "I expected to be harassed more or to be stared at more or just more fearful, but I felt most people just kind of left me alone, and that surprised me." Unfortunately, such positive experiences were not always the case for some of the female participants, as it will be shown later.

Some participants had thought of NAC as a spiritual stronghold of Islam and expected fierce and even violent religious oppression. They were surprised to see little of those when they first arrived. They had expected a darker, more negative overall impression of the country due to the image they previously had about Islam. Still, the friendliness of the local people changed their minds. They had also arrived with concerns of safety and security due to their conception of extremist Muslims. Instead, they felt surprised by a sense of safety and security due to the hospitable local people. Selective reporting of violence in the Muslim world by the mainstream media is perhaps not the only culprit for invoking fear among these Christian workers. For example, the website of an international mission organization, of which fourteen of my participants were members, showed grim photos of Muslim women and children in a dark background when I visited their site during this study. These images seemed to portray Muslims as oppressed people living in darkness who needed saving.[1] While this view is not entirely false, a monolithic understanding of Muslims can certainly misconstrue the reality. Overt generalizations and one-dimensional caricatures of a vastly diverse group of people can lead to a misunderstanding at best and, at worst, their demonization, even if the depictions are done with good intentions. They can create a barrier to healthy mission practices that catalyze human flourishing among people with a Muslim background.[2]

Building relationships with local people during their initial weeks and months had a significantly positive influence on the participants' sense of local adaptation. These connections occurred when participants were invited by local people into their homes and offered tea, sweets, or meals. Jessica, an American, expressed her amazement when she said, "You would just go to somebody, and they would have you come in and eat and want you to stay and then invite you to come [back] . . . ." This kind of hospitality by their Muslim neighbors repeatedly surprised my participants who did not grow up in such a welcoming, friendly environment back in their home countries. These stories of Muslim hospitality toward foreigners perhaps provide good examples of what Christian hospitality could look like, especially toward aliens and foreigners in a place such as the United States. When these Christian workers experienced local people's acts of hospitality and kind gestures in early weeks and months, they saw much of their fear of Muslims and the distrust toward the cultural Other that they held in their minds dissolve.

Having a good bonding experience with a local host family also played a significant role in several participants' initial adjustment to the local context. Myungsook reminisced how she became an adopted daughter in a local family, thanks to a kind introduction by another ICW who had a family-like relationship with this family. Susan, a single American woman, said that being included in the life of a local family was helpful to her initial adaptation. She said, "It was really good for me to see a father who loved his wife and loved his daughters . . . . They had a great relationship, and I probably would have made some pretty brash assumptions based on my experiences

1. See Abu-Lughod, *Muslim Women Need Saving?*
2. See Reisacher, *Dynamics of Muslim Worlds.*

with [local] men . . . about men and their relationships with women. So it was really good for me to see a . . . healthy family and marriage relationship . . . ." Similarly, Franco and Camila said, "She [their local host] was . . . she really took care of us. So that was really, really . . . very positive. The lady could have been our mother." In general, most participants observed hospitality and friendliness of their NAC local neighbors, landlords, and newly met friends as part of their essential early experiences. It was indicative in their comments that these experiences led them to lower their guards and removed fears regarding their social life in their new setting.

Learning Local Language(s) and Social Norms

Virtually all participants of this study devoted themselves to language and cultural learning during their first year in NAC. Many of them engaged in full-time language studies. They attended language courses or took private lessons to learn the local Arabic dialect. While the language learning methods varied among the participants, it was common for them to spend fifteen to twenty hours per week in classroom or private lessons. Some participants had a strong desire for local cultural immersion and not spending much time with other foreigners in their city. Two of them explained their intentionality for cultural immersion when they said:

> Our one philosophy that we try and let guide all of our days is [to] keep meeting people, keep getting out of the house, as much as you can. Whether individually or together, as much as we can with our days, we get out, and we meet people. (Ryan)

> We were very intentional with only being in relationships with locals [NAC nationals], intentionally not going to the expat church there. So we were just 100 percent as close to it, focused in [NAC] relationships. (Joseph)

Members of several different mission organizations mentioned that they used a method called Growing Participant Approach (GPA) developed by linguist Greg Thomson.[3] It seems that GPA has become the most popular language-learning method among the participants, replacing the previously popular LAMP (Language Acquisition Made Practical) method developed by Thomas and Elizabeth Brewster.[4] GPA focuses on listening and speaking rather than reading or writing. It is known among

---

3. See Thomson, "Growing Participator Approach (GPA)."
4. Brewster and Brewster, *Language Acquisition Made Practical*.

ICWs in NAC to be effective for building comprehension and fluency in a relatively short time.

During their first few months, many participants realized that the local social norms were in stark contrast to what they were used to in their home countries. Besides language learning and cultural immersion, Philip and Marie had to learn the basics of everyday life in the new environment, such as taking the trash out, how local people approached time, and finding a house to rent. Coming from a Western European country, they were surprised how easy it was to join and meet a friend at a café or a restaurant without making a prior appointment. What they experienced was a massive change in many details of how to conduct daily life. The social norms in the local setting were very different from what they were used to in Europe.

These differences in social life came as a shock to some participants. Caitlin was shocked by how different her local women friends were in their perspective of marriage and singleness. In recalling a conversation with a local friend, Caitlin said:

> She [her local friend] can't imagine why I would prefer single-ness above this lifestyle [getting married to a wealthy man as a second wife]. Why would I rather be single and not married, if I can be married and have this life [of being a second wife]? I can't understand why you want to be the second wife to anyone? And just understanding the differences between us, it's not just religion, it's a very different worldview, that my views are probably as strange to her as her views are to me, you know.

These social differences, especially ones related to their core values, often kept them at odds with their neighbors and friends, causing them to feel shocked or disoriented in NAC during their first year.

Stress of Adjusting to Local Living

When I asked them about their difficulties during their initial adjustment period in NAC, the participants mentioned several things. Depending on their marital status or family situation, they mentioned different types of stresses. Families with young children tended to say something related to their children's adjustments and schooling. Some children were woken up scared during the night because of the loud sound of *adhan*, the Islamic call to prayer. Claudia, a mother of two school-age boys, found it very difficult to see her children struggle to fit in their new local school. Emma, whose daughter was sent to a local school, was shocked to find out that Christmas Day was a typical school day, and her daughter even had an exam on that day. Emma had grown up in a Christian community in West Africa where Christmas was a widely celebrated national holiday. It had not occurred to her until that moment that her children would be required to attend school on Christmas day.

Ryan and Melissa, who had an infant child, found it difficult when local people interfered in their parenting and gave sweets to their baby without their permission. When they realized that the local neighbors did so out of good intentions, they decided that this was one of the things that they needed to adjust. According to Johannes and Noa, who were parents to four daughters, because everything was so new to them and they did not understand the local language, they often felt vulnerable. They felt that their emotions were not always stable during the first months.

Haejin, a single woman in her early 30s, came with her fears of local people due to the stereotypical image of Muslims as being violent and dangerous. It exacerbated her stress level during her initial adjustment period. She quickly became homesick. She also found it quite tiresome to adhere to local social customs, especially when visiting her local friends, who always asked her to stay overnight. When she attended weddings, which usually started in the evening and lasted till the next morning, she was physically and mentally worn out.

Mila was a business professional with a long corporate career in North America before she sensed a calling to serve as an international Christian worker. Coming to NAC from a place where punctuality and keeping one's words were golden, she found it bothersome when local friends did not keep appointments with her. It seems, however, that she might have equated these personal meetings as a part of her work since establishing relationships was a part of her main ministry activities at the beginning of her time in NAC. However, the local persons might have felt that these were out-of-routine social meetings that could be flexible and rearranged as needed if there were other more pressing needs.

Despite the general agreement among many participants about these difficulties, not everyone felt stressed by the local living. Youngcheol, a Korean, said, "The [local] culture is actually quite similar to our culture. So, it . . . was not a huge issue for us." Joseph and Rachel, an American couple, said they had no living stresses during their initial year. They arranged to have a nanny from the US live with them and hired a local house help so that they could solely focus on language studies. Their kids, who were very young at that time, did quite well too. Joseph recalled how amazed they were that things were going so well for them. He recalled, "[once] we sat down and talked a couple of times, our nanny and just the two of us, of like . . . where is the culture shock? We should be freaking out. This is going too well!" Rachel remembered that she added at that time, "This should be hard. Why isn't it hard?" There might be several reasons that they did not have as stressful an experience as others had. It seems that they expected hardship and adjusted their mindset accordingly. They also appeared to possess a large capacity to adapt and remain flexible. The smart living arrangements they made early on, in addition to previously living a hectic and stressful lifestyle before coming to NAC, seemed to have contributed to their sense of successful and enjoyable transition.

One of the most significant stressors was having unpleasant encounters with some local people. Franco recalled a time when a taxi driver was not honest with the fare. Mila was physically attacked on two different occasions by local men. Johannes and Noa had their house broken into while traveling and their valued personal items stolen. The shock of these events was amplified because they had never experienced these types of incidents in their home countries. Susan recalled some horrible experiences with local men. In a city where she once lived, she was often harassed by local men. Before she came to NAC, she had served as an ICW in a country in eastern Africa where she never experienced this kind of agitation. She equated this experience to "the whole living in a Muslim culture in general." She said, "It took me a long time to get comfortable with that to a certain extent."

Unfortunately, being harassed by men on the street was a common experience among women, especially single women. Brittany had a horrifying experience on her walk to the beach one day. She was followed and verbally harassed by four different local men along the way. She felt that she behaved in a culturally appropriate way, and yet this still happened. She seemed to think that dressing up in a certain way and avoiding eye contact with local men were sufficient measures to ward off this kind of undesired attention. She did not seem to be aware that the time, location, or the modes in which she behaved might have changed the nature of social contacts. Regardless of the cause for this event, it had a lasting negative impact on her adjustment to the local social life.

In an earlier interview, Linda, who had never met Brittany, provided a perspective on situations like the one experienced by Brittany. Linda said, "You shouldn't say . . . 'What am I doing wrong?' Of course, somebody could be doing something wrong. They could be smiling at men or wearing the wrong clothes, but usually, the girls who were getting hassled, they were not doing anything wrong. It's just the culture, and that's what guys do in this culture." Linda was generalizing the behaviors of local NAC men. She mentioned that only a small fraction of local men behaved in this way, harassing women on the street. However, these personal experiences seemed to have formed strong opinions in these ICWs about the overall social picture of their local context.

Some participants who were Asians had experienced racism in NAC. Myungsook, a Korean, remarked, "Once we are out on the street, we are all Chinese, aren't we?" She was often ridiculed and called "Jackie Chan," "Madame Jackie," or "Bruce Lee" on the street. She said that at one point, she was fed up with neighborhood kids calling her by names, so she grabbed one of them and sternly told him to bring his mother. She said that the kid cried in shock and embarrassment, and it made a big scene, but these kids in the neighborhood never ridiculed her again afterward. Claudia seemed to be referring to this type of rowdy behavior by local kids when she talked about her son having a hard time making local friends. She said, "It's challenging to find local friends because [local] kids are very rough. And my boys are rough too, but rough differently . . . . We don't have many kids in the neighborhood, but the encounters they've had in the past, especially my older one—he's ten—and he's been afraid of local kids." While not all local kids are perhaps bullies, her son's limited experiences in the local setting made him respond more carefully. However, many of these negative experiences seemed to have resulted from a misunderstanding, a lack of experience in the local context, or not going with the rhythm of local daily life.

Another significant factor that added to the participants' initial stress was their inability to communicate with local people. They described their frustrations as follows:

> Yeah, I think initially, I struggled quite a bit, mostly because of the language. I struggled with my language studies. I am not . . . such a fast learner, and it took me a while to communicate well. I'm also quite an introvert, so I struggled to find my voice, I think, and a way that I can connect with [people of NAC] that are true to who I am. My first few years was really hard for me to build friendships. (Caitlin)

> I didn't realize this until recently how isolated I've been feeling by lack of language. (Cheryl)

> Although the more I think about it, the more I realize it's very hard to be friends with someone who doesn't have a lot of language. You have to be really patient. So it takes a special [NAC person] to be willing to have someone who can't communicate with them. (Ashley)

According to Haejin, it was challenging to build relationships with local people due to communication difficulties that led to awkwardness and having to expend so much energy. For Stefanie, not understanding what was happening increased her sense of anxiety and vulnerability. These reflect the view that language ability is integral to building relationships. While not speaking the local language fluently would not stop them from making local friends, it still limited their ability to connect with people.

When participants attended a local language school that was not well organized (Junghoon, Eunyoung) or worked with an incompetent language tutor (Philip, Marie), it was quite frustrating and discouraging. Although understanding French had merits in many situations in NAC, many of these Christian workers chose to focus on learning the local NAC version of Arabic because of a desire to speak the heart language of the people. It was also a strategic decision for them since many felt it was essential to minister to local people in their heart language. They wanted to pray, teach the Bible, and worship in the local people's heart language. Philip arrived in NAC, knowing neither Arabic nor French. He chose to focus on the local Arabic and tried to practice with shopkeepers and neighbors. However, he was annoyed that local people would often speak to him in French, although he was not speaking to them in French. This was a common frustration among many foreign Christian workers trying to learn and practice the local Arabic. The language issue did not end after the initial year or two but was on-going throughout their entire time living in NAC. It will be discussed again in a section below.

In summary, international Christian workers generally had favorable first impressions of their local setting in NAC. Many of them enjoyed the warm hospitality and welcoming gestures of their neighbors and newly made local friends early on. Virtually all the participants focused on learning the local language and social conduct during their first year in NAC. Many struggled with differences in social norms and not being able to communicate well with local people. Some even persevered racism, verbal harassment, physical attacks, and a robbery. Some of them, however, felt that their local adaptation went very well. They did not find adjusting to the local culture to be too difficult but rather enjoyable.

ON-GOING SOCIAL LIFE IN THE LOCAL SETTING

Local adaptation by these Christian workers is not completed after the initial adjusting period of one to two years; it merely begins. They have to continue to learn local idiosyncrasies and grow in their language and communication skills. A part of the learning process demands that they learn to negotiate social interactions with the local people. They also need to deal with the constraints of local social structures. As foreigners, this is not an easy process to go through. Without this process, however, it would be difficult for them to develop personal resources to navigate the local living.

Adapting to Local Social Norms

Participants indicated that they had to change and adapt their behaviors and lifestyle to local sensibilities. These included adjusting their responses to local norms concerning time, hospitality, physical touch, and communication style. They largely accepted the social norms in the local context, adopted them as a part of their new lifestyle, and attempted to identify more closely with the local people. In most cases, they had to set different expectations in their relationships with local persons.

A common challenge among many participants was ambiguity in social situations. This was displayed most concretely in their attitude toward time and structure. ICWs with corporate or professional backgrounds were often frustrated by many local people's loose time orientation and a seeming lack of work structure. Camila worked as a teacher back in her home country. She showed signs of adapting to the time orientation of the local people when she said, "We would say five [o'clock], and we'd meet at 5:30 or quarter to six. I mean, that's okay. And I wait, I wait so there is some things . . . that . . . I don't mind adapting or just behaving like [the local] people do or . . . [They] don't drive me crazy anymore."

Julia, a German who spent well over a decade working in NAC, had adapted herself to be much more flexible with her expectation of time orientation and structure when working with local people. Even in communication, she had learned to gauge subtle meanings behind what local people said or did. She could tell when local people really meant something, or they were simply saying things to save face. Stefanie, a Swiss, acclimated herself to the "touch-culture" of the local people who often greeted her with cheek-to-cheek kisses. It was not something with which she felt comfortable because it felt as if her physical space was being intruded; feeling the cheeks of another woman felt a bit too close physically for her comfort. She also mentioned that local people were "so much people-oriented" that it was easy to forget the time or quality of work when working together with and among local people.

Junghoon, an Asian male in his early forties with a graduate degree from North America, used to get upset that local co-workers were always late to meetings. He began to think of his preference for punctuality as perhaps "a bit too Western." He consciously adjusted his expectations and even intentionally pushed back his own arrival time for scheduled activities. He was determined not to be frustrated by his local NAC colleagues not being punctual. He decided to accept it as a part of their daily life, understanding that this was how things were done in NAC. He concluded, "They were not necessarily doing this out of disrespect toward me."

Simon, a professional from West Africa with advanced graduate degrees from Western Europe, was shocked when strangers came up to him and asked how much he paid for his car or monthly rent. It was something that he had to accommodate as a part of his life in NAC. He said:

> You got to adjust that because you don't want to offend people. If it was my country, someone asks you a question like that, you can respond and tell you, what's your business? Why do you want to know? But here, if you say that, then you know . . . you can't put that kind of a wall . . . . So if . . . I don't want to give the amount. I just give a long [explanation] at least to keep the conversation going.

Many of these ICWs learned to accept and even put up with what they deemed as negative aspects of living in NAC. John, a Northern European, saw numerous shouting matches and fistfights out on the street between some local people. Although he rarely saw anything like these in his home country, they were no longer strange or alarming to him. John recently heard an intense fight break out at two o'clock in the morning on the street outside his home. He said that he and his wife did not think much of it. He observed his own reactions:

> The next morning we went out, and there's blood on the car. And I don't know if there were punches. I don't know what happened, but for us, it didn't affect us. I was just commenting, imagine we just arrived [in NAC], and we came out [of our home], and there was blood on our car. We would have been like, where are we living? What is this place? Because it's been four years . . . it wasn't a big deal, but anyway, that's just kind of adjusting to the culture.

When asked about difficulties in adapting to the local setting, Johannes said it was in "the area of trust." He noted, "People [in NAC] don't usually trust each other. So in our cultural background—and I think that's a very positive thing—we assume trust unless the opposite is proved." It was an on-going challenge for him as he was brought up to trust people, whereas, in his current setting, people kept telling him not to trust anyone.

The type of social adjustments made by ICWs depended largely on their particular local context since there were variations of social norms around the country. These variations were apparent as I traveled to six different cities of varying sizes that had different histories during my fieldwork. People I encountered in one particular city known for strong Islamic traditions came across to me as more aggressive and less friendly than those I had encountered in similar public settings in other cities. From taxi drivers to restaurant servers, they were not as warm, and they did not treat me, a foreigner, with the kind of friendliness typically found in many other cities. This could have been my subjective experience. However, some of my participants confirmed these variations of social behaviors across different cities in NAC.

Interactions with local people can vary depending on the social status and relationship one has with the person. For example, when I accompanied Jaehyuk, an Asian who owned a business, to his office, a couple of local female employees did not greet me and acted as if they did not see me. They perhaps saw me as an accomplice of their boss. The boss did not introduce me to them. It was an unusual, awkward experience even though I had been in various social situations in NAC. I thought this was telling of Jaehyuk's relationship with his local staff. He was clearly above them in social status as the boss and was not obligated to introduce me, his friend, to his employees who were at a lower social standing. I was not sure whether this was an Asian, local, or his way of doing things. Although he knew that this was my first visit to his office, he did not find it necessary to introduce me to his office employees. It felt like he was putting an intentional distance between himself and the staff. He was "all business," talking with them in French only about matters related to their work. The office atmosphere felt cold and task-oriented. Perhaps differences in class, status, position, and gender played a part in this situation. Jaehyuk later confided that he sometimes struggled to find the best way to present me to his local acquaintances since I was also an ICW. This whole situation shows the complexity of social life among these ICWs who live and work in NAC.

Another significant factor in the local adaptation by these workers was learning from local friends and neighbors. Julia spoke about how she learned so much from one of her local co-workers in social service work. She said, "Just seeing how she responds to people in need and her generosity, I think, has been a big part of me understanding that part of the culture." For Stefanie, it was a local believer who had taught her much about the NAC culture and provided "a safe place to ask questions." Bruce mentioned how he was surprised by his neighbors and street guardians' watchful eyes, who constantly monitored and made sure things were well with him and his wife. It taught him how the people in the neighborhood were working together to keep the area safe. ICWs' local adaptation was more than just a way to fit in and adjust to a new environment. It was also an opportunity to learn and grow in how to relate to people. This was apparent in comments by John, a professional from Northern Europe. One of the positive things he learned while living in NAC was the hospitality of local people, who put their relationships before other things.

Although learning the local Arabic language was generally a positive experience for most participants, it was often a struggle not knowing the language well. Especially for those who had lived for less than two years in NAC, learning the local language was a huge part of their local adaptation. For Junghoon, who lived in NAC for nearly a decade, his relative lack of language skills was one of the biggest stressors. His first few years in the country were marred by internal conflicts within his team, making it difficult for him to focus on language learning. He was now well established in his local ministry and was finding open doors for his projects. Some local NAC friends and colleagues were coming to him to inquire about his Christian faith. Still, it had been frustrating for him that his limited language ability had somewhat prevented him from seizing these opportunities for having a deeper spiritual impact on them.

The language situation in NAC is complicated for long-term ICWs. They have to deal with two or more languages that are widely used in the country. Linda, who spoke the local version of Arabic fluently, felt that she had somehow missed out by not having had an opportunity to study Modern Standard Arabic (MSA) seriously. It was one of the country's official languages as well as the language of choice of many NAC national believers for reading and studying the Bible. Wishing she had had a stronger foundation in MSA early on, she said, "I think it [MSA] makes . . . you a lot more effective in church work because you have a Bible language which is the same as the local people."

When Myungsook joined her IMO, she had to learn four different languages—English, Spanish, French, and Arabic—in a span of just three years. While it was a struggle for her to learn all these languages simultaneously, she eventually enjoyed learning the NAC version of Arabic. She said, "I was very encouraged when I was learning [the NAC Arabic dialect]. Every day, when I went out and practiced what I learned, I got responses from people right away." Jessica, an American, was also learning multiple languages. When she came to NAC, she was already proficient in French. Then she learned the local NAC Arabic, and now she was taking private lessons in one of the Berber languages.

As for Emma, learning the language was a part of adjusting to the culture. She said, "For me, culture is also linked to the language. The more you know the language, the more you dig into the culture, and it will make you like the culture." Heather emphasized the significance of understanding the language in one's cultural adjustment. She said, "Personally, I would say, if you have language, it's the key to families and relationships . . . ." Stefanie expressed the importance of language when she said, "For me, language is a big part of belonging here . . . " She mentioned how local people were impressed with her language skills when they found out that she had lived here for long. She said, "A few months ago, I was in the market, and then he [the shop keeper] said something, and then a lady translated immediately in French to me, and then the shopkeeper said: no, she's wonderful. She has [the local NAC Arabic.] She understands. Yeah, people know that I speak the language." It gave her a sense of belonging in the local community, which was an important contributor to her local adaptation.

Constraints and Changes in Local Social Structures

Many of the stories shared by the participants in this study indicated changes taking place in NAC. It is a reminder that, for better or worse, no society remains the same. The NAC society is not standing still but is changing, just like the rest of the world. It is not surprising then that NAC's social structures that influence the lived experiences of ICWs also go through changes over time.

Some of the participants felt that there were constraints to living and working in NAC. While they had made major changes to their lifestyle and adapted to the local living, these constraints still made life in NAC quite challenging. Schooling was an issue for many families with school-aged children. Some sent their children to local private schools; others sent their children to international schools or homeschooled their children. A couple from Western Europe had a hard time finding local friends for their home-schooled daughters. They tried to have their daughters connect with the girls who lived in their neighborhood, but they found it difficult. Their mom simply observed, "The [NAC] girls don't play outside."

For Emma, whose children attended a local private school, changes that happened around the month of Ramadan put extra strain on her. During Ramadan, she could not find certain household items, and changes in the price of goods entailed buying many things before Ramadan began. She had to adjust the family's daily routine to fit the changed local schedules and take care of as many administrative matters as possible before the month began. It put much pressure on her and her family.[5]

Some of the female participants saw that abiding by the socially acceptable dress code was, at times, challenging. Olivia usually wore

5. Ramadan refers to a month-long period in the Islamic calendar during which Muslims are required to fast from food and drink during the daylight time.

conservative attires back in her home country in Europe, but she now felt that she had to dress even more conservatively in her area in NAC. It made it quite challenging for her. Heather also shared this sentiment and felt greatly restricted. She said, "For women, the freedom to wear certain clothes . . . is affected by where you live geographically." When she worked in a professional environment in a large NAC city, she did not have to think about her "reputation for purity" as much and had more freedom in her social conduct. Now that she moved to a smaller town, she felt her freedom was greatly restricted. She explained that her team had a specific dress code for women to ensure that the members presented themselves well in public and respected the local customs.

These statements by participants show the importance of the local environment on how ICWs adjust their physical lifestyle and social interactions. Depending on whether they lived in a rural area, a large urban setting, or a town in between, ICWs had to adapt differently. For example, in a newly developing town on the outskirt of a large city with a mix of the urban and the rural, I met an entire MCT of ICWs. In observing their local setting, I realized that it would be hard for these workers to live here without a personal vehicle. It was difficult to get around since public transportation options were limited. The rapid real estate development in the area was ahead of the public management and planning for this town. What would this physical environment do to ICWs who settled here? They were forty minutes away from a large city by car. It was a small town with an odd mix of the new and the old, the wealthy and the poor, the developed and the developing.

With rapid real estate development, it seemed that gentrification was taking place here. There was an influx of the wealthy who owned second or third homes along the coastal area. These wealthy people drove expensive German cars. While taking a walk around this town, it was not hard to see Audis, Porches, Mercedez-Benzs, and BMWs on the roads. The owners of these cars would live in gated luxury communities, speak French, and dress and behave in "Western" ways. With the influx of the wealthy in this town, there would be a demand for serving their needs—house maids, gardeners, security guards, restaurants, and shopping. ICWs in this town were learning [the local Arabic dialect] instead of French, lived in a modest area in town rather than in those gated villas, drove modest cars rather than expensive European cars, and regularly spent time, not with the wealthy but the poor— those who provided services to the wealthy. Foreigners behaving in this way would be a strange sight since this was a small town and there were not many foreigners living here. As these workers navigate these social, economic, and cultural ebbs and flows, they might experience something very different from what they might experience in an urban context.

I noticed that the local people in this area did not follow the official time in NAC. At the time of the research trip, the entire country of NAC was on daylight savings time. However, people came for breakfast at cafes at nine-thirty or ten, even eleven in the morning, and then sat there until twelve or twelve-thirty. People came to eat lunch at two or two-thirty in the afternoon. These meal times were at least an hour behind the normal schedule for NAC people. Coffeeshops opened late in the morning. They were not following the country's standard time. This would have been hard to imagine in the busy downtown area in a major city in NAC. People in this town seemed to follow a more traditional way of life, oblivious to things like daylight savings time. What would this kind of environment do to ICWs? How would ICWs who came from highly time-oriented settings respond? Adapting to the rhythm of life in this setting would not be easy for some ICWs.

I went to a restaurant in this town for lunch and noticed that the servers spoke to me in French. They seemed to assume that I could speak French because I was a foreigner. Many NAC people are conversant in French; far fewer people are as proficient in English. I observed that the language spoken was linked to social class. Speaking French fluently did not mean that one was in an elite class, but the elite class certainly spoke French fluently. Some people in business spoke English well. Thus speaking English and French and associating with foreigners could give NAC citizens a boost in their social standing. It might take a long time for ICWs to learn these social nuances. It was obvious to me that some of my participants were unaware of these. Some never seemed to learn at all. When ICWs speak the local version of Arabic, it would be necessary for them to be aware of the social context in which they are speaking. They should be mindful of the social situation of the person they are speaking to and the unequal, extraordinary social dynamics brought into the situation by their own presence as foreign nationals, whom the locals would view as people with power, wealth, and privilege.

My field research trip took me to six different cities and towns in NAC—four major cities and two small towns outside major cities. While each locale had its distinct characteristics, it was undeniable that the cities I visited, and perhaps the entire NAC, were experiencing various degrees of change. Most notable were the changes happening due to real estate development in NAC. These were most visible in the two small towns I visited. According to Joseph and Rachel, who had lived in Town F for many years, the neighboring major city was growing so rapidly that their small town, which had always remained more rural than urban during their time, was being consolidated into it. In NAC, the type of law enforcement agency with jurisdiction over an area was the marker for whether it was designated as either urban or rural. They mentioned that the administrative boundary line used to be many kilometers away from where they lived, but at the time of the interview, this line ran along inside the town, much closer to them than before. It seemed that cities, both large and small, were becoming larger and getting their turn of development, internal migration, and urbanization.

Town C's situation was slightly different from Town F's since it was still about an hour and a half away by car from a major city. Nevertheless, this town was experiencing changes as well. In a fieldnote, I made the following observation about Town F:

> I took an intercity taxi from [City B] to [Town C]. It was efficient—it took only an hour and fifteen minutes in a two-year-old car. Normally, these taxis functioned like a tiny bus, taking in up to six passengers. I booked the entire taxi to myself, paying about thirty US dollars, which seemed to be a fair deal to me, not having to wait for other passengers to fill up the taxi. A large segment of the road to Town D had been paved anew. It didn't feel very far from City B. The road [to Town D] was empty and straight.

In NAC, there had been major constructions of roads and intercity highways during the past decade. As these local environments changed, these ICWs would also need to adapt to these changes around them. How would these changes influence their local living experiences?

The changes experienced by ICWs are not only economic or physical but also social in nature. Some participants reported major changes in people's attitudes toward religion, especially among the country's youth. Heather excitedly shared, "I feel like . . . this new generation of young people and the access that we have to technologies and different ways of doing things . . . I feel like there's a . . . paradigm shift that's happening . . . . " She also felt that previously isolated local women were becoming more accessible by Christian workers. She said, "[NAC] in particular never used to be open to foreigners because it [foreignness] was associated with Christianity, but now people seem a little bit more ready to accept the fact that . . . their way is not the only way. And so, they're more open to other ideas. So, there's just a different atmosphere in [NAC]." I learned that this was a narrative circulated by both ICWs and national believers in NAC. Although it is difficult to gauge what was actually happening, it seemed that social norms were changing. It appeared that people's values and attitudes were more open to change; more wide-ranging values and attitudes could be found among the general populace compared to the past.

It is crucial for the participants to establish legal means of residing and working in the country for the long haul. Many of them were worried that they might suddenly be forced to leave the country by the local or national authorities. They were aware that their mission work, especially evangelism and church planting activities, could jeopardize their long-term stay in NAC. Junghoon mentioned the on-going stress and fear among his team-mates. He said, "We always live under the stress and tension when going in and out through the [national] border [when traveling]." His residency card was about to expire at the time of my visit. He was not sure whether his residency renewal application would be approved.

Susan mentioned that the authorities began more strict enforcement of tax laws that enforced foreigners to pay required income taxes, which they did not usually have to pay in the past. She and her team were trying to determine its implications. She asked, "What does this mean for the future for people like us here?" These immigrant laws and legal issues add to the stress of living with the consciousness that the authorities might question and scrutinize their motivations for coming to live in NAC. Franco described this tension when he explained, "Here, you are afraid of things. You are insecure, the police calling you and asking you questions . . . . They're going to ask you and even the neighborhood around you. Everybody wants to see what you are doing." The uncertainty and unpredictability of their long-term prospect in the country was an important issue for many ICWs. It led some to become overly sensitive about how they were viewed in the eyes of the local community.

The expatriate community in NAC was an important social group for some research participants; it provided vital support. For Myungsook, the expatriate Christian community, in addition to her team, served an important role in her life. She said, "When I first arrived in [NAC], [name of her international church] provided a sort of a buffer from culture shock." She recalled that when she first arrived in her city, her new friends in this community helped her see NAC in "a very positive, very beautiful light." Myungsook also described her initial social surrounding as culturally very diverse. She was surrounded by English-speaking Christians in the international community while she had classmates from other African countries in her French class at a local university.

Not everyone thought that the expatriate community was only positive. Some ICWs saw foreigner communities as a hindrance to their ministry and tried to distance themselves. One main reason was that expatriate churches were not good models for national Christians in NAC to replicate. Joseph explained:

> There was very much a focus on 'We want to do a church that's reproducible.' We want to have it in small groups, not go to the big expat church that [NAC nationals] will never be able to be a part of. And just having that idea of we could come and be studying [the local Arabic dialect], and then get sucked into the [international] church life and the foreigner expat community.

Heather provides an explanation for Joseph's point. She thought that the international expatriate community had a different sub-culture. She explained, "You don't experience that in America really. And also, the worker community is another dimension." ICWs were already part of their MCT and the greater ICW community. It is an additional burden for them to immerse themselves in an expatriate community such as an international church and make another adjustment to its sub-culture.

Joseph's view was not held only by Westerners. There was a Korean ICW who had similar thoughts. He avoided being entrenched too deeply in the Korean expatriate community. Although I did not interview this person as a participant, I observed that he did not want to be mired in potentially turbulent relational situations in NAC in an expatriate community. He and his wife took themselves out of the expatriate setting and mainly focused on their work among NAC nationals. Sara, another Korean ICW, said that she avoided meeting with other Koreans because she felt that it could create relational issues.

While attending a worship service at an international church in NAC, I asked myself, "What might be the role of an international church for members of MCT?" I wrote in a fieldnote, "This is a larger neutral group that can provide relational contacts and social ties—something much needed for everyone, but especially for single women." I also noted that the worship service at this church was like a *bricolage*. It had a mixture of different worship styles—enthusiastic singing inspired by worship experiences in West Africa, a liturgy inspired by a reformed theology of its White American pastor, and a Pentecostal style of preaching by a guest preacher. It seemed to be a home away from home for these ICWs, but it would likely be a *strange* home.

NEGOTIATING SOCIAL NORMS WITH LOCAL PEOPLE

How ICWs negotiated their social relations with NAC nationals was complex. These negotiations took place in a variety of social situations. These workers were not merely making adjustments to their behaviors to fit the local norms but actively shaping their relationships with nationals. In other words, they were not passive bystanders on whom the "local culture" was being imposed; they were participants who were involved in the culture-making project along with those nationals with whom they repeatedly came in contact. These intercultural social negotiations did not take place in a vacuum. They depended on many factors such as where and in what ways these encounters took place, with whom, and in what context. The following narratives illustrate how participants were negotiating social norms. Sometimes, they were successful in leading the local people to adapt, to a certain extent, to their ways of doing things, but other times, ineffective and frustrated while trying to manage these relationships.

Dealing with Dishonesty and Cheating

There was a common notion among some participants that as foreigners without intimate local knowledge, they could easily be preyed upon by dishonest local people with their cheating tactics. Kevin was disheartened by these experiences. He came to NAC to love the local people. However, from early on, Kevin ran into conflicts with NAC nationals, not unlike many other foreign workers. He felt that people often tried to cheat him. Perhaps because he was compelled to love them and expected to nurture deeper relationships with locals, Kevin often felt betrayed, became angry when they tried to inflate the price of goods and services and was sad that the only way to fight against cheating was to yell and make a big scene. When someone took advantage of him, he quietly severed the relationship afterward. The whole situation was very unpleasant for Kevin. He compared these experiences in NAC with his prior experiences in another country where he served. He determined his current situation to be far worse than the prior one.

In the end, he said that he might give in to the demands of nationals and pay higher fees for services and goods he purchased. It led to his dislike and distrust of the local people. In a sense, he seemed disappointed in himself not only for letting them take advantage of him but also for the growing frustration and dislike of the local people—the very people with whom he came to share God's love. Through these experiences, he became more resolved to challenge local people whenever he sensed that they were trying to cheat. He still struggled with his dislike of NAC nationals.

Kevin was not only adjusting to life here but negotiating relations in the local marketplace. In the process, he went through a whirlwind of negative emotions and even developed a negative attitude toward nationals. Now equipped with the past experiences of these dealings with local people, he seemed to have become more aware and ready to confront them in conflict situations. This, in turn, would perhaps surprise nationals and lead to a shift in the way they dealt with Kevin.

Junghoon also had similar experiences. At his workplace, he found great joy in training people and seeing their improvement. But the unfair and unrealistic expectations of the local leadership brought challenges to him. According to him, these local leaders lacked a basic work ethic and often treated him and his trainees poorly. They cut off funding to the training program without any prior warning and then expected Junghoon to use his personal funds to run the program. From time to time, they canceled prepared events without consulting with him in advance. Their antics made Junghoon quite frustrated at times. He did not trust them. In the end, the repeated toxic ordeals made him quite tired and worn out emotionally.

On the surface, these dealings at his work seemed to be ordinary workplace conflicts and had little to do with cultural differences. However, had he run this program in his home country, he might not have experienced many of these incidents that came across to him as non-sense. He constantly had to negotiate his role and navigate the situation that involved his responsibilities as a trainer, his long-term vision of developing his work-based ministry in NAC, his genuine aspirations for his trainees, and his relations with the local leaders.

Dealing with Identity

Soon after he got married, Thomas joined the MCT in which his wife had already been a member for a year. Being part of this team did not fulfill his need for belonging; something was missing in his initial years in the country as a married man. Others on the team had been in the country longer and had more advanced language skills. While his wife had a well-established work and ministry, he lacked a clear professional identity. All these contributed to his feeling of isolation and loneliness. He needed a job, an identity, and a sense of belonging locally without too much pressure. His dissatisfaction with not having a clear role grew over time. Fortunately, he had an opportunity to be trained as an English teacher and took it. Then he received a job offer that gave him a clearer local identity and a chance to practice what he had just learned. As he and his wife pursued their dream of working in a more remote area within the region, they found an opening in a small city where they could partner with a local non-profit organization. They ended up moving closer to that city, which gave them a fresh start in a new city in their roles as an English teacher and an NGO worker.

Thomas's past struggle with his identity seemed more pronounced than other workers whom I interviewed. One's identity is socially constructed and shaped in context. Thomas was a foreigner who entered this North African context without a clear professional role. His role as an ICW was not an acceptable identity in NAC. He had to develop his sense of social and professional standing to function well in the local context. The process of developing his local identity was stressful, de-motivating, and humiliating for him, but his perseverance paid off. He was now well established as a respectable professional, working in a credible position with a non-profit organization. His story shows that negotiating one's identity in the NAC context requires a prolonged period of reassessing one's self-view, understanding local people's views, and persevering to find and shape a role that is both clear and acceptable to the local people.

Dealing with Differences in Time Orientation

Many participants mentioned that they struggled with the time orientation of local people in NAC. They said that locals would often be late to appointments or not even show up. In Mila's previous life in the corporate world of North America, punctuality was basic professional etiquette. When she came to NAC as an ICW, her goals were to lead nationals to the Christian faith and discipleship. To do that, building relationships with local people was of high priority. When she met new people, she invested in them and tried to spend time with them. She would make appointments to meet with them, but many did not show up and came late to these appointments without any notice. It made her frustrated. One of the ways she coped with this was to manage her expectations. She accepted this as the norm in the local context. She kept at building relationships with NAC nationals but with changed expectations. She was now the manager of a business that hired local employees and offered services to foreigners. She would emphasize to her employees how their foreign customers would demand punctuality.

Mila's is a paradigmatic story representing many other workers who come from places where punctuality was expected. Her case illustrates the tendencies of ICWs to see these relationship-building efforts as a part of their job. They unconsciously held onto their task-oriented habits and approached their relationships with locals with unrealistic, business-like expectations. However, these appointments were normally casual meetings that required local contacts to go out of their daily responsibilities. Out of politeness to these new foreign friends, they would rarely say "no" to their faces when ICWs asked to meet them, even when they could not accommodate them. It might have helped ICWs in these situations to come and join the local person's daily routine rather than making these separate appointments in meeting locations unusual to them. It was interesting that Mila attributed the cause for these un-kept appointments to the local culture. However, many people in corporate and government jobs in NAC have strict working hours. They would normally keep professional appointments, albeit with perhaps a bit more flexibility than ICWs. Nevertheless, in her business practices, she was enforcing punctuality among her employees. Overall, Mila was negotiating these relational dynamics with local people by adjusting her expectations regarding time orientation and also demanding punctuality from local people whom she meets.

STRATEGIES FOR NAVIGATING LOCAL CONTEXT

Many of the ICWs who participated in this study showed a penchant for socially engaging local people in their setting and making needed adjustments to their social behaviors and lifestyles. This adjustment process was on-going but not linear. It involved continual observation, intentional learning, and adjustments to the feedback they received directly or indirectly in their social situations. As they pursued this self-adjustment process in their local setting, they came up with strategies that helped them make better adaptations in their context.

Establishing Local Platforms

Most of the forty-nine participants interviewed for this study had established businesses, worked at local educational institutions, or served at non-profit workplaces. For foreigners to reside legally in NAC, they must file an application for residency in which they need to show their legitimate reason for living there. Some obtained teaching positions at existing schools or non-profit community development organizations; others started small businesses. Among the participants, twenty-three—nearly half—had either already established or planned to start a business.

After a brief stint as a NAC sales representative for a foreign company, Philip decided to start his own business to establish long-term, viable work in NAC. He recruited a married couple from his home country to join him in the business. Philip's team leader encouraged him and other teammates to either find a job or set up a business so that they could obtain residency for the long haul. Another couple in his team was already involved in getting a business started, and now Philip and his wife were about to begin a new venture. These Christian workers' motivation to start a business often came from the need to obtain legal residency and build credibility in the local community. Joseph explained his reasoning for starting his own business: "We don't want to just be here, sitting around . . . that's not good.

We have to have a legitimate reason to be here, and we want to be in the community and out with people."

However, many ICWs wanted to go beyond obtaining residency or establishing a credible identity through their business. Claudia and her husband planned to start a leisure sports business, but their motivation was more than just obtaining a long-term visa. Claudia envisioned the business to provide a platform upon which other ICWs could come and work. She hoped that the business would enable them to invest in the local community and share their faith in everyday life. She added, "We don't want to just have it as a company by name. But actually, we want to make something that people see how businesses are run with integrity . . . applying good principles, and also to give people . . . an income as well."

Claudia's ideals of how business should be run represent some of the theories and practices popularized by proponents of Business as Mission (BAM). Jo Plummer and Mats Tunehag define Business as Mission (BAM) as "a growing global movement of people embracing and practicing business for God's glory and the common good," and describe it as "a concept, a practice, and a global movement."[6] Ever since the term was first coined at a missions conference in the 1990s, BAM has grown and become a global movement involving many Christian organizations and networks worldwide. Although practitioner literature on the subject is growing, there is not much empirical academic research.[7] Doing BAM in practice may not be as simple as the concept. Several participants in this study who had attempted BAM attest to the enormous challenge of BAM practices. In several interviews and personal conversations, some ICWs shared details of their challenges while running businesses in NAC. Although it was not my focus in these conversations, these ICWs frequently shared stories about their professional or business experiences when discussing their intercultural social experiences in NAC.

Starting and running a business takes a toll on these Christian workers. Philip explained that he felt much pressure from having to do so many intense activities at once. He had to start and run a business, continue to learn the local language and grow in cultural skills, and sustain personal evangelistic ministries. It was clear to him that he needed help from others who bought into his vision for both ministry and business. Youngcheol, who had taken over a business started by another ICW who left the country, was burdened and stressed by all the activities, financial details, and intricacies of running a business in his setting.

---

6. Plummer and Tunehag, "Growing Global Movement," 32.

7. Lee, Fung, and Fung, "Doing Incarnation Business as Mission."

There are, however, opportunities for these workers in business in terms of Christian witness. When I visited him, Youngcheol was working on his presentation at a foreign international development agency's meeting with NAC national partners. He said that he had been asked to give a presentation based on his experiences as a consultant to about eighty to a hundred people attending the meeting. Youngcheol was optimistic that this presentation might lead to doing business in several small cities, developing meaningful relationships with people in those cities, and increasing the potential for a gospel witness.

Twelve of my participants were working with local or international non-profit, non-governmental organizations. For example, John and his wife worked with an international development organization in public health, and Julia worked with a local non-profit community center that served those with disabilities. These non-paid works provided them legal residency, standing with the local authorities, and credibility in the local community. There were only two participants whose primary profession was in education. Still, at least eight of the participants had, at one time or another, worked as teachers in international schools or local institutions that taught foreign languages.

Another important function of having a reputable profession was developing a transparent identity in the local community. Although these ICWs' ultimate motive for moving to NAC was to engage in Christian ministries, they had a dilemma; they could not reveal their religious motivations to local contacts without being misunderstood, or worse, being accused of illegally proselytizing or serving as agents of Western imperialist countries. Having a clear role and position with a legitimate business, school, or relief and development organization provided natural opportunities for these ICWs to interact with and build trust with local people. For example, Mila felt tension during her first few years in NAC, during which her professional identity was not clear. When she started working for an educational institute, she felt more confident that she could present and express herself better in the local society.

Whether through business, education, or community development, these ICWs in NAC put in much effort to establish their work platforms, seizing the opportunity to positively impact the local communities where they lived. This was a widespread practice among the participants as well as among others in their organizations. Far more important than financial gain was developing relationships with local people, making positive contributions to the local community, and utilizing their marketable skills, professional credentials, or educational background. In the process, they were attempting to gain trust among NAC people and establish long-term platforms for themselves and, potentially, other team members.

Discerning Ministry Direction

ICWs faced many decisions after they arrived in NAC. Even after they had successfully completed the initial adaptation stage, they continued to face situations that required on-going discernment of the direction of their ministry, major decisions involving the direction, and new adjustments for following through those decisions. Marcelo and Olivia provide a good example of the discernment and decision-making process experienced by many ICWs. After spending some time in NAC as singles, they were married and wanted to return to NAC with the same MCT in which they were members. They had a strong desire to live in a certain section of a city with no Christian presence. Marcelo strongly felt that he was called to live in this part of the city. He said, "This is where we need to be because nobody is working in the [name of the section], so I feel a very strong desire to be in [name of the section]." His greatest motivation for living in this neighborhood was his sense of calling to this area in the city. In my conversation with Marcelo, he mentioned several times his sense of personal calling to this area. He had a strong conviction that this was where God wanted him and his family to be.

Similarly, Joseph and Rachel attributed their decision to move to their town to God's intervention. Joseph once taught at an international school in a large city in NAC. He said, "The Lord opened up an opportunity for me to work at [name of the international school], an American school here in [name of city]." While Joseph had some opportunities to connect to the students' families, he found access to these families quite limited. He also did not find the kind of spiritual openness he longed to see among the wealthy local people he met through the school. That led him to resign from the school and move his family from a large house to a smaller home in a working-class neighborhood. He explained, "And that, looking back on it, it's definitely God stepping in." He and his wife strongly felt that this decision they had made many years ago was the right one.

Developing Resilience to Overcome Obstacles

Most ICWs I interviewed had the mindset of continually adapting and adjusting themselves to their surroundings. A part of it was negotiating social norms with local people, as mentioned previously. What stood out was their intentional, purposeful efforts to make these adjustments. They anticipated challenges in so doing. To cope with them, they relied on both internal and external resources available to them. They willingly made adjustments to their lifestyle. They changed how they related to people and behaved in public. They coped with the difficulties involved in doing so. Camila, who had lived in NAC for four years at the time of the interview, expected difficulties ahead when she said, "We definitely do things for the first time very frequently. [laugh] We always find something new here . . . . We are more adapted, and there are things that we feel we know now, but there's always something that surprises us." Anticipating toils ahead helped ICWs such as Camila to be mentally better prepared as they faced new challenges of living interculturally as ICWs in NAC.

Ryan and Melissa were a young married couple with a newly born. Ryan had lived in NAC for several years as a single man while Melissa was new to the country. As a young family with a baby, they felt limited how much they could focus on language and cultural adaptation. They still had to make many adjustments to spend time with the local people and continue to grow as effective ICWs. Ryan explained, "Melissa goes to language school for four hours, and I would just be with [their son's name] here. Sometimes me and [their son's name] would go out, but not often. Then Melissa would come home. We'd enjoy a meal together, and then I could go out. And I could sit somewhere, and I could study the language." This seems to be a good example of ICWs actively responding to the constraints in the local situation, their limited life structure, and their need for language and cultural learning. They adapted to what was given to them and took the initiative to do what they could while maintaining their primary focus.

When the situation increasingly became challenging, some of these workers relied on their reservoir and simply persevered. Jaehyuk is a good example. He did not easily waver at challenging circumstances. He faced several intense difficulties while running a business. For a few years, he had worked hard to develop a new educational program for professionals within his field of expertise. It was physically challenging since he had to overwork with very little sleep for an extended time. He had faced two different unfounded lawsuits by two of his former employees. Kyungja, his wife, said that Jaehyuk put all his efforts and energy into this program to bring spiritual impact on those he trained. Still, it was disheartening for him to see the trainees not responding.

Moreover, the employees he trusted had betrayed him. The level of discouragement and stress for him was indescribable, said Kyungja. She continued, "During the twenty-six years that we've been married, I've never seen him like this before." But Jaehyuk, without displaying much emotion, calmly said, "That's why it's now important that I finish this training program well."

As I learned much later, a few months after the interview, Jaehyuk had an acute illness that almost cost him his life. For sure, there were times when he reached the end of his resources. Jaehyuk admitted that he had gone over and beyond his physical and emotional capacity and was on the verge of a burn-out. In a moment of honesty and vulnerability, he confided that he sometimes felt like running away from NAC to a place far away. Despite the exceedingly difficult circumstances he faced, Jaehyuk still continues to work in NAC today. He displays courage and resilience uncommonly found even among ICWs.

Becoming Neighbors

While many Christian workers on MCT may make successful adjustments to their adopted society, it does not mean that they become just like NAC-born native citizens. These ICWs accepted certain social practices of NAC while rejecting others. They sometimes mixed and blended what they already practiced with what they newly adopted.

Linda's local adaptation led to creating what she referred to as her own "Linda culture." She said, "I think everybody creates a bit of a culture around them. They adapt the culture to fit what they need to know." She observed that one of the advantages of being a foreigner in NAC was social flexibility. She interacted daily with local people from "a wide range of social classes." She commented, "Being a foreigner means that you don't really have a social class with local people. So, you can mix with the poor. You can mix with the rich depending upon where the Lord has placed you." Linda's comments show the possible roles ICWs can play in NAC as outsiders who enter this society.

Some ethnographers indicate that in various parts of North Africa, kinship tends to provide both possibilities and boundaries of one's socioeconomic advancement; families and clan relationships likely determine one's social status.[8] As foreigners, ICWs do not have existing kinship connections, which might limit their opportunities. Neither are they limited by assigned social status based on their kinship. It allows them to move into any social space without suffering much consequence. The experiences of my participants, especially those who had lived in NAC for a long period, support this idea of social neutrality of ICWs and resulting opportunities for building local relationship networks.

As foreigners living in NAC, they had made mistakes and done things that might offend local people. Linda found that NAC people could

8. See Holmes-Eber, *Daughters of Tunis*; Scheele, *Village Matters*; Newcomb, *Everyday Life in Morocco*; Bourdieu, *In Other Words*.

be rather forgiving when she or other foreigners did things that were not in line with local customs. She said, "They can think, 'Oh, she's a foreigner,' you know, put up the things that otherwise they would find unusual." Julia agreed with Linda when she said that the local people were, in general, "gracious to foreigners" and "forgiving for cultural mistakes." Linda felt that people of "NAC were generally welcoming to foreigners," and they would find foreigners interesting.

Despite all the "unusual" things they might have done, there was one thing that these ICWs on MCT had in common with local people in NAC. Just like the people of NAC, hospitality played a significant part in their lives. They practiced hospitality toward their local friends and their team members. It was a vital aspect of their adapted social practices. During my field study trips, I was frequently at the receiving end of many ICWs' generous hospitality. They provided meals, tea, and coffee, and if needed, a place of rest and sleep.

For Philip and Marie, a German couple, their home was to be a place of hospitality toward their neighbors. During the interview, Philip enthusiastically shared his plans with their new home where they had recently moved. He said, "So we want to use this apartment to have an open house. And some [NAC] friends told us if you open your door to invite people, so it's like *dar as-salaam*, so it's like a house of peace. This was what we were searching for, a house where we could invite people, and also a peaceful home for our own." Caitlin, a single woman in her late 30s, lived alone in a large, spacious home with an open floor plan. She said that she wanted her place to be used as a place for other single female Christian workers around the country to come and rest. Such practice of hospitality toward neighbors and strangers was not uncommon among the ICWs whom I met.

SUMMARY AND CONCLUSION

This chapter described the influence of the surrounding environment of the North African country (NAC) on the intercultural experiences of international Christian workers (ICWs) on multicultural teams (MCTs). Through careful coding and sorting exercises of the collected data, I probed several areas that helped present the participants' lived realities in the context of NAC. These Christian workers' initial experiences in NAC set the stage for their ongoing social adjustments. As they continued to experience life with and among local people and communities, they became more adept at living and working in this new environment and could even negotiate new relational, social terms with their local interlocutors. They also learned and developed tangible personal strategies to navigate social situations in the local cultural context.

Through these experiences, these Christian workers were, in a sense, becoming more "local." They actively learned the local language(s) and social customs, developed relationships, were accepted by the local people, grew in their cultural understanding, and found ways to navigate the local social settings. Descriptions of the participants' experiences of living and working in the NAC context paint a picture of the local people and their society through their eyes. As a qualitative study incorporating ethnographic methods, the goal of this study is not to depict an ethnic culture but a process of "culture making" among a group of people who came to NAC for a common purpose of Christian missions. Describing how these Christian workers processed and understood what they saw, heard, and felt is an important step in understanding how they created their own "MCT culture" in this ministry context while constructing a model of the local NAC culture.

The next step is to understand what they experienced through working and building relationships within their multicultural teams. In the next chapter, I will discuss the participants' intercultural social experiences with their multinational, multiethnic colleagues on their teams.

5

Intercultural Social Experiences
in Multicultural Teams (MCTs)

THIS CHAPTER FOCUSES ON the intercultural social experiences of international Christian workers (ICWs) within their multicultural teams (MCTs). It addresses the second research question of how working with their multicultural team mediates these Christian workers' intercultural social experiences. This chapter presents five different categories sorted and selected from the data. It will describe the participants' initial experiences of joining their multicultural teams (MCTs), their accounts of the MCTs' structure and organization, the intercultural social dynamics in these teams, their social relationship with their MCT members, and their strategies for navigating the team and organizational life. These categories also describe some aspects of international mission organizations (IMOs) as the backdrop for these MCTs. The findings help explain how multicultural teams' social and organizational structures influence intercultural social processes that result in personal changes in these ICWs.

INITIAL EXPERIENCES IN MCTS

The participants' initial experiences in MCTs mainly involved making adjustments to teammates who were from different countries. Many participants received support and help from their team when they first arrived in the North African country (NAC). In many cases, the team provided a robust environment to build trusted relationships and meet their social needs. Some participants, including all members of one particular organization, were given an initial orientation and training program. Overall, MCTs functioned as a protective support structure for these workers in their most vulnerable time in NAC. They also faced many challenges within MCTs. They shared about conflicts within their teams and struggles with communication. Eventually, these workers made necessary adjustments to their team life, and the process of adapting to the team was a formative learning experience for virtually all of the participants.

Receiving Team Support

Many participants mentioned the support they received from their team during their initial time in NAC. They recalled how their teammates provided practical help during their initial period of adjustment in NAC. Laura and Kevin had joined a team riddled with conflicts. Having known some of the issues before their arrival led them to have low expectations for the team. They were surprised and quite grateful for how warmly their team leaders received them and how much practical help these leaders offered. Laura said, "So he [the team leader] helped us a lot with settling when we first arrived. He knew a lot about culture and language." Kevin chimed in and said, "We experienced more blessing than we had expected, especially in those first three, four months when we were here, we had more help . . . than we . . . thought we would have."

The help participants received from their teammates was practical in nature, such as providing a temporary place to live, finding a house to rent, and supplying local information on transportation and shopping. Due to travels by many ICWs during the summer, team members were not always around to offer help to newly arriving ICWs. For Bruce and Cheryl, having only one teammate who stayed in town to help them settle in the new country was a huge relief. He said, "The teammate that was here helped us get phones, made sure we knew how to get food and the necessary things to keep going, and she was here most of that three months." In Jessica's case, one of her teammates helped her meet a NAC neighbor almost immediately after arriving in NAC. Connecting with this neighbor, who was a mother of two girls, early on in her time in the country helped Jessica maintain a sense of purpose and find a new belonging. Melissa summed up these positive experiences when she said, "I'm very glad that we don't have to do this alone . . . . They're always just a phone call away. Life would be very hard if we didn't have them."

For some of the participants whose English was not fluent, it was helpful for their adjustment to the team life when teammates who were native speakers of English offered gestures of inclusion and showed cultural sensitivity toward them. Haejin appreciated that her teammates were accommodating toward her. They made sure that she felt included and understood in conversations and team meetings. She attributed this inclusive quality in her teammates to their past experiences of working with non-native English speakers. Similarly, Myungsook recalled how generous and accommodating their British team leaders were when they first arrived in their city. Sara was impressed with her Western teammates, who were respectful and intentional about listening to her, even though she struggled to express herself with her limited English. She said, "When I speak, I feel sorry to our team because . . . for them to understand my words, it must be very difficult. And yet, because of their desire and willingness to listen, I feel very thankful."

Not everyone received needed help from their team, however. In some situations, team members or leaders were unavailable to provide an orientation program or practical help when they first arrived. Philip said that his team's absence when he and his family first arrived forced him to grow in a short time, but he still wished he had more help. He said that he was afraid to go out because he was unsure about the local customs and did not understand the local language. He wished that someone had shown him how to do simple things and helped in his transition. His wife Marie also expected the team to be more involved with them. She could not hide her disappointment when she said, "I thought I had more help from our team and from our team members that we are stronger together, but it was more that we all do our thing separately. So, that was for me the hardest experience."

When these Christian workers joined their teams, they immediately gained access to a robust social environment. They quickly became friends with their new team members. It was almost a built-in function of becoming a part of their team. In her interview, Ashley repeatedly said how good it was to meet her team members, spend time with them, and learn from their experiences, especially how to persevere the initial shock with language and culture. Her local team was a part of a larger field team; these built-in relational connections within her larger field team also provided her access to a network of resourceful people. She also gained a valuable sense of belonging to a larger group of people who shared a common purpose.

Some participants appreciated the encouragement and fellowship within their team. Eunyoung and her husband experienced so much discouragement from relational turmoil within their team that they considered leaving NAC. But at their organization's regional conference, they were greatly consoled by their colleagues whom they had just met for the first time. For Ryan and Melissa, the informal times they spent together with their teammates gave them strength. Johannes emphasized the importance of having a fellowship within his team. He said, "To have a group of people here in [City E] that you can express your thoughts and your emotions, and your fears freely, that's something of incredible value. Yeah. So that's a great, great benefit to have people like ourselves here to fellowship with."

Some of these ICWs were provided with a structured orientation or initial training program, while others had a more informal one. Some did not have any team orientation or training at all. Ashley was surprised that the initial orientation provided to her was minimal. Haejin came with an expectation that a more well-structured training program would be offered. She was not sure whether some of the training sessions she participated in were helpful.

In Camila and Franco's case, their organization had a four-month training program with a locally experienced colleague assigned to them as their trainer. The program focused on language learning and cultural adaptation. They were asked not to see other foreigners during the program since it might hinder their cultural adaptation. When I probed the nature and function of this training program, Camila seemed hesitant and uncomfortable to talk more about this experience. Eventually, she candidly shared how their trainer's negative attitude toward the local society made them afraid of the local people. Strikingly, Camila said that they had to "unlearn a couple of factors" they learned from this trainer later on.

These participants' experiences indicate room for improvement in initial training and orientation within their teams. While larger, well-established teams had a well-structured training program for their newly arriving team members, it was difficult to expect the same from smaller teams with relatively little experience in the country.

MCTs of some participants served as a protective buffer from the pressures of the local context and even from other team members. The team provided a structure and safety net for many of the ICWs. Youngcheol, a veteran ICW, metaphorically compared those who first arrived in NAC to young children. He said that the team was "absolutely necessary at the beginning" for newly arriving ICWs. He commented:

> When we look at it in the long run, we can say that those who grow and mature under the team's protection are just like children who are born to and grow up under mom and dad, who are good parents. Once they grow up, they don't really need the team anymore. But there are still many benefits we can have within the boundary of the team . . . . Anyhow, initially, team life is very important.

Haejin was grateful that her team's presence ensured her safety and security. She said, "Rather than being isolated by myself, I think being with a group of people who share the same purpose and goal is actually nice."

Myungsook also recalled that her team functioned as "a buffer" from culture shock when she first arrived in NAC. Those team members influenced her to see the people of NAC in a very positive light. She was thankful that her team leader protected them from criticism and pressure from strong-minded colleagues in their regional team, who believed in a more aggressive, intense training regimen and pushing new members to their limits.

Initial Challenges in MCTs

Despite much help and support provided by their teams, MCT members still faced some difficult initial challenges in their team life. One that MCT members faced early on was conflicts with their teammates. In most such cases, conflicts were with their roommates. Many single, unmarried workers lived with a housemate or two to share the housing cost and provide support and accountability to one another. However, these arrangements did not always go smoothly. Linda recalled her first two years in NAC and said that the hardest issues she faced were "flatmate problems." She wondered if the conflict was due to cultural differences because they were from different countries in Europe or age differences since Linda was twenty years older than her housemate. Ashley also recalled when she had just arrived in NAC and moved into a house where two other single women on the team lived together. Three of them were from three different continents. Ashley quickly learned that her two housemates were not on good terms with each other. The tension between the two boiled over, and it became a difficult situation for all three.

It was notable that many of these participants were not entirely sure of the cause of their conflicts. While each of them wondered why they experienced these issues with their housemates, they did not blindly attribute them only to cultural differences. Jessica, an American, said that it was difficult for her to pinpoint the cause for the conflict with her housemate from Western Europe. She said that it was more comfortable settling in the local culture than adapting to her housemate's "international culture." She added, "You were never sure what was the source [of the conflict] because there were so many different factors going on."[1]

---

1. During this interview, I sensed that Jessica was reluctant to talk openly about her experience with her former housemate. There were many factors in this interview situation. She had just met me for the first time, but she knew that I knew her former housemate. I was a male in his late 40s. She was a woman in her 20s. Researcher reflexivity was a critical factor in this interview. I had to earn her trust and not make her feel too uncomfortable. I empathized with her and assured her of anonymity. In the end, she was gracious to share her experiences candidly.

When conflicts were with those in leadership, they created turmoil within the whole team. Participants who joined teams with existing leadership issues went through some challenging times. Junghoon said, "Personally, I had no honeymoon period when I came to [NAC]. There was no honeymoon season . . . . We had some very intense struggles within the team. We had no energy left to focus on making adjustments locally here." Noa also remembered how a serious leadership issue created chaos within the team and affected her and her family. She said, "There was not a good atmosphere in the team when we came. That was what we felt. And, people were not trusting each other." Her husband, Johannes, described it as a crisis. In the end, outside leaders had to intervene to resolve the conflict within the team. He did not want to give too many details of these painful events. He simply said, "Much more came to light, and that is beyond what should be recorded." The leadership factors in MCTs will be discussed in the next section when I describe the inner workings of MCTs.

Some participants mentioned the difficulty of communicating in English with team members as one of the challenges during their early days on their teams. Among the eleven multicultural teams to which forty-seven participants belonged, ten teams (forty-five participants) used English as their team language.[2] This is a common practice among international mission organizations that operate around the world.[3] However, the majority of my participants who were members of MCTs (62 percent; twenty-nine out of forty-seven) were not native speakers of English. Communicating in English was a significant issue with no simple solutions. Some of the participants who arrived in NAC without attaining a high level of English felt distressed; their inability to communicate clearly in English often led to their passive participation in team life. Some resorted to mostly listening and not speaking in team meetings.

The graph in Figure 2 shows the first languages of the participants who were members of multicultural teams and the number of native speakers for each of those languages. The largest first language group was English, with eighteen native speakers. It included citizens of the US, Canada, Australia, and the UK. The second-largest first language group

2. The remaining team with two participants uses Spanish as their team language. Their organization mainly recruits and sends ICWs from countries in Latin America.

3. There seem to be two main reasons for English being used as the team language in these international mission agencies. First, it is the convenience of English being the most widely used international language; secondly, many large international mission organizations have historical roots in the English-speaking world. The founders of five of the seven mission organizations whose members were interviewed for this study were either American or British. They continue to draw heavily their personnel and resources in the US and the UK.

was Korean, with thirteen native speakers. Then there were nine other first languages distributed among the remaining sixteen participants. This graph shows a general picture of the complex language and communication issues present in these MCTs.

Figure 2. First Language of Participants Who Were Members of MCTs

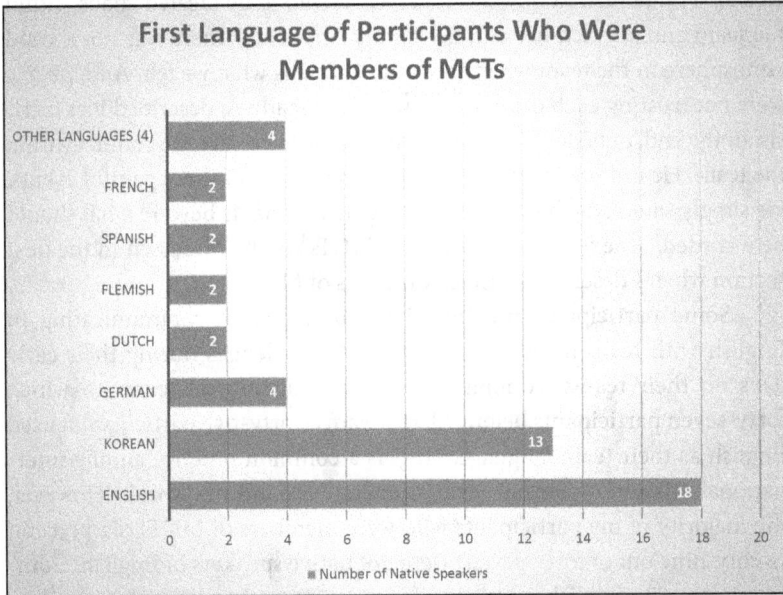

Philip, who initially arrived with limited English, said, "My English wasn't good, and right now it's a little bit better, but it was hard . . . . I feel like a baby because I can't speak. I can't speak what I want." Haejin said that it was very stressful for her to communicate in English, especially in team meetings when people directed questions to her in front of everyone. She often avoided talking with team members who did not understand her English well. She only wanted to talk with those who understood her. Julia, who was from Europe, initially had an American roommate. She said, "I could kind of understand what she was talking about, but couldn't respond." Also, for Kyungja, the most difficult part of team life was communicating in English. She felt that it was the only thing that was missing since she enjoyed being part of her team. Since these participants could not express themselves well in English, they were often seen as passive or indifferent by other team members.

The issue with English was two-sided, however. Participants who spoke English fluently also struggled to connect with non-native English speakers. Ashley said, "It was difficult that I couldn't communicate well with Haejin because she didn't have as much English. It was just frustrating because I like communicating. I like talking. I like listening." She also observed a relational rift developing between two teammates due to miscommunication. She thought that a part of the cause was one person not speaking English well. She thought that one felt distrusted while the other could not clearly communicate what she wanted.

Communication issues among team members often led to misunderstanding and sometimes relational conflicts. The story of Caitlin and Haejin, housemates of Ashley, illustrates this point well. Caitlin wanted to have a close relationship with Haejin, who was her new teammate and a housemate. From the beginning, however, something did not click between them. Caitlin wanted to include Haejin in almost every decision about decorating their house. She wanted Haejin to feel at home and feel like she was a part of the household. Haejin, however, kept withdrawing from the relationship. Many puzzling incidents with Haejin confused Caitlin and led to further deterioration of the relationship. Caitlin felt that all her efforts to build trust with Haejin miserably failed. The whole situation was devastating for Caitlin, who said she had never had this type of relational issue in the past.

However, the real issue might have started somewhere else. In interviewing Haejin, I discovered that she felt a lack of financial transparency in the team. She also saw Caitlin's friendly gestures as uninvited intrusions into her personal boundary. What complicated the matter was that Caitlin was also Haejin's team leader.

Based on what Caitlin and Haejin said in their separate interviews, it was obvious that there was a misunderstanding between them. Caitlin did not provide clarity and transparency that Haejin expected; Haejin did not respond to the kind of relational bonding expected by Caitlin. Haejin needed clarity, transparency, and separation of personal and business matters; Caitlin needed relationship, emotional support, and connection. Neither received what they expected from the other, which caused a loss of trust and straining of the relationship. It seems that things might have been better between them had they established early on a clearer boundary as housemates and teammates. The tension experienced by these two ICWs does not seem to be caused by a language or cultural issue or a personality conflict; it was a combination of several things accumulating, causing a relational rift.

The experiences of Asian members in these MCTs were noteworthy. There were fifteen ethnic Asians among the participants. Some of them mentioned their initial discomfort with the team culture. Several participants said they felt more comfortable with "the local NAC culture" than the "Western team culture." Jennifer and Chris, Asian Americans who were part of a predominantly White American team, felt that the culture within their team was unfamiliar to them. Jennifer said, "I think, rather, adapting to the American culture [of her team] was more difficult [than the local culture]." Both Youngcheol and Myungsook, who were with another organization, found it easier to adjust to the local NAC culture than their MCT's organizational culture.

It was not just the foreignness of their team culture that was difficult for these Asian ICWs. It also had something to do with dealing with multiple cultures at once. Jaehyuk said that the organizational culture of his MCT was strange to him. He also felt the local culture of NAC to be distant. Both the NAC context and his MCT context felt unfamiliar to him. He said, "Both in the local setting here and within the team, it was regrettable that I could not feel any intimacy . . . . That wasn't because the people were necessarily bad . . . . It just felt very foreign to me." Haejin also mentioned her cultural stress. She said, "In the team meetings, it was the Western culture, and [when I was] among the people I would meet, it was the [NAC] culture . . . . Since I am a Korean, a bit of it [stress] was coming from both sides so much so that I didn't even want to talk . . . in team meetings." Jennifer also mentioned the challenge of having to learn the local NAC culture, "the American culture" within the team, and a Korean colleague who was "very much Korean in her mentality."

Many of these Asian ICWs had to deal with simultaneously learning multiple languages, including English. Youngcheol and Myungsook, who are Koreans, provide an extreme example. In their first team in NAC, they had to adjust to British and Australian English accents within their team while studying Arabic and French in the local setting. Indeed, learning at least two languages simultaneously—normally, English and the local Arabic dialect—was one of the biggest challenges when these workers joined an MCT.

Making Adjustments

During the initial period in NAC, these ICWs had to make many adjustments to fit in with their team and the other team members.

Their adjustment to the team life sometimes involved becoming aware of relational dynamics and making intentional connections with their team members. For example, soon after joining her team, Ashley noticed that some team members were being left out in some social interactions, so she made an effort to include them in group settings. She noticed the cultural diversity in her new team and considered how it affected the whole team dynamics. She said, "I was looking forward to it, but I think, also apprehensive, just knowing that cultural differences make life difficult in lots of ways . . . or make life more complicated." She was aware of her own traits and thought about how her actions might be perceived by those with different cultural backgrounds. She realized that her verbally dominating personality could intimidate others, especially those who did not speak English fluently. So she intentionally talked less, made adjustments to her body language, tried to listen more, and invited her teammates to meals. Since she was still relatively new in NAC and did not have many local friends yet, it seems to have motivated her even more to make these efforts to connect with her teammates.

Chris and his wife Jennifer are Asian Americans. Although they had lived in the US since they were teenagers, most of their social life took place within the confines of their ethnic Asian church context. Chris thought it could be difficult for him and his wife to transition into a team with mostly White Americans. He thought it might also be a challenge for his team members to receive more Asians into their team. Thus, before leaving for NAC, they initiated an online conference call and tried to convey their concerns to their team leaders. Chris recalled telling them that although he had lived in the US for more than two decades, he was still culturally Korean. He said that he told them, "I have never worked with Caucasian people. That will be a culture shock for me to learn about your work ethic and everything, and it will be a culture shock for you as well because you've never had a 'Korean-Korean' before." He was intentional and proactive about making his relationship with his new team members go smoothly despite cultural differences.

These adjustments were not always easy to make, especially when the participants had recently arrived in NAC; everything felt so new to them, including all these new relationships on the team. In a sense, it was a strange experience for them since such adjustments would be so unnatural in other settings. Brittany reflected on her first months on the team and said, "To come into a team where these are now my people, and I am relying on them for everything and . . . they're pretty much the only people in my life. They're my teammates and my friends, and also . . . my TLs [team leaders] are sort of my boss . . . . So there are all these different aspects of our relationships . . . . But . . . at three months, they're kind of still strangers."

The participants told many stories about adjustments they had made to fit in with their new MCTs. Youngcheol told a story about his former team leader, who exemplified intentionality in adjusting to and accommodating other MCT members. When Youngcheol arrived in NAC with his wife, they stayed in the home of their team leader couple, who were British and Australian. Youngcheol, who grew up in a small town near the Eastern Sea in South Korea, loved to go out to the beach and catch octopus. His new city in NAC was near the coast, and he went to the beach with his wife one day and caught an octopus. He brought it to his host's home, hung it on a clothesline to dry the dead octopus, and enjoyed this delicacy for days. His host family did not say anything to him or his wife about it. Several years later, when Youngcheol learned how repulsive his actions could have been to his host family, his heart was filled with gratitude. This former team leader couple were patient and understanding even to say nothing to them about this incident. Youngcheol learned much from this couple and cherished the lesson he learned from them about being willing to accommodate people with very different cultural backgrounds.

STRUCTURE AND ORGANIZATION OF MCTS

For many of these international Christian workers, their ongoing social life with their teammates took place within the bounds of their team structure and policy. The information shared by the participants about their internal team matters can be categorized into two kinds: organizational issues and social dynamics. This section deals with organizational issues such as team structures they had in place, how they developed team ministries, how their international mission organization functioned, and how leadership worked in their MCTs.

Support, Accountability, and Team Policies

For describing the team relations, many participants talked about how their teams were structured. In most cases, teams provided accountability and support and established appropriate rules and policies for their members. In most cases, the team structure was reinforced by holding regularly scheduled team meetings.

Several participants mentioned that the main benefits provided by their teams were accountability and support. Joseph and Rachel, who had served as team leaders for almost a decade, described the accountability and support structure in their international mission organization. Explaining that their organization was "field-governed," they said that the team leaders made all strategy and operation decisions. They had a leader in another country who kept them accountable. This leader regularly checked with them and helped them maintain their spiritual, emotional, and physical health and ministry vision. Rachel said, "We set the goals, and they hold us accountable. 'This is what you said you wanted to do. How's it going? What help do you need? What support do you need? What training do you need?'" They showed appreciation for the level of support and accountability provided by their leader.

Some participants could not emphasize enough the importance of team for ICWs. Youngcheol, a veteran worker with decades of experience with MCTs in NAC, emphatically said, "I think, first and foremost, that *team is everything.*"[4] When new team members arrived in NAC, the team would help them with literally everything. He explained, "That's because everything in my whole life is taking place within the boundary set by the team." He compared new team members to young children, describing how the team was "absolutely necessary" for newly arriving workers; it provided an environment for these new workers to grow, learn, and receive care. In his view, once they have adapted to life in NAC, the team becomes more of a place of belonging, a security blanket, and a space in which they could begin to contribute to other team members. Youngcheol felt that until then, this supportive function of the team was needed for these team members. Brittany, who had been in the country for less than two years at the time of the interview, seemed to concur with Youngcheol when she said, "Team is pretty much all I have here . . . . There have been other relationships both with ex-pats and [NAC nationals] that are formed, but my core support is my team."

Forty-seven of the forty-nine participants were full members of eleven different MCTs that belonged to seven IMOs. Every team had team policies by which the members were expected to abide. Some teams had comprehensive policy manuals covering areas ranging from local living standards, language acquisition, and ministry strategies to personnel policies such as dating for singles, vacation, and finances. Others had short, concise documents of several pages. In either case, there was a consensus among participants that it was important for them to follow these rules to ensure their well-being.

Most of these teams mandated a conservative dress code for their members. Heather, who had lived in three different cities and towns in NAC, said, "For women, freedom to wear certain clothes . . . is affected by where you live geographically." Each town she lived in had somewhat different local norms of what was appropriate for women to wear. It should be noted here that these teams not only applied their policies but also interpreted their local social contexts and provided social behavior guidelines. In other words, team policies were largely influenced by their understanding of socially acceptable norms in the local community where they lived. Most of these teams had established basic social behaviors required for their team members to follow

---

4. Emphasis is added.

while going out in the local community. Based on their personal experiences and responses from local people, these MCTs made further adjustments to their social behaviors and team policies.

During some interviews, I found out that at least two of the seven IMOs had a conflict resolution guideline for their team members to follow. One participant, however, raised some concerns about whether these conflict resolution guidelines were necessarily applicable in complex intercultural relationships involving persons with different cultural backgrounds, especially if non-Western members were part of the conflict. This complexity in intercultural social life is becoming a crucial issue for these IMOs; increased complexity in global missions tends to relativize and even subvert much of the interpretive framework they had long utilized. This issue will be discussed more later.

A widespread practice among these MCTs was to have regular team meetings. Most teams met weekly in the home of one of the team members. I attended a weekly team meeting where the team focused on spiritual input and mutual encouragement. Among the six members, one was absent, and five attended this meeting. It was a typical home gathering for this IMO's teams in NAC where members would gather, share coffee, tea, and pastries, have a time of worship and devotion together, spend some time in a Bible study, and discuss team business. After the meeting was over, the hosting couple prepared and offered a meal to everyone.

Junghoon, the leader of a different MCT, described his team's meeting format, which was not very different from the one I attended. His local team was composed of three families. He explained that they met every week, the meeting was conducted in English, and everyone enjoyed meeting together. Each family had their own professional work that kept them busy. Sharing about each other's life and ministry was the central focus of their meetings. Laura, who was on a different team, described her team's weekly meetings. They borrowed a room at an international church building for a two-hour afternoon meeting. Members took turns facilitating the meeting and preparing refreshments. They decided in advance what they were going to focus on each week. They normally alternated their prayer time between focusing on personal matters and organizational or regional prayer concerns.

Other participants mentioned how, in their teams, they tried to be flexible with the frequency and content of team meetings depending on their situation. In general, these team meetings provided a structure and regularly occurring robust social settings for these teams. Many of the participants considered these meetings vital for their teams to maintain strong teamwork and healthy ministries.

Team Ministry

Several participants mentioned that developing team ministries was of high importance to them. Many of them said that developing local ministries together as a team would be ideal, whether doing evangelistic activities in particular neighborhoods, ministering to the needy, or partnering with NAC national believers and house churches. Religious and social restrictions in NAC were identified as a partial cause for the difficulties of these Christian workers in developing concrete ministries together with their teammates.

Some of the participants were focused on church planting (CP) and ministry practices associated with Disciple-Making Movement (DMM). While scholarly literature on DMM (Disciple-Making Movements) is rare, a recent article by Warrick Farah provides a balanced perspective.[5] Participants associated with one particular organization had a more unified, intentional focus on CP and DMM. Joseph, a team leader who was a member of this organization, said that his team's priority was to help a movement started in their town. He described his team's ministry strategy as getting out in the local community and gaining access to people's homes where his team members would actively share their faith. He explained, "So it's not about us entertaining people, having all the hospitality and people in the room. But it's us finding 'people of peace,' and going to them, and meeting in their homes." Joseph and Rachel explained that the idea of "a person of peace" or "POP" came from the Gospel of Luke. It is "somebody who welcomes us and our message and opens up their network." They explained the importance of persons of peace since they saw these persons as the ones who were the key to facilitating and nurturing a new movement toward Christ.

Most of these Christian workers faced the difficulty of maintaining their long-term residency in NAC. When they talked about "team ministry," it could mean ministry activities in which they were engaged together, shared professional or business platforms, or a combination of both. The boundary between professional work and Christian ministry seemed to be blurred in their context of ministry. In many cases, a whole team could not work together on either ministry activities or professional platforms; each team member had to develop their own ministry activities and professional platforms. This was sometimes a cause for disappointment in some ICWs since they did not work together with their team or even spend enough time with them.

The eleven MCTs to which my participants belonged varied in their style of engaging in team ministries. Claudia compared her team to a soccer team. She explained that two of her teammates worked together in a business,

5. Farah, "Motus Dei."

another was an artist, and she and her husband were trying to get a new business started. Nevertheless, they all studied at the same language school, had weekly team meetings together, and shared the common vision of reaching their city with the gospel. To her, this was similar to a soccer team in which its players individually moved around with greater freedom while having a level of coordination and collaboration between them.

Linda's team functioned differently. She mentioned that her team was never singularly focused on one thing. She said, "I think we've never really had a single focus team . . . in terms of ministry. So there have been a lot of discussions about whether that is desirable and whether we need that . . . ." Linda seemed to prefer this kind of flexibility in her team, whereas to Mila, who once served on the same team as Linda, this seeming lack of singular focus was frustrating.

Some of the participants talked about what they identified as challenges of doing ministry with their team members. These largely fell into two types of issues—team management issues and personnel issues. Concerning team management issues, Mila felt that a lack of standards and accountability hindered developing team ministry. She attributed this to "the culture of a non-profit charity." As someone who came from a professional career in the corporate setting in North America, it was not easy for her to adjust to an international mission organization. She said that in the business world, there were clear expectations and standards in place. However, there were other things to consider in her mission organization, such as relationships and showing grace to one another. She felt these created a frustrating situation for ICWs who wanted to pursue clear ministry goals. The biggest question for her was accountability. When would it be appropriate to apply organizational standards for the teams and team members? At the time of the interview, Mila was serving in a key leadership role in her organization. In my conversations with other members of her field organization, they pointed out that Mila's discomfort with a lack of standards and accountability in the organization was a significant factor in her decision-making process and her style of dealing with team members.

Some participants pointed out that the intercultural nature of MCTs made it difficult to develop team ministries. According to Amy and Laura, due to the inefficiency resulting from language and cultural differences within their teams, it took more time and effort to get things organized and implemented, which limited the development of a robust team ministry.

When it came to personnel issues, Susan thought that the biggest challenge to developing team ministry was the high turnover rate of team members. When all her teammates left the city where they all lived, it was not feasible for her as a single woman to live and work alone in an isolated town, so she was required to relocate to another area.

Many factors influenced the departures of Christian workers in NAC. Some left due to family issues, children's education, or ailing parents back in their sending country. Others left due to the local situation becoming unstable or the project they worked on discontinued; occasionally, some were forced to leave by NAC authorities. Still, others left when they felt that it was time for them to move on.

Johannes pointed out one of the most significant reasons ICWs shied away from working together on the same platform was the security risk. He thought that team members working on the same project risked further scrutiny from the authorities and could jeopardize their long-term work in NAC. Other participants gave other reasons such as logistics, busyness, and simply juggling many responsibilities as challenges to developing strong team ministries.

Transnational Organizations

The participants' descriptions of their teams revealed the transnational nature of their international mission organizations. These organizations recruited their workers from six continents and placed them in multicultural teams around NAC. For these ICWs, the transnational aspect of their organizations was a significant factor in their intercultural social experiences.

All seven mission organizations, in which my participants were members, provided intercultural training before their workers were sent to a field. These training programs seemed to have an enduring impact on these ICWs. In the case of Philip, what he learned in his pre-field training was still vivid on his mind. He recalled one particular instruction. He recited what he learned in his training, "Don't be like a German or like an American . . . . Try to adapt [to] the culture and to find out how you can live in this culture . . . like a [NAC national], not like a German. So, don't build your own culture in another country." Ryan, a worker with a different IMO, said that the training he received at his home office devoted a large portion to understanding cultural differences. He had to read books and take classes on cultural differences. He said, "There's one specific book that basically lists every nation in the world and has a paragraph or two on them, trying to describe what they're like." Ryan explained that the class materials included information about every nation represented in his mission agency and the kind of things one could expect from people from these nations.

Some of these ICWs received an initial orientation and training in their MCT when they first arrived in NAC. This type of program usually focused on cultural adaptation. Youngcheol preferred the kind of training that emphasized experiential learning, required newly arrived ICWs to try various new things independently, and led them to make direct observations of NAC people out on the streets. He lamented that much of the experiential training modules within his organization had now been replaced with lectures and seminars.

Some participants had ongoing training opportunities through their IMOs. Linda recalled participating in a course on cultures. She said, "Probably it's not something we tend to do at the beginning, but somebody brought resources . . . [on] cold culture, hot culture, this way of looking at things. I think that's useful, but it's also probably not. It's not necessary initially, I think." Some years ago, Myungsook went to a two-week intensive course that dealt with personal life and faith issues for Christian workers. It was a transformational experience for her. She said, "When I took [the training course name], all the heavy burdens of life were lifted." Laura recently attended a workshop where she learned how to listen to people from other cultures and use different forms of communication to people from different cultures. One organization even offered an English as a Second Language program at their headquarters in North America for non-native speakers of English. At the time of their interview, Joseph and Rachel said they were taking a course through their organization on how multicultural teams worked. This course was being conducted via online video conferences. Rachel explained the content of this training module:

> So it's primarily talking about spectrums, like in decision-making or low-context, high-context . . . . Korea, Japan are high-context cultures where you read between the lines. Germany and the United States are low-context where I say what I mean, I mean what I say. And the disconnect that comes from that, individualist versus collective, the spectrum. So the US is very individualistic. Mexico and [NAC] are very collective with regard to decision making. So it's mostly talking about where do all of the countries fall on this spectrum? How . . . do we communicate? If being individualist is our typical decision-making style, how do we work that with the Koreans on our team who are maybe more collective in their decision-making style?

Joseph and Rachel found this course helpful, especially since their team had become more multicultural and their plan was to recruit more members from different countries.

Some of the participants shared their organizational policies and how these were implemented. Their policy manual required the participation of their members in regular retreats and conferences, specified the process of selecting leaders and the terms of the selection process, and established channels of communication through which they can raise issues. It also had sections on conflict resolution, peacemaking, and regional organizational structures.

Kevin and Laura provided detailed information about their regional structure in North Africa. Kevin explained that their regional team spanned several countries in North Africa and Europe. They annually attended the summer conference at a location in Europe. This was an important event to which all of their team members looked forward every year. They talked about how leadership selection happened through a democratic process of consensus building. In vivid details, they shared the inner workings of their mission organization, which is perhaps neither necessary nor appropriate to include here. However, what was striking about how they described their organization was the enormous amount of time and effort their IMO invested in supporting their workers spiritually, emotionally, and logistically.

Johannes, a member of this organization, appreciated the structure and accumulated wisdom of his IMO and its regional body. Initially, Johannes did not fully understand why such a large, complicated organizational structure was needed. After having worked through a team crisis with the help of organizational leaders from outside, he saw the significance of the international structure of his mission agency that ensured his own team's wellbeing.

However, it was not difficult to see that there were limits to these transnational structures. For example, the IMO mentioned above had a management challenge due to its regional team spanning a large area composed of several countries. Laura felt that the purpose and functions of a transnational organization needed to be defined more clearly. There were logistical issues with operating a transnational regional team. Laura explained:

> Things are complicated. Like just . . . trying to get everybody to meet together becomes more difficult. It's harder for us to find people willing to serve in leadership positions because being a leader in a transnational field requires that you travel to the other country for the . . . meetings. So there's lots of . . . practical things that have come up that people are not sure about, and I don't feel like . . . people want to necessarily change. They may decide, in the end, it's still worth it to be a transnational field, but I think they want to understand more, like what are they gaining by being a transnational field as opposed to a sort of the sacrifices that are involved in being a transnational field.

Due to scheduling conflicts between team members who lived in different countries, it was increasingly difficult to organize their annual conference in Europe. Also, since their members lived and worked in different cities in NAC, they increasingly felt a need for more country-focus plans. Still, the discussions at these annual conferences were usually on the entire region, which increased frustrations among their colleagues.

Leadership Matters

Leadership was not a topic that I intentionally explored in this study, but participants shared about both effective and ineffective leadership. They described what they thought as characteristics of an effective leader. Two leadership qualities stood out—character and executive capacity.

Leaders' character was often displayed in the way they encouraged their team members. Among some participants who served as team leaders, there was an indication of ongoing personal growth in this area. Thomas and Mikyung saw that providing genuine encouragement was a vital part of their leadership role. They recognized that each of their team members had a different need for encouragement and motivation. They had to learn the best way to encourage and motivate each team member. Reflecting on this learning process, Mikyung said that helping people find what they enjoyed, something that gave them energy was a crucial part of leadership.

When their team leader position was vacant, Joseph and Rachel filled in as interim leaders, thinking they would do this only until permanent leaders came along. However, they ended up becoming permanent team leaders. Rachel quipped, "Nobody's ever come along! [laugh]" to which Joseph responded, "So, we're still coming along!" It was not difficult to see in this leader couple humility and openness to learning.

Executive functions such as decision-making and team management were considered as qualities needed to be effective leaders. Rachel emphasized how she and her husband had always tried to make the best possible decision. She said, "We have never made a decision that has only been in the best interest of our family. We have always looked at the [NAC people] involved, the team members involved, our family, ourselves, the future, the impact. And then, we make a decision." In Mila's view, identifying and bringing together team members for a specifically focused mission was key to leadership. Sometimes it required her to make tough decisions, including rejecting well-equipped Christian workers who applied to join her team. She once had to decline a mature couple when she determined that her team was not ready to receive new team members. A serious personnel issue could harm these potential team members. So, she made a difficult and unpopular decision to protect those workers.[6]

Jaehyuk, a former leader of a country-wide team, described how he established new team rules and policies. In some cases, he had to make the tough decision to cut ties with some existing members who were unwilling to commit to and abide by the new team policies. He said that it was very taxing for him to make and implement those decisions. In the end, Jaehyuk was able to get the job done. His experiences of navigating highly intense circumstances in his past professional career and ministry situations seemed to be significant personal resources that he relied on to take these decisive actions. His co-leaders were, however, indecisive and unable to make tough leadership decisions. This difference in leadership style did not seem to be due to cultural differences or "power distance"; the main difference seemed to be on leadership competency. It seems that leadership style is often confused with leadership competency. Jaehyuk had leadership competency that made him an effective leader.

It would be obvious that a lack of character and executive capacity would make leaders ineffective. In one team situation, the team leader's insecurity and character flaws proved to be costly. In another case, a leader's disconnect with the actual on-the-ground work caused a rift with the team members, making him ineffective in his role.

Several participants described painful experiences they had with dysfunctional leaders. These ICWs were initially reluctant to provide the details, describing their situation only generally. After interviewing several people on the same team and making connections between their stories, it became evident that their former leaders had major character flaws that negatively affected the whole team. According to one interviewee, the team was still reeling from this "trauma." All eleven participants who were part of this team testified the difficulty they had with their leaders. Piecing together what these participants shared in the interviews, I suspected that these former leaders, who were no longer with the organization, might have been emotionally unstable; they were manipulative, controlling, and even verbally abusive at times. Although this was an extreme case of dysfunctional leadership in an MCT, it was a sobering example of how much impact, both positive and negative, leadership could have on ICWs in MCTs.

A sense of not being heard was another important leadership issue pointed out by some participants. They felt disappointed that there was a lack of two-way communication and a space for discussion between the

---

6. These workers ended up joining a different organization. At the time of the interview, they were well settled in NAC and were in a healthy situation with another team.

leaders and members. In their view, the voices of many team members were not being heard, and there was a disconnect between the team members and the leaders.[7]

Many of the participants revealed complex challenges involved in leading a multicultural team of an international mission organization. One of the issues was the leadership structure. Eunyoung, who served as a team leader with her husband, observed that the regional leader could not properly care for all the regional team members. She saw this as a structural weakness. Suppose a team member had an issue with the team leader and reported it to the regional leader. In that case, the regional leader would put pressure on the team leader to resolve the issue. But this could backfire on the team member who reported the issue with the team leader. In Eunyoung's view, it was not realistic for the team leader, who, as a facilitator, did not have much power or authority, was expected to fulfill the responsibilities of caring for all the members.

When a new recruit had an unresolved issue, and it was not properly identified and dealt with during the application process in the home office of a sending country, the receiving field team suffered. That was what Mila experienced with one of her team members. It was a complex situation in which a new team member with unresolved emotional issues caused much pain and hurt. It ended up getting many people involved, including the leaders and members of several teams, the sending home office, another mission organization in which the person was previously a member, and personal counselors. In the end, the subjected team member left the organization, but the emotional toll on the team was not small.

Some of the participants also shared about the challenge for Korean leaders in MCTs. This was mentioned by both Koreans and Westerners. Junghoon, a Korean, said, "There is unique leadership characteristic that only Koreans have. I've seen this leadership characteristic not being in good harmony within international organizations." He mentioned being hierarchical and authoritative as general characteristics of Korean leaders. He observed that Korean leaders tended to impose their will on team members; they would often feel the need to display a charismatic leadership style. Junghoon said that his Western teammates raised a concern with a Korean leader because he did not spend much time listening to team members. He commented, "We have a system [in the organization]. He [the Korean leader] knows all about this system. But it's in his nature, so he keeps imposing [his will]. It's very uncomfortable."

7. It should be noted that, due to the sensitive nature of discussing leadership issues in these teams, I only include here a general description of leadership issues without mentioning specifics of the individuals involved.

A Western couple observed the subtle relational dynamic between a senior Korean leader and a junior Korean leader. They recognized that the junior leader struggled with the senior leader because the junior leader could not speak about an issue directly or raise a concern with the senior leader "because he feels bound within his culture." However, this couple felt free from this type of relational entanglement because they were Westerners, so they would politely but directly speak to the senior leader about their concerns. The husband explained further complexity. The international guidelines in their organization are usually interpreted and implemented from a Euro-centric perspective. With an increasing number of their leaders coming from the Global South, he was concerned about how their guidelines would be understood. This is an insightful observation about the complexity of leadership in international mission organizations. There may be international guidelines that are assumed to be aligning their mission practices, but different interpretations of these guidelines could change everything.

So far, in this section, I have described myriad issues related to the inner workings of multicultural teams with international personnel. There was a team structure that provided accountability and support for the participants. IMOs established team policies that guided the social conduct of their workers. Their regular team meetings reinforced their core values. Many of these teams adopted Church Planting Movement (CPM) or Disciple-Making Movement (DMM) as their core strategy and tried to align themselves with tasks required to pursue these movements. While participants faced challenges of establishing viable long-term platforms, they also experienced constraints of working in a country with religious restrictions. Frequent turnovers of team members and lack of strategic focus were mentioned as factors that impeded developing team ministries. The intercultural, multicultural nature of the team and its ensuing inefficiency were also pointed out as key issues.

The participants described the transnational aspect of their teams and the impact of leadership. Each of these organizations had its own unique structure, but overall, there were many similarities in how they all functioned. Connections with their international organizations provided needed support and training for these teams, but there were limits to how they could influence ICWs in their local ministry settings. Participants also identified effective and ineffective leadership and gave examples from their experiences.

INTERCULTURAL DYNAMICS WITHIN MULTICULTURAL
TEAMS

The international Christian workers who participated in this study had a
significant portion of their social life revolving around their multicultural
teams. In this section, intercultural social relationships within multicultural
teams will be addressed. I will describe how intercultural practices in these
MCTs mediated social norms within these teams. This section also looks at
the impact of using English as the team language and the perspectives of
Korean participants about MCTs and IMOs.

Negotiating Social Norms through Multicultural Team Practices

With the rules and policies of their teams in place, participants were active
players in creating and negotiating social norms within their teams. While
each of these teams seemed to have unique social dynamics at work, virtually all of them wrestled with cultural diversity present within them. Despite
cultural differences, MCTs, at their best, seemed to work well because common values were sufficiently shared by the team members.

Some participants described how interactions among their team
members and efforts to adapt to the local social norms in NAC helped create unique dynamics in their teams. Brittany said, "It's good for us to have so
many different perspectives . . . , but then trying to meld together into this
[NAC] culture . . . ." She thought the diversity within her team was a positive
aspect of her team because she and her teammates could "pull from our
own . . . cultures or our own experiences growing up . . . to add and bring to
relationships here, and . . . to [NAC] and within our team . . . and even meld
together better as a team." Brittany seemed to be describing here a process
through which the members of her MCT were building their team's unique
cultural and social norms. They would bring from their own life experiences, add different cultural elements, evaluate how they are received by
their team members, make appropriate adjustments, and "meld" and "pull
together" something new—their unique team culture.

Myungsook and Mikyung, members of the same mission organization, both pointed out the uniqueness of the culture in their mission
organization, which was considered one of the most culturally diverse in
the world. Mikyung commented that members of a monocultural team
would more easily understand the words and actions of the other members. However, in her team, *everyone and everything* was so different. She
said, "When ten people gather, there are ten nationalities! We are all so

different, and yet all of us think that we are right." She implied that the variety of perspectives existing within her team inevitably created quite a unique team culture. Thomas also felt that these different views within the team led to increased awareness of cultural Other. He mentioned, "If you, within your teams, just have all these different cultures . . . I think we learn how it's really not about . . . right and wrong. It's just about it's different. Doesn't mean it's wrong just because it's different." He explained that these differences felt and experienced by ICWs within their MCTs prepared them well for living in an entirely different culture. He concluded, "I think that's a clear strength of the multicultural teams."

Jaehyuk had been a part of several MCTs across two different international organizations in NAC. He expected these teams to be culturally "more Western," but he realized that each local team or each organization had a distinct culture of its own. He felt that the local context made the team culture or organizational culture different in each locale. He observed that the team culture also depended on the team members' distinct experiences and personalities. Rachel seemed to concur with Jaehyuk's view. She said that even though all her team members were US citizens, her team's culture was quite different from the mainstream White American culture. She thought it was partially due to her team having cultural diversity among its members and fully immersed in the local NAC context.

On average, each of the eleven MCTs, of which my participants were members, was composed of team members with just over three nationalities. Some had up to six different passport countries represented on their local team. Although there was a varying degree of cultural diversity present in each team, many participants saw it as the most significant team characteristic. They mentioned that there were different kinds of diversities on their MCTs, affecting their team's social dynamics. They identified not only cultural diversity but also diversity in generations, personalities, and theologies. The participants generally agreed on the challenging nature of having all these diversities, even as they showed an enormous appreciation for them.

Recognizing the complexity of the diversity present within her mission organization, Mila said there were "multiple ways of being different and diverse" within MCTs. Diversities in her organization could not easily be reduced to simple terms. MCTs in which my participants were members were diverse culturally and in various other ways. Mila thought that the great diversity of her former team made it difficult to focus on the team's primary mission. She said, "There's so many different personalities, different cultures . . . , language difficulties and . . . different layers . . . . And I think that was the challenge because of the diversity. It was hard to . . . come to an agreement for what we were trying to do together . . . ."

However, she also saw the benefits of a diverse group, comparing it to a tapestry. She explained, "Each one of us bringing our parts and . . . instead of just this design or this color, it . . . has a lot more different designs, different colors, and gives a different picture." She thought that being confronted with different ways of thinking and behaving challenged MCT members to reflect on their ways of doing things and areas they needed to change. Similarly, Laura commented, "I feel like I have learned a lot of things in there to see things in a lot of different ways that I would never have had a chance to if I . . . hadn't been part of a multicultural team."

Joseph's team was composed entirely of members who were US citizens, but there were differences in age and backgrounds that affected their group dynamics. He had team members in their sixties and members in their twenties and thirties. Some used to be farmers in the Midwest, while others worked as professionals in Southern California. They had members who grew up in cosmopolitan mega-cities and rural areas, domestically and overseas. It was notable that Joseph and his team members emphasized the significance of differences in age and personal backgrounds in their team.

In contrast, members of other MCTs with more passport countries represented tended to frame their observations around cultural diversity in their teams. One member of Joseph's team also shared about different theological perspectives on the team. It shows that diversity affecting this team was more complicated than it seemed.

It would be important to note that the membership in these teams was constantly changing. Over time, existing team members left, and new members joined. Depending on who was on the team, the team dynamics changed. For example, when Joseph and Rachel first joined their team during the late 2000s, they had South African, British, and Latin American teammates, whereas all of the current team members were US citizens.

Working in teams was a core value held by several mission organizations in which my participants were members. Despite various diversities existing among them, it was striking that most of the ICWs participating in this study lived by similar codes of conduct. For example, virtually all of them dressed modestly and conservatively on purpose; they all learned or were trying to learn the NAC Arabic and tried to interact with local people as much as possible; they tried to share the gospel message with their local friends whenever they had opportunities; they were cautious in relating to persons of the opposite gender, whether foreigners or NAC nationals; they tried not to be in situations where they were alone with a person of the opposite gender in an enclosed room or a car unless it was their spouse or family member.

Chris, one of the participants in this study, helped me set up interview appointments with two of his single female team members. He arranged these interviews in a manner that kept to these codes. He opened his home to be used as the location for these interviews, and he made sure that he, his wife, and his children were present at home when the interviewee and I were meeting. In this way, the single woman interviewee would not have to be alone with an adult male, which would violate their team code of conduct. It also ensured that their neighbors and people in the local community would not be suspicious of any inappropriate relations between the woman and me, protecting her reputation in the local community. This was a standard social protocol among all forty-nine participants as if they had all agreed to such conduct even though they were with different teams and organizations and lived in different cities throughout NAC.[8]

In terms of lifestyle, most participants lived at an economically modest level. During my fieldwork, I visited seventeen different homes and five different offices of ICWs. While they neither were in a run-down condition nor showed signs of economic scarcity, compared to international expatriates who worked for large corporations or foreign diplomatic missions, these homes and offices were simple and modest. They had almost a bland, unremarkable appearance. On the outside, no one would be able to tell that these places were occupied by foreigners. Unlike traditional missionary compounds in other regions, their living spaces and workplaces were well integrated into, not isolated from, the local community and its people. They all had local NAC people, not foreigners, as their neighbors.

There seemed to be a general agreement among these ICWs on conducting themselves socially in the local context. These shared social codes among these workers across many organizations were striking, considering their vast cultural diversity. It seemed that these ICWs shared a lot more in common than one might have imagined. Cultural differences seemed to pale compared to the common purpose, goals, and social codes of conduct shared by them. Focusing on the same shared values seemed to be an effective way for these Christian workers to negotiate and establish the relational and social norms within their MCTs.

It was notable that the vast majority of them used a similar coded language related to their Christian mission work. Some of these terms were: workers (missionaries), TL (team leader), cousins (Muslims), M-work (mission work), E-work (evangelism), company (mission organization), CP (church planting), CPM (church planting movement), DBS (Discovery

---

8. There was such an agreement worked out by representatives of various international mission organizations and NAC national churches during the 2000s. It was developed by a network of ICWs and NAC national churches.

Bible Study), and DMM (Disciple Making Movement). These coded words and acronyms were used by these ICWs to minimize the risk of being seen in a negative light as "missionaries," a term generally understood in the NAC society as Western imperial agents who bought religious converts by offering financial and other incentives. None of these ICWs wanted to be identified as such an agent; they wanted to be known as Christians or followers of Jesus, who loved God and people.

During interviews, I asked interviewees whether they could send me copies of their recent newsletters; many of them positively responded. It was notable how all ICWs whom I interviewed, no matter which country's passport they carried and whichever culture they came from, regularly wrote newsletters to their supporters and churches in their sending countries. Then it struck me that there was an incredible level of consistency in the way they practiced Christian missions.

Julia, one of the participants, pointed out that since everyone on her team was Christian, even if there were tensions between them, she knew that they were perhaps due to personal or cultural differences, not faith differences. What she essentially pointed out was that she and her colleagues shared the most critical element with the potential to eclipse other differences—their Christian faith. It is a significant insight when one looks at how, in Christian missions today, cultural differentiation tends to exaggerate differences between people. Rather than learning about arbitrary differences, perhaps it would be more beneficial for mission workers to focus on the commonalities they have in Christ. A pragmatic, utilitarian view of Christian missions tends to maintain differences between cultural groups and social segments for the sake of "reaching the unreached."[9] In so doing, rather than uniting Christians, they risk causing rifts among them. If Christian fellowship is a spiritual reality already fulfilled in Christ, as Bonhoeffer writes, it would be worthwhile to ask how the theological reality of Christian unity can be embodied in everyday mission practices.[10]

Consequences of English as Team Language

Among the forty-seven participants, forty-five were members of MCTs that used English as the team language. In these teams, all official communications were carried out in English. Using English as the team language was the cause for some complex issues for these Christian workers and their teams.

9. See Lee and Park, "Beyond People Group Thinking."
10. Bonhoeffer, Life Together.

There were ongoing communication challenges within these teams. As I have already mentioned in the section on initial challenges in MCTs, the communication difficulty between fluent English speakers and those with limited English was neither a one-sided issue nor a temporary one. It was frustrating for both those fluent English speakers and those who were not fluent. Linda, a native English speaker, learned that not being able to communicate with a teammate well was personally taxing. To her, it was not just about understanding words but understanding the person and the person's culture. Mila felt that the language barrier was one of those unavoidable consequences of working in MCTs. Likewise, John quickly found that emails and long text messages did not work well with his team members who were not fluent in English. John began to communicate more through face-to-face meetings and short messages.

The situation with John's team was more complicated than simply a language issue, however. John and his wife, who were the team leaders, had achieved the highest level of graduate education in their respective professional fields in their home country. They had a certain preferred style of communicating and interacting with others, which their team members did not share. On top of these, their team members did not have a strong command of English. It should be noted that language was only one of several factors to consider in assessing the communication issues within this MCT.

Ryan, a native English speaker, said, "I know language and culture are closely tied, but far more than cultural behaviors, the biggest barrier is language definitely." Although he was sympathetic toward those who were not fluent in English, he seemed frustrated with communication difficulties with his teammates. He felt that his teammates' lack of English language skills was one of the biggest barriers within his team. He explained, "It's not uncommon to spend twenty-five minutes just trying to correctly communicate a very simple sentence, so it's kind of like, okay, we have two hours to make a decision, and we waste so much time just trying to . . . understand what thoughts are being shared . . . ."

Stefanie, who was not a native speaker of English, was once in a group setting where a native speaker was giving a seminar. She said that the speaker spoke very fast and used some unfamiliar words, so it was difficult for her to follow the seminar. She said, "It can be quite frustrating . . . because I know it could be different." Stefanie pointed out that when she was under pressure, her level of English dropped considerably and made her prone to more mistakes than normal. Others had seen her use English at a high level before, so they expected her to speak and understand at that high level at all times. She felt burdened by these expectations.

Jaehyuk and Kyungja's MCT used to be composed almost entirely of native speakers of English. This had changed in recent years, and now most of the team did not speak or understand English well. According to Kyungja, it was difficult to conduct team meetings due to the language barrier. While they continued to conduct team meetings in English, it was not easy to get much done during these meetings. As a result, some team members who were native English speakers were distressed that they no longer wanted to attend these meetings. This was of great concern to Jaehyuk and Kyungja, who had served for years in leadership.

Using English as the team language also somewhat hampered the development of teamwork. In Junghoon's MCT, although none of the team members were native English speakers, they still used English as the team language. Junghoon felt that their interactions often lacked necessary depth, and discussions stayed shallow. It was not convenient for them to use English as the team language, but there seemed to be no other viable alternative.

Mikyung, a veteran Christian worker, recalled an incident during her first couple of weeks with her MCT. There was a colleague who was constantly saying jokes to the teammates. All her new teammates, who were fluent English speakers, laughed at the jokes, but she could not join in the laughter because she did not understand them. It made her feel left out and isolated in the team. She could understand matters related to team business or ministry training but not this teammate's jokes. Her story shows a need for MCT members to be more sensitive about telling jokes to those from other countries, especially if they are not fluent in English.

The use of English as the primary language of communication had another unintended consequence—inequality. Ashley, a native English speaker with previous international experience, shared a perceptive observation about her team. She noticed that she possessed more power than her teammates simply by being a native English speaker. She said, "Because I can make myself understood to others, my views can be heard or will be heard more easily. So I think it's completely a difference in power." She was aware of her privilege. Ashley said that she had power because she was born in a country where English, the most dominant language in mission and theology, was the main language, although she did nothing to deserve it. It seems that the unequal level of influence one can exert based on one's abilities to speak English was a hindrance to these MCTs in developing meaningful teamwork.

The language barrier also created inefficiency in these teams. Although Ryan had a strong desire to include everyone on the team, the inefficiency of team meetings bothered him. He wondered if teams might be better off by dividing by language groups. He said, "It just makes the most sense as far as efficiency goes." It seems that these members of MCTs all sought equality, inclusion, and efficiency. But they found it impossible to have all three; to have equality and inclusion within the team, they had to endure inefficiency. If they wanted efficiency, it was obvious that the team could not afford to put equality and inclusion first. It was a dilemma for these MCTs. However, it makes one wonder whether efficiency was ever a biblical value or a requirement for a Christian community in mission.

Using English as the team language had an emotional toll on those team members who were not fluent in English. Because of the limitation of expressing themselves, team meetings could become quite frustrating for them. John was observant of these about his German teammates when he sympathetically said, "We feel for them . . . sometimes they really get frustrated because they know what they want to say, but they can't get it out." For some, being unable to express themselves fully in English was humiliating as they often felt like little children. Stefanie decried, "I'm not a baby!" Although she was a capable adult ICW in NAC, her feelings often betrayed her stature.

The language barrier sometimes created awkward experiences for everyone on MCTs. At a team meeting in City "B" in which I participated, Haejin shared her understanding of a Bible verse in English as best as she could. But it was obviously difficult for her teammates to understand what she was trying to communicate. When she sensed that the team did not understand what she intended to communicate, Haejin nervously laughed, seemingly trying to mitigate the moment's awkwardness.

Some of these ICWs valiantly went the extra length to include and communicate with teammates who were not fluent speakers of English. This took much extra effort on the part of these native speakers. For example, John and Amy decided to change how they communicated to non-native English speakers on their team. They spoke more slowly than they normally spoke. They stopped writing long text messages or emails to their team members but instead wrote short, simple text messages. Still, it was personally taxing for John and Amy being unable to communicate and share at a deep level with their team.

Some teams try to remedy some of these negative consequences of using English as the team language. Joseph mentioned that he had seen a team in another country forced to use the local language as the team language because the team members did not have a shared common language. He suggested using the NAC Arabic as the team language might resolve many of the issues found in many MCTs in NAC. Indeed, this is a suggested solution by some mission practitioners.[11] However, such measures could

---

11. E.g., Roembke, *Building Credible Multicultural Teams.*

lead to unintended consequences as changing the team language might re-create the same dynamics. For example, the best speakers of the new team language are likely to be dominant in influence and power; those who are not fluent in the new team language might suffer regardless of the efforts they made. The issues of inequality, exclusion, and inefficiency could be repeated in different forms. Using the local language might still be a good alternative to using English as the team language, but it is also likely to result in a different set of consequences.

Perspectives of Korean Members of MCTs

For the participants who served with global mission organizations, working with international personnel from every corner of the world was a source of both joy and distress. These international organizations that established multicultural teams in North Africa had many Korean members. Among the participants in this study, Koreans made up the second-largest national group after the US. Some of these Koreans described the challenges of being part of a multicultural team of an international mission organization.

One of the things they mentioned was the uneven practice of multicul-turalism by their international mission organization. Some Korean partici-pants pointed out that their organization was too "Western." Chris worked with an organization that had its sending bases concentrated in Western Europe and North America. He attended the agency's international confer-ence, where all of its members from around the world gathered together. According to him, 95 percent of all attendees were White. He commented, "They [White ICWs] don't know what to do with us [non-White ICWs]." As one of few Asians who attended this conference, Chris said that he experi-enced varying reactions from Western Christian workers. Some responded to him with an overreaction of welcome; others tried to avoid him. He felt that some were talking down to him; some attendees at the conference gave him the impression that they felt superior.

For Junghoon, who worked with a different IMO, it was not fair that his organization's standards and policies were following a certain "West-ern" style. He did not feel that his organization had room to implement some of the "Asian ways." He pointed out, "In principle no single culture should be above or below another culture. But it seems that there remains this appearance." He said that when he was going through initial training in North America, he was told that the organization was multicultural, and every member had to learn multiculturalism. He said, "I felt that they were telling me to learn *their multiculturalism* over there."[12] Junghoon

12. Emphasis is added.

thought that true multiculturalism would have an even mix of cultural practices. Still, he often felt that a Western model was being imposed on members from the Global South.

Junghoon also discussed another related issue. He said that his IMO had developed a peacemaking manual for conflict resolution between team members, which suggested several steps of evaluating and implementing peacemaking. Junghoon felt, however, this was not how he or other Asians would approach peacemaking. He said that some Westerners on the team were aware of the incompatibility of their peacemaking manual with some non-Western cultures and tried to re-evaluate the manual. However, Junghoon did not think that they were going to make any significant changes to the manual. When I asked why he thought so, he replied, "That's because they don't know. They haven't really been burnt by it."

Sara once tried to introduce to her teammates "the Korean style" of group prayer, during which everyone would pray out loud in their native language altogether at the same time. She did not think it went very well. She said, "They are not used to this. So, I should adjust to them since that's how the team culture is. I should adjust to them." When her entire regional teams gathered together for a summer conference, almost half of all members were Koreans. She noticed that the group prayer sessions were still done in a typical "Western style." When she realized that she was going against the team culture, she decided not to try the Korean style anymore.

There was also a representation issue on some of these mission organizations. For example, Junghoon's organization had an increasing number of Koreans joining them while the number of Western workers decreased steadily. He said that some people within his organization suggested that more Koreans take on the leadership roles since they were becoming larger in numbers, but he disagreed. He thought that such thinking was more aligned to politics, not Christian mission. However, he still thought that there was an embedded inequality between Westerners and Asians within his mission agency. He received the impression that Westerners were fine with Asians joining and working under them while they did not want to work under Asians. Both he and his wife felt that this was very much a current reality in their IMO.

Jaehyuk talked about the challenge of integrating other Koreans into his MCT. When he and his wife joined their NAC team in the mid-2000s, they were the very first Koreans to do so. Since then, their country team had gone through many changes. Most of their previous team members left NAC, and new members had arrived. Within his local city team, there were now more Koreans than Westerners. The issue was not just in the number but also in that the new Korean members were not culturally attuned to their international social norms; their English skills were also rather limited. They had regular team meetings together, but the communication was difficult, and the meetings were not very productive. It became quite stressful for the Westerners on the team, and they no longer wanted to join regular team meetings with all the Korean members present. The Westerners on his team suggested to Koreans that they have their separate team meetings speaking their language. Meanwhile, they would have a time of fellowship with only Jaehyuk and his wife once a month.

It should be noted that Jaehyuk had rich previous international experiences, had served on the country leadership team, was fluent in English and French, and was well regarded within his organization at the international level. According to Jaehyuk, most Western team members felt comfortable with him and his wife. The challenge of Korean integration into MCTs in NAC was not an isolated incident for this organization but was prevalent in many other places around the world. Jaehyuk explained, "In other places, Koreans isolate and go out by themselves, saying they will form a team only by themselves." Kyungja said that because of Jaehyuk's influence, new Korean members kept joining their MCT rather than forming a separate Korean team in NAC. Although they wanted to make the team function in a healthy, more integrated way, they found it increasingly difficult with the intercultural social dynamics at play within the team.

So far, in this section, I have explored intercultural social dynamics in MCTs experienced by ICWs. Being in teams with people from different cultures created unique social dynamics within these teams. ICWs gained from rich diversity but also struggled with differences. Despite challenges, many participants believed that diversity in their teams was a positive experience that led to growth and learning. There was a common code of conduct closely followed by ICWs across teams and organizations. It showed that although these ICWs had very diverse backgrounds, they still had more shared values and commonalities than previously recognized. While the common practice of using English as the team language had consequences, no teams could find a good alternative solution. Some Korean participants expressed their concerns with uneven multicultural policies and challenges of Korean integration into MCTs. Each of the issues described in this section and the previous one portrays a complex and dynamic social context of multicultural teams in which structure and agency are entangled in complicated intercultural flux. The next section will further explore how social relationships unfolded in the MCT context.

SOCIAL RELATIONSHIPS WITHIN MCTS

The participants described various relational experiences with their team members. Although these accounts revealed the relational challenges in multicultural teams, they also displayed how social life within MCT was a rich ground for learning and personal growth.

Relational Issues: Conflicts, Misunderstandings, and Disagreements

Many participants shared numerous stories of interpersonal issues within their MCTs. These stories highlighted the nature and extent of interpersonal conflicts, misunderstandings, disagreements and how these ICWs responded to them.

The majority of participants who shared examples of conflict understood the cause for conflict was not entirely cultural differences or language barriers. It was clear that Linda recognized this when she commented, "I think it's not always nationality; it's not always language. It's also personality. It's the things that happen. People have conflicts." When Mila saw some serious unresolved emotional issues in a team member, she tried to help her by initiating a conversation with her on the issues, but it did not go very well. The person did not initially admit them. By the time her team member became more willing to address the issues, there was already a deep rift in their relationship, making it far more difficult to tackle the issues.

Several participants who served on the same MCT brought up a conflict they all had experienced with a couple who were now their former colleagues. In separate interviews, they corroborated some disturbing incidents that took place with this couple. On one occasion, this couple became so angry to the point that they raised their voices, yelling and shouting at other team members in front of the whole team during a team meeting. Through numerous examples and stories told about these former colleagues, a picture of persons with serious emotional issues emerged. It appeared that unresolved personal issues had marred the minds and hearts of these Christian workers and led to a painful conflict that ensued for several years and harmed the team.

Among all the stories of interpersonal conflict, one of the most intriguing was the one told by Junghoon. When asked about how people from different cultural backgrounds responded differently to conflicts, Junghoon shared an example of a team member who shall be called Dirk. Dirk was a Western European worker who lived in a different city from Junghoon. When Dirk had a sudden family emergency in his home country, he had to leave his family behind in his city and travel back home. Junghoon, as Dirk's team leader, wanted to make sure that he was well supported and cared for, so he quickly communicated to his whole team and regional teams what had happened and asked for prayer support. Some of them even made financial contributions toward Dirk's travel. In the middle of his already-packed schedule, Junghoon did everything that he could think of to help and provide support for Dirk. Then Junghoon thought that things would be well for Dirk, despite the circumstance. He expected that he would hear from Dirk when he returned to NAC after attending to the family needs.

Junghoon did not hear back from Dirk, but then about three weeks later, he was shocked to receive a long message from Dirk, who did not hide his deep disappointment with Junghoon and his inactions as the team leader. Dirk was upset that no one from the team, including Junghoon, called or cared for his wife and family while he had been gone. Junghoon immediately realized that for some reason, he did not think to call or provide care for Dirk's wife and children while Dirk was traveling. He did recognize his mistake and apologized to Dirk. Nonetheless, Junghoon could not help but feel rather unappreciated and misunderstood. Although he had forgotten to contact his wife, he went to extra lengths to support and provide timely help for Dirk in a time of personal emergency. Junghoon said that he felt a deep emptiness. All that he had done for Dirk went unnoticed and unappreciated. As the team leader, he still felt responsible for his lack of care for Dirk's family during his absence, so he decided to let go of the negative feelings. Junghoon chose to apologize sincerely to Dirk and avoided an escalation in this conflict. At the time of the interview, Junghoon mentioned that he had a good relationship with Dirk. Junghoon seemed glad for the actions he had taken when he found Dirk upset. At the same time, he regretted that the conflict was so one-sided. Although he apologized for his lack of attention to Dirk's family, Junghoon did not feel that Dirk showed enough appreciation for the things Junghoon had done for him in a time of distress.

Through this incident, Junghoon said that he got a first-hand experience of a Western European person who expressed his displeasures in a shockingly explicit and direct manner. Junghoon, a Korean, was taken aback and emotionally rattled by this direct confrontation and accusation. While he tried to understand how his Western colleagues approached relationships, for Junghoon, this was a good example of how non-Westerners had to adapt to Western social and cultural norms. It was apparent that Junghoon wished that his Western team members, including Dirk, would develop a deeper awareness of how Asians preferred to relate and resolve conflicts. He hoped that they would adjust their social conduct when they dealt with Asians. Unfortunately, Junghoon saw such efforts neither in this incident nor in the overall organizational culture of his IMO. It was ironic since his IMO emphasized multiculturalism; it raised the question of whose multiculturalism its members practiced.

The above example of the conflict between Dirk and Junghoon was partially caused by a misunderstanding due to differences in "languaculture," a term coined by linguistic anthropologist Michael Agar to denote that language and culture are inseparable.[13] Junghoon had studied and read about the general social inclinations of Westerners. Thus he was able to suppress his feelings of hurt and anger and willed himself to empathize with Dirk in his disappointment. It should be noted that Dirk's approach to resolving his issue with Junghoon would certainly be seen as rather disrespectful or even selfish by other Koreans. Junghoon said that even though he felt offended by Dirk's confrontation, he tried to understand why this Western European friend might have behaved in such a manner.

Caitlin talked about her experience of misunderstanding and conflict with a Korean housemate. Caitlin thought that the source of the conflict was a misunderstanding due to the language barrier. She said, "I think a big thing was maybe language, that we misunderstand each other a lot. I've never, never felt so misunderstood in my life, hearing things I've never heard before. I'm thinking, 'Wow, really? Is that how you experience me?'" Jaehyuk was once contacted by a Western team leader in another region because of a misunderstanding with Koreans who were on the team. A Korean couple on the team had just given birth to a child. The Western team leader wanted to congratulate and celebrate with them, but the mother informed them that she could not come to team meetings for four weeks. The team leader was concerned whether he had offended her in any way. He did not know that it was customary for Korean women who had just given birth not to go out for a month to recover from delivery. However, when the team leader was informed of her planned absence, he got the impression that she was upset with him about something. It was a misunderstanding that Jaehyuk had to help clear up.

These misunderstandings due to language and cultural differences are, however, more nuanced and subtle than they might appear. An example is my email exchange with a German couple whom I was to interview. I had sent an email to them to arrange a time for an interview but had not heard back from them for several days. When I finally heard from them, they said that they could interview in less than twenty-four hours later. This short notice put pressure on me due to a tight schedule, but I had no choice but to go ahead with this interview. From the emails, the

13. Agar, *Language Shock; Culture*, 2019.

husband came across as blunt and direct. I was unsure whether it was due to his style of English, which was not his first language. The impression I got from his emails was of a man who was stubborn, straightforward, and somewhat rude. However, when I met him in person, I realized that I had entirely wrong assumptions. He was soft-spoken and came across as introverted, sensitive, and kind. I realized that I might have been misled by my unconscious bias of his nationality.

However, misunderstandings between Christian workers on MCTs were not always due to cultural or language differences. Several participants showed that interpersonal dynamics, personalities, and character flaws contributed to various misunderstandings between team members. In one case, the misunderstanding was between people from the same country. What complicated the issue was that while there were both linguacultural and interpersonal differences that led to misunderstandings, it was difficult to isolate one from another since these were thoroughly mixed in everyday interactions. For example, Jessica recalled an occasion when a team member from another country who was not fluent in English said that ever since coming to NAC, Jessica looked as if she had plastic surgery. Despite this seemingly rude and offensive remark, Jessica did not come to a conclusion right away but wisely probed and asked follow-up questions to this teammate to understand what she was trying to say. Then Jessica realized that it was a compliment; the teammate meant that Jessica looked happy, beautiful, and blossoming. Jessica commented about this teammate: "There were lots of things she would say . . . to other people as well, and I think if they didn't ask the follow-up questions, it would either be . . . very offensive . . . or it wouldn't make any sense."

There were many instances of the participants disagreeing with certain team decisions, policies, or styles of operation. Chris showed frustration with what he deemed as inefficient decision-making within his MCT. He said, "We could reduce our team meeting time by 70 percent if we discussed just for 5 minutes, and the team leader made the decisions, and everybody followed them." Thomas recalled how he struggled with a decision made by his leader to send some of his team members to another city and form a new team there. It was difficult for him because it was decided without his consent, and yet he and the remaining team members were the ones who suffered the consequences of the decision—a smaller, weakened team with few members.

Sometimes, disagreements between team members were over local social norms and how they were supposed to behave as foreigners. Many years ago, Mikyung, a single woman at that time, had once invited a dozen single Christian workers to dinner at her home. She later found out that the senior members of the team were disapproving of this event. They strongly felt that it was culturally inappropriate in their context for young single people to host a social gathering by themselves without a presence of a mature family or a married couple. Later, she was told to come by the house of the team leader. There were two senior couples on the team who reprimanded her. Mikyung felt that these senior members did not necessarily trust young single workers. She thought that she had gained their trust through her exemplary and impeccable track record in her ministry in the country. She felt, however, that the senior members still saw her immature and lacking in judgment. Mikyung recalled that it was quite hurtful to her.

There was a case of team members who did not agree with team policy. A married American couple felt quite limited in their freedom because of their team policy requiring approval from the team leaders for travel outside their town. The husband said, "It's very frustrating at our age. We've been married longer than most of them [their team members] have lived, and we know we can go to [the name of another city] without a problem for a couple of days." In a separate interview, even though I did not ask about it, the team leader couple talked about how and why such a team policy was necessary. They explained that as the team leaders, they were ultimately responsible for the well-being of all their team members. The wife leader said, "The American culture . . . says, 'I'm independent. I make decisions for my family. I don't have to think about how this is going to affect somebody else.' That doesn't work on our team." She explained that, with the level of commitment required to work as a team in NAC, it was not easy for someone "with the American mindset of culture" since "it clashes with the kind the community and the culture that we have on our team."

Frustrations, Disappointments, Loneliness, and Exclusion

Many participants often felt frustrated or disappointed while serving with MCTs. Several different factors were identified as the cause of these emotions. One was a sense of not being heard, especially by the leadership. Thomas felt a deep disappointment when he felt that he was not being heard by the leadership. He had disagreements and concerns about letting some of his team members move to a different city, leaving a smaller and weakened team behind. Thomas recalled, "We felt a strong disconnect in understanding." He was certain that he sufficiently communicated his concerns to the leaders, but his voice was not heard. He did not see careful consideration by the leaders of the issues he raised.

One of the greatest disappointments for some participants was dysfunctional leadership. Junghoon felt that the invaluable window of time for adapting to the new culture during his initial years was wasted because of the tremendous stress and a large amount of energy spent on working through relational issues with his former team leaders.

Communication difficulty was another point of frustration for a majority of the participants. There were many cases of this kind. Jessica mentioned that whatever she intended to communicate was somehow misconstrued by her housemate. It was not only due to the language barrier but also that her housemate was unwilling to accept whatever Jessica was trying to communicate with her. For John and Amy, doing team life with non-native speakers of English had also been challenging. They did their best to accommodate and involve their team members, but it was somewhat frustrating when they frequently had to withhold themselves, unable to express themselves fully. Amy said:

> Yes, it can be hard because there's a part of us that represses a bit of how we connect because we're not sure that they can do that fully with the language that we commonly use. The email thing is for real, for sure, for John. He communicates great by email. It's really easy for him. He can get a lot of content across, and that would be a brilliant way for him to communicate extra things for the team—practical things of just encouragements and things . . . but he can't.

Some participants were disappointed when they did not find a family-like team life. Marie explained her expectations of her team before she arrived in NAC. She said, "We thought . . . to live like families together, that we spend more time, that it's more open. We can visit each other. We can help each other if we have problems." These expectations were largely unmet. Claudia also said, "It was so hard that we weren't more [of] a team, like more into each others' lives a bit." Olivia shared a similar view when she said, "Our team is not so much like . . . [a] family, to be honest . . . our team leaders are really nice and they take really good care of us, but the family part . . . I think it's because maybe we just meet once a week for two hours." Cheryl said, "I thought that we would be spending a lot more time together as a family and doing more things together." Rachel recalled how she wished she had a deeper community within her team when she first arrived in NAC. She said, "Everybody's doing their own thing, and we get together once a month to kind of encourage each other, but there wasn't too much in the way of like community doing life together."

Feeling lonely was a common experience among some of the participants, even while working with their teams. This sense of loneliness seemed exaggerated among single women and those who lived in geographically isolated locations. Jennifer, who was married and had young children, observed that many of her colleagues felt lonely. She was surprised when she learned that single women in her team felt so much loneliness. She said, "They struggle so much and appeal about the constraints they have as singles. It's not just one or two singles. The ones I met at [her organization's regional conference] were also." Chris recalled when a single female colleague shared her experience of being a single person in the group setting. Chris reported, "She said, 'It sucks to be a single!" She said that . . . . 'I'm so lonely.' And then she got angry with those of us who weren't singles!" Jennifer and Chris's observations were corroborated by some single women participants. Brittany said that being a single woman contributed to her loneliness. She was a part of an MCT that had families and couples. She said that all of her team members had already been in the country for a long time, had many local relationships, or had a spouse or family members. But for her to arrive in NAC by herself and join the team as a total stranger was difficult. She said, "There were lots of different points where it just made me feel more alone and isolated . . . that I was a single woman, that I was coming in alone." She also mentioned how living in a smaller town heightened her sense of loneliness.

Stefanie, who lived in a larger city, felt alone because she was the only ICW from her home country. She said that couples had each other, but "People like me who are just alone with my culture in a team, it's different, I would say." Heather came to NAC when she was a single woman in her twenties. She wished that she received more care and attention from her organization. She confided, "You know . . . I still have a desire for marriage. I still have a desire for real, real, authentic relationships . . . ." She longed for intimate relationships, but due to the cultural context and her ministry focus, there were limitations on how to go about developing those relationships, especially with men.

While Thomas had a fulfilling ministry, living and working in a remote town was difficult, especially during the first year of moving into that town. The nearest large city was about an hour and a half away by car. He said, "Well, it was quite . . . lonely in the beginning because even though [City B] is close, it was . . . still . . . felt lonely. It was an adjustment to be so alone and having people [colleagues] quite far away." His wife, Mikyung, shared her experiences in more detail. She said, "It's lonely. It's very lonely. Of course, people who serve in the line of work that we do would experience loneliness. Those in cities would feel lonely, but in smaller places like here, it shows even more. Loneliness . . . it runs very deep."

The nature of MCTs with a unified team language of English and Western-oriented social norms made some ICWs from the Global South feel excluded. Mikyung recalled a feeling of exclusion when everyone in the team laughed, but she could not. She did not understand the joke told by a colleague. It was at that moment that she felt excluded. She said, "As I lived together with them, things got better because my understanding improved, but at first, it was hard . . . that . . . I alone couldn't laugh. I couldn't pretend that I understood [the joke] . . . ." Ashley, a White Australian, was sensitive toward this kind of exclusion experienced by non-native speakers of English. She observed that verbally dominant English speakers often made non-native speakers of English feel excluded. She explained, "It's not intentional. It's unintentional, but just realizing that everyone had almost their backs to them [Asian team members], and so they were quite isolated in group settings." Ashley was perceptive to grasp what these Asian team members might have felt. She remembered a situation in which native English speakers dominated the group conversation and how Asian team members reacted to it. She perceptively observed, "And they were silent . . . (a long pause) And they were silent. . ."

Chris recalled having a conversation with a German colleague at a regional conference. After watching a soccer match on TV together, Chris said that this German colleague confided with him about his struggle to fit in. Chris said, "What this friend told me was, 'I feel lonely.' So I asked why. Then he said, 'I'm German, and my English is not good. And when they were preaching, especially when he [the speaker] breaks a joke and everybody is laughing, and I don't understand.' It was an inside joke, but he didn't get it."

It was not only the language barrier that made members of MCTs feel excluded. It was also a social and cultural gap that led to feelings of exclusion by these workers. For example, Caitlin felt shunned out when her Korean roommate would spend all her time with other Korean team members while not engaging with her. While it might have been unintentional on these Korean team members' part, it still came across to Caitlin as being exclusive. Caitlin, nevertheless, empathized with them. She knew how it might feel to be part of a group in which English speakers were dominant. She said:

> I've experienced this so many times. When I'm the only African in the room when you're with a group of Americans and they talk English, and . . . my English is fluent or good enough that I can hold a conversation, but I have no idea what you're talking about because they're talking about books they've read or things in their country or their history or any topic that is related to their culture or their country. An outsider feels excluded.

She related that experience to her current team dynamics in which three dominant English speakers were often talking about something from their country and how it often left the Korean team members excluded from the conversation.

Rich Learning Experience

Despite a heap of relational issues and negative feelings experienced, many participants mentioned that the social life within their MCTs had provided a rich learning experience for them. Among the things that participants mentioned, cultural diversity was singled out as the most significant factor in their learning and growth.

Cheryl, who grew up in a farming community in the Midwest in the United States, said, "I didn't know I was going to learn about not only the [NAC] culture but the Chinese culture as well!" Learning about the "cultures" of their teammates was considered by many participants to be a major benefit of working with an MCT. The extent to which participants were exposed to other cultures was dependent upon who their teammates were. During their first few years in NAC, Youngcheol and Myungsook were exposed to multiple cultures. Youngcheol recalled, "When we came to [NAC], our surrounding culture was [NAC] people, the team culture was . . . although we had British people, in reality, our team's most influential majority culture was the Latin culture. There were many Latinos on the team." Myungsook, who grew up in a conservative Presbyterian church in a rural area in Korea, recalled how shocked and horrified she was at the sight of some Latin American team members hugging each other and lying down on the floor during a corporate worship time. As shocked as she was to witness these different expressions in worship, it helped her learn to accept those who were very different from her.

Various participants described the benefits of working with multicultural teams. Table 2 includes direct quotes spoken by seven participants with seven different cultural backgrounds about these benefits. Despite these positive aspects of working with an MCT, virtually all participants were still very aware of the challenges. Stefanie summed it up when she said that although there was beauty in the diversity of MCT, there was always a high price to pay—so much effort and time were required from all team members to make an MCT work. Nevertheless, many participants thought that MCTs were worth it. Eunyoung represented these thoughts well when she compared relationships within MCTs to a marriage relationship. She said, "So when we get married and live together, due to all the daily grindings and frictions, it's actually quite hard. But when two persons try to adjust something in them, then their horizon gets expanded. Then they become ready to give birth to a child, and their scale gets bigger." She said it was likewise for MCTs; working with MCTs expanded the horizon of her understanding and comfort zone.

Table 2. Participant Comments on Benefits of MCT

No	Speaker	Cultural Background	ParticipantQuote
1	Linda	English	You get a wider view on the world, certainly more interesting. I didn't come to [NAC] just to stay in a little English group, you know . . . Because when you have this international focus . . . and you're working with [NAC people] and other foreigners . . . for me then, to be in a multinational team is very normal. We learn from each other.
2	Julia	German	I'm thinking, like even the knowledge that you'd get [about] other places. Like what I know about Korea or Switzerland or England, that's so much increased. This [is from] just being with people from those countries.
3	Amy	Northern Irish	Maybe you have this hunch that something happens in these kinds of teams, and you're definitely changed as a result. That is absolutely true for us. We . . . have . . . no regrets at all about the fact that we have had this multicultural team experience. It's been incredible, and it's been very challenging as well in some ways, but it's so rich to get that experience.
4	Myung-sook	Korean	We are very rich . . . [like a] very rich sauce, the "sauce" is very rich.
5	Thomas	Scandinavian	More than anything, I think the multicultural team is a strength . . . our team thinks differently about things, it makes us more aware and accept that [NAC people] think differently, and that can be okay.

No	Speaker	Cultural Background	ParticipantQuote
6	Laura	Canadian	I feel like I have learned a lot of things in there to see things in a lot of different ways that I would never have had a chance to . . . if I hadn't been part of a multicultural team.
7	Noa	Dutch	You get all these different viewpoints from people with different cultural backgrounds. I appreciate that a lot. It makes you always challenge your own cultural, how you would behave or how you think, and it challenges you because it makes you think like okay, is this because I am European or Dutch or is this how I should think, or is it maybe more biblical to do it in another way?

Being Encouraged and Empowered

Although many participants had challenging relationships within their teams and experienced negative emotions, they testified that their teams, nevertheless, empowered and encouraged them to continue their work in NAC. Myungsook recalled how she learned to be generous and sacrificial from her very first team leader in NAC. She and her husband experienced warmth and protection from this leader. These experiences were still an inspiration for them. She said, "While there's a general impression in Korea that a team leader is thought of as someone who instructs and sets boundaries and limits people, but here, he [the former team leader] helped us bring what we had and unfold them quite a lot."

Julia appreciated the fact that her team encouraged its members to take initiatives and develop their ministries. She said, "Everyone in their individual place, it's very much encouraged to move forward, women or men or young or old. I think . . . that is really strong in our company that people that [have shown] . . . individual strengths . . . are given a lot of trusts that they are able to do things [on their own]."

Eunyoung shared about the abundance of encouragement she received at her organization's regional conference. After a tumultuous first year in conflict with her team leaders, she and her husband went to this conference quite discouraged and hopeless. She said, "But from the first day, I received so much encouragement that I kept weeping. At that first conference, I cried so much. I was so thankful to those people when they comforted me and empathized with me about my struggles." Her colleagues and leaders whom she met at the conference were encouraging and provided practical wisdom in how to go about dealing with relational conflicts and decision-making within the team.

For Ryan and Melissa, having a close teammate couple living nearby was a huge encouragement. These teammates supported them in processing their spiritual journey. He said, "Having that closeness, so you don't have to get in a taxi and make a half-hour trip, it's been really, really nice. They're neighbors, and that's really helped our team dynamic." After someone broke into their home while they were away and stole many of their personal things, Johannes and Noa were quite rattled. However, they were greatly encouraged by their team members. The whole team came alongside them and listened to them, just being there and supporting them. Johannes commented, "They're a mirror that shows what has happened to us is terrible, and it's difficult. They validate the emotions you have or the experience you had. So for us, being with a team is of incredible value. I don't think that we would've been here without a team."

In this section, I tried to provide nuanced descriptions of the kind of social interactions and interpersonal relationships among ICWs of MCTs. Conflicts, misunderstandings, and disagreements, which many participants experienced in their team relationships, were often driven by personality differences or character flaws. They were, however, sometimes caused by cultural differences in how one approached certain social situations. Many participants experienced varying degrees of negative emotions, from frustrations and disappointments to loneliness and feeling of being excluded. Nonetheless, most of them appreciated the multicultural team that empowered them in their intercultural learning and growth. In the next section, I turn to the strategies used by ICWs in navigating the murky waters of their team and organizational life.

STRATEGIES FOR NAVIGATING TEAM AND ORGANIZATIONAL LIFE

When asked if she had anything else to add to what she had shared so far in the interview, after a long pause, Mila said, "I was just thinking that . . . we say as an organization, we are multicultural, and they promote . . . diversity . . . and I think it's good for the locals to see . . . the diversity of the body. But I'm also wondering . . . How are we navigating that . . . as an organization . . . ?" This section describes how the participants navigated the social world of their MCT and/or transnational mission organization.

Mila's question is a significant one. After everything that had been said, it is of critical importance that these MCTs and IMOs have carefully thought through plans to help their workers navigate their complex social space. Rather than answering this question at an organizational level, this study has focused its attention on the participants' individual, micro-level tactics and strategies. This study found that these ICWs navigated their team life, with mixed results, largely by making sense of differences among their team members, responding to these differences, and approaching their team life relationally.

Making Sense of Differences

While looking for repeating patterns and meaningful categories in the interview data, I noticed that the data showed participants frequently trying to make sense of the seeming differences between themselves and their MCT members. Their attempts to make sense of these perceived differences became not only a way of doing life together with their teammates but also a means to navigate the liminal social space in their intercultural organizational life.

The most common pattern among the participants was to make comparisons between what they thought as cultural differences across places of origins or nationalities. The most frequently juxtaposed cultural groupings among the participants were "Asian" and "Western." It is understandable since, among the forty-seven participants who were members of MCTs, those who could be categorized as "Westerners" (twenty-eight participants) formed the largest group while the second-largest were "Asians" (fifteen participants). A vast majority of the team members of the participants in this study were Western Europeans, European-heritage people from North America and Australia, and Asians; there were very few Africans or Latin Americans within my participants' teams except for two married couples who belonged to an organization based in Africa and another in Latin America, respectively.

According to these ICWs, one of the most significant differences between Asian and Western team members was in how they related to one another. Many participants mentioned differences in conflict resolution, communication style, leadership and authority, and personal interests resulting from cultural backgrounds. It should be noted that the majority of these observations on cultural differences between "the East" and "the West" or the Global South and the Global North were made by Asians about Westerners.

During interviews, I asked open questions about the challenges they faced within their teams. Many participants talked about cultural differences. The fact that many Asian participants mentioned cultural differences as the greatest challenge in their teams seemed to show the magnitude of impact these differences had on them. On the one hand, I, the researcher, am an Asian. In interviews with Koreans, I spoke in Korean. The natural camaraderie and identification with the researcher might have disarmed Korean and other Asian participants and perhaps removed any reluctance of sharing something critical about their Western team members. It might have led these Asian participants to identify me as "Us" and feel safe to share about "Them."

On the other hand, the researcher's identity might have prevented some Western participants from openly sharing their thoughts and feelings about cultural differences they experienced with Asians. Additionally, in these teams, English was used as the team language, and people from the Global North still formed the most dominant cultural grouping. This could also have affected the outcome of these interviews. I tried to be attentive to these subtle sensitivities during interviews. In some cases, I sensed the reluctance of the participants who were European-heritage North Americans or Western Europeans to share anything negative about their Asian teammates. Only after earning their trust, emphasizing protection of confidentiality and anonymity, and coming across to them as more "Western" than their Asian colleagues through a display of my command of English and cultural inclinations had I sensed these participants finally disarming and honestly sharing their experiences.

Some Asian participants pointed out the difference between how Western members and Asian members of MCTs related to others. Mikyung said, "When it comes to being considerate of others . . . That's a bit different. Asians and Westerners are a bit different in the way they are considerate of others." For example, when she and other team members went out for a group picnic, everyone brought their own lunch. However, she and another Asian team member packed and brought extra food to cover for everyone in case someone did not bring any lunch. She said, "We were trying to be considerate. But normally, foreigners [non-Koreans] brought only the food they were going to eat. (Laugh) We always packed extra food for others." She also mentioned that when she and her teammates traveled together, she and the other Asian teammate were the only ones to bring extra food and share it with the rest. She pointed out that even when Western members offered their food or snack to others, they usually said, "If you want" or "if you'd like." To her, that came across as a bit selfish and cold-hearted.

When MCT members experienced a conflict, there was a difference in how Westerners and Asians resolved it. Junghoon said:

> When Koreans have some problems [with someone else], they apologize, and if an apology was accepted, the other person would usually respond by saying, "I'm sorry too. I already forgot it all." But Westerners cannot forget. They say apology accepted. So, one person apologizes, and the other receives the apology. The one who apologizes was at fault, so he apologized. Then the other accepts this apology. This is what we keep learning in the organization since ours is also an international organization. But the more we do it this way, the more I think about how we Koreans don't do it like that. If I apologize and say sorry, then the other person should also say, "I'm sorry too."

Junghoon felt that he understood how Westerners went about the conflict resolution process, but it always felt it lacked something, and it kept bothering him. He felt that it was unfair how this way of peacemaking was imposed on Asians, although he did not think this was the best way to approach peacemaking with Asians. Mutuality was absent; there was only the offender and the offended; nothing in between. In his mind, both sides—Asians and Westerners—should adjust their conflict resolution style, adapting to the other side, but only Asians always had to adjust their style to Western norms.

Some of the Western participants spoke about differences between Asians and Westerners in communication styles. The difference was identified as mainly being direct or indirect. Susan, who was training new Asian and Hispanic team members, said that the communication style of these new teammates was much more indirect than hers was. These Asian and Hispanic teammates were actually US citizens. So, Susan initially expected them to be more direct in their communication. Referring to an incident when a major miscommunication took place with her teammates, she said, "That was probably like my first moment where I thought we were not all quite as Western in our communication styles."

Chris, an ethnic Korean, compared differences between Asians and Westerners in decision-making style. He observed that the decision-making process in his team led by Westerners was thoroughly democratic. He said that for those with an Asian background, it would be natural for the leader to listen to different opinions, but in the end, make the final decision and ask members to follow. But for Chris, his team's decision-making process seemed unnecessarily democratic. He was frustrated when the leader weighed in on every input from every team member for what he considered to be a simple decision. He articulated the cause of his frustration as cultural differences. He said, "It's individual rights . . . . That is, wow, very strong . . . ." He said his White American teammates prioritized their individual rights to a point where they were not willing to yield to the collective good. Chris thought that it was almost ideological. In his view, his teammates did not want to give up their rights for fear that doing so might lead to further erosion of their rights and freedom in the future. He thought that this difference was not displayed in just individual preferences but also in organizational processes.

Sara had dual membership in both an international mission organization (IMO) and a Korean mission organization. Naturally, she compared her experiences in both organizations. There were clear differences. She described the following as the characteristics of her IMO in contrast to her Korean organization: taking the time and going slowly with decisions; more democratic; horizontal, not hierarchical in leadership and authority; listening to everyone more important than getting things done quickly; "being" more important than "doing." Although she saw many strengths in her IMO, she thought the decision-making process in her IMO was not very efficient; they unnecessarily wasted too much time.

Based on the information provided by several participants, it seemed that an MCT was experiencing what I would refer to as a "multicultural dilemma." In this team, Laura and other Western members faced situations where they were puzzled by how one of their leaders conducted team business and made decisions. They were reluctant, however, to raise the issue because the leader was an East Asian. These Western members were unsure of themselves when working with this East Asian leader. Laura explained, "As a Westerner, I feel like I would like to say something, but I'm often wondering . . . is it because I don't understand something culturally that if I understood that culturally, I would see this differently?" When the East Asian leader did something or behaved in a certain way that did not make sense to them, they were unsure whether it was wise to ask him about it since it might actually be due to his culturally Asian inclinations.

It seemed that they did not want to come across as ethnocentric or culturally insensitive by questioning the East Asian leader's leadership style. If they were correct in thinking that the issue at hand was mainly due to his cultural background, then withholding judgment might have been a wise choice. However, if issues of real concern were present, then not pointing them out would have been costly for the whole team. This was a dilemma for Laura and other Western team members. Based on their intercultural training, they thought of East Asians as hierarchical and "high power-distance."[14] It made them reluctant to confront the leader and raise concerns directly with him. Instead, perhaps wisely, they went to other East Asian team members to make sense of what was happening with the leader.

Comparing and Differentiating Differences

There were several other comparisons made by the participants about the differences between cultures. John and Amy, who were from Northern Ireland, described the difference between "the American culture" and "the German culture" based on what they observed in their colleagues and friends. They had read that the best way to see the difference between these two cultures was to wear an outfit that did not match and then go to an American friend and a German friend to ask them what they thought about the outfit. They explained that an American would say that it looked great while a German would say that it did not match, speaking candidly. John said, "Even if they don't think it looks great, they [Americans] won't want to tell you. Then, you go to your German friend and ask them, and they'll say, 'Oh, that doesn't fit.' Because they love you, and they want to tell you that it doesn't work." As crude as their example might be, it seemed to me that John and Amy were genuinely trying to make sense of their colleagues and understand where they were coming from since they worked with both Americans and Germans.

Camila, who came from a Spanish-speaking country in Latin America, said Brazilians did not speak the same language as her. Still, their values, work habits, and ways of managing time were similar. She also said that those who came from the northern part of Latin America, such as Mexico and Colombia, had a very different communication approach. She mentioned that she had to be careful and use sensitivity when writing emails to them. Her husband Franco added, "You cannot speak to them in a direct way. You have to . . . speak around, around, around, before we arrive at the point."

Rachel and Joseph talked about differences of sub-cultures within the United States. They had team members from four corners of the United States who behaved very differently from one another. They talked about the difficulty of team chemistry caused by these different US sub-cultures represented on their team. However, it is possible that these differences, which were assumed to be cultural in nature, could have instead been attributed to their individual or personal idiosyncrasies. Although it was not entirely clear what was really happening in this team, it seemed to be a situation that

14. Refer to Hofstede et al., *Cultures and Organizations.* for the definition of "power distance" and other dimensions of national culture.

needed to be scrutinized further. Perhaps, these differences should not have been automatically attributed to differences of sub-cultures within the US. However, Joseph and Rachel seemed to be interpreting these differences between team members as cultural differences. But the question remains whether cultural differences could explain all these differences.

In making sense of differences between team members of MCTs, some participants tried to distinguish cultural factors from personal factors. They recognized that much of people's behaviors had to do with both their personal dispositions and their cultural backgrounds. James and Donna, who had worked with English and Australian team members in the past, said that they wished they had known the personality profiles of their teammates earlier. They thought that the differences in their team and the resulting tensions were not driven by cultural differences but more by personality differences.

However, several participants indicated that distinguishing between cultural and personal characteristics was difficult. Julia said, "I think it's confusing for me, difficult to . . . I mean, I know three Koreans now on the team and one Swiss. And then one British . . . . I mean some of the things I notice . . . [are] more cultural, but then also they're all . . . personal . . . ." Thomas had a similar experience that he was unsure whether his American teammate's behavior was due to his personality or the American culture. Noa had a difficult experience during her first year in NAC with some of her teammates. She was unsure whether a serious issue she saw in them was caused by their personality, culture, spiritual matters, or emotional issues. It was confusing to her. Ryan said that people could make excuses by blaming their personal issues, character flaws, or even sinful behaviors on their own culture. He explained:

> There was sin, meaning there was pride or arrogance or just hostility or lying. There was sin, but it was disguised as culture, and I think . . . I've seen it a number of times. That's an issue. When there's sin in the heart or hatred, rather than repenting of it, it's "Oh, sorry, I'm such and such. I'm this culture. I didn't mean to offend you." In this case, I think it was . . . "I didn't mean to offend you. I'm just Korean," is what one person said. Yet time and time again, that was the reason, and eventually, it came out that there was a cause for hurt. There was an intent to hurt. And all this time, it was excused by being called a cultural thing, and it was not cultural. It was a sin.

Youngcheol said that when he looked back, much of what he used to think of as cultural differences between people from other cultures were actually due to their personal tendencies. He had been in a team with a Swiss and Vietnamese. Knowing their background helped him understand the Swiss husband's frugal, thrifty lifestyle and the Vietnamese wife's scarcity mentality, but not entirely. He recognized that these characteristics were not exclusively cultural but deeply personal.

There was a pattern among the participants to attribute behaviors and actions by someone to that person's cultural background or nationality, at least at the beginning. Then, as they gained more intercultural experiences over months or sometimes years, they tended to distinguish between behaviors that they deemed as cultural behaviors and others as personal; they created distinct categories between these two levels of attributions.

Some participants mentioned that there were other kinds of differences between their MCT members. John and Amy thought that the differences in their team were more of a language issue than an issue of cultural differences. They were more comfortable verbally communicating with their American friends who were not part of their MCT because they all spoke English as their first language. However, John and Amy felt that they were more culturally aligned to their Western European team members than their American friends. Although communication was more challenging with their Western European teammates, they still behaved and responded in ways that were more conventional to them. At the same time, the Americans did not act in ways that they anticipated. In talking about these people in this way, they were inadvertently isolating culture from language. It seemed to be a way for them to make sense of the confusing situation in which they found themselves with their team.

A similar observation was made by Mikyung, who had served in a mediator role between those in a conflict situation within her team. She said this particular conflict situation was not mainly caused by cultural differences but by value differences. She did not give many details of this case due to the sensitivity of the matter. Based on what Mikyung shared, she seemed to be dealing with a complex case of interpersonal, intra-team conflict that involved issues that extended over many areas. She was also trying to make sense of the situation by isolating value differences from cultural differences. In so doing, she was preventing herself and other team members from viewing the situation as a cultural conflict that would pit one culture against another. It made sense when I considered her role as a peacemaker in this situation.

The above stories illustrate the complexity of social life among ICWs who are part of MCTs. Whether the way by which they made sense of their situations was correct or not, the complexity of the issues they faced caused confusion, misunderstanding, and, in some cases, intense dejection among them. In these culturally and socially entangled situations, these ICWs seemed to be trying to frame the differences they experienced in a way that gave them a reference point from which to begin to address the relational issues at hand.

Responding to Differences (1): Simplifying, Generalizing, and Stereotyping

In addition to trying to make sense of, comparing, and differentiating differences within their MCTs, the participants tended to respond to the complex social realities by utilizing a reductionistic perspective of culture while also developing a nuanced understanding of cultural realities. When discussing cultural issues, the vast majority of the participants used concepts and languages that simplified the complexities of cultures. In many cases, they tended to stereotype cultures by national characterizations. They reduced cultures down to their essence, blamed certain team issues on cultural differences, and generalized their own culture. It was notable that they used the notion of culture in an inconsistent and sometimes contradicting manner.

The most common pattern among the participants in their use of the culture concept was defining each culture by its national characters. When they talked about a culture, it was usually depicted as the culture of a nation. For example, Germany would have a German culture, Korea would have a Korean culture, etc. The important thing to note here is not whether these perceptions were accurate or not, but how these perceptions played out in their everyday relationships and social interactions within MCTs. Sometimes, the participants used a culture concept in light-hearted humor; other times, the act of stereotyping damaged relationships and hurt others' feelings. It seems that these notions of culture partly grew out of their personal experiences and interactions with people and partly from learning certain materials on cultural content widely distributed among these teams through intercultural training offered by their IMOs.

Several different national archetypes were used by some participants during their interviews. These were mentioned by those who were not of the nationality being stereotyped. Some participants who were not Americans stated that Americans came across as arrogant, overemphasized individuality and their rights, and tended not to say things that might offend others even if they were true.[15] The Dutch were seen as direct, blunt, putting a high value on time, clear on what they wanted or disliked, and having strong opinions. Some mentioned that being on time was very

---

15. They did not specify but seemed to imply that they were thinking of White Americans when they spoke of Americans.

important to Germans. A person from a European country said that Germans were more direct, rude, spoke faster, and came across as arrogant due to their speech style and accent. While making appointments for my interviews, one of my contacts sent me an email about some potential German participants for this study. This contact person wrote, "We can figure out the details by WhatsApp closer to the time. *But they are German, so they like to know these things a bit ahead of time ;)*."[16] It was clear that no harm was intended by this comment, but it was obvious that this person associated Germans with a need to plan ahead.

Some made comments about the Irish. One person said, "I noticed Irish people are more closed and not living so openly. I think they are also . . . more private." A common understanding of Koreans was that they were hierarchical, and their leadership style was more top-down. One participant also said that another person was smart because that person was Asian. There was also a notion that Koreans were very good at having regular prayer times in the early morning hours. Another person also observed that Mexicans had strong communal living and spent much time in fellowship with one another.

Linda and Youngcheol, both with decades of intercultural, transnational ministry experiences, had some words to say about why some Christian workers might stereotype others. During a group interview, Youngcheol was a little sarcastic when he said, "I felt sometimes people who studied too much and [were] too bright . . . easily make . . . stereotypes [of] other people . . . ." To Youngcheol's comment, Linda replied, "It might not be a matter of being bright. It might be . . . that the person's thinking is more black-and-white. Some people think very black and white. I mean, I don't know who this person is . . . but . . . some people think this is this, and that is that. And they . . . divide things as black and white, positives, and negatives."

The act of essentializing a culture usually works by reducing a culture down to some concrete characteristics or its essence. Stereotyping can be seen as a form of essentializing. However, an essentialist view of culture would be broader and applies to a general concept of culture.[17] The practice of essentializing cultures was widespread among the participants. One ICW said, "I love Korean culture. Some of my best roommates have been Koreans, where we really got along well." Such a view represents the idea

16. Emphasis was added. Note the wink symbol within the quoted email text. It adds much meaning to this text.

17. For a good discussion on acts of essentializing cultures and how they affect studies of culture, see Werbner, "Dialectics of Cultural Hybridity," 1997; Baumann, *Multicultural Riddle.* By "essentializing," I do not mean a philosophical view but the practice of reducing a culture, a society, or a group of people to its essence.

that "culture" has a clear boundary and real content. It would be difficult
to define Korean culture since culture is an abstract concept. Thus, when
someone says that they love Korean culture, that person is essentializing it.
The same person said, "We have seven cultures in our team." However, the
cultural boundaries within her team were quickly blurred when she added
that one of her team members was both North American and Asian, and
another was both Western European and Australian.

Culture was often generalized by my participants for the convenience
of communication. For example, as Ashley explained the difficulty of integrating team members who came from different countries, she generalized
culture by saying, "[Some team members] know the *Western culture* well,
and so we end up talking just *Western things*."[18] This type of generalization
was a common practice among the participants. Donna also commented
that learning about other cultures was an important facet of working with
an MCT. Rachel had been taking a course on multicultural team ministry. When asked about it, she described her course content. She gave me a
quick summary of the training as follows:

> It's primarily talking about spectrums like in decision-making
> or low context, high context . . . . Korea, Japan are high context
> cultures where you read between the lines. Germany, the United
> States are the low context where I say what I mean, I mean what
> I say, and the disconnect that comes from that, individualist ver-
> sus collective, the spectrum. So the US is very individualistic.
> Mexico, [NAC] very collective with regards to decision making.
> So it's mostly talking about where do all of the countries fall on
> this spectrum? How can we . . . communicate? If being individu-
> alist is our typical decision-making style, how do we work that
> with the Koreans on our team who are maybe more collective in
> their decision-making style?

From what Rachel said, it is obvious that these training materials
were based on Hofstede's model of dimensions of national culture.[19] The
practice of essentializing cultures seemed to be widespread at the individual level among ICWs and at the organizational level in their IMOs. The
essentialist cultural perspective in mission organizations finds its support
from cross-cultural management literature, especially Geert Hofstede,
Fons Trompenaars, and GLOBE studies.[20] These works are widely cited in

---

18. Emphasis was added.

19. Refer to Hofstede, *Culture's Consequences*; Hofstede et al., *Cultures and Organizations*.

20. See Hofstede, *Culture's Consequences*; Hofstede et al., *Cultures and Organizations*;

introductory missions books on cross-cultural leadership and multicultural teamwork.[21]

Ryan, a Canadian, reported that his organization had heavily emphasized learning about other cultures. He mentioned that this emphasis was "pumped into" all new members. He said that his IMO stressed the importance of learning about other cultures in its training program. Based on what Ryan said, a practice of essentializing cultures seemed to be a foundational method of intercultural training in this organization. In fact, reviewing the intercultural training materials used in Ryan's IMO and two other large IMOs reveals that their training materials are based on an essentialist view of culture. More specifically, they use concepts such as dimensions of national culture, culture map, and cultural intelligence (CQ).[22]

It was notable that some participants were not essentializing only other cultures and people of those cultures; they were also generalizing and stereotyping people of their own culture. In comparing cultures of different Latin American countries, Camila and Franco said that people of their home country in Latin America tended to be more direct in the way people communicated and related to others. Mikyung, a Korean, described Koreans as having a "group culture," while Ashley, an Australian, pointed out that Australians were verbally dominant. Noa, a Dutch, also said, "Dutch people are very direct. You say what you mean, and you mean what you say, and that's it. So you're very clear in communication." John said the Irish humor was "very self-deprecating," and the Irish were more direct and brutally honest. Junghoon and Sara both indicated that their Korean culture was hierarchical.

Responding to Differences (2): Developing a Nuanced Understanding and Contesting Stereotypes

Although the participants often essentialized cultures and readily used cultural stereotypes in their description of colleagues from other countries, many displayed a growing cultural understanding, which was nuanced and complex. Some participants recognized the limitation of an essentialized view of culture. Junghoon was aware of cultural variations and diversities that existed within each country. He did not think that national culture types

---

Trompenaars and Hampden-Turner, *Riding Waves of Culture*; House et al., *Culture, Leadership, and Organizations*.

21. See McConnell, *Cultural Insights*; Moreau et al., *Effective Intercultural Communication*; Moreau et al., *Introducing World Missions*; Plueddemann, *Leading across Cultures*; Plueddemann, *Teaching Across Cultures*.

22. Lee, "Reimagining 'Culture.'"

always worked with everyone. He mentioned, as an example, a former Dutch teammate who did not fit the cultural profile of the Dutch. He did not elaborate on how or why this teammate did not fit the profile, but when asked whether he thought these culture profiles were accurate, he replied, "No, they are not. I haven't really looked at people thinking about those culture types. A person has many different facets. Each situation is different, each reaction is different, and when a person reacts in a certain way, people might say, 'Oh, he was a Korean after all.' But that person may not always be like that." Junghoon indicated that cultural seminars and training helped him not to stereotype people by their national characterizations.

It was ironic that Junghoon learned not to stereotype people from the intercultural training course offered by his IMO even though the materials used in this IMO's training program adopted an essentialist view of culture. While the training materials in this IMO explained culture by national characterizations, they also emphasized a learner's attitude and were critical of stereotyping practices. The reasoning behind these materials seemed to be that these national characterizations provided a baseline for people to begin their intercultural learning. They provided a starting point, but ICWs needed to recognize that persons did not always match these categories. However, this approach seems problematic since it simultaneously stimulates and dissuades stereotyping people according to their national characterizations.

Just as an essentialist view of culture did not afford an adequate picture of social realities, some participants also suggested getting to know a few people from a country neither provided a full picture. Julia pointed out how meeting one or two persons from a country only gave her minimal exposure to that country. It would be impossible for members of MCTs to know what a country's culture was like based only on their limited experiences with a few colleagues from that country. Nevertheless, much of these ICWs' knowledge about other countries seemed to be highly dependent upon their experiences with teammates from those countries and how these colleagues presented their countries to them.

Franco and Camila, who were from the southern part of Latin America, shared their view of Latin America and its cultures, which showed great cultural diversity, a complicated history from its European and African migration, and contemporary societies that resulted from the accelerated blending of various cultural elements from Europe and Africa. When I asked them why they felt that the southern part was very different from the other parts of Latin America, they attributed it to the Italian and Spanish migration to the southern area. They explained that the culture of countries such as Argentina was heavily influenced by immigrants from Southern Europe.

They also said that "the native people" were a little different; countries such as Chile and Uruguay, which had no native people and only immigrants from Europe, tended to be more European in their cultural tendencies. They explained that many African people were brought into countries such as Paraguay and Brazil, so they were different in their culture. On top of these, there was also the language divide between Spanish and Portuguese.

Their brief commentary on Latin America was an intriguing blend of both essentialist and constructivist views of cultures. They recognized how cultural flows moved and mixed to form today's various Latin American cultures. At the same time, they generalized and essentialized cultures by countries, by origin in Europe and Africa, and by language. Their view of cultures seemed to reflect how many ICWs on MCTs tended to describe cultures, cultural differences, and cultural changes taking place.

The participants also showed signs of actively seeking ways to address perceived differences with team members from other cultures. From what they shared, I identified three general methods used by the participants in dealing with cultural differences.

First, they tried to find common ground. Some participants recognized that they shared many common experiences in life and ministry in NAC with their teammates. Chris, who was initially shocked by the cultural differences he found on the team, mentioned that he eventually concluded that there were not that many actual differences. He said:

> They all grieved over the same things. For example, [names of team members] miss their grandchild and are sad. My parents are also sad because they miss their grandchildren. My parents also cry. [names of team members] also cry. And another friend struggles with loneliness. We also struggle because we feel lonely. Someone lied, the local people lied, and a team member took a loss and fumed over it. We also fume over such things.

He saw more things in common with his co-laborers in Christ, who were toiling together with him in a challenging intercultural ministry context. He added, "Wow, we feel the same things. There are, of course, some things that are due to different cultures, but in general, we are all similar."

Secondly, the participants took up a humble attitude. When I asked all participants at the end of each interview whether they had anything to add, several of them emphasized the need for humility and learner posture to work through all the differences present in their MCTs. Joseph and Rachel showed a passion for leading MCT well and how to do life together with people from many different cultures. Referring to her team, Caitlin said, "We're Koreans, we have Europeans, we have Americans, we have Africans, we have all the different cultures. I think that's something very special. But I think with that comes a lot of challenges, and it's good to learn how we can grow and overcome some of these things." A strong desire to continually learn and think of ways to improve relationships with her teammates was evident in her words. Other participants also mentioned that they wanted to serve their teammates with a humble attitude.

Thirdly, they contested essentialist views of culture. Some ICWs were aware of the negative side of an essentialist view of cultures that might lead to stereotypes. This awareness helped them make conscious choices to resist it. Thomas described how an essentialist view of cultures could lead to judging people. He recalled a relational tension with his former leader. An outside mediator told him and his wife that the cause for the tension was their indirect communication style. They were told that they did not make their view clear to the leader, perhaps due to being Asian.[23] Thomas felt that a label was wrongfully used to clear a misunderstanding. According to him, the result was further misunderstandings and a growing sense of isolation for him and his wife. He thought that it was unfair to be labeled in that way.

Thomas wished that he could explain himself without being viewed as an "indirect communicator." He also shared how he had been on both sides of this kind of labeling. He explained that many NAC people who saw him assumed that he was rich because he was a European. On the other hand, he also admitted, "I . . . have stereotypes of some of the people. So, sometimes if I explain a certain personal action, I might include the cultural background they have." While he consciously contested essentialist perspectives on culture and stereotyping people according to their common national characterizations, Thomas recognized that he still used an essentialist view on occasions. It was contradictory and yet seemed to be a common practice among many ICWs.

Approaching Team Life Relationally

One of the most effective ways for the participants to navigate their MCT and transnational organizational life was taking a relational approach to team life. Whether they subscribed to an essentialist view or a more nuanced understanding of cultures, or both simultaneously, building relationships with teammates who came from different cultures and working through relational difficulties were crucial to living in this complex social space.

An important part of the relational approach to team life was developing mutual relationships through which MCT members gave and received support and encouragement. When Brittany was going through a

---

23. Thomas is a Scandinavian. His wife is an Asian.

tough period in NAC, the relationships within the team helped her come out of it stronger. She said, "I don't have anything that I can pinpoint and say this was what pulled me out specifically . . . , but I think I tried to be very open about the fact that I was struggling, and . . . I had my teammates . . . rallying around me and praying for me and asking how they could help me." Youngcheol recalled his early years in NAC and said that a strong sense of belonging to his team helped him feel more at ease. Myungsook named the couple who were her former team leaders as her sponsors in her initial years in NAC. She said, "If it weren't for [names of the leader couple], we couldn't probably have stayed in NAC for long." Her relationship with this couple taught her many lessons about faith, ministry, and life as ICWs in NAC. It was foundational to her later role as an encourager and mentor to many ICWs.

Some veteran ICWs were willing to support and encourage others, especially younger workers or newly arrived NAC members. Some younger women came to Linda and confided in her. She said she would listen, and if God gave her some counsel, she would share it with the person who confided in her. This kind of encouraging role was what Mikyung thought most needed for her colleagues. She said, "Everyone has left their own country . . . . They came because of their dedication. But living here itself is the beginning of suffering. So, whether they do well or not, whether they fit the program [of the team] or not, I think they are living a life that needs a lot of encouragement."

Some workers shared about playing a mediator role between people in conflict or those who had relational issues. Kevin had arrived in NAC and joined his team when the existing team crisis was coming to its end. Kevin had a unique position as someone who understood the situation and was not negatively affected by the crisis by joining the team toward the end of the crisis. He was able to bring "a bit of a neutral element in the team" and an outsider-insider view that helped the team sort through issues.

In conflict situations, persons who could facilitate the conversation with some authority and objectivity were usually asked to be mediators, and they seemed to be effective in that role. It was especially true for conflicts between persons from different countries. The persons who were in a leadership position and had worked in NAC for many years could mediate effectively in complex interpersonal issues.

Another important function of a mediator was being the voice for underrepresented members. Laura and Kevin found themselves in a situation where they had Korean leaders and Korean teammates. Laura said that being non-Koreans on a team with many Korean members naturally made them "a voice piece" for their Korean teammates who could not object or raise concerns with the Korean leader. They noticed that even when their Korean teammates had something that they wanted to discuss in team meetings, they were reluctant to bring them up for their discomfort of raising an issue with their elder Korean leader. Laura added, "Because we're outside . . . of Korean culture, [we] have the freedom to do that on their behalf when they themselves are unable to . . . say something." It was not only a group of Koreans for whom they would be a voice. They often stood and became a voice for team members who were singles. They both sensed that this was a role to which God called them for the time being.

When my participants were involved in a conflict, they had various responses. Some simply apologized to the other person for any hurt or harm done. There was once a case of serious conflict that could have escalated further between two fellow team members over an incident at their workplace. In a relationally fragile situation, the person involved in this conflict was wise to avoid provoking the other person. It took some time and a few rounds of conversations between them and involving two other leaders, but in the end, they were able to apologize to each other and move on from the incident.

In one case, two workers who were roommates had many relational issues and misunderstandings. By walking through an interpersonal conflict resolution process established by their organization, these members could see beyond their differences and learn to respect and love each other. Still, they realized that their personalities and preferences were the main reason for these clashes, so they agreed that they should no longer be roommates. They parted ways in terms of living arrangements, but they became much closer in their friendship and supported each other mutually.

Another way of resolving interpersonal conflicts between Christian workers was talking openly about an issue with the party that caused the grievance. When Thomas had a conflict with a team member that resulted from a misunderstanding, he simply talked about it with the member. It led to a better understanding of each other and more open conversations about how they understood each other. Similarly, when Marcelo thought that his team leader was too dominating in making team decisions and how to go about doing their ministry, he confronted the leader. Immediately, the leader apologized and explained that it was not his intention. It became clear to them that it was a misunderstanding, and they were able to clear quickly any hard feelings that remained with the leader.

SUMMARY AND CONCLUSION

In this long chapter, I have described the factors related to multicultural teams (MCTs) that influenced the intercultural social experiences of the participants. The analysis of field study data led to the construction and selection of five salient categories: participants' initial experiences in MCTs, their experiences of intricate inner workings of MCT structures, intercultural dynamics within these teams, their social relationships within MCT, and their strategies for navigating their team and organizational life. These five categories were analyzed in this chapter.

First, Christian workers' initial experiences in their MCTs showed a process of adaptation that involved receiving support and protection from their team, experiencing interpersonal conflicts ensuing from misunderstandings, and struggling to communicate in English. Secondly, the intricate inner workings of MCTs were described. MCTs were described in terms of their formal and informal structures and leadership. Transnational connections to the broader organization and leadership-related issues were significant in their experiences of MCTs. Thirdly, intercultural dynamics within these MCTs show how unique social norms are negotiated and created. The impact of English as the team language was explored, and perspectives of Korean members of MCTs were discussed. Fourth, participants shared stories about the relationships within their teams. These included accounts of various relational issues and negative emotions and stories of empowerment and enriching learning experiences. These were analyzed in detail. Fifth and lastly, the participants described their strategies for navigating the tumultuous team and organizational life. They tried to make sense of differences with their team members by applying a cultural framework based on national characterizations. They responded to the perceived cultural differences with pragmatic multicultural understandings. It was found that they framed their cultural understandings in somewhat contradictory manners by using both essentialized and nuanced articulation of cultures.

These descriptions of the social and structural dynamics of MCTs and strategic responses by ICWs suggest an ongoing intercultural social process in these team environments. As these Christian workers navigated their culturally entangled social context, they managed and coped with the tension between agency and structure.

Among the participants, forty-seven were part of eleven MCTs that belonged to seven different international mission organizations (IMOs). As it may be expected, their experiences in these MCTs were complicated and multilayered. The participants also displayed remarkable similarities and common themes in their experiences despite cultural diversity and a variety of backgrounds among them. It seems as if they were going through an assimilating process as they dealt with their team and organizational structure and their social relationships with people from different cultures. Although they were part of different teams and organizations, the participants were strikingly similar in their operating principles and practices. Additionally, due to their experiences in MCTs, they seemed to be actively constructing a team culture even as they were being influenced by it. This process of "culture making" will be addressed more in chapter 7.

So far, the complicated intercultural social life of ICWs has been investigated and described. This chapter discussed the MCT factors in the ICWs' experiences, whereas the previous chapter dealt with the contextual factors related to living and working in the North African country (NAC). The next chapter will investigate the changes that take place in these ICWs as an outcome of having gone through these intercultural social experiences.

6

Intercultural Living and Personal Change

In this chapter, I describe personal changes in international Christian workers (ICWs) who work with multicultural teams (MCTs). These changes seem to occur as an outcome of their intercultural social experiences. Throughout this chapter, I will make an attempt to answer the third research question, "What are the personal outcomes of their intercultural experiences?" I present here four kinds of personal changes the participants perceived as the outcomes of their intercultural social life. The most noticeable changes were in their personal dispositions and social behaviors. I discuss the nature and extent of these changes. Many participants also felt that they gained a new cultural "home" while they lost their old "home"; some developed a sense of loss, referred to as *cultural homelessness*.

Deciding which changes were personal changes was tricky since the analysis inevitably relied on participants' self-perception. It was also inferred that these outcomes were related to and even caused by participants' intercultural social experiences. Steps were taken during the data analysis to address the inference. First, a careful coding procedure was used to comb through the data to identify the indicators that pointed toward significant personal changes. These indicators were sorted and organized as codes, which eventually produced the four categories of personal changes presented here. Secondly, the analysis did not solely depend on the participants' perceptions. Insights were drawn from field notes and my experiential knowledge as an international Christian worker (ICW) who worked with multicultural teams (MCT) in the research site in North Africa for over a decade. Thus, this chapter is not only descriptive; it includes interpretive and explanatory components as well.

CHANGES IN PERSONAL DISPOSITION

Several participants discussed notable changes in themselves. They attributed these changes to their intercultural experiences. These changes seemed to have happened at a deeper level than simply changing some behaviors; they greatly influenced their lives. Among extant social theories, Pierre Bourdieu's notion of *habitus* seems to provide plausible explanations for these personal changes.[1] To describe the extent of these changes, I will use the term "disposition," a word Bourdieu uses to elaborate on *habitus*, to refer to the aspects of these participants' changes. The *habitus* concept will be revisited and further explored in chapter 7.

While analyzing the collected data, I coded numerous participant comments and research memos that contained my observations that indicated significant changes in the participants. As I sorted the select data, some sub-categories especially stood out; these seemed to describe the notion of personal disposition well. Among those sub-categories, I identified transnational identity, intercultural social awareness, and personal values as central to a working definition of personal disposition.

Developing a Transnational Identity

Some participants expressed a feeling that they were no longer fully aligned to attributes of their cultural heritage. For example, some explicitly said that they were no longer "English" or "German" or "Korean" in their cultural disposition. They often used the language of "I am not XYZ anymore," with XYZ being their nationality or cultural background. They also emphasized that they were now international or multicultural persons.

Developing a new transnational identity sometimes meant that these ICWs had lost part of their cultural identity. During the interview, William casually said, "I'm probably becoming less English. I just feel it when I'm home."[2] Losing his sense of being English was closely related to his sense of "cultural homelessness," which will be discussed later. In Jaehyuk's case, although he was a Korean, he said that he did not understand the Korean way of thinking and relating. He had some puzzling experiences with other Koreans within his IMO. It led him to state, "I am no longer a Korean." Having lived interculturally for almost two decades, it seemed that his social norms and personal dispositions had changed. Although he could not tell

---

1. See Bourdieu, *Outline of a Theory of Practice*; *Distinction*; *The Logic of Practice*.

2. "William" is a second pseudonym for one of the participants. He is actually not English. His nationality was arbitrarily changed here to ensure his anonymity.

whether his cultural changes had more to do with his MCT experiences or living in NAC, he was aware that he had changed.

Both Jaehyuk and his wife Kyungja mentioned another Korean worker who had spent many years in NAC and worked with MCTs as a good example of a Korean who had become very "un-Korean." They thought that this worker was not very Korean in his values and social preferences. They felt that his pragmatic style and his unique perspectives reflected more Western norms. They observed that this Korean worker had clear boundaries and could answer "yes" or "no" to demands and requests by other Koreans. In their view, these were signs that he was not a typical Korean.

Several other participants also discussed the loss of one's previous cultural identity. In a group interview with an MCT, Myungsook teased Julia, who was present at the meeting and said, "She, Julia, was very German at the beginning, but now I think she's losing a bit of Germanness (laugh)." To that, Linda chimed in by meaningfully stating, "You lose some of your English-ness, German-ness, Swiss-..., Korean-ness when you live abroad so long." Everyone in the group nodded in agreement with Linda. They recognized changes in their teammates and themselves after years of living in NAC and working with an MCT.

In this group conversation, Linda said that she was not very English but had become more of "an international person." She explained:

> I think from the fact that I've lived abroad for a third of my life ... is another reason why I'm not very English .... So, I might feel English compared to you, but when I go home, my people around me may think, "She's not very English." But I will look English because I dress English. But then maybe something about my behavior, something about the way ... I think about things which may not be very so-called English ... because I like to think of myself as *an international person*. I've been abroad mixing with other nationalities so long, you know.

Looking back on his experiences as an Asian who had lived in the US, Eunseok defined himself as "a bat," implying his dual national identity.[3] Although he had a US passport, he did not feel that White Americans saw him as one of them. The irony was that other Korean workers in NAC told him that he was not very Korean; he was told that he came across as a bit cold since he did not read between the lines very well and appropriately responded to other Koreans' unspoken expectations. He explained using

---

3. "Eunseok" is a second pseudonym for one of the participants. He is a citizen of a Western nation, but is not a US citizen. These changes were made in order to protect his identity.

a Korean expression that translated as "I've drunk a little bit of Western water . . . ." He thought that he had unconsciously adopted many social customs of the US. Interestingly, he still felt more comfortable socializing with other Koreans than Westerners.

Julia indicated her multiple belongings. She said that while she could identify more with NAC people, she was still a German. She said, "Germanness is so deeply rooted. It's . . . never going to be completely lost." However, she also saw herself as an international person. Her friends and family members in Germany thought that she was different. Her case shows an example of becoming an in-between person, someone who was now living between cultures.

Growing Intercultural Social Awareness

Some participants perceived the increase in their cultural and social awareness through their intercultural experiences. This awareness included knowledge about other countries and cultural contexts, a self-awareness that displayed reflexivity, and social discernment in various intercultural situations.

Most veteran Christian workers who participated in this study appeared to have cultural knowledge accrued over years of interacting with and engaging people from other cultures. Linda described it well when she commented, "I think it's accumulative. You get to know people and then you understand something about their culture. And it helps you with somebody else down the line who you're going to meet as well." Although Heather had received advice and read books that helped her understand local NAC social norms, she admitted that much of her current cultural knowledge was gained experientially through trial and error over the years.

Linda showed her nuanced understanding of the local context when she commented, "I don't see [NAC] as a mono-culture at all." She had gotten to know local people in both the elite upper class and the lower class. She had realized that, depending on their background, the local people in NAC thought and behaved very differently. She mentioned that people in the elite class whom she knew were highly educated, spoke French and English well, not very religious, and quite open to new ideas.

For Laura and Kevin, serving with Koreans on an MCT helped them understand why Korean leaders led in certain ways. Laura said, "We're still learning, but I often had experiences of something being said or done by a [Korean] leader and feeling like I didn't quite understand what it was or why it happened that way." She would ask her Korean teammates to explain what was going on and gain a better understanding in that way. Kevin and Laura were sympathetic toward Korean leaders in their organization who faced many cultural challenges. Kevin tried to see things from the Korean leader's perspective. He said, "It's difficult, for one thing, if you're a Korean background to discuss in English . . . , but also . . . from a leader's point of view, the leader is actually supposed to make the decisions. We don't necessarily need to or should discuss that." At the same time, he and Laura wondered about the best way forward as a team because, in their observation, there had not been many open discussions about team issues ever since a Korean became their leader. These insights were an accumulation of their experiences of Korean team members and their organizational life.

Some participants showed a sign of growing in their understanding of their own social and cultural situatedness and its impact on their relationships and environments. This kind of inner reference point is what is often referred to as *reflexivity*, which British sociologist Margaret Archer defines as "the regular exercise of the mental ability . . . to consider themselves in relation to their (social) contexts and vice versa."[4] Among these ICWs, reflexivity was often displayed in their self-awareness, understanding of their cultural tendencies, and the impact of their tendencies on the people of NAC as well as their MCT members.

Julia said that she was gaining a better understanding of her German cultural tendencies and how they had impacted her life. Experiencing differences with her team members and local NAC friends helped her learn more about herself and grow in her understanding of what might constitute her "German-ness." She also commented that her intercultural experiences taught her not to rely on her initial understanding of what people who come from other cultures might say. Instead, she learned to double-check the person's meaning before making a conclusion. These were the kind of words that a seasoned social researcher might say.

William thought about his past experiences with MCT and commented:

> If I was just with English people, I would probably be less exposed and be more difficult for me to see the value of cultural differences and see it's just [NAC people] being weird. But, if it's [NAC people] and Koreans and Americans, they're all weird, then maybe it's just me who is weird. It [Being in a MCT] helps you examine yourself in a different way than in a monocultural team.

Claudia shared William's sentiment as she declared, "My way isn't the only way." The reason for her openness to different ways of life, she said, was the fact that she was "exposed so much to different cultures" in MCTs and her experiences as an ICW.

---

4. Archer, *Making Our Way*, 4.

Through their MCT experiences, some Christian workers developed an awareness for distinguishing culture and personality/character. Ryan heard one of his colleagues once explain that her seemingly erratic behaviors were due to her culture. However, as he grew in his understanding and awareness of cultures, it became clear that her culture was not responsible for those hurtful behaviors by this team member; they were consequences of her personal flaws.

Some ICWs talked about learning to read subtle, unspoken messages by those from other cultures. William, who worked in local NAC communities that held more conservative, traditional values, initially struggled to read social situations while meeting the local people. It took time for him to learn the signs and subtle messages given by the locals. After many visits and encounters with these people, he became more discerning about these social settings. His intercultural experience was his teacher.

Julia shared her concern that different cultures could be misrepresented even by interculturally experienced people. She explained how ICWs could misinterpret the local context despite their years of experience because of their biases. She warned that people needed to be more cautious about their theoretical knowledge and needed to scrutinize their experience of a culture, no matter how much time was spent. Mila also described her culturally adaptable capacity acquired through many years of intercultural living. She had developed a capacity to gather and sort through a mixture of cultural information while suspending judgment. She explained it as her "cultural orientation." She said, "I hope I have become more gracious to myself and to others, but also to . . . be more quick to suspend judgment and to pull myself away and say, okay, what's happening here?" It seemed that she had almost taken on a new propensity to think, react, and behave in these culturally savvy ways.

Shifting Personal Priorities and Values

In addition to developing a multicultural identity and heightened social awareness, the participants also saw changes in their priorities and values. Some of these ICWs indicated that they now had some new values in them. Brittany identified being more compassionate toward others, including her teammates and local NAC people. On the other hand, Jessica began to see the importance of self-care after having ministered in NAC among needy people.

Others no longer valued the things that they once cherished. James thought that many things which were valued by his family members back in the US—mostly material things—were no longer important to him. John and Amy mentioned that on their last visit to their home country during the Christmas season, they found the way people celebrated Christmas "unbearable" and too materialistic.

For Julia, a major change in her value system was how she saw the truth and false. She said that they were not as clear-cut as before. She added, "I have allowed them [her values] to shift a little bit or to expand . . . . My values are . . . not necessarily that German anymore." She saw more grey areas emerging in her relationships with NAC people. In situations where she would have judged someone as lying in the past, she was now careful not to come to those conclusions too quickly. She adjusted her priorities to the social norms of NAC people and tried to avoid shameful situations. Franco also mentioned that he had more respect for other points of view, and Linda indicated that acceptance was now a strong value for her. She said, "Of course, we can't accept every behavior, but in a sense, we have to accept people [as] how they are according to their cultural background and things like that . . . maybe we have more of a challenge in that because we're a multicultural team . . . , but . . . I think acceptance is a big, big thing to me."

CHANGES IN SOCIAL BEHAVIOR AND ATTITUDE

Many participants recognized various changes in their own social behaviors. Some mentioned that their teammates also noticed them. Julia, a German single woman, seemed to behave, relate, and socialize more like a local NAC person. She had thoroughly adapted to the social world of her MCT and the local context of NAC. After more than a dozen years of living in this way, Julia felt that her social behaviors had significantly changed. She noticed that she no longer thought or behaved in a "black-and-white" fashion so much. When she said, "I . . . sometimes miss being able to think black and white . . . . I wished I could make the world more simple again," she seemed to be recognizing how her world had become more complicated not just due to external changes, but internal changes in herself. Her social attitudes and behaviors had changed. Things that she regarded in the past as very important, such as clarity and punctuality, were not as important to her now.

Mixing Cultural Elements

A major change in the participants' social behavior was the daily practice of mixing and blending various cultural and social elements in their lives. The easiest one to notice was food. When I attended a team meeting in City B, the evening started with dinner. Haejin had prepared *bibimbap* using cooked vegetables, tuna, eggs, and Korean chili paste. I noticed that all the team members, regardless of nationality or ethnic background, enjoyed this distinctly Korean food. It was obvious to me that they all had tasted this food before and somehow learned to like it. On another occasion, in the lunch that followed a team meeting in City A, I noticed that the meal provided by the Asian hosts was a mixture of traditional NAC food, European sweets, NAC pastries, and some Asian side dishes. The members of this team, who were of four different passport countries, enjoyed all of the food items without saying much or paying special attention to the kind of food in front of them as if this was a normal meal for them.

Some participants were routinely blending two or more languages in conversations with one another. Youngcheol was aware of his own pattern of mixing words and phrases from several different languages. He said, "When I sit down and talk with my wife, . . . probably between two of us, with the base of a Korean sentence, we would have twenty to 30 percent of English words, French words, 20-25 percent, [NAC Arabic] 20-30 percent, and then 5-10 percent of Spanish words . . . . Many languages are mixed in there." It was notable that he and his wife communicated in this way naturally and unconsciously. He explained that he often used expressions or phrases in any language that left a strong impression on him. These were expressions heard and used in past situations that engaged him emotionally, regardless of which language the words came from.

Emma, who was from a country in Africa and spent a decade and a half in another African country and NAC, said that she was adding her favorite cultural elements from these other cultures to her own lifestyle. She named hospitality as such an element. She described this act of blending as adding to her own culture. She said, "I would say, for me . . . it's [not] changed, but it's enlarged. I have my background and everything, but I think whenever I'm somewhere, I take what is good from their culture and . . . I kind of like to blend. So I see I have my own culture, but also what I learned from [other cultures] . . . which is also part of me now." What Emma described here seems to be a case of micro-level experiences of cultural hybridization—blending and using cultural elements from each culture in which she had lived before for her benefit.

Similarly, Linda had created a breakfast routine that was neither of NAC nor of her native England. She called this routine "my own Linda culture." She described it as sitting each morning at an outdoor cafe in her neighborhood, where no woman would usually be sitting alone and having breakfast and tea. She said that she had invited other women to join, asking them, "Would you come and join the Linda culture?" She then explained, "So I think everybody creates a bit of a culture around them. They adapt the culture to fit what they need."

Becoming More Flexible

Another change that the participants noticed in their own social behaviors was their increased flexibility. Participants felt that they were more flexible and accommodating in terms of personal lifestyle, relating to other people, and the general structure of life. Some of them also found themselves more relaxed in their attitude toward time than before.

Myungsook thought one major change she saw in herself over the years was being more accommodating to differences she saw in other people. She made a distinction between "accepting" and "tolerant," explaining that *accommodating* fell somewhere between those two. She felt that she was now more willing to embrace people who behaved and thought differently from her. Youngcheol also mentioned that some of his personal characteristics had changed. He said that he could accept diverse people who lived different ways of life, especially those he might have criticized and questioned in the past.

Some participants were not clear whether they had changed or not in the way they related to people. Brittany said that she did not notice any changes in her during the two years of living in NAC and working with an MCT. She, however, admitted, "But this [living in NAC] has been the most adaptation that I've ever been through. So I think maybe even though I've been adaptable . . . , that's grown even more, being able to adapt. And maybe my patience and compassion toward others." Nowadays, she reminded herself whenever she experienced differences with other people that being different was not necessarily bad or wrong, or even strange. She added, "So I think . . . just trying to stay really mindful of . . . the things that I don't quite understand or even the things that I am forcibly against and do not agree with, they're just different." It was not clear to me why Brittany did not think she changed. It seemed that she had experienced much change in herself while adapting to life with an MCT in NAC.

Several participants mentioned that a major personal change happened in their attitude toward time orientation (Junghoon, Simon, Noa, Johannes, and Julia). They were more relaxed than before if people did not keep an appointment time or when they had to decide things at the last minute without advance planning. When I was spending several days with members of an MCT in City A, it was notable that Julia, who used to be known for always being on time and never being late, came several minutes late to the team meeting. I noticed that she had also come late to a separate meeting, and she again came late to our interview appointment. This was surprising and had me thinking that something had changed in her.

The change in how one treated time can be most vividly seen in a story told by Johannes and Noa, a Dutch couple, about their last visit to their homeland. I asked them how they found people's approaches to time and schedule while visiting their home country. They said that they were often frustrated by the need to make appointments with their friends and relatives because they could make time available only if scheduled at least three weeks in advance. They realized that they used to do the same in the past, planning everything well in advance. Now they did not enjoy a lifestyle with tight scheduling. They saw this as a major change due to having lived in NAC for several years and adapted to a new life.

Another change mentioned by some participants was their flexibility toward structures and standards. Mikyung recalled how her team in the past put a heavy emphasis on certain standards, such as how many hours one spent on language learning and how well a person was doing in going out to spend time with local NAC people. She remembered how team members were evaluated upon these standard measures. If someone on the team did not meet the standard, there were harsh criticisms within the team. She had changed in her view of these standards; she did not think it was good to impose such standards on her team members.

Amy, who was a professional in Northern Europe, struggled with a lack of structure in her life in NAC. She confessed, "I am quite a rigid person. I'm quite a rigid thinker, and I love structure and routine. Everything about this kind of lifestyle [in NAC] makes that really hard." It was an honest admission of her struggle with the lifestyle required of ICWs living and working in NAC. Even though she struggled with it, it seemed that she was accepting the challenge and learning to be more flexible. For Stefanie, life in NAC was a balancing act between being flexible or being structured. She was learning to hold onto both in balance. After pondering for a while, she said, "Sometimes we need structure, and sometimes you have to let structure go."

Some participants mentioned concrete personal patterns such as driving habits or spiritual practices when talking about being flexible. Others talked about their attitudes, such as embracing ambiguity or becoming more open to new ideas. Although different participants talked about different personal changes, they all pointed toward a flexible mindset, putting a high value on being more open to new things and relaxed about rules.

Julia told a story of how she had grown increasingly comfortable with ambiguity. For example, when she was invited to an event by local NAC friends, Julia did not tell them immediately that she could not come even though she knew that she could not. "You don't say, 'No, I cannot come.'

You just say *insha'llah* [an Arabic phrase for "God willing"] or . . . something like that right there," she said.

Camila and Franco, who grew up in a conservative church in Latin America, said they experienced drastic changes in their mindset. Camila said, "Once you go and live abroad, you get more open-minded, definitely. So when you go back home, there you see things differently because you've been able to experience another culture." Franco added that even his theology changed. Experiencing a world outside his conservative Christian denomination in another cultural context opened his mind. He said, "Now, we can see that probably the church is a little bigger than your denomination. And even . . . the way to sing, the way to [do] meetings, the way to worship could be in a very different way."

Relating to People

Some participants indicated that they experienced a change in the way they related to people. This change involved their style of communication and social interaction. It was especially striking how some participants had changed in the way they communicated with others. Johannes, a Dutchman, noticed that he was often misunderstood in his home country because he communicated to people ambiguously. For example, he would say something like, when translated literally into English, "Maybe it's an idea for you to come this Saturday afternoon," but the person who heard it would misunderstand him by thinking that it was just an idea, not an invitation or a request, even though he wanted the person to come and visit his family at home. His wife also mentioned that when people in the Netherlands asked her something in a straightforward, unequivocal manner, she somehow felt offended. She said, "But that's how I always used to do it, but now it feels like, 'Oh, okay, so you're mad at me or something?'" These were major changes that they recognized in themselves.

Thomas, from Scandinavia, realized a major change in himself after having lived in a rural area in NAC for several years. On his visits to his home country, when friends offered him a cup of coffee, he would automatically respond by saying, "No, thank you." Because when he visited the rural people in NAC, they always offered him a drink. The culturally appropriate response was to kindly decline the gesture at least two or three times. If they kept insisting, then he would accept the drink only reluctantly. After several years of behaving in this way, this became his automatic response when he was offered something by someone. Even when he liked and wanted things offered to him, from a cup of coffee to expensive electronic gadgets and even financial support, he responded automatically by declining them. He said, "That's just how I . . . Without even thinking, it becomes . . . the right thing to do. I have to decline. So, that's a way I've been culturally changed by being here."

Living in NAC for many years seemed to have changed the way Linda, an English woman, spoke her English. She said, "I tend to speak a lot more slowly than . . . a lot of English speakers . . . . I do it somehow . . . naturally now because I'm teaching people whose English is not their first language, and also because I'm mixing with a lot of foreigners. But sometimes I go home [her home country] and speak to a group, and they said, 'But Linda, you speak so slowly!'"

It was not just the communication style that changed. Johannes noticed that the way he interacted with women had changed. While back in his home country for a summer, he went to pick up his children at school. While waiting, the mother of one of his children's classmates started talking to him and asking him questions. This made him quite uncomfortable. He said, "I felt off guard, and I didn't know how to respond because I thought, 'Why are you talking to me?' Then, of course, the second thought is, 'Oh, no, I'm here, this is completely normal, I can talk to a woman that I don't know, and it's not a problem.'" Unconsciously, Johannes had adopted a traditional NAC social code of conduct of not speaking in public with a woman he did not personally know since it was considered inappropriate. Noa also mentioned how awkward she felt when giving a customary kiss on the cheek to a male church member who visited her home. According to both Johannes and Noa, this feeling of awkwardness in male-female relationships gradually grew in them. The longer they lived in NAC, the more awkward they felt about the whole issue. It seemed that Johannes and Noa experienced some major changes in their social patterns, especially in communication, time orientation, and gender relations. The traditional social norms of NAC to which they became accustomed were drastically different from what this Dutch couple used to practice. It was remarkable how they had changed so much in their social behaviors and preferences in just a few years.

Another change for Johannes and Noa was their practice of hospitality, which often defied the high value they placed on privacy. Noa said that in the Netherlands, without a prior appointment, they would have never offered people who stopped by or came for other reasons to stay and join them for dinner. Neither of them recalled their Dutch parents ever doing such a thing in their entire lives. However, they now routinely offered visitors and guests to join them for a meal, even if it was not on the agenda or they were not prepared.

One tangible change Youngcheol saw in his interactions with people was that he now had a habit of shaking someone's hand and then unconsciously putting his right hand on the left side of his chest. It was a common hand gesture of NAC nationals that showed respect to the other person when greeting them. It was not uncommon among ICWs who had lived in NAC for a while to develop this habit.

Some participants also mentioned how they related to people in a more [NAC] way. Philip used to get straight to the point when he got in touch with someone, but now he first asked about the person's family and exchanged pleasantries before getting to his main agenda. Julia used to feel guilty when her local friends asked her why she had not visited them in a while, but in a reverse of roles, she now does the same to her local friends, asking them why they had not visited her in a while, putting the blame back on them.

NEW CULTURAL "HOME"

Many international Christian workers (ICWs) felt they had gained a new "home" after having lived and worked in NAC for a while. A majority of them mentioned NAC as their adopted home and felt comfortable living in NAC. Many of them also felt that their home was among other international people like themselves. Some of them also indicated that they now had multiple homes due to living cross-culturally for many years.

International Setting as "Home"

Some participants indicated that they felt most comfortable among circles of ICWs. Youngcheol felt most comfortable in an IMO environment because it had been his social environment for about three decades. Linda, who was about to retire and return to her home country, shared a similar feeling and said, "I've been in international work so long . . . whether for friendship or ministry, [so] I'll be looking for internationals when I go home. I think it's natural that I will do that." She indicated that her preferred social environment was a multicultural or international setting. She said that it was "because of its variety and also challenges." She repeated that she liked the diversity in international teams and found it more interesting. Julia also said that she felt most comfortable in the international setting because she liked its wider perspective. She now found it more difficult to adjust to monocultural environments. Stefanie felt more like a normal person in the international setting where others were like her. Mila also indicated that she felt comfortable with "a mixed group of people" with cultural diversity regardless of the geographical location.

During her home assignment in Switzerland, Stefanie felt that she had a strong belonging with her teammates and local colleagues at work in NAC. This realization came when she saw that many of her Swiss friends and family members could not fully understand her experiences of the past several years in NAC. It became even more apparent when an American teammate came to visit her in her home country. She fondly remembered this friend's visit. Even though this team member was an American, Stefanie could talk to her about her struggles and "felt more understood." As she and her colleagues shared many personal issues and challenges in common, she felt closer to this colleague than her friends back home.

As it has been shown, the main reason that many participants considered an international environment as their most comfortable social setting was the friendship they had with their teammates from other cultures. For the vast majority of the participants, their teammates were more than co-workers. They were considered first and foremost as brothers, sisters, and friends. Claudia described her friendship with her teammates when she said, "So there is friendship there for me, and I know I can always count on them if I need help. I know they're there for me, and I want to be there as well for them." Eunseok talked fondly of a former Dutch colleague who suddenly left NAC and returned to his home country. He even went to visit him in the Netherlands because "he was still our friend." Eunseok said that this team member and his family left NAC because they did not want to pretend to be happy and calm while they often got upset at the behaviors of some local NAC people. Eunseok continued the story:

> They so suddenly left, and my expectation was that this friend should become the leader. He was so fluent in the language and had a lot of abilities . . . . But they said they were washing dishes in a restaurant after returning to the Netherlands. So my eyes got so teary when I heard that. And I said, "Why are you guys cleaning the floor and washing dishes over there?" I think I understand them. They couldn't deceive themselves . . . .

It was clear that this Dutch colleague was more than just a co-worker to Eunseok. He was a brother in Christ and a cherished friend.

Julia described her relationships with her teammates over the years. They were quite diverse in their range of nationalities and backgrounds. She seemed pleasantly surprised at how she built such deep friendships with those who were so different from her. She indicated that these colleagues and friends, with all their differences, were the most significant factors in her personal changes. Similarly, Johannes also reflected and shared that when people from different backgrounds and nationalities chose to be united, it would bring glory to God. He said that such glorious moments were often found "in small things." Then he told a story that illustrated how, for him and other ICWs who worked with MCTs, friendships across cultural and ethnic boundaries were a source of great encouragement and became their desired cultural home.[5] Johannes said:

> A long time ago, we were having this team outing to a swimming pool, and Chulsoo . . . , a Korean, was sitting at the edge of the swimming pool. He had his long hair tied up in a knot, and there was this one piece of hair just going down over his back. And he was sitting there, very Asian. His posture, and . . . he sat straight back, and he was having his legs out, crossed. So he was there, and I was looking at that picture from the back. That was a very Asian view. Then there comes my little blond daughter, and she sits right next to him, and she started . . . looking up at him. And she starts this conversation with some childish talk. I don't know what it was about because I was far away, but I just saw it happening. And I thought, "Isn't that beautiful?" He's there, being very Asian. And then this little blond girl is just feeling so comfortable sitting right next to him starting this conversation, and they've been sitting there for quite some time. And I thought this is where it all breaks down—nationalities, backgrounds, and it's just that moment of joyful interaction. And I don't intend anything pluralistic or universalistic with this statement, but it was something beautiful. What I do mean is that there is unity in the body of Christ, and when it shows, it's really beautiful.

It was not only team members with whom these participants had built relationships. There were other ICWs who were part of different Christian organizations. There were also NAC national believers with whom these Christian workers developed close relationships. There were also some Christian expatriates who came to NAC for their corporate or diplomatic assignments or university studies. Many of these people attended international churches in major cities. ICWs often crossed organizational, team, and occupational boundaries and connected with them regardless of their citizenship or ethnic background.

There were also intricate networks of ICWs in NAC. These networks included people who were associated with many different international and foreign mission organizations, national house churches, Christian

---

5. I am including this story in its entirety because it is a paradigmatic story that illustrates how intercultural relationships and communities become a new cultural home for these ICWs.

denominations, and various local and international fellowships. They were somehow interconnected through a complex web of formal and informal relationships. Being an insider—a "like-minded" worker—to this ICW network would give ICWs access to valuable information, people, and resources. Naturally, this created a large social group with whom ICWs in NAC could relate, socialize, and collaborate for ministry purposes.

Many participants had friendships with other ICWs across organizational boundaries. It was not known how many ICWs were working in NAC. Some speculated that there were several hundred ICWs spread out around the country. Nevertheless, these international Christian worker networks within NAC had formed a large, country-wide fellowship that provided ICWs with relational connections and social contacts outside their teams. It seemed that this was a much-needed community for most, especially unmarried singles. It was not unusual for a Christian worker to have these connections outside their team or organization. When I was visiting an Asian Christian worker at his home, he received a phone call from the European director of a community development project established and supported by foreign Christians. Then the wife of this worker received a phone call from the wife of a NAC national Christian leader. This was an example of how these Christian workers were socially connected to diverse people across organizational and cultural boundaries.

NAC as "Home"

Many participants indicated that they felt comfortable living in NAC. Linda, who was often invited by her NAC local friends, said, "I do quite like this culture actually. I like the way that families include." When Linda visited a friend at her home, her friend's whole family and sometimes extended family would be involved in conversations and interactions with Linda. It made Linda feel very much at home. Both Youngcheol and Julia agreed that they felt at home in NAC when local people did not treat them differently but regarded them just as local persons. It made their daily life in NAC feel "normal."

Those who were relatively new to NAC tended to equate being comfortable in NAC to knowing how to do basic things in daily life. Claudia (one year in NAC) said that she felt at home in NAC. She explained, "Now we feel like we've put the roots down, and you know your way around, you know where to get things. You know who to ask for advice, and you have some friends." Marie and Philip (two years in NAC) also repeated a similar sentiment. Brittany (two years in NAC) said, "I think there . . . probably always will be some things that I just kind of shake my head at . . . . You get used to it, but it's still so different . . . , but I feel comfortable. I know this neighborhood, and the people around me know me. I feel completely comfortable going and doing all of the daily things that I need to do. Buying groceries, paying bills, taking a taxi into town."

Having adapted to life in NAC in many ways, Amy (four years in NAC) also felt comfortable with how things worked in NAC. She commented, "I feel very comfortable in [NAC]," said Thomas, who had lived in NAC for more than ten years. He made it hard to ask any further questions on this when he said, "I mean, we feel at home. We are very comfortable here. It's good being here. So, we're very comfortable, very comfortable, and we love being here . . . ." Mila said that she was comfortable in NAC to the point where she identified more with NAC people and would use the pronoun "we" whenever she talked to foreigners about NAC. A few participants even indicated that they felt more comfortable in NAC than in their home countries.

While visiting Town C, I observed Thomas and Mikyung's interactions with their neighbors and people in their local community. They seemed to have cordial relationships with their neighbors. When people saw them on the street, they often stopped to greet them with a handshake or kisses on the cheeks. Thomas always graciously greeted them with a big smile. His knowledge of the local language and cultural norms was impressive. This couple seemed well established as respected members of the local community.

Thomas confirmed my observation when he told me, "In many ways, we really felt much more belonging here with people than we did in [name of another city]." He found that it was easier to relate to the local people in their town compared to the large city where they had lived before. Mikyung said that their relationships in the local community were much deeper, and their interactions were much more rich and frequent because the local community was much smaller than the large city where they had lived. When there was a family emergency in their home country, which required them to travel on short notice, their local friends quickly came to help with packing and looked after their young children. Mikyung said, "Without them, living here would be hard. Our relationship with them is continuing to deepen, and I feel it is very meaningful."

The sense of NAC as their home seemed to have much to do with these ICWs finding belonging in the local community and building close relationships with local people. Whether meeting neighbors or co-workers or even random encounters on the street or at cafes, these workers intentionally developed relationships with the local people. Rachel shared her story: "So we were in that home for eight years, and had people knocking on our door, night and day, 'My husband kicked me out of my house,' abusive situations, crazy situations, death, hate, 'Come sit and mourn with us.' Just really deep, deep relationships in that neighborhood."

Some participants fondly talked about how they were taken in as a part of the family by some local people. One participant remembered a local family in her old neighborhood, particularly the mother, who adopted her as her own daughter. On the scheduled wedding day of the local family's youngest daughter, this participant had to travel to attend her organization's conference in Europe, so she could not attend the wedding. When she told this family, they did not hesitate to postpone the wedding date so that this participant could attend it. It was a huge honor for her. It affirmed that she was indeed an important part of this family. Such experiences solidified their sense of belonging in NAC. It was the same for Linda. She was very close to a local family who considered her as a family member. She said, "I think for me it's about those times with friends, particularly like [A] and [M]'s family, if there's an event like a couple of weeks ago, it was very special because everybody was there and just to feel a part. [. . .] And it was just a wonderful being a part, knowing everybody, knowing the children . . . ."

Multiple "Homes"

When some of the participants discussed about their "home," they were not merely talking about a place in which they felt culturally and socially comfortable. They also had practical concerns of a physical place to live, financial resources needed, or close relationships to fall back on. Several participants specifically mentioned that they considered both NAC and their sending country as their "homes." Susan, a single woman who had spent about thirty years outside her home country of the US, said that both the US and NAC were her home. When I pressed her to choose her most comfortable place in terms of cultural context, Susan found it hard to decide. In the end, she chose her home state in the US because her aging parents still lived there. Mila, another single woman who had been in NAC for nearly two decades, also had difficulty choosing between her home country and NAC as her preferred home. She said that she went back and forth between the two and felt quite at home in both countries.

For Claudia, NAC was her third country of residence. She said that she had many homes. She explained, "We're settled in. This [NAC] is home now. Like this is what we refer to home. And when we say Australia, I mean, it's home too, Germany is home too, it just gets confusing." Then she clarified what she meant when she said, "But I think home is now where the family is, and it's just this weird concept. I mean, I still call Germany home, I call Australia home, I call our house in [City B] home."

It was hard for Kyungja and Jaehyuk, who were from Korea and yet spent almost two decades outside Korea, to imagine going back to Korea to live. It was mainly due to logistical issues and the resources needed to live there. For now, Kyungja felt that NAC was more comfortable and felt more like home, but Jaehyuk thought they could move and live anywhere in the world. To them, "home" seemed to be a relative term that depended on their ministry and calling.

Despite their sense of comfort in NAC, when asked where they felt their home was, some participants perceived their sending country as their home. Simon represented this view when he explained, "I have my friends, I have my family. Your food. I still like it. (laughing) So when I'm there, I'm fine. It's not like . . . I'm not fine here. But it's different. Here [NAC], I know that I'm in a kind of secondary culture, so I have to adjust, and I have to make things work. But when I'm there [home country], I'm very . . . Well, I'm happy." These perceptions of ICWs about the place of their true home showed the kind of sacrifices that these Christian workers made in order to serve in NAC.

CULTURAL HOMELESSNESS

"I kind of feel . . . I am homeless . . . ." It was striking to hear these words from William. William was well established in his ministry in the local community. He was highly respected by his colleagues for his faithfulness in ministry and his strong relationships within the local community. He also had strong connections with family and friends in his native England.[6] And yet, he felt like he had no place he could call home. This sentiment can be described as *cultural homelessness*, a term coined by psychologists Navarrete Vivero and Jenkins to explain a phenomenon often observed among immigrant children and multiracial children in the United States.[7] Cultural homelessness refers to "the unique experiences and feelings that have been observed in certain multicultural individuals: their struggles to belong and to reconcile their conflicting frames of reference, and their difficulties attaining membership in the group(s) in which they aspire to be accepted as members."[8] The accounts of some of the participants showed a sense of loss of home, a struggle to have a sense of belonging anywhere, and a feeling of living in between cultures.

6. Again, I would like to remind the reader that "William" is a second pseudonym for one of the participants. Although he is not English, I changed his nationality and some details to maintain his anonymity as much as possible.

7. Vivero and Jenkins, "Existential Hazards"; Navarrete and Jenkins, "Cultural Homelessness, Multiminority Status"; Hoersting and Jenkins, "No Place to Call."

8. Navarrete and Jenkins, "Cultural Homelessness, Multiminority Status," 794–95.

These sentiments expressed by these ICWs sounded strikingly similar to the above description of cultural homelessness.

Being a Stranger in Home Country

For some participants, it was surprising or even shocking to realize that they were like strangers in their homelands when they visited their sending countries. William expressed this feeling when he said, "I feel like a stranger. Yeah, I feel like a stranger in my country." This sense of being a stranger in his home country came from simple things as not knowing how the new public transport system worked. He said, "I come, and I feel stupid because I don't know how to take the bus." Such trivial things could still trigger a feeling of being a stranger, which then led to a sense of loss.

Some participants felt a loss of social status or standing in their home country. For Youngcheol, who usually visited his native Korea every other year, each visit reminded him that he was an outsider. He said, "In reality, when I visit Korea, I cannot enter deeply into the Korean society because I don't really know it." Stefanie said that she struggled to find her place in Switzerland when she went back to visit after a couple of years of working in NAC. Having no role or position in her home community and being financially dependent on others' giving made it difficult for her to find her place socially. She was honored and shown respect as an ICW appointed and commissioned by her church community, but she did not feel that she could be herself; she found it burdensome to be put on a pedestal.

Myungsook shared a story about her first visit to Korea after serving abroad with her mission organization for her initial term. The trip took place after she had very intense intercultural experiences—for two years, she lived in three countries and learned four different languages. While transiting through airports, she had a strange experience of being confused and disoriented. For some reason, she had trouble with memory, and everyone she saw at the airport in Korea appeared to her as someone she knew. Thankfully, this did not last long, but it was a frightening experience for her.

However, social awkwardness was not the only thing experienced by some of these participants; they also felt a sense of loss in financial and logistical matters. Linda said, "No one knows me in the UK." She implied that she had no credit history in her home country that made it very difficult for her to rent a house or get a credit card. She was asked to pay rent for six months upfront to sign a lease agreement. Jaehyuk, who had a professional career in Korea before coming to NAC, wondered if he could ever get back into his professional practice in his home country because of both changes in himself and in his home country. He was not sure whether he could adapt to these changes. I was surprised to hear his words. After all, he was someone who had coped well with very intense cultural and social adaptations to serve as an ICW in NAC.

Some participants returned home for a visit and found themselves disappointed with their friends and family members. It was largely due to seeing the lifestyle of people back home in such a contrast to what they strove for in NAC. It is not that this lifestyle was entirely foreign to them; their intercultural experiences made them more acutely aware of the disparity of wealth, consumerism in the West, materialistic lifestyle, and, in some cases, unenthusiastic attitudes of people back in their home country.

On the first visit to her hometown in the US after her first term in NAC, Jessica struggled to hold back her feeling of anger. It was disconcerting for her to see that people did not appreciate the freedom they were enjoying. She recalled, "I remember I went to meet with friends. We went to a coffee shop, and it was really chill, and of course, it gives so much freedom, and I remember just thinking like people don't even know how much freedom they have here. [. . .] I felt like they just didn't value the freedom that women have!"

John did not hide his disappointment with the spiritual apathy that he witnessed among Christians during his home country visits. He shared his honest feelings when he said, "For me, it's the church, it's Christians that annoy me. People who are living very comfortable lives and aren't really engaged with God, and are kind of sleepwalking . . . their faith." He added, "I struggle with how to relate to those people because I want to just tell them to start out fresh." Caitlin had a similar experience in her native South Africa. She said, "When I go back home . . . , I find it very difficult. People's mindsets are different, hard to have conversations, and almost like, people have no interest in your work or your life . . . ."

These negative experiences might be what some call "reverse culture shock" or "reentry stress."[9] These disappointments seemed to represent a growing gulf between these Christian workers and their home countries. These ICWs seemed to experience a strong feeling of being isolated, estranged, and even marginalized in their home countries.

Sometimes strained relationships with family members or friends were a cause for their growing emotional distance from their home countries. In some cases, this was a natural development that was unavoidable as people went through changes in the season of life. For example, Stefanie found some of her friends now had babies or young children, which made them unavailable to meet with her. In other cases, family expectations or even conflicts

9. See Austin and Beyer, "Missionary Repatriation."

with family members seemed to take away their sense of belonging in their home countries. Balancing between expectations of family and meeting their own needs was a difficult and stressful act for these workers.

Being Tired from Life and Ministry in NAC

Eunseok was an international Christian worker well known to me. I looked forward to this interview since I was interested in what transpired in his life over the past several years since I left NAC. When I visited Eunseok at his home and saw him, I immediately noticed some changes in him. I remembered him always being well-groomed and neatly dressed. On this day, however, he did not seem to care so much about his looks. He also appeared weary and tired. It was hard to pinpoint what it was, but there was something noticeably different about him. He was a coffee enthusiast who used to be meticulous about roasting and grinding his own coffee beans and then carefully brewing them by hand dripping. He never offered his guests anything less. Now he was serving me instant coffee. He said that this was so much more convenient, so he stopped making hand-drip coffee. That was an obvious change in four years. But what exactly happened to him? Why did he look so tired and weary? Then he mentioned a need for him to take a leave. He dryly said, "I want to get out of NAC." Through stories he unpacked, a picture of someone tired of the lifestyle, demands, and emotional grind of serving as an ICW in NAC and working with an MCT emerged.

It was not only Eunseok, however. Other participants, especially those who had worked in NAC for many years, confided that they were tired and needed a break from NAC. It was not always clear what made them tired, and each person had a different situation, but a common theme was that they were tired from doing the life and ministry in NAC for the long haul. It took an emotional and mental toll on them. Linda spent well over two decades in NAC, actively engaging many local people and leading several local women to faith. Always friendly, energetic, and people-oriented, she had many local NAC friends. But it was becoming impossible to maintain contact with all of them, so she intentionally dropped some. She said, "It's not that I ever want to lose relationships, but I wasn't able to maintain them all." She noticed more recently that she was increasingly annoyed by her local friends leaving the television on all the time while she was visiting them. But it was never an issue for her in the past. She said, "I lost patience with the TV being on, people talking about things that I didn't know what they were talking about, but I think it was just for me just tiredness quite honestly." It was notable that during the interview, she repeated the word "tired" several times. She added,

"This is an aspect of living cross-culturally, which is more tiring than just living in a simpler world of your own culture."

Julia agreed with Linda's statement about the toll of intercultural living. On a recent visit to her home country, she realized that it took more energy to live in NAC than her homeland. Despite her fluency in the local language and deep understanding of the local people, Julia still found life in her home country easier than in NAC. She said that the things that took energy in NAC had now become so normal for her that she did not recognize the tiring aspect of living in NAC.

Mikyung talked about the experience of burn-out several years ago. She and her husband had moved to a more remote, isolated area with their young children without any team members. This was not long after she had given birth to their second child. She admitted that she might have had postpartum depression at that time. Despite fulfilling the dream of moving into that town to serve God, moving to this rural area took a toll on them. There were so many changes to their life, and the new environment was too unfamiliar. They also felt lonely. She said, "I think living itself was extremely difficult . . . . We were struggling to cope with and manage our ministry . . . ." What sustained them during this period was taking regular times outside NAC for rest and recovery. She said that these breaks had greatly helped her and her family cope with the stress of living and ministering in NAC.

Uncertainty of North Africa as Home

Another factor contributing to the participants' sense of cultural homelessness was the uncertainty of their stay in NAC. Due to the unpredictability of obtaining the residency visa, many participants expressed anxiety and concern about their long-term future in NAC. Myungsook, who had become more relaxed about this matter in recent years, recalled that she used to have a lot more anxiety about her long-term future in NAC. She said, "For some reason, I always thought that this was not a place to stay but to leave any time, so in some ways, there was not much sense of stability psychologically." Susan also expressed this uncertainty when she said, "I'd be very interested to stay here, but I don't know. Things always happen here that I don't think it's going to work for me to stay here long-term . . . ." When asked about how long they planned to work in NAC, many participants mentioned that they wanted to stay for a long time, but they were unsure. Many wanted to continue their work and thought they would be there for the foreseeable future, but they also felt unsure about their long-term future in NAC. The uncertainty seemed to sap the energy out of them. It required them to have a contingency plan for unexpected emergencies. After all, their next application for residency renewal could be rejected; they could suddenly be deported from the country by the authorities.

Franco said that he and his wife were living like immigrants. He explained that they had to show the reason for being there in their application for residency, but they did not always understand what was going on with the authorities. He said, "You will always be a frog from another pond because . . . you would be a foreigner all your life. Even if you speak the language . . . ." Camila added, "I think being a foreigner makes it very vulnerable."

When I visited City E to conduct several interviews, I visited an ICW couple whom I knew. I happened to catch the husband the day before leaving for Europe to help one of their children transition to a Western European university. He and his wife were from a country in East Asia. Their two older children studied in colleges in the US. Their youngest was now moving to Western Europe. And yet, they were living and working in NAC. They had worked in another country in the Arab world for several years but had to leave when the local government did not renew their residency. Their story illustrates the uncertainty and the toll it takes on Christian workers and their families serving in this part of the world. It showed the reality that the lives of these international workers were, in a sense, like those of temporary migrants.

Responding to Cultural Homelessness

Responses to a state of cultural homelessness by my interlocutors were two folds. First, their sense of personal calling reminded them of their ultimate home in heaven and their purpose of living in NAC. Secondly, they became more intentional about seeking relationships with their MCT members and local NAC friends.

When asked where they felt their home was, some participants replied with a spiritual answer. Claudia confidently said that it was heaven. Susan said, "My home is an eternal home. That's all I know. (chuckle) So ultimately . . . my goal really is [to be] with Jesus, the place he's preparing for me . . . ." Similarly, William, who talked in length about his sense of homelessness, also said, "Only the Kingdom of God is my true home." They were not merely reciting a theological concept but putting all these things in perspective by focusing on their faith in God, whom they trusted and believed to have led them thus far amid uncertainty and difficulties they had faced in NAC.

They also tried to inspire themselves and their teammates by appealing to their purpose of living in NAC. Bruce and Cheryl said that they were accountable to their grandchildren. When I asked them about it, they explained that they gave up their privilege of being with their family, especially their grandchildren, by choosing to live in NAC. This brought great sadness to them. Even as they were sharing this, they became quite emotional. Since they knew that they were serving in NAC at great personal cost, Bruce and Cheryl turned their sadness into a motivation to be fruitful in their work of seeking God's kingdom in NAC. Thomas and Mikyung were able to cope with the long process of moving from City A to City B, and then finally to Town C. They experienced isolation, intense loneliness, depression, and uncertainty of serving in their remote rural town. It was clearly their sense of purpose and calling from God that helped them through it all. Thomas said, "We came with a very clear purpose. We knew we were going to go to Town C, and we were in City B to establish the relationships here. [Town C], I think the sense of clear purpose was really helpful." Heather, a single Asian American woman who had worked for over a dozen years in NAC, was emphatic when she reflected, "Yeah, like . . . the purpose of life was stronger to live out here than to see what other options there were in the States."

While I worked on coding an interview transcript, I came to a sudden realization that there was a God-element to every interview. God's leading played the most significant role in how these participants ended up where they lived and worked. How can this not be a critical element in the intercultural social processes among these ICWs? Why would they go to a place like Town C, City E, Town F, or City B, endure hardships, and persevere through uncertainties and personal struggles? Why would they stay there? It was all because they believed that God wanted them to be there. There were meaning and purpose that came from discerning God's calling for their lives. As they discerned God's direction for them and followed it, they gained enough strength to endure the challenges of adjusting, learning, adapting, and changing. Without this sense of calling and purpose, one wonders if any of them would have been able to stay there long enough to experience any of these personal changes. It would be easier to live where one grew up and had lived for years. Why did they leave all those comforts in their home countries in exchange for these difficult challenges in NAC? It was because they saw tremendous value in going through these hardships. Without their faith motivation, they would not have relocated to these places and lived there for so long, doing the work that they did.

It seemed that having strong intercultural relationships, if not completely erased a feeling of cultural homelessness and being outsiders, consoled these Christian workers and became a source of their encouragement. As previously described, these ICWs developed friendships with various people—members of their MCTs, other Christian workers, foreigners in the expatriate community outside their teams, NAC national believers, and local NAC people. It was evident that these ICWs maintained close contact and relationships with many of these people. These relationships gave them the strength to continue to work in NAC. Being intentional about building these relationships helped them cope with their sense of loss and grief.

SUMMARY AND CONCLUSION

This chapter described the personal changes in the participants as outcomes of their complex intercultural social life. By undertaking careful analysis of the collected data, this study produced an understanding of personal changes as perceived by and observed in the participants. Among the patterns recognized and ideas generated during data analysis, four categories of personal changes were most meaningful.

First, there were changes in the personal disposition of many participants. These changes seemed to take place at a deeper level in the lives of ICWs. It possibly indicates some profound changes in their self-concept. The changes in their personal disposition seemed to be mainly manifested in three areas: developing a transnational identity, the growth of intercultural social awareness, and altered personal priorities and values.

Secondly, many participants also experienced significant changes in their social behavior and attitude. Many became much more flexible in their relational style, their regard for structures, and their mindset. A more flexible, accommodating propensity was displayed in the way they related to people, especially in their methods of communication and social interaction. Some showed that they practiced mixing and blending various cultural forms and elements available to them to enhance their lives.

Thirdly, the participants developed a sense of a new cultural "home." Many felt at home in international, multicultural settings. They developed deep friendships with their multicultural team (MCT) colleagues and others outside the team, including those with different cultural backgrounds. These relationships contributed to their growing ease with multicultural social settings. Some also found their belonging in the North African country (NAC); they strongly felt that NAC was their home. Some also indicated that they had multiple homes, both culturally and literally.

It leads us to our fourth and last category, which shows that some participants experienced a sense of loss of their home. This sentiment can be described as a form of *cultural homelessness*. Some Christian workers felt like strangers in their home countries. The uncertainty and fatigue of living and working in NAC took a toll on them. However, they could cope with their cultural homelessness by focusing on their calling and developing strong relationships across cultures, both with their team members and local NAC people.

In this chapter, personal changes were analyzed as outcomes of intercultural social experiences described in detail in chapters 4 and 5. Based on the findings, I argue that personal changes in these international Christian workers (ICWs) were significantly influenced by their intercultural social experiences in the NAC context as they lived and worked with and among NAC people and in their multicultural team (MCT) context. In many of these cases, the extent of personal changes was not insignificant. Some participants showed signs of drastic changes in their personal disposition and social behavior. These changes seemed to have happened at a considerable depth and breadth.

The data strongly support a link between intercultural social experiences and these personal changes. The causal relationship between these two, however, does not seem to be in a single direction. It seems that there is a more complicated relationship between intercultural social life and personal changes; they may be influencing and being influenced by one another. This indicates a possible change model in individuals, small communities (e.g., MCTs), and even larger organized groups of people (e.g., educational institutions, religious organizations, etc.). Interactions between the participants and their complex social contexts seem to engender a process by which a mental model or discourse of an MCT culture and a general NAC culture are constructed. During this process, ICWs seem to experience personal changes and the boundaries between agency and structure seem to be blurred. This conceptual model regarding personal changes will be explored further in discussions of *diasporic habitus* in chapter 7.

7

Further Interpretation and Synthesis

CHAPTERS 4 AND 5 described how the context of the North African country (NAC) and the context of multicultural team (MCT) settings mediated the intercultural social experiences of the participants. Then in chapter 6, I presented an analysis of personal changes in these international Christian workers (ICWs), which resulted from their unique intercultural social life. These were mostly descriptive summaries of the coded data. While parts of these chapters provided some interpretive analysis of the phenomena being observed, especially in chapter 6, these mainly focused on describing the experiences of ICWs. In this chapter, I further analyze the findings from the previous three chapters, interpret their meanings, and synthesize a working conceptual model of intercultural social processes and their impact on the socialities of individuals and groups in intercultural, multicultural settings.

Throughout data analysis, I sought to make meaning out of the categories and sub-categories that I discovered, extracted, and constructed from the data. I thought of possible connections between these categories and existing theories. While many analytic categories could have been investigated further, I came to see a central motif that could bring together and connect many of the patterns recognized in this study. I refer to this central motif as developing *diasporic habitus* through continual engagement in complex, intercultural social processes interwoven into the fabric of everyday life. This phrase will need to be unpacked. This chapter is devoted to explaining and proposing this theoretical model for explaining complex intercultural social processes.

UNDERSTANDING INTERCULTURAL
SOCIAL PROCESSES

This study attempted to understand how living in a North African country (NAC) and working with multicultural teams (MCTs) mediated the intercultural social experiences of ICWs. By research design, these two experiences were treated separately during the data collection and analysis. Interview questions were specifically designed to ask separate questions about their social experiences with people of NAC and with their team members in MCTs. Then the raw data for each realm of experiences were analyzed and categorized accordingly. These resulted in detailed descriptions of these two different realms of experiences in chapters 4 and 5, respectively. It was intentionally done to spare the participants from making analytical connections between experiences in one realm with the other themselves. It is the responsibility of the researcher, not the participants, to produce critical insights from each realm of experiences and make the analytical link between the two realms. This was done by "an iterative-inductive approach," moving back and forth between the data, analysis, and thinking about the meaning.[1]

At an earlier stage of the research, I determined that the best way to learn about complex intercultural social processes was to focus on these two dominant intercultural experiences in the participants' everyday life and treat them as two separate processes. Once the raw data were sorted into specific categories that described nuances of both realms of experiences, I looked for empirical evidence, extant theories, and logical connections that showed how these two distinct experiences might be related to one another.

Characterizing Intercultural Social Process (ISP)

Intercultural social experiences of ICWs take place in the cultural "contact zones" of NAC and MCT.[2] Their experiences show consistent patterns of intentional cultural adaptation and social negotiations that result in changes in their social dispositions. In this research, these patterns are identified as *intercultural social processes* (ISPs). As the term indicates, these processes have both intercultural and social aspects that mediate the lived realities of ICWs in their cultural contact zones.

The research participants, without exception, engaged in language learning and cultural adaptation when they first arrived in NAC. While they experienced the stress of these adjustments, they were negotiating

---

1. O'Reilly, *Ethnographic Methods*, 29–30.
2. Pratt, *Imperial Eyes*.

social relations with the local people of NAC and coming up with strategies to cope with their new life in NAC. Although the way they went about taking actions and giving responses differed from person to person, there were noticeably similar patterns across the vast majority of the participants. These patterns resulted from their intentional actions and reactions to inadvertent outcomes of living in an unfamiliar context. The same can be said about their experiences in working with an MCT. As they adjusted to life with their MCT, they also negotiated relationships, coped with straining experiences, and developed means to navigate their team life. These patterns indicate that a set of complex social processes are at work in the everyday life of ICWs.

Some social researchers view the social experiences of immigrants in their newly settled country as a process of adaptation, conflict, and negotiation. Studies of immigrants to Australia provide good examples that show parallels with this study. Sociologist Greg Noble shows how immigrants in Australia experience disorientation and reorientation while resettling in Australia.[3] He reports that it leads them to develop social awareness that embodies their social awkwardness and in-betweenness. Similarly, in an ethnographic study in the suburbs of Australia, sociologist Amanda Wise explores how racial tensions and intercultural anxieties arise in everyday encounters between Chinese immigrants and long-established White Australians in the context of rapid, immigration-driven demographic changes in local communities.[4] These studies of international migrants provide support for the approach taken in this project to interpret the experiences of ICWs in NAC as part of distinct intercultural social processes (ISPs) that lead to changes in their embodied personal and social dispositions.

Interwoven Dual Process and Construction of "Culture"

Distinct intercultural social processes (ISPs) that ICWs go through while living in NAC and working with an MCT suggest a need to analyze each of these two realms of intercultural experiences as separate social processes before bringing the two processes together as an interwoven process. During data analysis, I intentionally isolated these two realms, which I will refer to as "the NAC process" and "the MCT process." The NAC process represents social patterns related to living with and among NAC people, while the MCT process describes patterns that emerge within MCT.

Each process was described in detail in chapter 4 and 5. In each process, there are dynamic interactions that mediate the everyday life experiences of

3. Noble, "Habitus, Field and Migrant."
4. Wise, "Sensuous Multiculturalism."

ICWs. My analysis shows that each process contains seemingly complete, enclosed experiences. For example, for our analytical purposes, we might isolate the experience of Marcelo and Olivia in having a lovely visit with their Muslim neighbors in City B from their experience of having a time of heartfelt worship with their MCT composed of members from three different passport countries. In reality, however, these two experiences cannot really be separated. When Marcelo and Olivia meet with their team, they would share with their teammates about this visit to their Muslim neighbors. They would talk about what they observed, felt, and thought about the experience. They would ask the team to pray for these neighbors. Later on, the other team members might get a chance to meet these neighbors of Marcelo and Olivia in a social gathering. They might also become friends with them and, naturally, spend time together. Eventually, these neighbors could become interested in the faith of these ICWs, and they might begin to study the Bible together. The two intercultural social processes, which were considered separate, have already merged in reality.

Although this was a hypothetical example, it was not uncommon to hear this kind of story from the participants. The key point here is that, in reality, it may neither be possible nor helpful to distinguish these two processes; nor is it the ultimate goal of this research. A holistic view of their experiences would see these processes as intertwined and interwoven with each other, taking place at the same time. These two processes would not be mutually exclusive. Therefore, it would be logical to think of these two as interwoven processes that continuously influence one another. These ICWs go through daily life as they live among the people of NAC. Still, these life experiences in NAC are mediated—corrected, affirmed, interpreted, given meanings—by their interactions with their MCT and its members. The opposite is also true. Their interactive learning and adaptation practice is influenced by their experiences and interactions with NAC people. Thus, the NAC process happens in conjunction with the MCT process, and the MCT process takes place in the context of the NAC process. They affect each other, and it might even be said that one is embedded in the other. Indeed, it might be best to see them as an interwoven dual process. I will call this interwoven process "the NAC-MCT process."

Through this dual interwoven intercultural social process, the ICWs seem to construct two cultural models—a cultural model of NAC and a cultural model for their MCT—that make sense to them. These intercultural social processes can be viewed as culture-making processes. Linguistic anthropologist Michael Agar provides a helpful explanation of how "culture" should be understood when he explains that a description of another "culture" is, inevitably, "my mental model of your perspective."[5] In other words, a simplified description of culture is only a mental model created from someone else's positioned view. It represents neither objective realities nor emic perspectives. As Agar puts it, "it is *our* model of *them*, not *their* model."[6] In a sense, this is how my participants were constructing cultures. They seemed to produce a workable mental model of the NAC culture, which they believed was the actual, real "culture" of NAC. They also seemed to create an MCT "culture." This team culture emulates an interactive social space with its own rules, structures, and accepted code of conduct. This space is influenced by and incorporates the ICWs' mental model of the NAC culture. These two mental models seem to go through a continuous revision on an individual and corporate basis based on new experiences and information. Instead of saying that these ICWs learned the NAC culture and adapted to the team culture, for our purposes of social analysis, it would be more beneficial to say that they created a mental model of culture for the country of NAC and another for their MCT.

This dual process could be observed in the experiences of many participants. It was easier to see this process at work among newly arrived ICWs. For example, Chris and Jennifer had been in NAC for less than a year when I interviewed them. After they arrived, their MCT members picked them up from the airport, helped them find an apartment, and arranged their language learning lessons. They also gave them an orientation to the local living situation and trained them on how to relate to their Muslim neighbors. While they were given many opportunities to learn and experience the local setting on their own, their team gave them timely feedback on what they were experiencing so that they could make sense of their experiences. In other words, their team was mediating their intercultural experiences of the local social context. There seemed to be a close relationship between these two processes and how they played out in Chris and Jennifer's early experiences in NAC. Their initial adaptation and adjustment seemed to be happening rapidly with the NAC-MCT process. Also, I could say that their NAC process would also influence their MCT process as they gained more local experiences and interacted with their team, sharing their experiences.

5. Agar, *Culture*, 2019, 87.
6. Agar, *Culture*, 2019, 87.

Locating Intercultural Social Process (ISP) in the "Third Space"

Where do the intercultural social processes (ISPs) take place? Where can we locate the NAC-MCT process? The notion of the intercultural social process developed in this study is an abstraction of complicated, entangled social realities of ICWs. As I have elaborated in chapter 2, the conceptual framework of this research utilizes Homi Bhabha's theory of cultural hybridity.[7] One of his ideas that provides a key for exploring complex human processes is the notion of the Third Space. For the sake of analysis, let us assume for a moment that the location where intercultural social processes take place is in what Bhabha refers to as the Third Space, the in-between space of cultural contact zone where cultures are "enunciated."[8] Bhabha states that it is possible to conceptualize "an *inter*national culture" only in the Third Space of cultural contact zones.[9] He writes, "It is in this space that we will find those words with which we can speak of Ourselves and Others."[10]

In an ambiguous language, Bhabha provides a postcolonial critique of Western societies of the late twentieth century. It should be noted that Bhabha did not develop his notion of hybridity for empirical social research. While his work is interdisciplinary, his academic home is in comparative literature. Thus, it is difficult to apply his theory in an empirical study such as this. This difficulty is not, however, for the lack of sophistication or complexity of his arguments. There is simply a limit to how his social imagination can be directly translated into social research.

Nevertheless, his conceptualization of hybridity caught the attention of scholars in various disciplines, including cultural and social anthropology. It resonated with what they were already observing in a far more complex world than they previously thought. While many scholars have used his theory as a point of departure for their cultural analysis, few empirical studies used his approach as the main framework. The reason is not hard to see. Cultural hybridity is an abstract meta-theory that critiques the broader societal and cultural trends, albeit highly sophisticated and nuanced narratives. While it is not an empirical theory, it still has provided scholarly inspiration for multiple studies, including this one.

However, this research is not about his postcolonial critique or nuanced discussions of the relationship between the colonizer and the colonized. Instead, the contribution of Bhabha's theory to this study is in

7. Bhabha, *Location of Culture*.
8. Bhabha, *Location of Culture*.
9. Bhabha, *Location of Culture*, 56.
10. Bhabha, "Cultural Diversity," 157.

providing a conceptual point of departure for further investigation into a social phenomenon uncovered by the research findings. This study has focused on understanding intercultural social processes in a sophisticated intercultural setting that can shed new light on intercultural mission theory and practice. Bhabha's notion of the Third Space as the location of salient cultural production provides insight for missiological reflection and research. While it is hard to pin down and define the Third Space, in the context of this study, it can be seen relationally as an imaginary space between people from different cultures who come in close contact with one another. Putting the findings of this study and Bhabha's notion together gives us a plausible empirical model that shows intercultural social processes taking place in this imaginary Third Space. In this intercultural contact zone, people from different cultural backgrounds interact and create new cultural practices, social codes of conduct, and social dispositions. In the case of my research participants, it can be assumed that the NAC-MCT process takes place in the liminal Third Space of cultures, which opens up around them as they live meaningfully in the given context. These contribute to their changed personal dispositions and social practices.

Intensity of Intercultural Social Process and Its Outcome

The term intercultural social process (ISP) is an umbrella term I coined for various patterns I have observed in the lives of the ICWs who participated in this study. While each person's unique experiences can sometimes be generalized as certain analytic categories, it does not mean that these processes are uniform across different people and groups. The intensity or magnitude of these social experiences can differ significantly from person to person and from period to period. Although the research data show many variations across the cases, the most salient emergent patterns in the data suggest that the larger the cultural and language gap, the higher the intensity of the intercultural social process will be. For example, ICW's initial experiences in NAC and their MCT described in chapters 4 and 5 show that their initial adaptation period in NAC was far more volatile than their later period. Also, those who spoke English fluently had experienced less disorientation in their MCT life than those who did not; The Asian participants tended to have more intense adjustments in MCT and less intense experience with people of NAC than the Western participants.

Anthropologist Hans-Rudolf Wicker provides a helpful image of culture as "the river, forever changing within given perimeters of space and time," highlighting its fluid, flowing nature within its historical and geographical confines.[11] Taking this metaphor further, we may see ICWs' intercultural social experiences in the cultural intersection of an MCT in the NAC context as the river made of and shaped by many smaller streams. The flow of this metaphorical "river" is influenced by torrential rain (flood), powerful streams merging (whirlpool), or a sudden drop in the terrain (waterfall). This gives a picture of what ICWs went through as they moved into NAC (cultural waterfall), joined an MCT (cultural whirlpool), and faced an onslaught of never-seen-before issues in everyday living (cultural torrential rain and flood). The intensity and volatility of these processes would dramatically change, depending on the factors present in the local setting and within the team. One can expect that factors such as cultural and language diversity on the team and the gap in social norms between the local people and ICWs can significantly impact the intensity of intercultural social experiences that make up these processes. It can be anticipated that the greater the cultural difference and diversity, the stronger the "turbulence" in intercultural social processes.

Multicultural Teams and Différance

The multicultural team context that unfolds in North Africa is highly complex. Many different factors influence the everyday life of these ICWs. Depending on who is and is not on their team and who they meet and develop relationships within the NAC context, the intercultural social processes can take very different turns. For example, a South African married couple with teenage children would bring life experiences different from a single Asian woman who has an immigrant background in Australia or a White Canadian man who has a German-Russian Mennonite background and lived his entire life in rural central Canada. These are not some arbitrary cases but real ICWs in NAC whom I had met in the past. Also, ICWs would experience a very different NAC society if they met and interacted mostly with wealthy, secular, upper-class, highly educated NAC nationals instead of those who were religiously devoted, lived in a rural area and struggled to make a living.

What seems to be clear is that these diverse social factors do influence ICWs to learn, adapt, and change their way of living and reorient their perspectives. Although many of these idiosyncrasies might play out differently for each ICW, the fact that they go through a social process over time that changes them is undeniable. Although the intercultural social process mediates unique experiences and produces distinctive changes in these individuals, the pattern of how these processes unfold is strikingly similar

---

11. Wicker, "From Complex Culture," 39.

among these ICWs. It does not end up with these ICWs being assimilated or homogenized into a single uniform culture, but it adds a "thick layer" of shared experiences and common practices. After many years of leading meaningful lives through the intercultural social process, these ICWs still retain their differences. Still, it is questionable whether these unique traits found in these ICWs can be dubbed as cultural differences based on pre-determined national characterizations. In other words, after years of experiencing this process, could the aforementioned South African couple, the single Asian Australian woman, and the White Canadian man be understood by applying generalized national culture traits of South Africa, a country in Asia, and Canada, respectively?

It is likely that arbitrary boundaries only increase perceived cultural differences between people. One wonders then if focusing on cultural differences, especially superficial ones that are capriciously constructed to represent some content of a bounded culture or an essentialized national group, could help these ICWs and their MCTs build stronger ministries and teams. Sharp cultural differentiation does not seem to represent reality well. Instead, it creates a false reality imagined and reinforced in people's consciousness that hinders building relationships across cultures.

In thinking about how these cultural differences are often portrayed in missionary circles, I find Derrida's idea of *différance* helpful in re-imagining how to explain cultural differences among those who go through complex intercultural social processes. *Différance*, "is literally neither a word nor a concept," writes Derrida. It is an ambiguous term that suspends over between its meanings and states.[12] It is a clever wordplay with an intentional misspelling that replaces "*e*" of *différence* (difference) with an "*a*." He thus creates an ambivalent word that does not exist in the French language, and yet, seems to mean both "difference" and "deference," and the gerunds, "differing" and "deferring." However, it is and means none of them. In French pronunciation, *différance* (non-word) and *différence* (difference) sound the same, so the listener cannot know the difference between these two words. The difference is noted when one sees them in written forms. But in speech, the real meaning of the word continues to be "deferred" because to tell the "difference" between the two words, it becomes necessary to use other words to qualify them.[13]

Both Stuart Hall and Homi Bhabha take up this linguistic dilemma of *différance* and bring them into the sphere of culture, identity, and

---

12. Derrida, *Margins of Philosophy*, 3.
13. Derrida, *Margins of Philosophy*, 3–27.

multiculturalism in their reflections of postcolonial times.[14] Hall's comments are especially helpful. Hall sees *différance* as "a marker which sets up a disturbance in our settled understanding . . . of the word/concept. It sets the word in motion to new meanings without erasing the *trace* of its other meanings."[15] He states, "It is a 'weave' of similarities and differences that refuse to separate into fixed binary oppositions. *Différance* characterizes a system . . . . Meaning here has no origin or final destination, cannot be finally fixed, is always *in process* . . . ."[16] The act of cultural differentiation of cultural Other can work in this way. When we see someone from another culture who comes across as *different*, we may notice the *difference*. As soon as the difference is noticed, however, the true meaning of the person is postponed, which puts us in a perpetual catch-up mode. This is an intercultural dilemma that has no easy answers.

We find a hint, however, from Stuart Hall's insights. Hall's cultural interpretation of *différance* has a bearing on ICWs in MCTs. He highlights the contradiction, ambiguity, and in-betweenness symbolized by *différance*. It unsettles our understanding of the Other, signaling incomplete but new meanings while acknowledging historical entanglements present in the MCTs of IMOs. It needs to be remembered that intercultural social practices within MCTs are shaped by contingent cultural elements around ICWs. Lived experiences in the liminal space of an MCT can convince ICWs to refuse the fixed notion about a culture or a group of people. Rather than defining cultural differences into fixed binary opposites, they can recognize and maintain multiple layers of similarities and differences interwoven into the fabric of their everyday interactions lived out in their multicultural teams. Rigid views of culture and people often employed by intercultural Christian missions can lead to a reification of essentialized cultures that reduce and demean friends and colleagues from other cultures. As they admit that they do not fully understand the meanings of their teammates from other cultures, they also need to accept the cultural complexity, resist the urge to settle for a simplistic model and think more deeply about the paradox and potential of multicultural team life.

What About Same-Culture Teams?

The discussion thus far has focused on intercultural social processes related to ICWs who worked with multicultural teams. It raises a question

14. Hall, "Cultural Identity and Diaspora"; Hall, "Multi-Cultural Question"; Bhabha, *Location of Culture.*

15. Hall, "Cultural Identity and Diaspora," 229.

16. Hall, "Multi-Cultural Question," 216.

about how these processes would be different for a same-culture team in which all team members have a similar national, ethnic, and language background. The model of intercultural social processes I have developed thus far assumes that there is a strong influence of the social aspect of the team on the process itself. In an interwoven dual-process model, ICWs' experiences in their MCT would mediate their experiences with people of NAC, and vice versa, thus producing a more acutely accelerated process of social adaptation and negotiation that leads to greater changes in the personal and social disposition of ICWs.

In a monocultural or same-culture team setting, one can anticipate that these experiences would be more moderate. The team would still mediate all intercultural social processes taking place in the lives of its members. However, with less cultural and/or ethnic diversity, more shared social norms, and common cultural scripts among the team members, one can expect the intercultural social process to be less volatile and more predictable. One can anticipate that the complexity of intercultural interactions will be reduced for a monocultural team, and the cultural contact zone will also be smaller and narrower for the members.

Since this research aimed to explore the intercultural social experiences of ICWs who worked with multicultural, multinational teams, ICWs who worked on same-culture teams were not considered in the research sample. However, I included two cases of ICWs who were members of same-culture teams. The reason I chose to interview them was to strengthen the credibility of the research findings. By interviewing two ICWs who were members of two different same-culture teams, I could compare them with MCT members, the primary research population. Although the sample is small and limited, I anticipated that the qualitative data gathered from them would be sufficient to show similarities and contrasts with MCT members.

I interviewed two persons of same-culture teams: Corey, a White American male who worked with a team of White Americans who mostly came from the same church group in the States, and Sungmin, a Korean male who was with a mission team sent out by a Korean mission organization composed only of Koreans. At the time of the interview, Sungmin was nearing ten years of service in NAC, and Corey had been working in NAC for four years. I intentionally asked them the same line of questions as I had asked members of MCTs, probing their local NAC experiences and team experiences. I went into these interviews expecting that there would be both similarities and differences between these two interviewees and those who were members of MCTs.

I was surprised, however, to find more pronounced differences than I had initially anticipated. When I asked Corey and Sungmin about their team life, there was no mention of cultural tensions on their teams. It was a non-issue. They talked more about personality issues on the team or problems with their NAC national co-workers. Their "cultural" focus was entirely on NAC people, not on any cultural issues found within their team. There was little sign that they had spent time or put effort into thinking about their own culture or cultural tendencies. All of the cultural comparisons made by these two workers were between their own culture and the local NAC culture, even though I asked the same line of questions as other participants. There seemed to be an absence of a frame of reference concerning intercultural issues. It was plausible that these workers had a cultural framework very different from that of MCT members. When I tried to probe their intercultural experiences, neither of them interpreted their experiences in NAC in terms of culture or cultural experiences.

Although it could be that their unique individual experiences or idiosyncrasies led them to answer my questions differently than MCT members, it seemed obvious that they had not struggled with cultural differences or language issues within their team; they did not experience the level of frustrations as MCT members did.

From these data, as limited as they were, some observations can be made about the MCT context in juxtaposition to the same-culture team context. Regarding intercultural social processes, the MCT context seems to be more complex than a same-culture team context. MCT members seemed to pay far more attention and spent far more energy on intercultural issues, communication, and team-building than their counterparts in same-culture teams. MCT members could not focus all their energy on local ministry in NAC due to being preoccupied with their MCT issues, so they appeared less efficient than members of same-culture teams in achieving their ministry goals. The ongoing social interactions with teammates who were different from them resulted in more tiredness. Still, they seemed to develop a higher degree of intercultural awareness and more pronounced changes in their personal disposition and social behavior. As for intercultural social processes, the data generally support my argument that ISPs of MCTs are more volatile and multi-dimensional than ISPs of same-culture teams as they went through a more intense intercultural social adaptation and negotiation process.

In summary, let us briefly review what has been discussed in this section. In this study, intercultural social processes are defined as processes of cultural adaptation and social negotiation by international Christian workers that result in changes in their social disposition. These processes mediate their interpersonal experiences in cultural contact zones in NAC and their MCT. There are multiple processes at work when people from different cultures come in contact with one another. These processes are interwoven and intertwined to the point that, in reality, they cannot be separated. In the lives of ICWs of MCTs in NAC, their two most dominant ISPs are the NAC process, which occurs in intercultural contact with people of NAC, and the MCT process, which happens in the intercultural contact between them and MCT members. It is assumed that these processes take place in an imagined Third Space between cultures. These processes influence one another; one mediates the other and vice versa. While this study presented analyses of these two processes separately, in reality, neither process happens in isolation from the other.

It must be noted that the changes in individual ICWs affect not only themselves but also their immediate communities and social groups. The people who go in and out of the Third Space of ICWs are, inevitably, part of the NAC-MCT process. Thus, these changes seen in ICWs are not self-contained individual changes; they are social, communal, and relational by nature and affect their social group. All the multiple layers of changes would affect one another, forming a combined sociocultural structure and agency. It would be a complex system of social agents, structures, and cultural flows continually moving and shifting. This "system" merits further thought and will be discussed in the following section.

DIASPORIC HABITUS

Chapter 6 described the nature and extent of personal changes in international Christian workers (ICWs). Based on the evidence from the body of data, I argued that these changes resulted from their intercultural social experiences in North Africa and with their multicultural teams. It would be easy to label these changes as "cultural changes." However, this way of explanation—making "culture" responsible for so much—neither adequately characterizes the rich complexity of these changes in them nor provides helpful insights for understanding intercultural social processes. It requires a more nuanced concept to explain and interpret the nature of these changes in people who have endured a complex and sometimes painful intercultural social life while participating in intercultural missions.

I propose "diasporic habitus" as a notion that explains the lived realities of these ICWs. This term seems to have been first coined by British social researcher David Parker in his discussion of the Chinese immigrants in Britain, centered around their everyday life at a Chinese eatery.[17] He writes, "The term diasporic habitus facilitates the exploration of specific modalities governing the social practices of transnational collectives, operating 'away from

17. Parker, "Chinese Takeaway."

home."[18] Then Ien Ang uses this term in her review of Stuart Hall's posthumous memoir to sum up Hall's prolific academic career and his life as a diasporic intellectual figure.[19] It is a phrase that combines Hall's lifelong work on diasporic identity and Bourdieu's notion of *habitus*. Although Ang does not elaborate it, she perhaps does not need to; the term is already packed with meanings that deeply resonate with the lived experiences of ICWs revealed thus far in this study. Thus I propose a working definition of *diasporic habitus* as a system of internalized dispositions and schemes acquired through repeated practices by those who live *meaningfully* in a country or culture different from their own. This notion is discussed next.

Personal Change and Habitus

Individual changes in the research participants could be seen in their personal dispositions, social behaviors, new cultural "homes," and a sense of cultural homelessness. Most participants had developed a cultural identity transcending their national or cultural backgrounds. In many cases, they understood themselves as fitting better in international, multicultural settings. They displayed growing awareness of their positioned, unavoidably biased perspective. Many of them displayed a change in the way they related and socialized with people. Some felt that they were culturally homeless, feeling entirely at home neither in their home countries nor in NAC.

I can make a few observations about these changes. First, there is a relational, social aspect to personal changes in ICWs. Intercultural social processes happen in intercultural contact zones where prolonged personal interactions and relationships with the cultural Other lead to specific changes in ICWs' personal and social dispositions.

Secondly, there is a structural aspect in these changes. ICWs develop transnational, intercultural self-concepts. They gain increased cultural and social awareness and revise their behavioral patterns. It should be noted that all these changes feed into their daily social contact with their MCT members and local people in NAC. In the process, they establish a personal structure related to their lifestyle, team life, organizational policies, and social conduct in the local NAC setting. The changes in them influence more than just themselves; they would affect the interactions and general social behaviors of people and groups with whom they regularly spend time.

Thirdly, there is an agency aspect in these changes in ICWs. Personal changes do not happen as once-and-done events. As ICWs actively participate in their intercultural, multicultural social life, personal changes become

18. Parker, "Chinese Takeaway," 84.
19. Ang, "Inhabiting the Diasporic Habitus"; Hall, *Familiar Stranger*.

ongoing. With new knowledge attained through their lived experiences, their dispositions and social inclinations go through changes, but these changes are not only imposed on them; they are active in selectively accepting, rejecting, and blending new social and cultural elements at hand as they continue to revise their social conduct. They are not passive bystanders as these changes are forced upon them; they actively shape and reshape them within the purview of their lived experiences in NAC. These different aspects of personal changes indicate that the changes taking place in these ICWs are part of a significant social phenomenon that needs further investigation.

There are many parallels between how Bourdieu characterizes the concept of *habitus* and the nature of and circumstances that bring about personal changes in ICWs.[20] In his early characterization, Bourdieu explains *habitus* as follows:

> The structures constitutive of a particular type of environment . . . produce *habitus*, systems of durable, transposable *dispositions*, structured structures predisposed to function as structuring structures, that is, as principles of the generation and structuring of practices and representations which can be objectively "regulated" and "regular" without in any way being the product of obedience to rules, objectively adapted to their goals without presupposing a conscious aiming at ends or an express mastery of the operations necessary to attain them and, being all this, collectively orchestrated without being the product of the orchestrating action of a conductor.[21]

Habitus is a paradoxical concept. It includes the role of both social structure and agency, producing an ecosystem-like entity that acts, reacts, adjusts, and reforms itself. Bourdieu seems to emphasize that the development of human social practice is not a mechanical, predetermined program while recognizing the ongoing influence of the preexisting systems of dispositions on human behavior. It is not a concept that can easily be reduced down to a one-sentence definition. Bourdieu devotes hundreds of pages in several volumes to explain how he sees *habitus* working in the social world. Among many of Bourdieu's qualified elaborations of *habitus*, more refined, shorter versions appear in his later book, *The Logic of Practice*. He explains that *habitus* is "constituted in practice and is always

20. Bourdieu, *Outline of a Theory of Practice*; Bourdieu, *Logic of Practice*.
21. Bourdieu, *Outline of a Theory of Practice*, 72.

oriented towards practical functions."[22] It is "embodied history, internalized as a second nature and so forgotten as history."[23]

In a seemingly circular logic, he explains that *habitus* is both a producer and a product of history, constrained by "schemes generated by history."[24] As "an acquired system of generative schemes," *habitus* is also "an infinite capacity for generating products—thoughts, perceptions, expressions, and actions—whose limits are set by the historically and socially situated conditions of its production."[25] As can be seen in these explanations, Bourdieu constructs the notion with paradoxical opposites. It is *a structured structure* and *a structuring structure*. It is a product and a producer. It is limitless and limited. These seemingly contradictory depictions of *habitus* are perhaps its genius since they remove false dichotomies while maintaining conceptual tensions. Critics of Bourdieu reject his notion for its deterministic leanings.[26] However, it is worth noting Brubaker's perceptive comment, "Bourdieu was not . . . defining but rather was characterizing the concept of habitus in a variety of ways in order to communicate a certain theoretical stance or posture, to designate—and inculcate—a certain sociological disposition, a certain way of looking at the world."[27] Through *habitus*, Bourdieu provides a way to understand the social world by exploring how everyday practice shapes and is shaped by people's embodied social schemes.

Characterizing Diasporic Habitus

The concept of *habitus* helps explain the social phenomena so far discussed in this research. Despite Bourdieu's enormous influence, however, social sciences have not sufficiently addressed the nature and extent of how *habitus* could change in diaspora or immigration settings.[28] Bourdieu himself rarely discussed or even mentioned culture as if he was trying to avoid using the term at all cost. For our purposes, it would be helpful to apply the concept of *habitus* to intercultural social situations of the research participants. ICWs come to NAC with their cultural identity and social disposition developed in their previous social field—the social settings in their home countries. As they enter NAC and join their MCT, they are now situated in a

22. Bourdieu, *Logic of Practice*, 52.

23. Bourdieu, *Logic of Practice*, 54.

24. Bourdieu, *Logic of Practice*, 54.

25. Bourdieu, *Logic of Practice*, 55.

26. Brubaker, "Social Theory as Habitus"; Sayer, "Reflexivity and the Habitus"; O'Reilly, *Ethnographic Methods*.

27. Brubaker, "Social Theory as Habitus," 217.

28. Noble, "Habitus, Field and Migrant," 345.

new, very different social field where their *habitus* or their durable dispositions, the inclinations that helped them in the past, betray them. By aban-
doning or revising some of their old schemes of social behaviors, taking up
some new, and practicing a mixture of old and new through trial-and-error,
their *habitus* goes through changes over time.[29] While retaining some of
their prior dispositions, ICWs must develop new ones alongside the old in
order to survive in their new social environment. Over time, some of the
newer dispositions—communicating and socializing in Arabic or French
or English, discomfort in relating to people of the opposite gender, or automatically declining friends' offers—eclipse or even replace the old ones. Of
course, much of the past still remains, but some new sets of social dispositions are blended with old ones to generate new social practices. According
to Sayer, *habitus* includes the practices that succeed in a particular social
field where the person's social life is situated.[30] Therefore, social practices
that were part of the previously carried dispositions will be limited in a new
social field. Unless they develop new social strategies and tactics soon, they
would inevitably suffer the consequences.

And suffered the consequences they have. ICWs' experiences in NAC
were often characterized by confusion and disorientation. It took a while
for them to learn to negotiate social norms and adjust their practices. Their
social life in MCTs was mixed with both positive and negative experiences. While many of them saw much growth and learning, they also had
heartbreaking experiences of conflicts and misunderstandings with their
colleagues. *Habitus* of these ICWs is reshaped over time to the point that
their preferred social field is no longer in the country of their birth and/or
earlier life. However, they also develop a better understanding of themselves
and others. Their values and even identities are changed after having gone
through a long period of highly intense intercultural social processes. In
the end, few of them have a clear answer to the question of where they now
belong and where their true home was.

Sociologist Zygmunt Bauman writes, "One thinks of identity whenever one is not sure of where one belongs; that is, one is not sure how to
place oneself among the evident variety of behavioural styles and patterns,
and how to make sure that people around would accept this placement
as right and proper, so that both sides would know how to go on in each
other's presence."[31] This is true of these ICWs. As they think about who
they are now, ICWs realize that they are no longer who they used to be;

29. Sayer, "Reflexivity and the Habitus," 110.
30. Sayer, "Reflexivity and the Habitus," 109.
31. Bauman, "From Pilgrim to Tourist," 19.

they do not have clarity about where their "home" is anymore. This leads them to think about their eternal home in heaven, even as they find reasons to be grateful for their new "home" with their MCT in NAC, and also grieve the loss of their "homeland." These experiences are, in many ways, similar to those of many transnational migrants.

These diasporic sentiments by ICWs are well articulated by two of the most celebrated postcolonial scholars, Edward Said and Stuart Hall. Both lived and worked in the diaspora as minority scholars in the dominant majority society in the United States (Said) and the United Kingdom (Hall). Their self-reflections, especially on their diasporic experiences, describe lived realities of a life in exile and perhaps in a state of cultural homelessness. It is entirely fitting that their memoirs produced toward the end of their lives (for Hall, posthumously) are titled *Out of Place: A Memoir*[32] and *Familiar Stranger: A Life Between Two Islands*.[33] The titles alone meaningfully empathize with the kind of life experienced by many transnational migrants, including international Christian workers. While experiences of ICWs in NAC may not precisely replicate the lives of these prolific scholars, ICWs do have sentiments of being out of place or becoming a familiar stranger; in-betweenness and sense of cultural homelessness were staples in the lives of ICWs. In all their dispositions, proclivities, sentiments, and capacities, these intercultural, diasporic social realities would constitute what I would call *diasporic habitus*.

A Participant Case of Inhabiting Diasporic Habitus

I have so far developed a concept of *diasporic habitus* in relation to international Christian workers who worked with multicultural teams. I inductively drew out patterns of personal changes from the research data and thought about these patterns with the notion of *habitus* and how the term was previously used by others. It would become more vivid if *diasporic habitus* is shown through a case of a research participant. I select the case of Youngcheol because his interview was perhaps among the most insightful and rich in content. He was an incise cultural critic. His persona seemed to display what it meant to "inhabit the diasporic habitus."[34] Through an account of his intercultural life, we might see how *diasporic habitus* plays out in a person's life.

Youngcheol was born and grew up in a rural town in South Korea. After the Korean War, his father had moved to his village to lead a "rural

32. Said, *Out of Place*.
33. Hall, *Familiar Stranger*.
34. Ang, "Inhabiting the Diasporic Habitus," 4.

enlightenment campaign." His hometown area was heavily Confucianist, but his family was part of a strong local church-based Christian community. He said, "We lived in the rural area, but in a sense, we lived cross-culturally. We lived in a different culture." After completing his first year in a seminary, he joined his mission organization, thinking he would gain overseas ministry experience for a couple of years and return to finish his seminary education. He wryly said, "It got a bit longer like this . . . ." It had been twenty-eight years since he left Korea.

When he joined his IMO, he went with an open mind and eagerness to learn. He came from a unique family culture in which directness and clarity were typical; they had no trouble answering yes or no to questions and requests from others; no strict rules were imposed on him by his parents. He said that Koreans who came from a "face-culture" might have been offended by him and his family.

As he joined his IMO, he participated in a training program for Koreans along with thirty other Korean trainees. The program was held in the UK. He said that he felt more uneasy with other Koreans than the British people. After the training program, he went to a small city in Spain to join a multicultural ministry team. He learned Spanish and worked among migrants for a year. He recalled how warmly his neighbors in Spain received him. Interestingly, none of them were part of the majority culture but were immigrants themselves. During this time, he experienced a conflict with a teammate from Europe. He understood then that it was not due to cultural differences but differences in personality and values.

After serving in Spain for a year, he moved to NAC. Although he had joined a team led by an Englishman, he said that his team culture was dominated by Latin Americans. In a short span of two years, he studied English, Spanish, Arabic, and French. At one point, one of his team members insisted that Youngcheol should not be allowed to eat rice so that he would adjust to cross-cultural life. He contested it by saying that it was cultural discrimination. He said that what you ate at home was not the issue; having the capacity to enjoy whatever NAC people or teammates from other cultures shared with him were far more important to intercultural living.

There were myriad insights he freely shared during the interview. Almost in passing, he mentioned that he felt that the NAC culture was similar to his own. Adapting to NAC was practically a non-issue for him. However, in contrast to what other Korean participants have said, he did not say that his adaptation to his MCT was more difficult; his counter-cultural upbringing and learner posture helped him cope well with the stresses of multicultural team life. He regretted the cynicism of some Christian workers about NAC people; he lamented a lack of intercultural awareness among some ICWs from the West. After nearly three decades spent in North Africa, he continued to learn new things about NAC. He said, "Culture is something that's alive because it comes from living people." In his mind, cultural adaptation was "ongoing" and "present-progressive." He said, "That's why even now I keep falling off my chair with surprises again and again." At the time of the interview, he was learning NAC young adults' perspectives on dating, sex, and marriage. He was critical of how some ICWs saw the NAC culture as some rural, old traditional culture instead of urban, global culture going through continual changes, especially among the youth. Because of ongoing changes in NAC, he felt that it was important for ICWs to get out of their office or home, walk the streets, hang out in cafes, and maintain "a feel for NAC."

He said that having spent decades in the social environment of his IMO, he felt most comfortable in that setting where he shared a common vocational, religious language, experiences, and themes. Reflecting on the influence of the NAC context on his MCT life, he said that if he and his team were in Europe, Latin America, or Southeast Asia, his life and ministry would have looked very different. "Things change drastically according to the spiritual, social, political, or economic atmosphere," he said, and then added, "Our team culture would have been very different had we not been in NAC." He saw that ICWs came to NAC with two "extreme orientations." One was the view that NAC was "a closed country," and the second was treating NAC as "a Muslim country." He thought that these two assumptions had a negative influence on how ICWs lived and worked in NAC. In speaking of changes in people, Youngcheol recognized that no ICW could fully become a NAC person but more of a hybrid. He saw that some changes in people were natural, organic, and analog; other changes were imposed, inorganic, and digital. He preferred the organic, natural, and analog; he thought these presented a better option for ICWs.

Many elements in Youngcheol's story highlight *diasporic habitus*. His insights were unique; his perspectives were uncommonly refreshing with a ring of truth. The interview was in Korean, but he frequently used phrases and expressions in four other languages. The capacity to understand and speak multiple languages, thus various ways of life, seems to be a part of *diasporic habitus*.

Youngcheol was known for his unique sense of humor. I have seen Youngcheol joke with people from many different countries, speaking in various languages. From his life story, it is apparent that he came with a unique background. To those who do not understand the unique setting in which he grew up, he might have come across as "just another Korean." However, he was known among other Korean ICWs, including some of the participants in this study, as a "not very Korean-like" person. Provided that he did develop a unique *habitus* over many years of living and working in NAC, it seems that he still brought his unique internalized dispositions to NAC and into his MCT.

No one comes to a new social setting with a clean slate. Everyone comes into new social fields with their existing *habitus* intact. Bourdieu was clear that past experiences were actively present in people's *habitus* or scheme of daily life practice.[35] Youngcheol's personal history was very much a part of how *diasporic habitus* played out in his life. His initial few years with his IMO as a Christian worker were tumultuous. He experienced intense, volatile intercultural social forces at work in just a few years, living in a few different countries, learning several languages, and being in a community with people with very different inclinations. If we used the imagery previously used, his new experiences were hit with an intercultural social flood, whirlpool, and waterfall all at the same time. How he survived the volatility and chaos of those years is astonishing. Perhaps his inner character and resilience, ingrained in his *habitus*, helped him withstand the pressures of cultural vectors in his early years as an ICW. One last point to be made is that he used the term "culture" in quite an expansive manner, including both essentialist and processual views of culture. He used popular renderings of culture while displaying an uncanny ability to articulate the most scholarly insights on the construct called "culture." This dual discursive use of the term "culture" will be briefly discussed later.

Diasporic Habitus and Cultural Hybridity

Looking at the findings of this research through the lens of Bourdieu's practice theory had helped me articulate the notion of *diasporic habitus*. Considering the fact that Bourdieu devoted his entire career to elaborating the notion, it is obvious that the idea of *diasporic habitus* will undoubtedly require more nuanced discussions than this study can allow. I submit that *diasporic habitus* can initiate constructive conversations in missiology.

Now I return to the original conceptual framework of this study, namely, the theory of cultural hybridization. While Bhabha's hybridity theory had an influential role in envisioning this research, the foundational concept for this project came from Nestor García Canclini's argument that "the object of study is not hybridity, but instead the processes of hybridization."[36] This would be a good place to discuss the limit of cultural hybridity theory and how a notion of *diasporic habitus* might help fill the gap.

35. Bourdieu, *Logic of Practice*, 54.
36. García Canclini, "State of War," 43.

Cultural hybridity theory withstood many attacks from critics and was established as a bulwark in postcolonial scholarship and beyond. As mentioned in chapter 2, Werbner raises a concern that inorganic, "interruptive hybridity" could threaten the existing order and end up harming minorities and migrants.[37] Her concern is a practical one as it deals with the implications of cultural hybridity in the public sphere. There are also concerns about whether cultural hybridity theory has relevance as a robust social theory in the thick of globalization well into the mid-twenty-first century. I raise here three issues about cultural hybridity theory.

First, while the differentiation between the organic and inorganic hybridity theorized by Bakhtin is lauded by Bhabha and Werbner as a helpful perspective for cultural analysis, it is difficult to distinguish empirically between these two.[38] Participants in this study have gone through some intense intercultural social processes. Much of what they experienced was intentional, inorganic by design, while they also experienced unintended, organic consequences (e.g., cultural homelessness). However, the distinction between the two types of hybridity inadvertently hides that these two might be inseparable and intertwined. While analyzing the data, I looked for indications of either kind of hybridity. There were signs everywhere of hybridity; however, it was not easy to distinguish which type. Distinctions of the organic and the inorganic seemed to be only arbitrary and superficial. The theoretical difference between the two might help us understand how the process of hybridization happens, but in reality, organic hybridity and inorganic hybridity are intermixed.

Let us consider Youngcheol's case once again. The most visibly inorganic, intentional hybridity he displays might be his capacity to speak multiple languages. It took years of hard work to reach fluency in three different languages and conversational proficiency in another. But was it solely his voluntary, "inorganic" hard work that resulted in his language capability? It took numerous encounters, interactions, opportunities, and chance meetings that allowed him to learn and grow in his language skills. The environment for his linguistic growth was not purely intentional, inorganic, or conscious. It took years of living in a combined conscious and unconscious hybrid environment to acquire his current language *habitus*. It is impossible to isolate the organic from the inorganic in his experiences. It seems that hybridity always occurs in a combination of both organic and inorganic. Intentional, conscious hybridity may take place along with

37. Werbner, "Limits of Cultural Hybridity."

38. See Bakhtin, *The Dialogic Imagination*; Bhabha, *The Location of Culture*; Werbner, "Dialectics of Cultural Hybridity," 1997.

unintentional, unconscious hybridity. As scholars point out, hybridity always entails ambivalent meanings. It is always double-voiced. This characterization of hybridity should also be seen in a blurred distinction between organic and inorganic hybridity.

Secondly, it is notoriously difficult to "operationalize" the hybridity theory in empirical research. It is a type of meta-theory that functions as a cultural critique, especially of the realities in the former colonies and the resulting multicultural societies in the postcolonial West. Since the theory was not intended as an empirical social scientific theory, it is surprising how much impact it has had in various fields of social and human sciences. Nevertheless, the theory's abstract narratives have gaps that make it challenging to use in empirical studies. One way to mitigate this weakness might be using the cultural hybridity theory in conjunction with the practice theory. García Canclini suggests that the concept of cultural hybridization can have "*explanatory power*" and be used as "a *hermeneutic* resource" when it is used alongside other salient social concepts.[39] Partnering the concept of *diasporic habitus* with cultural hybridization theory shows the potential to narrow this gap between the hybridity theory and its empirical approach and everyday practice. Embodied schemes of diasporic dispositions can be the point of convergence for theory and practice, as this study has shown.

Thirdly, cultural hybridity, born as a literary analysis in colonial encounters and their aftermath, has been viewed as somewhat limited in its applications to migrants and minorities in the West.[40] Its application for the colonial context should not be too easily generalized or transferred to other diasporas without carefully evaluating the context. This difficulty further justifies this study's call for an empirical approach to cultural hybridization.

This study is an example of an effort to apply an abstract, macro social theory to empirical investigations of complex phenomena. The best means to bridge the gap between an abstract theory and empirical research may be what Nederveen Pieterse calls "a multilevel approach" or "the elevator approach to theory."[41] It means moving between a macro theory and practical empiricism grounded in field data. This study represents such an approach in which the researcher went back and forth between cultural hybridization theory, empirical data, and other existing theories that produced working models of intercultural social process and *diasporic habitus*.

39. García Canclini, "The State of War," 42.
40. Papastergiadis, "Tracing Hybridity in Theory," 273.
41. Nederveen Pieterse, *Multipolar Globalization*, 193.

Trajectory of Diasporic Habitus

International Christian workers come to NAC with a particular way of rendering the world in which they live. While they navigate, negotiate, and interact in their NAC-MCT process, they accept (e.g., learning new languages and developing ministry strategy), reject (e.g., the religion of Islam), adapt (e.g., social conduct), maintain (e.g., certain practices from home country) and blend (e.g., food, music, gestures, facial expressions, dress code, cultural expressions, lifestyle, daily schedule) certain social elements in team life and the local context. As a result, they go through a change in their internalized system of social schemes or *habitus*. This phrase, *diasporic habitus,* represents these changed dispositions that take on an intercultural, transnational character.

Through complex intercultural social processes (ISPs), ICWs shape and reshape their *diasporic habitus*, which continually mediates and is mediated by those ISPs. While how *diasporic habitus* manifests itself might differ from context to context, person to person, group to group, and time to time, the internalized, structured and structuring scheme is likely to display increasing consistency as individuals settle in their intercultural social processes. This would explain the consistent social patterns found at multiple levels across the vastly diverse participants. This conceptual model shows the complexity of intercultural social dynamics and the means to simplify the complex phenomena to gain a better understanding.

The discussions thus far still leave many questions unanswered. For example, why did some ICWs experience so much change in themselves while others did so less? Was it a matter of the intensity of ISP and the length of time in these new social conditions? How do the following contribute to the shaping of *diasporic habitus*: primary socialization, personal faith, prior life experiences, ideological and/or theological elements, spiritual experiences, characteristics of their international mission organization, a sense of their calling, and level of involvement with NAC national believers? Since these questions are beyond the purview of this study, I will not further address them here. They indicate, however, a potentially fruitful future research trajectory for this conceptual model.

PRACTICE OF DOUBLE DISCOURSES OF "CULTURE"

One of the findings of this study was that many international Christian workers (ICWs) who worked with multicultural teams (MCTs) showed a tendency to use one of the two different ways of thinking about "culture." One way was what is sometimes referred to as "essentialist" in that the research participants attributed people's behaviors, tendencies, and traits to their "culture." They tended to reduce a culture down to its immutable characteristics. They appeared to hold a view that culture had internal cohesion while it kept an external boundary. Culture was often attached to a particular ethnic group or a country, region, or continent. They displayed a view that each country or nation-state, and sometimes an entire continent, had a culture with specific dimensions or characteristics practiced by its members.

The other way that they thought about culture is sometimes called "constructivist" or "processual." Sometimes they recognized the diversity and variations in each country that contested essentialist views. They resisted stereotypes and were careful not to judge people based on their "culture" while recognizing that cultures changed. These two diametrically opposite ways of using the word "culture" by ICWs were described in chapter 5 in detail.

It seemed that most participants leaned toward one view or the other when they talked about culture. However, some of them used a combination of the two contrasting views depending on their situation. They tried to make sense of and respond to the confusion that stemmed from differences that they saw in people of NAC and their fellow MCT members. It seems that they were attempting to reconcile the seeming contradiction of these two cultural discourses in their everyday practice.

Essentialist and Processual: Two Discourses of Culture

In the late nineteenth century, Edward B. Tylor famously wrote, "Culture or Civilization, taken in its wide ethnographic sense, is that complex whole which includes knowledge, belief, art, morals, law, custom, and any other capabilities and habits acquired by man as a member of society."[42] Since then, the notion of culture has gone through many changes. About one hundred years after Tylor's book was first published, Clifford Geertz defined culture as "the fabric of meaning in terms of which human beings interpret their experience and guide their action."[43] Geertz's view of culture was an innovation at a time when those under positivist traditions considered him too radically constructivist and too deviant from the classic anthropological perspective.[44] Since then, most anthropologists have moved further away from the classic definitions of culture for nearly a half-century, even making Geertz's view appear outdated. The notion of culture has received major push-backs for its inadequate and problematic uses, as documented by numerous

42. Tylor, *Primitive Culture*, 1:1.

43. Geertz, *The Interpretation of Cultures*, 145.

44. Ortner, *The Fate of "Culture."*

anthropologists.[45] Indeed, it is hard to imagine any anthropologist today subscribing to a classic notion of culture, such as Tylor's. Agar gives a good explanation of the classic notion when he states:

> The old concept carries connotations of a closed system, frozen in time, with a comprehensive and consistent image of what a person is and how he/she should act. No more. Nowadays the term of art is "globalization," as it is in many other popular and professional conversations and writings around the world. And globalization means we have to rethink the old idea of culture when we talk about a particular person or a particular group. A person nowadays isn't just wrapped in a single culture. A person nowadays is wrapped in . . . what?[46]

It is this "what" question that seems to cause much confusion among academics and non-academics alike. Then it is not surprising that there are different kinds of perspectives on culture which people use in their daily lives. In general, these perspectives broadly fall into two types: the essentialist perspective and the processual perspective. Scholars in anthropology and cultural studies I cite in this study show the difficulty of holding onto essentialist views in a globalizing world; they would rather describe culture as a process.[47] Some missiologists share this perspective. Schreiter recognizes the necessity for a theology of culture to foreground the processual aspect of change and culture construction.[48] Rynkiewich shows that the "standard missiological model" widely circulating in missions tends to reify bounded, essentialized cultures.[49] He suggests a complementary model that incorporates the understanding, "Culture is contingent, culture is constructed, culture is contested."[50]

With this background, I now turn to an ethnographic study by anthropologist Gerd Baumann, whose work has many parallels with the findings of this study.[51] He conducted field research among "so-called immigrants"

45. E.g., Abu-Lughod, "Writing Against Culture"; Abu-Lughod, *Muslim Women Need Saving?*; Kuper, *Culture*; Ortner, *The Fate of "Culture."*

46. Agar, *Culture*, 2019, 5.

47. E.g., Ang, *On Not Speaking Chinese*; Appadurai, *Modernity at Large*; García Canclini, *Hybrid Cultures*; Nederveen Pieterse, *Globalization and Culture*, 2015.

48. Schreiter, *The New Catholicity.*

49. Rynkiewich, "World in My Parish."

50. Rynkiewich, "World in My Parish," 315.

51. Baumann, *Contesting Culture*; "Dominant and Demotic Discourses"; *The Multicultural Riddle.*

in Southall, a densely populated multicultural suburb of London.[52] He found that the residents of Southall used two different discourses of culture. He calls the first one "the dominant discourse" and the second one "the demotic discourse." Baumann explains that the dominant discourse sees "culture" as the reified essence of an ethnic group.

In contrast, the demotic discourse weakens, if not abandons, the link between an ethnic group and its "culture."[53] He notes that while Southallians maintained their ethnic community boundaries, they also moved around across the boundaries and formed their "culture" inside and outside these lines.[54] He observes, "Southallians engage the dominant discourse as well as the demotic one. They reify 'cultures' while at the same time making culture. Even when they explicitly engage the demotic discourse, the faultlines of the dominant one are effective and, more than that, empirically visible."[55] He notices that the use of these discourses of culture was varied "depending upon their judgements of context and purpose."[56] These selective decisions were influenced by the Southallians' perceived social advantage or usefulness at the moment.[57] These insights help us understand how people utilize both an essentialist and a processual discourse of culture in their everyday social practices.

Who Used Which Discourse and Why

Many participants in this study talked about culture as an essentialized, bounded, and integrated whole possessed by a national or cultural group. They tended to assign certain qualities to a specific cultural group or generalized cultural traits of people to a particular country. Table 3 below displays "cultural" statements made by ICWs, either in direct quotes or summary forms of words spoken by different participants about other cultures. These are snippets of what the participants said in their interviews. There were many other instances in which participants talked about culture in this manner. As these words show, they were generalizing national traits to that country or regional ones to that region. When they saw someone behaving in a certain way, they often concluded that the person's culture was the cause for that behavior. Also, culture became objects that could be learned, loved, celebrated, or possessed.

52. Baumann, *Contesting Culture*, 1.
53. Baumann, "Dominant and Demotic Discourses," 209.
54. Bauman, "From Pilgrim to Tourist."
55. Baumann, "Dominant and Demotic Discourses," 214.
56. Baumann, *Contesting Culture*, 189.
57. Baumann, *Contesting Culture*, 195–96.

Table 3. "Culture" Statements Made by Participants

No.	Culture spoken of	Speaker	"Cultural" Statement
1	Dutch	European	It's the Dutch thing to have a very strong opinion on something.
2	Dutch	N. American	"Dutch people can be quite blunt."
3	Dutch	Asian	They were "so Dutch."
4	Korean	N. American	Korea has a hierarchical culture.
5	Korean	European	"Koreans are very good at having regular prayer times, like in the morning."
6	German	European	Germans are harder. They tend to speak faster.
7	German	European	Being punctual is very important to Germans.
8	American	European	Americans tend to come across a little bit arrogant.
9	American	European	"Americans would never say the kind of things that we say."
10	Mexican & Colombian	Latin American	Mexicans and Colombians are very indirect in their communication.
11	Irish	European	Irish culture is more private and not so open.

However, many participants simultaneously displayed a nuanced understanding of culture and a keen intercultural awareness described as a processual perspective. I have already highlighted elsewhere Youngcheol, Thomas, and Linda as examples of international Christian workers who have developed an astute understanding of intercultural issues. Then why did these ICWs describe cultures in these contradictory ways? According to Baumann, the dominant or essentialist view was a default perspective of Southall residents that did not disappear even as they practiced their demotic, processual discourses of culture.[58] They would switch their language, discourse, and expressions about culture whenever they deemed one more

58. See Baumann, *Contesting Culture*; "Dominant and Demotic Discourses."

beneficial than the other. They were changing, expanding, and adapting their ethnic, religious, or cultural identity as needed.

In a sense, this is what ICWs who participated in this research seemed to be doing. In their multicultural team life, they experience much confusion and disorientation. In most cases, they simply tried to make sense of these social situations that involved vast cultural differences. They reified others' and their own cultures to their generalized, essential qualities so that they had a reference point around which they could re-orient their thinking and make their MCT life work. These efforts to make sense of the differences occur at the individual, team, and international organization levels, respectively.

In my review of intercultural training materials used in three IMOs in which 78 percent (thirty-eight out of forty-nine) of my participants were members, I found that these materials were based on national culture models by Hofstede and Trompenaars. However, Hofstede's national dimensions model is problematic due to its essentialist views and tendency to commit "ecological fallacy," which tends to apply national-level aggregates to subnational groups and individuals.[59]

In discussing cultural differences within their teams, some participants used parts of the framework called dimensions of national culture developed by Hofstede, by far the most dominant model used in the academic fields of cross-cultural management and intercultural communication. It was clear that some of my participants were influenced by this model, which tends to lean toward what Baumann would call the essentialist discourse of culture. They seemed to use this model as a reference point to understand intercultural social experiences within their MCTs. However, some realized that these cultural dimensions and national characters did not always match the individual team members they were getting to know. They developed an intercultural social stance that was mindful of the narratives of national cultures and yet transcended them in everyday practice with their diverse MCT members.

Using a Double Discourse of Culture as a Social Strategy

International Christian workers on multicultural teams in North Africa deal with a complicated and sometimes contradictory mixture of ideas about nationality, ethnicity, religion, and culture in their everyday experiences. In general, those ICWs who consolidate their intercultural social experiences

59. McSweeney, "Ecological Mono-Deterministic Fallacy"; Brewer and Venaik, "The Ecological Fallacy"; Messner, "The Misconstruction of Hofstede."

into a flexible and multi-layered framework of cultural understanding tend to develop a more robust processual or constructivist perspective in tandem with the standard dominant or reified view of essentialized culture. Those who had more intense, thorough, and diverse experiences of cultural reorientation are more likely to develop more multifaceted intercultural social capacities, including the ability to use both the dominant essentialist view and the demotic, processual view of culture. While further study is needed to confirm it, one can expect that these capacities are strongly correlated to their *diasporic habitus*, as a set of internalized dispositions attained through repeated practice by these ICWs.

As part of respondent validation, Jaehyuk, one of the participants in the study, provided feedback on the preliminary findings of this study.[60] While affirming the complex intercultural social influences interwoven into the fabric of the MCT and the NAC context that fed off of each other, he reiterated that he had certainly changed over the years, and he was "no longer a Korean." This exaggerated expression came across to me with much meaning. Understanding the intense intercultural social experiences he had as an ICW in NAC, I knew that these words were not just an essentialist discourse but had a ring of truth. He had changed for sure. He had no trouble using whichever discourse, whether an essentialist or processual because he had learned to navigate the tumultuous waters of intercultural social life. And he was not alone. Many participants selectively used either the dominant/essentialist or the demotic/processual discourse depending on the topic, situation, or context. The capacity to use this double, dual discourse of culture is perhaps one of the defining characteristics of international Christian workers who had a long engagement with intense intercultural social processes. Baumann helpfully writes:

> An ethnographic study of multicultural realities as lived in one place can produce new clues that fill in the theoretical gap we have noticed: the gap between people claiming reified identities and their everyday necessity of crosscutting identifications. People who live in a multicultural milieu need to do both to reach their personal, family, or community goals. What develops in such an environment is a double discursive competence: people know when to reify one of their identities, and they know when to question their own reifications.[61]

60. See Flick, *Managing Quality in Research*, 88–90; Merriam and Tisdell, *Qualitative Research*, 246.

61. Baumann, *The Multicultural Riddle*, 139.

This statement is a fitting explanation of why ICWs develop "a double discursive competence," to borrow Baumann's term, or perhaps why they end up with *diasporic habitus*, to use the notion developed in this study. Baumann argues that a higher level of engagement in intercultural, multicultural practices strengthens one's double discursive competence.[62] Therefore, it would be correct to assume that the contradictory practice of double discourses of culture still goes through continual improvement and revision. With new experiences and feedback from their teammates, ICWs continue to develop their "structured and structuring structures" of diasporic dispositions and capacities. MCT is a large part of this accelerated, intensified process that perhaps enables these revisions of one's existing cultural understanding, personal disposition, and social conduct. This is how multicultural teams in NAC would function as what Etienne Wenger calls "communities of practice."[63]

In missiological literature, the dominant, essentialist view of culture is well represented by concepts such as dimensions of national culture, homogeneous unit principle (HUP), the 10/40 window, and unreached people groups (UPG). The processual view is usually put forth by notions of migration, urbanization, and globalization. While one set of concepts seems outdated and the other more favorable, Baumann suggests that we should not see these two views as "two opposite theories and call one of them true and the other one false."[64] He argues that it is necessary to hold onto both in our thinking. There seems to be an inherent tension between the essential and the processual, fixity and fluidity, and the dominant and demotic. It reminds us that this kind of tension also exists between the particular and the universal, unity and diversity, "the Pilgrim principle" and "the indigenous principle."[65] This tension is ingrained in human societies because they have existed in some form at all times; we cannot rid either side of this tension. Baumann offers, "By viewing culture as the object of two discursive competences, one essentialist and one processual, we can study and appreciate the culture-making sophistication of exactly those people who are usually treated as the dupes of 'their' reified cultures."[66] Thus, the best way to go about intercultural social research might be to figure out how to hold onto both views in some ways to maintain the tension so that we get a better view of the complex and messy social world we engage in Christian mission.

62. Baumann, *The Multicultural Riddle*, 93.

63. Wenger, *Communities of Practice*.

64. Baumann, "Dominant and Demotic Discourses," 94.

65. Walls, "The Gospel as Prisoner."

66. Baumann, *The Multicultural Riddle*, 94.

SUMMARY AND CONCLUSION

In this chapter, the major findings of the study were further analyzed and interpreted. I developed my arguments using relevant literature as a conversation partner and revisited the research data to support the arguments. Three conceptual themes were developed and explained.

First, the complex processes occurring among international Christian workers (ICWs) were analyzed, and an argument for understanding intercultural social processes (ISPs) was developed. The participants' intercultural social experiences in the context of their multicultural teams (MCTs) and the North African country (NAC) showed consistent patterns of cultural adaptation and social negotiation that resulted in changes in their embodied social dispositions. It seems that the NAC process and the multicultural team (MCT) process have mediating effects on one another. A holistic view of these processes merges these two into an interwoven NAC-MCT process. This dual process leads the participants to construct two mental models of culture—a model for the NAC culture and another for the MCT culture. Intercultural social processes (ISPs) were seen through Bhabha's notion of the Third Space, connecting the research findings back to the original conceptual framework of this research. The intensity of ISPs and their impact were also considered. Two cases of same-culture team members were compared to the main sample of the study. Based on the relationship between the intensity of ISPs and their impact on the person and, ISPs experienced by ICWs in MCTs seem to be more volatile and multi-dimensional than ISPs experienced by ICWs on same-culture teams. Thus it seems likely that the extent of personal change experienced by ICWs in MCTs is higher than that of ICWs in same-culture teams. This point should be confirmed through a comparative study of ICWs in MCTs and ICWs in same-culture teams.

Secondly, a notion of *diasporic habitus* was proposed. It can help shed new light on the lived realities of ICWs. In developing and characterizing *diasporic habitus*, Bourdieu's concept of *habitus*, the analysis of participants' changed personal dispositions and social behaviors, and the understanding of intercultural social processes were utilized. A working definition of *diasporic habitus* is a system of internalized dispositions and schemes acquired through repeated practices by those who live meaningfully in a country or a culture different from their own. An exemplary participant case was examined using this notion, highlighting the points in the person's life that indicate his development of *diasporic habitus*. This concept was then juxtaposed with the cultural hybridization theory. I evaluated conceptual gaps in the cultural hybridity notion that could potentially be filled by utilizing the concept of *diasporic habitus*. I ended the discussion with some questions that could be addressed in future research so that this concept is further explored empirically.

Thirdly, I investigated the participants' practice of using double discourses of culture. Many participants were seen utilizing both the essentialist view and the processual view in their everyday practice. Relying on Gerd Baumann's empirical theory of double discursive competence, I analyzed how ICWs used both discourses. Some participants attained a capacity for selectively using one or both of the two discourses to their benefit. This ability seems to be a quality that can be included in the concept of *diasporic habitus*. Despite the salience of the processual discourse among social researchers, both essentialist and processual discourses are valuable in learning about the sophisticated culture-making projects that take place everywhere.

The ideas and concepts generated in this chapter show possibilities for further empirical research. The analysis of the research findings included in this chapter should be considered groundwork for introducing new concepts to missiology. Thus the extent of this report was limited to developing those three analytic concepts to only a moderate theoretical level. In order to develop these analytic themes further into working theories, it would be necessary to expand the literature base and make more extensive data comparisons. It may be possible to turn each of these three themes into a separate research project. I delimited myself from pursuing these efforts in this study since it would considerably expand its scope. The topics of intercultural social processes and *diasporic habitus* seem to warrant further empirical research in the future.

8

Conclusions, Implications, and Recommendations

THE PURPOSE OF THIS study was to explore the nature, contributing factors, and outcomes of intercultural social experiences of international Christian workers (ICWs) on multicultural teams (MCTs) that worked in a North African country (NAC). The conclusions in this chapter, drawn from the research findings and analyses, mainly address the three conceptual themes developed in chapter 7. Missiological implications are derived from these themes. First, the understandings gained about intercultural social processes (ISPs) suggest revisiting existing mission theories in light of complex processes occurring in mission contexts. Second, the bi-directional relationship between intercultural social processes (ISPs) and personal changes in international Christian workers (ICWs) has important implications for mission organizations in conducting member care and training for their ICWs. Thirdly, the practice of using double discourses of culture shows the need for reflexivity in missiology. Then recommendations for further research are made. This chapter, and thus the book, will close with some personal remarks.

INTERCULTURAL SOCIAL PROCESSES IN MISSION

One of the key analyses in this research is that both the context of NAC with its people, customs, and social structures and the context of MCTs, with all the various diversities of their members, influence the intercultural social experiences of ICWs and guide them in constructing their mental models of a NAC culture and an MCT culture. The two seemingly separate experiences represent a complex, interwoven intercultural social process that leads to personal changes in these ICWs. This study finds that the intensity and complexity of this process mediate personal changes that happen to these ICWs. It was argued that the factors within MCTs that cause intra-team tensions and conflicts also increase the degree of intensity and complexity of the intercultural social process. In other words, multicultural teams are likely to engender more *turbulence* in the intercultural social process.

With limited comparative data of ICWs of same-culture teams, I am careful not to state conclusively that ICWs who work with MCTs experience more significant personal changes. However, from the result of this study one can anticipate that personal changes experienced by those in MCTs would be, if not more or greater, at least *different* from those in same-culture teams. It would also depend on what kind of same-culture teams we are discussing. As shown throughout this project, "culture" as a moving concept is hard to nail down; it is not constructive to put it in a narrowly defined rigid conceptual jar. Some same-culture teams may have even more diversities than some multicultural teams. An important lesson to be learned here is that the more diverse or varied the group of people we study, the greater the need for different research tools to recognize the complexity and analyze the data accordingly.

A missiological implication of this conclusion is that there is a need to revisit existing mission theories in light of the fluid concept of "culture" and the complex intercultural social processes that are taking place in virtually every mission context. Building intercultural relationships or international partnerships in missions means understanding the intercultural contact zone as a liminal space of contestation in which complex and turbulent intercultural social processes occur. These processes are likely to bring significant changes over time to those engaged in the contact zone. Although the outcomes of these intercultural relations are often unpredictable and not guaranteed, going into these relations with a keen awareness of potential volatility and uncertainty would remind ICWs to maintain their humility and motivate them to retain a learner posture.

ICWs actively develop and build their cultural reality in the context of their lived experiences with multicultural teams—their teammates and organizations—and the local realities defined by social, political, relational, cultural, and religious dynamics. This study has shown that members of culturally diverse teams need to learn how to negotiate social norms and navigate through murky waters of disorienting social situations. An easy way out is to reify essentialized cultures and put a bulk of the blame on culture. In contrast, character flaws or interpersonal issues might be the actual culprit for the disharmony. This is why cross-cultural management theories based on an essentialist view of culture can be a convenient but poisonous solution to problems in multicultural teams. They may seem practical and even helpful in the short term. Still, it is difficult to imagine how a perspective that tends to turn people into an essentialized Other can help Christian workers build a vibrant Christian community together. It seems that "managerial" and utilitarian perspectives have penetrated some portion of missiological thoughts and trickled down into training materials for intercultural ministries.[1] It raises concerns about how such a view can have negative repercussions for these institutions and organizations in which many *ethne* have gathered together to serve in global mission. For these organizations, there needs to be a fresh perspective that considers the complexity of intercultural social processes as many *nations* and *peoples*, not only European-descent people, gather together to serve in Christian mission.

CHANGES THAT HAPPEN TO PERSONS IN MISSION

This study investigated the nature of personal changes in international Christian workers (ICWs) and found a robust bi-directional relationship between intercultural social life and personal changes in ICWs. They influence one another and build a capacity that sustains and perhaps further enhances certain dispositions in them. Personal changes in these ICWs are not only individually influential but also have a large impact on their multicultural teams (MCTs), which in turn affect the dispositions and social behavior of these groups and teams of ICWs. This understanding led to developing a notion of *diasporic habitus* as a system of internalized dispositions and schemes acquired through repeated practices by those who lead an intercultural, diasporic life. It accounts for the changes that ICWs experience in their lives over extended exposure to intercultural social living. The development of *diasporic habitus* among ICWs should be explored further through empirical research.

There is a lack of missiological research that investigates significant personal changes that occur to international Christian workers. While many mission theorists and practitioners are aware that intercultural living brings about personal changes, their understandings seem to be only anecdotal at best. The notion of *diasporic habitus* can provide an empirical, comprehensive theory of change in the person participating in intercultural missions. It takes into account the intensity and complexity of sociocultural influences upon the person. It shows that the changes in these persons are social and structural, as seen in the similar social code of conduct practiced by ICWs in NAC as part of their shared *diasporic habitus*. Being exposed to diverse people can raise questions about the

1. Escobar, "Evangelical Missiology."

reality itself. These internal questions raised in one's mind can have a powerful impact on the person's change in perspective, behaviors, and social outlook, which *diasporic habitus* represents.

Diasporic habitus has implications for missionary member care, normally approached from a counseling or psychological perspective. The notion of *diasporic habitus* has a strong psychological element to it since it foregrounds major changes in a person through intercultural social processes and how these changes continue to shape the person's life and sociality. Cultural homelessness, which becomes part of some ICWs' *diasporic habitus*, is a notion that resulted from psychological studies of so-called multicultural persons. Although relatively late in joining discussions on globalization compared to other human sciences, the discipline of psychology has come a long way in addressing intercultural issues.[2] Three relatively new and somewhat overlapping sub-fields of psychology show potential for helping missiological research on changes in persons. These are acculturation psychology, multicultural identity theory, and culture and psychology.[3] Insights from these sub-fields of psychological study can help us understand the development of *diasporic habitus* among ICWs.

However, there does not seem to be an active conversation between scholars in these sub-fields of psychology and cultural and social anthropology, the very discipline that pioneered the notion of "culture" and strove to tackle myriad related issues. Surprisingly, there is almost no dialogue between them; they rarely cite each other's works. It is not clear if they are aware if they are addressing some of the same intercultural issues. In its true interdisciplinary fashion, missiology can perhaps converse with these fields of study for fruitful research and even engender scholarly discussions across these academic disciplines.

REFLEXIVITY IN MISSIOLOGY

The third significant analysis from this study was the participants' practice of using double discourses of culture. They utilized an essentialist perspective of culture along with a processual view in their everyday life. This is an acquired adeptness that becomes part of their intercultural capacity, or perhaps *diasporic habitus*. Recognizing this pattern among *diasporic* persons is helpful in understanding culture-making projects within groups that inhabit complex intercultural spaces. There is still much that needs

---

2. Arnett, "The Psychology of Globalization."

3. See Sam and Berry, *The Cambridge Handbook of Acculturation Psychology*; Benet-Martínez and Hong, *The Oxford Handbook of Multicultural Identity*; Chiu and Hong, *Social Psychology of Culture*; Leung, Chiu, and Hong, *Cultural Processes*.

to be uncovered about how these happen in various contexts. This analysis leads me to think that missiological researchers need to become aware of both essentialist and processual perspectives being used in context. Unfortunately, these two perspectives often appear indistinguishable in missiological research. These two discourses are not given sufficient attention by mission scholars and practitioners. Some seem to subscribe to an essentialist perspective without carefully evaluating its cause, impact, or credibility. Indeed, the essentialist view seems to be deeply embedded in many international mission organizations' social structures and processes. Perhaps the easiest way to respond is to criticize and deconstruct such a view. It would be vital, however, that the essentialist discourse is not simply dismissed or downplayed as wrong. Instead, it needs to be actively engaged as a way in which these organizations and teams construct and perpetuate their model of social worlds, no matter how distant it may be from the realities on the ground. The motives and reasons that mission practitioners, scholars, and organizations use this framework of dominant, essentialist discourses of culture need to be investigated further.

New studies in missiology cannot merely recycle old mission theories without considering the assumptions of those theories and the contexts in which they were first developed. It is not that earlier mission theories are entirely irrelevant or not useful anymore. However, it needs to be recognized that those theories were developed to address specific issues in specific contexts from particular positioned views in the past. When mission researchers deal with new issues in new settings, they must first recognize their positioned perspective and recalibrate their reference point so that their biases can be accounted for before approaching new issues or new contexts in intercultural missions. When they do, they will perhaps see something entirely unexpected or different from the past views. Mission theories popularized in the past need to be seen as products of their particular contexts and evaluated as such before being reused and recycled in new missiological discourses. Unfortunately, past theories are too often taken out of their original context and applied to new settings without careful evaluations.

It is puzzling to see mission scholars who blindly subscribe to and perpetuate theories and concepts built on essentialist ideologies without a careful and thorough investigation of the trustworthiness of those theories. What immediately comes to mind are many popular applications of the people group thinking paradigm and the national characterization model by Hofstede and others. It is perhaps wise for missiologists to heed Baumann's advice and see mission contexts through a lens of double discursive competence.[4] It

---

4. Baumann, *Contesting Culture*; *The Multicultural Riddle*.

would also be beneficial to pay attention to Brubaker's compelling argument for distinguishing between categories of analysis and categories of practice, between tools of analysis and objects of analysis.[5] Tendencies of reifying essentialized culture in past missiological models should be seen as objects of our research, not instruments. Any mission practice that reifies culture should be treated as a category of practice, not a category of analysis and be examined as an object of missiological analysis.

It is known that humans cannot live without categories, for we are "intrinsically category-makers."[6] However, could simplistic, reductionistic categories too frequently used in missions, even if for the sake of promoting global missions, explain complex social realities? They simply cannot. Therefore, we must give a benefit of the doubt when we meet people whom we previously put in the categories, such as "high context," "low power distance," "Amazigh" or "Kabyle Berber." Some seasoned missiologists have pointed out that these simple categories and models can be a beginning point, a preliminary way to start thinking about social realities. However, it is necessary to question these constructed categories, even—perhaps, especially—the ones developed in this study. There are probably benefits as well as limits of these categories. What might those be? This is the question that we must ask before promoting these reductionistic categories. It seems that what we need is reflexivity, the type of self-awareness that incorporates an understanding of our positioned, situated, and biased realities due to our individual and collective history.[7] It seems that missiology has largely been lacking in this area, but it does not need to stay that way.

RECOMMENDATIONS FOR FURTHER RESEARCH

While thinking of possible recommendations from the results of this study, it occurs to me that this study is far from complete. It seems that it is ending as soon as it barely scratched the surface and began to uncover a tiny part of a much larger "thing." With this sentiment and the posture of a humbled learner, I make the following recommendations for further research for other missiological researchers and myself.

5. Brubaker, "Categories of Analysis"; *Ethnicity without Groups*, 2004; "The 'Diaspora' Diaspora."

6. Lee, "Interdisciplinary Reflections."

7. Bourdieu, *Distinction*, 467.

Investigating Different Intercultural-Multicultural "Fields"

First, it seems clear that more empirical studies are needed in various intercultural-multicultural "fields" of complex cultural flows. While it is a welcome view that there is an increasing number of research on migrants, refugees, and diaspora communities, many of them are conducted as studies of some ethnic migrant groups in some cities or countries as isolated, reified groups. They need to be studied in conjunction with other groups who occupy the same social space to capture the dynamic intercultural social processes taking place. Missiological research often focuses on particular ethnic, cultural, or religious groups as isolated cases. While much can be learned through these studies, they often become too predictable with their findings, providing few surprises and new conceptual insights. Conclusions seem to be already drawn before the actual research is conducted.[8] This type of analysis makes it difficult to see the connections, flows, and influences shaping those groups since they are continually reinventing themselves, are probably not bound by the labels we put on them and are unlikely to be internally homogeneous as they first seemed.

Studying Other Research Populations

Second, it would be helpful if similar research is conducted with different types of research populations. For example, a new study can focus on same-culture teams in NAC or investigate ICWs in multicultural teams (MCTs) who serve in a country or a region where religious freedom is rigorously protected by the law. How would the research findings be different if this study was conducted among ICWs in MCTs that worked in Manila, Sydney, Brussels, Montreal, Nairobi, or Bangkok? What could we find if it was conducted in NAC with teams composed only of Koreans, White Americans, or Nigerians?

Using Quantitative and Mixed Research Methods

Third, the findings in this research are preliminary results of studying personal changes in people who pursue intercultural living. Thus, this research can be expanded further to incorporate other research methods to develop theories. Other research methods can be tried, including case studies, quantitative methods using surveys, and mixed methods to advance knowledge. Various single case or multi-case studies can be designed. By changing the unit of analysis from individual Christian workers to multicultural teams or mission organizations, we may also broaden our understanding of intercultural social

8. See Baumann, *Contesting Culture*, 9–10.

processes. For example, one can attempt a multi-case study of several multicultural teams in the same country or region, a comparative case study of several teams in different countries of the same organization, or a single case study of a large international mission organization with global and historical significance. Questionnaires and surveys can be developed to quantify ICWs' dispositions, intercultural awareness, or cultural homelessness and test hypotheses drawn from the results of this study.

If cultural diversity, usually judged by the number of languages and nationalities, increases within an MCT or an international mission organization (IMO), do interpersonal conflicts increase? Is *diasporic habitus* more developed among those exposed to the diversity of cultures for a longer period? These are some of the questions that can be answered through quantitative research. Mixed methods that include elements of both qualitative and quantitative inquiry can also be employed. These can combine various data collecting methods, such as questionnaires, surveys, interviews, and focus groups. Methodological considerations must match the goal and purpose of the research project. This study was intentionally designed and conducted as an open, loose, and exploratory inquiry. Its results now present many possibilities for more focused, narrowed-down research that could produce new empirical theories.

Conversing with Intercultural Sub-Fields of Psychology

Fourth, as previously mentioned, bringing psychological sub-fields that focus on intercultural social dynamics in a conversation with anthropological and sociological theories shows promise. In this study, the intercultural social process was explored initially using the conceptual lens of cultural hybridization and later interpreting the data via Bourdieu's practice theory. I stopped short of further investigating the psychological results of these processes. There is a potential for fruitful research in the latest scholarship in the emerging fields of acculturation psychology, multicultural identity, and culture and psychology. These fields were beyond the scope of this study and not pursued.

However, it should be noted that there is little to no conversation between these emerging intercultural sub-fields within psychology and the schools of thought in which cultural hybridization theory and practice theory were developed. In other words, psychologists are generally not conversing with anthropologists and sociologists and vice versa about these complicated, entangled concepts about humans in an intricate, diversifying and globalizing social world. Perhaps missiology can—should—provide a space for these different human sciences to come together in ongoing discussions, along with historians, theologians, and biblical scholars for mutual benefits for the sake of *missio Dei*. Making connections between cultural hybridization processes at micro and meso-levels and insights of multicultural identity theories and/or acculturation psychology have room to grow for analyzing complex social phenomena that happen at the intersection of global cultural flows.

Exploring Practice, Community, and Hybridization

Fifth, this study shows the potential of using practice theory in conjunction with the hybridization theory for interpreting complex social contexts. This study was designed with cultural hybridization theory as its primary conceptual framework. Bourdieu's practice theory was only later incorporated during the analysis of the research data and interpreting the findings. As García Canclini argues, combining cultural hybridization theory with other robust social theories can be beneficial in analyzing complex sociocultural phenomena.[9] The use of cultural hybridization perspective and practice theory was found to be fruitful for this research. However, it was difficult to incorporate practice theory more fully in this study since I discovered its relevance only as I conducted data analysis and could only incorporate it into the study at a late stage. This is an area that needs further exploration and experiments in application to missiology.

Building on practice theory, Lave and Wenger develop a concept of "the community of practice."[10] Although it is not discussed in depth in this study, the research results imply that multicultural teams (MCTs) function as both formal and informal learning communities. *Habitus*, by definition, is a system of acquired or *learned* schemes of dispositions, capacities, and social behaviors. *Diasporic habitus* is not developed alone; individual ICWs do not learn and adapt in isolation. It is produced in ongoing social relations and social practice. This whole area of community and practice can be further explored both theoretically and empirically.

Revisiting Mission Concepts and Practices

Sixth, this research produces an understanding of complex intercultural social processes and their impact on how international Christian workers changed over time. If combined with some new potential projects mentioned above, the knowledge generated from this study can be used to compare, evaluate, or even revise existing concepts in mission theories. I have

9. García Canclini, "The State of War," 41–42.
10. Lave and Wenger, *Situated Learning*; Wenger, *Communities of Practice*.

previously mentioned branches of people group thinking and the national character model of culture as concepts that needed to be reevaluated and revised. There are also notions such as culture shock,[11] the Third Culture Kids (TCK),[12] and the bi-cultural bridge[13] that some found quite useful in mission practices. However, these concepts were developed many decades ago in particular contexts that were later generalized to other settings. Would these notions still be able to hold their ground today in different contexts? For example, would the Third Culture Kids notion, initially developed from observations of American children abroad, apply to Indian migrant children who live in the suburbs of London? Or could experiences of a child of American missionaries, born in Southern California, lived for ten years in North Africa attending a local school, and learned to speak four languages fluently, be explained or understood using the notion of the bi-cultural bridge? What if the child's missionary parents were actually Korean immigrants who went through their higher education in the US? How would these idiosyncrasies change things for this child? Could those dated notions be applied to people who live more globally and historically entangled lives? Therefore, it would be helpful to review the claims of these notions from the past with the following questions: can these concepts still be retained and used in today's contexts? Do they have weak areas that could be strengthened with the help of a more recent scholarship? What are the elements in these concepts that should be discarded or revised? Can the impact of their historical backgrounds be reevaluated in light of their context? These questions can strengthen where these concepts are lacking and provide more clarity in the areas where they are limited or even irrelevant due to their contextual factors. It seems more important than ever that complexity and reflexivity are incorporated in claims of both old and new mission concepts.

Further Application of This Research

Seventh and last, the results of this study can be used for further investigation of some topics intentionally omitted from this study. These omissions include intercultural leadership, the influence of gender, marital status, family situation, the spiritual impact on the lives of ICWs, ministry issues in a Muslim context, and missional theologies of these ICWs. Although they were not a part of my research focus, these factors were related to the sociocultural processes involved in the intercultural life of these workers.

11. Oberg, "Cultural Shock."

12. Useem and Downie, "Third-Culture Kids."

13. Hiebert, *Anthropological Insights for Missionaries*; Hiebert, *Anthropological Reflections*.

While some of these are briefly touched on in interviews and demographic questionnaires, they were not closely examined. Each area could be a separate research project in its own right.

There is also the issue of language learning and its impact on ICWs that could be probed further. Some ICWs had to learn both English as the team language and a local language simultaneously. Others only had to learn a local language. Some came to NAC as multilingual, adding Arabic, French, and/or one of the Berber languages to their repertoires of languages; others learned to speak another language fluently for the first time in their lives. These add further complexity to the social life of these participants. As these linguistic factors are very much intertwined with their intercultural social experiences, it would be worth paying closer attention to them to advance knowledge of intercultural social processes.

CLOSING REMARKS

My interest in this research topic began back in 2004 when I joined a multicultural team (MCT) of an international mission organization (IMO) and moved to a city in the North African country (NAC). During the decade that I lived there, I got to know over a hundred colleagues who served on several different teams scattered across the region. They altogether had more than twenty national or ethnic backgrounds. While I worked with these colleagues in various ways, I witnessed instances of misunderstandings, miscommunication, and conflicts unfolding in front of my eyes; I was even involved in some of them myself. Initially, I believed that implementing the standard cross-cultural ministry model of improving our understanding of cultural differences and adapting our communication style was the best solution to address these issues. Still, at some point, I began to sense that something was lacking in this model.

I realized after a while that shared experiences with these colleagues for an extended time helped us overcome the difficulties of having so much cultural and linguistic diversity within our teams. Differences in cultures were no longer stressed in team life so much; instead, it was what we experienced, felt, shared, struggled, and did together as a community with a common purpose and vision that became most central to us. In this process, what inadvertently happened was that we built a new hodgepodge of a group "culture." At the same time, individuals on the team, as they went through these communal experiences together, developed not only new skills and perspectives but also new ways of behaving and relating that contributed to shaping the social practices accepted by all of us. The social environment of the multicultural team was "a Third Space," the liminal space in which international Christian workers (ICWs) entered and were changed. Realizing these about our team life instilled in me a sense of gratitude and hope for the kind of community we could build, perhaps, in any intercultural social context.

There is something to be learned from anthropologist Abu-Lughod's observation of everyday lived experiences of Muslim women in the Arab world.[14] She insightfully writes:

> To think about the big picture means remembering that no person is an island. People are involved with others—with their families, their friends, their villages or neighborhoods, and their countries . . . . All of us are shaped by forces that engage wide groups and that go well beyond us. We all live in real time, our worlds marked by change, argument, and social contestation.[15]

Indeed, not one of these international Christian workers whom I interviewed was an island. They were deeply involved with their teammates, local NAC friends, and other Christian expatriates who shared similar values. Their social life was complicated. There were many sources of influence and a variety of social connections across cultural boundaries. The lived realities of these intercultural social experiences do not necessarily lead them to invoke and celebrate the idea of cultural hybridity. Rather than being "something" or "someone" to be scrutinized, hybridity reminds us to consider *the type of lens* we put on to look at the social world. In other words, cultural hybridity should be a tool, a lens, and a perspective of analysis rather than an object of observation and analysis. When the social world is seen in this way, it opens up new ways of interpreting social realities, which are complicated, historically entangled, and quite messy.

A few more words need to be said about cultural hybridity, a central concept in this study. This research shows that everyone is a cultural hybrid, but everyone is, with all their unique history and dispositions, a *different* cultural hybrid. This view makes essentialist claims about cultures and ethnic groups untenable. At the same time, it helps us guard against shallow multiculturalism or an increasingly ethnicized hybridism that seems to be the fashion of the day.

As noted by García Canclini, cultural hybridization may be too broad a term that it becomes too confounding with many kinds of social phenomena and processes placed under its single label.[16] Instead, it should be understood as an umbrella term that refers to a general process of incorporating

14. Abu-Lughod, *Muslim Women Need Saving?*
15. Abu-Lughod, *Muslim Women Need Saving?*, 224.
16. García Canclini, "Introduction: Hybrid Cultures," xxv.

and mixing various cultural elements in various contexts at various levels. When cultural hybridity is viewed in this way, it becomes a useful interpretive lens and even a salient conceptual framework that helps us understand social phenomena. This is the reason that in this study I try not to use the term *cultural hybridity* to refer to specific phenomena observed among international Christian workers or within multicultural teams; I limit my use of the term to more general, broader social processes. However, it can be understood as a particular social process if the researcher focuses on a micro-level phenomenon. Then the researcher must clarify the usage when utilizing this noun term in a micro-level social analysis.

I chose the title of this study as "Hybridizing Mission" to give an air of ambivalence to it in a manner similar to how others have used the word "mission." David Bosch's magnum opus most easily comes to mind.[17] This book title implies that Christian mission is both *hybridizing* and *hybridized*. This is really not a novel idea, although the language may be new. In their lifelong scholarship, both Andrew Walls and Lamin Sanneh have shown how, throughout its history, Christian mission has contributed to hybridizing cultures and cultures have contributed to hybridizing Christian mission and thus Christianity.[18] This study shows that current international Christian workers do reflect what Walls, Sanneh, and others have found in their study of the history of Christian mission. This research finds that Christian mission, through its entangled and complicated history around the globe, is not explainable apart from the idea of cultural hybridity and the cultural process of hybridization. Burrows recognizes the ubiquity of the hybridizing process in Christian mission when he writes, "[H]ybridity is not only possible but inevitable in the process of an individual's or a people's achieving mature Christian identity in a cultural setting such as Korea, Papua New Guinea, Costa Rica, the United States, Jamaica, or India."[19]

When international Christian workers enter a new cultural setting, they bring some of the cultural and social elements from their "old home," find new elements in their "new home," and incorporate some of them into their everyday life practice. They learn to accept, reject, mix, and blend these different elements at hand, and over time, some significant changes take place in them. In a sense, it may be somewhat crudely said that they are *hybridized*. Through interactions and negotiations in their social environment, the changes that happen in them catalyze and influence subsequent change processes among their colleagues, national Christians, their teams,

17. Bosch, *Transforming Mission*.
18. Walls, *The Missionary Movement*; Sanneh, *Translating the Message*.
19. Burrows, "Theological Ideals, Cross-Cultural Realities," 30.

and organizations. Perhaps slowly, but almost certainly, all these partakers in the social process experience changes in their individual lives and the larger social environment. It again indicates that Christian mission is hybridizing people and society. In this ongoing process that spans not just years or decades but perhaps many centuries, countless people have come in contact with the gospel. They would hear the theological statement that *Isa al-Masih* or *Yesu Grisdo* or Jesus Christ is *kyrios* from Christian messengers. This story continues in and through the lives of people like these ICWs in this North African country and others around the world.

The reality is, however, not that rosy and bright. This study contains many stories of interpersonal conflicts and tensions. There are not only examples in this study of what Jane Samson refers to as "brothering" and "othering," but also the joy of "being brothered" and the pain of "being othered" in the lived experiences of my participants.[20] I recently heard the news that between the time when interviews took place and writing these remarks, several participants have moved on, permanently leaving NAC and their MCTs behind. Some of them have remained in NAC, although they have resigned from their organizations. Others are struggling to establish a new business or renew their long-term resident visa in the country. It is hard to know the reasons for the struggles of some of these workers that drag on and the departures of some team members that seem premature. It is my understanding, based on what I know, that a variety of factors discussed throughout this study played a large part in their departures from NAR or resignation from their teams or other current challenges they may face.

The everyday life of an international Christian worker is often filled with inner struggles, relational tensions, and external challenges. It reminds us of Jesus' words about his disciples, "They are not of this world, even as I am not of it." (John 17:16) Jesus, who was in his earthly "tabernacle" for a while, experienced human tensions and conflicts in all their agony and viciousness. Jesus also said to his disciples, "As the Father has sent me, I am sending you." (John 20:21) What are the implications for these sayings of Jesus as they pertain to the pains and struggles these Christian workers experience? How do we serve as God's agents in this world as the body of Christ with so much diversity and differences?

There are no easy answers, but perhaps we can find a glimpse of hope in the words of Johannes, one of my interlocutors. He reflected on his relationships with his teammates. Then with the conviction and confidence of someone who had experienced it firsthand, Johannes said, "If people from different backgrounds, different nationalities can still choose to be brothers

20. Samson, *Race and Redemption*.

and sisters, and be one body, *that is something beautiful.* That, I would not want to miss. When you get to know people from other backgrounds, it's no longer a Korean or an American. But it is Seth, it is Chulsoo, it is somebody with a name that you know well that has become *a dear friend.*"[21] These inspired words remind me that I too have always been that somebody with a name, well known to my colleagues and teammates as a dear friend during the years of serving as an international Christian worker with multicultural teams. This timeless relational, communal foundation to Christian mission is perhaps the most needed piece to solve the complex puzzle of cultural differences and diversity in global missions.

21. Emphasis is added.

Appendix A

Letter of Informed Consent

Dear participant,

Thank you for your willingness to participate in this research. I am a PhD student at Trinity International University in Deerfield, Illinois, USA. The research in which you are about to participate is designed to explore various cultural processes experienced by cross-cultural workers like yourself. I will ask some questions about your personal experiences of cultural adaptation in this country and working with your multicultural team. Your thoughts and experiences will help me learn about how people in cross-cultural and multi-cultural settings experience cultural changes in their life, work, and relationships.

If you are participating in an interview, it will last about one hour. If you are participating in a group discussion, it will take about 90 minutes. These conversations will be audio-recorded so that I can focus on listening rather than taking notes. The recordings will be transcribed to be used later for this research. Audio recordings will be deleted at the end of the research process. I would like to ask your permission to record this interview. Please be assured that your identity will be protected. Any information you provide will be held in strict confidence. Please know that your participation in this research is entirely voluntary. You are free to withdraw at any time during this study.

At the end of the interview and/or the group discussion, I will ask you if I could receive a copy of your last three or four newsletters by email. Again, this will remain confidential and used solely for this research. Sharing your newsletters with me is also fully voluntary; you are free to decline this request.

Thank you once again for your participation in this research.

Best regards,
Peter Lee

"I acknowledge that I have been informed of and understand the nature and purpose of this study and I freely consent to participate."

Name: _____

Signed: _____

Date: _____

Appendix B

Interview Protocol

THIS SECTION INCLUDES SETS of interview topic guides used for interviews with individuals, married couples, and groups. As Joseph A. Maxwell points out, interview questions used in qualitative research should be seen as "the *means* to answering" the research questions rather than *translation* or *operationalization* of the latter.[1]

This field study took this approach of using these questions to guide the participant to share information regarding the subject of the research and to allow for flexible and spontaneous occurrences of interactive dynamics in these interview conversations. Depending on the changing circumstance or newly emerging themes during the field study, I adjusted on the spot in terms of line of questioning and varied questions to probe deeper into the lived experiences of the participants.

PERSONAL INFORMATION

I asked the participants to provide the following personal demographic information by filling out a secure online form. Forty-four out of the forty-nine participants responded and filled out the form online. For the remaining three participants who did not fill out the form, I filled in most of the remaining information myself based on my knowledge of the participants or the content of their interviews. The data was used for analytical purposes.

1. Name

2. Email

3. Age

4. Gender

---

1. Maxwell, *Qualitative Research Design*, 100.

5. Marital status

6. Passport country

7. Professions (current and previous)

8. Place of birth (City/Town, State/Province, Country)

9. Place of childhood (City/Town, State/Province, Country)

10. Ethnic background

11. Denominational or church background

12. Mother tongue or first language

13. Languages spoken

14. Number of years in the country

15. Number of years with the team/company

16. Number of members on the team

17. Passport countries of team members

18. Team language

INDIVIDUAL AND COUPLE INTERVIEW QUESTIONS (INITIAL)

Below are the questions and follow-up questions that I used as my interview guide in conducting early interviews during the initial field research trip that I took in May 2018. Depending on the person and the circumstance, the order, as well as the actual questions used, were changed. These were used for interviews with both individuals and married couples. My primary goal for asking these questions was to probe into my participants' personal experiences and gather rich data that answer my research questions.

Opening:

- Could you tell me your story of how you came to this country and how you ended up joining your team?

  [Follow-up] Could you tell me your earlier life? (your immediate family; how you grew up; your cultural background)?

Initial Adaptation Process:

- Could you tell me what your initial cultural adjustment was like when you first arrived in this country? Tell me some stories.

- What was most positive or enjoyable about your cultural adjustment process? Why? What were the results? An example?

- What was most negative or difficult? Why? What were the results? An example?

- Would you say that you are still culturally changing in some ways? How?

- How do you experience your home culture when you return to your home country? What are some factors that contribute to that experience?

- Can you compare yourself before coming here and the present time and tell me any significant cultural changes that you (or your spouse) notice in yourself after living and working here? (or what are the major cultural differences in yourself between "then" and "now"?) Any change in your lifestyle? Change in the way you relate or socialize? Change in the way you do your ministry?

- What specific factors do you think contributed to these cultural changes that took place in your life?

- In what kind of cultural context do you feel most comfortable now? (Where is your cultural home, or where do you feel you belong culturally?) Since when and how did you begin to feel that way?

Mediation of MCT on Adaptation Process:

- Can you describe your team, team members, and/or your team life in general? What is your role on the team? Can you explain a little history of your team here—when, where, who, what, why, and how?

- What is distinctive about your team? How do they play out in team life and ministry? Any examples?

- What do you appreciate about your team, team members, or team life? Is there anything that you wish you could change about your team? What are they?

- In what ways did your team influence your initial cultural adjustment?

- In what ways does your team influence your current life and ministry?

- In what ways has your team influenced the cultural changes that took place in you?
- In what ways has the local culture/people influenced your team and team life? Examples?

Their Understanding of Culture:

- When you have a new team member, how would you explain the cultures of your team members and the local people? How would you explain cultural differences between them and how to address them?
- What were the most significant factors (personal experiences, training, or books) in developing your understanding of these matters?
- Could you tell me a bit about the kind of cross-cultural training program or education you've received, any books or materials you studied that you found helpful?

Closing:

- Is there anything you would like to add?
- Debrief: Is there anything you would like to ask regarding this research or this interview?
- Follow-up permission: If I have some further questions, would it be okay for me to contact you in the future?
- Newsletter permission: Would it be possible for me to receive by email your last several newsletters? (Explain confidentiality; it's only for the purpose of this study; totally voluntary)
- Training materials permission: Could you send me the training materials that you shared about? (Explain confidentiality; it's only for this study; totally voluntary)
- May I ask which "company" you are working with?

INDIVIDUAL AND COUPLE INTERVIEW QUESTIONS (REVISED AFTER INITIAL FIELD RESEARCH)

While conducting several interviews during the initial phase of the field research, I began to realize that some of the questions were more effective than others, and some were not as relevant. The line of questioning did not always flow well. More seriously, some items were imposing on the participants to provide analytical assessments rather than to tell concrete stories of their lived experiences. It was evident that some adjustments needed to be made. The following is the new interview questioning guide used throughout the second phase of field research.

Opening:

1. Could you share your story of how you came to this country?
   - If this didn't include personal, family, and cultural background, ask: what was your earlier life like? (Your immediate family, how you grew up, your cultural background)
2. How did you get to join your team?
   - Why did you join your current organization?
   - How attractive was the multicultural facet of team life?

Initial Adaptation Process:

3. What was your initial cultural adjustment like when you first arrived in this country?
   - Can you walk me through the first week of your arrival?
4. What were the cultural adjustments you had to make?
   - What were the results?
   - Examples?
5. Have you gone back to visit your "sending country"?
   - How did you experience your home culture when you returned to your home country?
   - What are some things that had an impact on that experience?
6. Do you notice any changes in yourself? Please explain.
   - Can you compare yourself before coming here and the present time and tell me any significant cultural changes that you (or your spouse) notice in yourself after living and working here? (or what are the major cultural differences in yourself between "then" and "now"?)
   - Any change in your lifestyle?
   - Any change in the way you relate or socialize?
   - Any change in the way you do your ministry?
7. What were some difficult experiences in adapting to NAC?

8. In what kind of cultural setting do you feel most comfortable now? (Where is your cultural home, or where do you feel you belong culturally?)

   – Since when and how did you begin to feel that way?

   – How comfortable do you feel living in NAC now?

Mediation of MCT on Adaptation Process:

9. Can you describe your team, team members, and/or your team life in general?

   – What is your role on the team?

   – Can you explain a little history of your team here—when, where, who, what, why, and how?

10. What were some prior expectations you had before coming to join the team?

    – What was different between your expectations and the actual experiences?

11. Could you describe the initial training you received in your sending country?

    – How about the initial training you received in NAC?

12. What do you do in team meetings?

    – Could you explain in detail a typical team meeting, team retreat, or gathering?

    – Could you describe the last, most recent team meeting?

13. Have you had any difficult experiences with the team?

    – Could you give me a specific example?

Involvement in the Local Cultural Setting:

14. In a typical week, with whom do you spend the most amount of time?

    – What do you do with them?

15. What is a typical day like for you?

    – What about the most recent typical day?

Closing:

16. Is there anything you would like to add?

17. Debrief: Is there anything you would like to ask regarding this research or this interview?

18. Follow-up permission: If I have some further questions, would it be okay for me to contact you in the future?

19. Newsletter permission: Would it be possible for me to receive by email your last several newsletters? (Explain confidentiality; it's only for the purpose of this study; totally voluntary)

20. Training materials permission: Could you send me the training materials that you shared about? (Explain confidentiality; it's only for this study; totally voluntary)

INTERVIEWING COUPLES

In many cases, it was more convenient to interview married couples together rather than interviewing them separately. While I used for married couples the same questions prepared for individual interviews, I adjusted the interview by treating the couple as "adjuncts of interviewing individuals."[2] It means that I gave due attention to each individual as she or he spoke and showed appropriate respect to the other, facilitating an open and active discussion with both of them. I engaged each of them in a conversational and interactive style, varying the questions and the mode of questioning—sometimes asking the same question to both, asking different ones to each, and asking one to respond to or elaborate on an answer given by another. I intentionally allocated about an hour and a half to interview a couple, whereas one hour was planned for each individual interview. The interactive dynamics of interviewing couples were different from interviewing individuals due to their life experiences as married couples and the conversation being a trilogue rather than a dialogue. This enriched data collected.

GROUP INTERVIEWS

The following questioning route was used in the group interview. At the beginning of the group session, I explained the purpose of and gave instruction for the interview and confirmed each participant's consent for participating and recording the interview session. Combining individual/couple interviews with a group interview aides in collecting rich data

---

2. Yin, *Qualitative Research from Start to Finish*, 148.

since perspectives obtained from these different arenas can improve the credibility of the findings.[3]

There are various issues to watch out for in group interviews. Desire to conform to the group consensus and unequal social power within the group could have influenced the results.[4] Past or present relational issues or conflicts within the team might inhibit honest sharing. It was challenging to identify some of these issues present while conducting group interviews. It is another reason that combining group interviews with individual/couple interviews could be beneficial as some of these issues may be identified.

If a group interview takes place before personal interviews of the group members, discussions that happened in the group might influence responses of participants in personal interviews. If it is conducted after personal interviews, the participants might be affected by others' responses and group interactions in the session; they might be affected by having previously thought about the topic in personal interviews. I determined during the fieldwork that it was simply impossible to control these factors or even account for all these issues in data analysis.

GROUP INTERVIEW QUESTIONS

Opening:

1. [Optional] Please tell us your name, how long you have been working in this country/on this team, where you were before joining this team and what you were doing. (5 min.)

Introductory:

2. Can you briefly (in less than one minute) share about how you came to this country and joined this team? (10 min.)

Transition:

3. Think back to when you first came to this country. What were your first impressions? (5 min.)

4. Can you describe what your initial cultural adaptation process was like? (5 min.)

5. What were enjoyable about adapting to this culture? What were not so enjoyable? (10 min.)

3. Mann, *Research Interview*, 179.
4. Saldaña and Omasta, *Qualitative Research*, 94.

Key Questions:

6. What was particularly helpful about being a part of an MCT? (5 min.)

7. What was particularly challenging about being a part of an MCT? (5 min.)

8. Are you any different because you have been a part of an MCT? If so, how? (10 min.)

9. Are you any different because you have lived in this country? If so, how? (10 min.)

10. [Optional] How might your MCT different from another MCT in another region? (5 min.)

11. [Optional] How might your MCT different from a monocultural team in this country? (5 min.)

Ending Questions:

12. Among everything we talked about, what was most important to you? Why? (10 min.)

13. [Optional] Is there anything that we should have talked about but didn't? (5 min.)

Appendix C

Profile of Participants

	Gender			Marital Status	
Male	Female		Single	Married
19	30		12	37

		Age		
20-29	30-39	40-49	50-59	60+
6	17	15	9	2

	Highest Level of Education Completed			
High School	Some University or Vocational School	Bachelor's	Master's	Doctorate
3	10	19	13	4

Number by Current Passport Country (By Continent)

Africa (3)	Asia (10)	Australia (1)	Europe (13)	N. America (20)	S. America (2)
South Africa (1) *W. Africa (2)	Korea (10)	Australia (1)	Belgium (2) Germany (4) Netherlands (2) *Scandina-via (1) Switzerland (1) UK (3)	Canada (7) USA (13)	*S. America (2)

Country of Birth
(Not Mentioned as Current
Passport Country)

*SE Asia	Korea
1	4

*Name of the country/language generalized to its region due to an increased risk of participants being identified.

Racial/Origin Categories[1]

Asian	Black	Hispanic	White	Two or more
16	2	2	27	1

1. Using these "racial/origin categories" to describe the participants is problematic. It clearly shows limitations and deficiencies of these constructs. Nevertheless, use of these categories is yet another effort to construe the complex entanglements that the participants live with. People do not seem to be able to live without these flawed constructs.

Mother Tongue/First Language		Total Number of Fluent Languages Spoken by Participants (Including Mother Tongue)	
English	18	Four or More	7
Korean	13	Three	11
German	4	Two	21
Dutch	2	One	8
French	2		
Flemish	2		
Spanish	2		
SE Asian*	1		
Scandinavian*	1		
Swiss German	1		
Afrikaans	1		

*Name of the country/language generalized to its region due to an increased risk of participants being identified.

Number of Years in NAC				
20 +	10–19	5–9	2–4	Less than 2
4	13	4	19	7

Number of Passport Countries Represented on Their MCT		Team Language among MCTs	
Six	1	English	Spanish
Five	7	45	2
Four	13		
Three	11		
Two	3		
One	12		

Number of Participants by City/Town

City A	City B	Town C	City D	City E	Town F
13	11	3	5	9	8

Occupation/Professional Platform in NAC

Business	Teaching	NGO	Student	Retired
23	2	12	10	2

Interview Types

Individual	Married Couple	Group
20	15	1

Language Used in Interviews

English	Korean
35	14

Language Profile of Participants who Interviewed in English

Native English Speakers	Speakers of English as 2nd Language	Speakers of English as 2nd language or beyond
18	14	2

*Name of the country/language generalized to its region due to an increased risk of participants being identified.

DETAILS OF INDIVIDUAL INTERVIEWEES

No.	Participant Pseudonym	Age	Gender	Marital Status	Passport Country
1	Youngcheol*	50-59	M	M	Korea
2	Junghoon**	40-49	M	M	Canada
3	Linda*	60-69	F	S	UK
4	Myungsook*	50-59	F	M	Korea
5	Julia*	30-39	F	S	Germany
6	Stefanie*	40-49	F	S	Switzerland
7	Susan	50-59	F	S	USA
8	Thomas	40-49	M	M	Scandinavia+
9	Mikyung	40-49	F	M	Korea
10	Jessica	20-29	F	S	USA
11	Ashley	20-29	F	S	Australia
12	Caitlin	30-39	F	S	South Africa
13	Mila	50-59	F	S	Canada
14	Claudia	30-39	F	M	Germany
15	Haejin	30-39	F	S	Korea
16	Sara	30-39	F	S	Korea
17	Brittany	20-29	F	S	USA
18	Heather	40-49	F	S	USA

* Also participated in a group interview.

** Also participated in a married couple interview.

+ Name of the country/language generalized to its region; this participant has an increased risk of being identified due to the rarity of such a person in NAC.

Racial Category	First Language	Years in NAC	Interview Language
Asian	Korean	20+	Korean
Asian	Korean	5-9	Korean
White	English	20+	English
Asian	Korean	20+	Korean
White	German	10-19	English
White	Swiss German	5-9	English
White	English	20+	English
White	Scandinavian+	10-19	English
Asian	Korean	10-19	Korean
White	English	2-5	English
White	English	<2	English
White	Afrikaans	5-9	English
Asian	Asian+	10-19	English
White	German	<2	English
Asian	Korean	<2	Korean
Asian	Korean	2-5	Korean
White	English	<2	English
Asian	English	10-19	English

DETAILS OF MARRIED COUPLE INTERVIEWEES

No.	Participant	Age	Gender	Marital Status	Passport Country
19	Emma	40-49	F	M	W. Africa+
	Simon	40-49	M	M	W. Africa+
20	Camila	40-49	F	M	S. America+
	Franco	40-49	M	M	S. America+
21	Marie	20-29	F	M	Germany
	Philip	30-39	M	M	Germany
22	John	30-39	M	M	UK
	Amy	30-39	F	M	UK
23	Marcelo	30-39	M	M	Belgium
	Olivia	30-39	F	M	Belgium
24	Kyungja	50-59	F	M	Korea
	Jaehyuk	50-59	M	M	Korea
25	Eunyoung	40-49	F	M	Canada
	Junghoon**	40-49	M	M	Canada
26	Kevin	30-39	M	M	Canada
	Laura	30-39	F	M	Canada
27	Melissa	20-29	F	M	Canada
	Ryan	20-29	M	M	Canada
28	Noa	30-39	F	M	Netherlands
	Johannes	30-39	M	M	Netherlands
29	Jiyoung	40-49	F	M	Korea
	Taeho	40-49	M	M	Korea
30	Donna	50-59	F	M	USA
	James	50-59	M	M	USA
31	Chris	30-39	M	M	USA
	Jennifer	30-39	F	M	USA
32	Cheryl	50-59	F	M	USA
	Bruce	60-69	M	M	USA
33	Joseph	40-49	M	M	USA
	Rachel	40-49	F	M	USA

** *Junghoon* also participated in an individual interview.

Racial Category	First Language	Years in NAC	Interview Language
Black	French	10-19	English
Black	French	10-19	English
Hispanic	Spanish	2-5	English
Hispanic	Spanish	2-5	English
White	German	2-5	English
White	German	2-5	English
White	English	2-5	English
White	English	2-5	English
Biracial	Flemish	2-5	English
White	Flemish	2-5	English
Asian	Korean	10-19	Korean
Asian	Korean	10-19	Korean
Asian	Korean	5-9	Korean
Asian	Korean	5-9	Korean
White	English	2-5	English
White	English	2-5	English
White	English	<2	English
White	English	2-5	English
White	Dutch	2-5	English
White	Dutch	2-5	English
Asian	Korean	2-5	Korean
Asian	Korean	2-5	Korean
White	English	10-19	English
White	English	10-19	English
Asian	Korean	<2	Korean
Asian	Korean	<2	Korean
White	English	2-5	English
White	English	2-5	English
White	English	10-19	English
White	English	10-19	English

+ Name of the country/language is generalized to its region; this participant has an increased risk of being identified due to the rarity of such a person in NAC.

DETAILS OF SAME-CULTURE TEAM COMPARISON INTERVIEWEES

	No. 34	No. 35
Participant Pseudonym	Sungmin*	Corey*
Age	40-49	30-39
Gender	M	M
Marital Status	M	M
Passport Country	Korea	USA
Racial Category	Asian	White
First Language	Korean	English
Years in NAC	5-9	2-5
Interview Language	Korean	English

*These two participants were international Christian workers (ICWs) who were not part of an MCT of international mission organization; Sungmin was part of a team composed only of Korean workers sent by a Korean mission organization while Corey was a member of an American team sent from an American organization. They were interviewed as a comparison sample.

Appendix D

Pilot Study: Intercultural Experiences
of Mission Workers

PURPOSE

The initial purpose of this pilot study was to gain a perspective on the nature of intercultural living that would help with my research design. This pilot probed into international Christian workers' experiences of entering and living in a cultural context different from their initial cultural upbringing. It sought to learn more about the effects on the international Christian workers. Due to a lack of prior empirical studies on sociocultural changes experienced by international Christian workers in connection to cultural hybridity theory, I decided that it would be beneficial to conduct a pilot study and incorporate its findings in the research design. By interviewing several persons who were similar to the research population for this research and asking them about their intercultural experiences, I anticipated gaining information that might help me make informed decisions on research questions and methods for my field study. After having completed field research, I discovered a second purpose for this pilot study and its data: to aid in data analysis and strengthen the credibility of the research. This pilot study report is re-written with these two purposes in mind.

METHODS OF PILOT STUDY

Between February 28 and March 5, 2018, I conducted individual interviews with five career international Christian workers. Four of these participants were current doctoral students at a theological institute in the Chicago area, and one was the spouse of a doctoral student. Before these interviews, I had personally known each of them. I recruited them by explaining the nature and purpose of this pilot study and asking for their participation. All five participants were very cooperative, expressing an interest in participating in this pilot study. In an ideal pilot study, the researcher would typically study a part of the actual research population. In this pilot study, however, it was not possible to work with people in the actual research population due to the scarcity and the limited number of those persons who were being identified as research subjects. Since the research mainly aims to explore social and cultural processes of international Christian workers who work cross-culturally in a different cultural environment on multicultural teams (MCTs) composed of persons of various cultures, it was decided that a pilot study of several international Christian workers who had similar experiences would be conducive to developing and implementing the overall research plan.

This group of participants, despite including only five persons, displayed a right level of diversity among them in terms of gender (two women and three men), countries of service (ten different countries in Asia, Middle East, Western Europe, North America, and North Africa), citizenship (three born US citizens, one naturalized US citizen, and one South Korean citizen), ethnicity (two White Americans and three ethnic Koreans), age (one in the 50s, two in their 40s, two in their 30s), years of field service (three with ten years, one with 11 years, and one with 17 years), their age when they left their home culture (three in their 20s and two in their early 30s), their marital status (one single and four married), and the type of mission team and mission organization they worked with (two were with two different US based organizations while three were members of multicultural teams (MCTs) of three large, international mission organizations). Four of the participants spent most of their growing-up years in culturally homogeneous environments while one grew up having to navigate between two different cultural contexts.

In these semi-structured interviews, I asked questions related to participants' cultural upbringing, initial cultural adjustments after arriving in the field of service, what role their mission team played in their cultural adaptation, any personal changes that were noticeable to them through these intercultural experiences, and where they currently found their "cultural home" or the cultural context in which they felt most comfortable.

Each interview lasted from twenty minutes to forty minutes, averaging about thirty minutes per interview. Three interviews were conducted in English and two in Korean. Because of my existing relationship with the participants and their familiarity with my PhD research, I could quickly move into core issues and collect relevant data even in short interview time.

During the days following the interviews, I transcribed all five interviews in their original language. The two interviews conducted in Korean were not translated since I had bilingual fluency in both Korean and English and could work with both languages at virtually the same academic level. I translated only those sections in the Korean interviews that I include in this report. I imported the transcripts into Nvivo 11 software and conducted an open coding of the five interviews. The initial coding generated several descriptive categories.

After having completed two separate field research trips in May and September 2018, I worked on preparing the collected data for analysis. During February 2019, as a part of my data analysis for this study, I was developing a coding strategy for more complex, extensive data collected from the fieldwork. At this point, I decided to revisit the pilot study data and went through a fresh new coding process, this time using the newer version, Nvivo 12 software. I considered the possible benefits of coding this pilot data again. There were several. First and foremost, it would allow me to practice coding methods; second, there might be helpful analytical insights gained through coding this set of data again; third, re-coding this dataset might generate analytical categories that could be compared with the primary data; fourth, this comparison could strengthen the credibility of my main study.

The new round of coding, just as the previous one, utilized open coding and then axial coding method. It resulted in categories that were related to but somewhat different from and more analytical than the ones produced by the initial coding from early 2018. In the next section, I present re-written findings that are generated through these two separate rounds of coding.

FINDINGS

Among several categories that could be generated through the initial and second round of coding, I chose four as most relevant and insightful for this research. First, the pilot study participants recognized their increased sensitivity toward people from other cultures and a growing awareness of intercultural issues. Second, they attributed their prior intercultural experiences as significant in cultural adaptation to their country of mission service. Third, they mentioned their ministry team as a source of both help and difficulty of cultural adjustments. Fourth, they mostly identified a change in their "cultural home" or a type of "cultural homelessness."[1]

---

1. Vivero and Jenkins, "Existential Hazards"; Hoersting and Jenkins, "No Place to Call"; Liu, *Hybridity and Cultural Home*.

Increasing Cultural Awareness

Four of the participants recognized an increase in their awareness of and sensitivity toward people of other cultures as a significant change in themselves. Eunju indicated that increases in empathy and compassion toward internationals were a substantial change in her. Krissy mentioned an increased openness toward and willingness to include people who were very different from herself. Nathan suggested that he was now more aware of the challenges faced by minorities, migrants, and international students here in the States, which he attributed to his overseas experiences. Stephen also mentioned how his overseas mission experience led him to appreciate his own culture more and helped him to see the cultural factors present in various social situations more clearly.[2]

Three of the participants shared their sense of marginalization and exclusion while serving overseas. Some were due to a lack of language proficiency in the team language or a local language. In addition, Krissy talked about how her missionary identity caused a type of marginalization as she served in a predominantly Muslim country. From what she shared, it is unclear what kind of impact their sense of exclusion and being marginalized had on their growth in cultural awareness. Stephen discussed his experience of being marginalized within his team because he was a cultural minority.

For Nathan, on the other hand, the experience of being excluded seems to have affected his cultural sensitivity and awareness. Nathan, a White American, explained his sense of exclusion went beyond language and had more to do with his ethnicity. He said, "I think . . . people in Asia always see me as different. . . . even when I get to know people, they would still sometimes refer to me . . . it's like a foreign devil or the typical way people refer to foreigners in [the name of the country of service]. So you always feel a little bit like, I'm not quite like you because I have white skin." This experience, while painful, seems to have contributed to developing a keen awareness of how minorities and migrants may feel as they enter a different culture, for he does not see this level of sensitivity among his siblings and parents.

Having Prior Experience of Other Cultures

One thing that the participants indicated as helpful to their cultural adjustment in the country of their service was their prior experience of other cultures. While four participants said that they had very little or no exposure to different cultures while growing up, all of them did have cross-cultural

2. All names have been changed to protect the privacy and security of the pilot study participants.

experiences during teenage years or college through short term mission trips, overseas study, or living overseas. Nathan described an overseas living experience he had during his adolescent years as "a very defining thing." While attending a culturally diverse international school abroad for two years, he recalls that he gained "a much broader picture of what different cultures looked like." Stephen, on the other hand, had a very different experience of growing up between two cultures as a second-generation immigrant in the US. He said, "I grew up Korean . . . in America. I was always jumping back and forth between cultures my whole life as I remember on my application to [the name of his mission organization], it asked how many years of cross-cultural experiences that I've had. I just put my age. It had been my whole life!" This experience of bicultural living in America seems to have had a significant personal impact on his cultural understanding.

Four of the participants had short-term cross-cultural experiences during their young adults or teenage years. Two went on an overseas study program in Europe during college. Three participants had gone on short term mission trips—two of them to countries in Asia and one to an American Indian reservation. One did not go on a short-term mission trip before her international assignment, but she had been on staff at the home office of a large international mission organization and had a chance to meet and interact with many international Christian workers from other countries.

The experiences of these participants suggest that their exposure to other cultures, no matter at what age or in whichever form, was a factor in how they related to people from different cultures and the way they viewed the world. Four of them explicitly gave credit to these prior cross-cultural experiences for preparing them in a variety of ways for their intercultural ministry.

Being Influenced by Team

The ministry teams in which the participants belonged presented both positive and negative experiences. Tension in interpersonal dynamics within the team was a detractor rather than a helper to their cultural adaptation, whereas healthy teams functioned as helpful and supportive resources in their cultural adjustments.

All five participants had something to share about their experiences with their team members and team culture. Eric served with a team composed only of White Americans. He had successfully adapted to the local culture and language and was leading the team. He was often bothered by some teammates who did not adjust well to the country and said negative things about the culture and people. Stephen, who is from an ethnic minority immigrant community in the United States, worked in a culturally diverse ministry context in Europe but with a culturally homogeneous team. He indicated that among all the cultures he was working with, "the White American, southern corporate culture" of his team was most challenging. When Eric moved to another country, he again found himself in a culturally diverse ministry setting. However, he often felt like an outsider when it came to his ministry team.

Eunju, who served in five different countries in Asia, North America, and Western Europe with a large international organization, said that she became used to her multicultural team culture, which she described as primarily "Western." Nathan, who was part of a multicultural team in East Asia, said that his team helped him learn the local language more quickly and provided much of his social needs. His team, which also included long-established citizens of the country where he served, was helpful in terms of getting him adjusted to the local situation. Krissy, who served on a multicultural team in Africa, said that her team provided much needed practical help, and their corporate experiences of the local culture were beneficial in learning and growing in her setting.

Although this limited study and its limited data may not be sufficient to make any finding conclusive, it is notable that three of the participants who reported cultural changes in themselves have worked with multicultural teams over a long period. Stephen, who did not work with multicultural teams, believes that his multicultural upbringing before going overseas helped him understand and successfully deal with situations in an immigrant church context abroad where he served as a pastor and again while engaged in a teaching ministry in a major city in another country.

Developing "Cultural Homelessness"

Four of the five participants explicitly expressed their social preference for culturally diverse environments. When asked about the cultural context in which they felt most comfortable and had the best fit, all five participants, who spent a decade or longer in places outside of their birth country, showed some level of *cultural dissonance* with or *cultural dislocation* from the primary cultural context of their childhood.

Two participants said outright that it was in an international, multicultural setting where they felt most comfortable. Krissy, an ethnic Korean, said that she felt most at ease in an environment where there were diverse people. She reported feeling uncomfortable in a setting where there were only Koreans, even though she used to feel comfortable in those settings in the past, or when she was among only White Americans because it made her feel that she did not belong there. She directly attributes this change to her multicultural, intercultural mission experience overseas.

Stephen, an ethnic Korean who was born and raised in the US, also shared a similar feeling. He reminisced about his experiences of living and working in a cosmopolitan foreign city where the vast majority of people living there came from somewhere else. He said, "I think for me, I always grew up my whole life feeling like an outsider. I'm not Korean enough for the Koreans, not American enough for the Americans, but finally in [the city name] was a place where I'm not an outsider." It seems that Stephen found a new "cultural home" in that city where he served. It also shows his cultural homelessness in both the US and Korea, two countries to which his own "cultural background" is linked.

Nathan expressed some weariness of the culturally homogenous lifestyle of his parents and siblings. Certain cultural traditions that his family maintained were no longer meaningful or relevant to him. Eric also felt culturally more comfortable living in his country of service, and he struggled when he came back to the US He said:

> I was there for ten years, and I loved the people and culture and country so much that . . . I felt such an attachment and huge part of my identity was there in [country name] and being a missionary, all ministry and leadership and things going on there. . . . our daughter going to [local national] school there. Yeah, so I think definitely my identity was there, and I felt comfortable there.

Eunju's comments somewhat reflect a state of "cultural homelessness." She did not have a preferred cultural home. She neither felt entirely at home in her birth country nor here in the States, where she had spent more than ten years now.

IMPLICATIONS

One of the goals for conducting this pilot study was to test the feasibility of my research design. I wanted to see whether the line of questioning I use for the pilot study participants could generate rich descriptions that could lead to analytical insights. Although this pilot study was limited in scope and scale, it enabled the researcher to collect rich data and generated several descriptive categories that could be more deeply considered for reflection.

Feasibility of Research Design

The successful completion of this research project may depend on the quality of descriptive data collected through personal interviews and the quality of data analysis that goes beyond description toward generating concepts, and even theories. There is no way to ensure that the data collected will be of high quality apart from personal hunches and triangulation built into the research methods design. While a pilot study does not guarantee the successful collection of rich data, it does provide practical ideas about research protocols that the researcher can try out and can help evaluate the strengths and weaknesses of the research design, so the researcher can address them if needed.

It was encouraging that the pilot study participants, who were veteran international Christian workers, were willing to share their experiences and provided information related to this study. These short interviews collected data that showed personal interpretation and conceptualization of their intercultural experiences. These participants, who resemble the research population for my study, articulated intercultural social experiences that they went through in a very personal language. Most importantly, out of these five interviews emerged recognizable and relevant categories. This pilot study, if anything, showed that interviewing international Christian workers about their intercultural experiences can lead to the collection of rich data.

Since four of the five participants were PhD students who were trained to reflect on and articulate complex concepts, the data collected in this pilot study may not prove that all international Christian workers that I interviewed in my field study would also be able to do so. Also, their views may be biased and shaped by their subjectivities. Nevertheless, the following facts support the argument for my research methods. First, the language which the participants and I used in these interviews were not highly technical. Second, international Christian workers of large international organizations receive extensive intercultural training and even some missiological training. Third, I have had in the past similar types of interactions with former colleagues about cultural and intercultural experiences.

This pilot study also reveals some of the dynamics of international Christian workers' cross-cultural experiences, changes in personal views, and social preferences. While it is not possible to conduct a rigorous analysis of such limited data and develop robust theories, it does raise analytical questions that might lead to research that produces an empirical theory of the sociocultural process of personal change.

Hybridization: Sociocultural Process of Change?

An underlying assumption of this study is that hybridization is an ongoing process in all social spheres where intercultural interactions are taking place. It implies it is happening almost everywhere and involves virtually everyone. The pervasive nature of hybridity has been theorized by several scholars, most notably Homi K. Bhabha,[3] Jan Nederveen Pieterse,[4] Ien Ang,[5] and Néstor García Canclini.[6] However, if we stop at describing every culture as hybrid and everyone as hybridized, the concept of hybridity will not retain much of its analytical power. Also, the hybridity concept remains meaningful so long as it is applied to existing boundaries.[7]

It should be noted that my research interest here lies not in an essentialized version of hybridity, but the cultural processes of hybridization. Hybridity and hybrid identities should not be prematurely—and sometimes too enthusiastically—seen as some "overly pleasant versions of *mestizaje*" that will magically resolve all issues of cultural diversity and differences.[8] It is not a particular static or fixed state of hybridity that helps explicate the empirical phenomenon in this study. This kind of static view would be too naïve for and does not come close to understanding the sociocultural reality on the ground. Hybridity is not a state to arrive at or a condition to manipulate so that we achieve some "easy multicultural and multiracial harmony"; instead, it is "a heuristic device" that can help us interpret complex social phenomena, especially under globalizing schemes.[9] García Canclini also emphasizes, "That is why it is best to insist that the object of study is not hybridity, but the processes of hybridization. In this way, one can acknowledge the extent to which these processes are destructive, and recognize what is left out of the fusion. A theory of hybridization that is not naïve requires a critical awareness of its limits, of what refuses or resists hybridization."[10]

In the pilot study interviews, I attempted to ask questions to the participants that might lead to their articulation of the process of adjustment, adaptation, and change. The data and findings in this pilot study show that

3. Bhabha, *Location of Culture*.

4. Nederveen Pieterse, "Globalisation as Hybridisation"; Nederveen Pieterse, "Hybridity, So What?"; Nederveen Pieterse, *Globalization and Culture*, 2015.

5. Ang, *On Not Speaking Chinese*; Ang, "Together-In-Difference."

6. García Canclini, *Hybrid Cultures*; García Canclini, "State of War"; García Canclini, *Consumers and Citizens*; García Canclini, "Introduction: Hybrid Cultures."

7. Nederveen Pieterse, *Globalization and Culture*, 2015, 108.

8. García Canclini, "Introduction: Hybrid Cultures," xxviii.

9. Ang, "Together-In-Difference," 149–53.

10. García Canclini, "Introduction: Hybrid Cultures," xxviii.

this line of questioning can lead to collecting valuable information and help us appreciate how deeply these sociocultural processes are embedded in the lived experiences of these international Christian workers.

Social Relationships with Cultural Other: Negotiation and Mediation?

The interview data, though inconclusive, shows the somewhat different articulation of changes in self between those who worked with multicultural teams and those who worked with culturally homogeneous teams. Three participants who were on multicultural teams talked about a substantial change in themselves, about becoming more aware of people from other cultures. They could attribute this change partially to their multicultural teams. The two participants who were with monocultural teams did not say much about the change in themselves concerning their mission experiences. One of these two, however, mentioned how his upbringing of navigating between two cultures helped him understand and relate to people from other cultures better than his colleagues with culturally homogeneous upbringing. Anecdotally this perhaps makes sense, but it needs to be investigated further in an empirical study whether multicultural team relationships do play a role and if they do, what kind of role they play.

García Canclini suggests that hybridization can be seen as "a process of intersection and transaction" that enables democratic cohabitation of different cultural groups.[11] In other words, hybridization involves complex processes of negotiations on which cultural elements, both new and old, are accepted, rejected, adapted, mixed, and further combined to produce new cultural products, both tangible and intangible. When international Christian workers enter a new cultural context, they would be entering into a process of these interactive transactions with local cultural elements. But how might the international Christian workers' team influence this process? It can be explained by socialization theories, but socialization is usually studied among children and adolescents, and the kind of processes that these international Christian workers go through would be addressed by overlapping theories of acculturation.[12] Acculturation theories, however, are inadequate to explain these complex processes experienced by international Christian workers on multicultural teams since it only looks at interactions between two cultures and does not explain how a

---

11. García Canclini, "Introduction: Hybrid Cultures," xxviii.
12. See Grusec and Hastings, *Handbook of Socialization*.

third culture—which includes several different cultures or some of their combinations—might influence the process.[13]

The participants' answers raise further questions about whether there may be a mediating effect of culturally diverse social relationships within the mission team on the international Christian worker's cultural hybridization process of negotiation and transaction in a new cultural environment. The reverse may also be happening that the transaction process with the local cultural elements has a mediating effect on those social relationships. A third possibility is that these negotiations might also be taking place in the social relations within the team. Exploring these triple processes of cultural negotiations—international Christian worker, multicultural team, and local context—would be a worthwhile endeavor for missiological research.

SUMMARY AND CONCLUSION

Through this pilot study, I was able to get a glimpse of some of the cultural processes that international Christian workers go through when they enter and live in a cultural context different from their primary cultural upbringing. By interviewing five career international Christian workers with diverse experiences and backgrounds, I learned that these participants could reflect and articulate their cross-cultural experiences. It is also crucial for empirical studies to focus on the dynamic process of hybridization, not a static notion of hybridity. This distinction must be maintained throughout the research process. Lastly, the mediating relationship between international Christian worker, mission team, and the local context needs to be distinguished from one another and be carefully examined. It may hold the key to discovering specific factors and the extent of how the cultural dissonance or dislocation among international Christian workers takes place as a result of these international Christian workers' cross-cultural experiences.

13. See Berry, "Acculturation."

Appendix E

Coding Process

The following describes my early coding experience during this study. I include this information here so that the readers can get a glimpse of my analytic thinking process and gain a better understanding of how I developed my categories and themes through data analysis.

ESTABLISHING A CODING PLAN FOR SYSTEMATIC ANALYSIS

Before beginning to code the data, I decided to establish a specific plan for coding. It was due to the amount of data and the nature of this inquiry. At first, it was hard to decide what kind of coding methods I should use. The size of the dataset was enormous. Ambiguity and uncertainty were paralyzing. I was not sure how and where to begin. It was a moment that I had to invoke some courage and patience.

While the literature on qualitative data analysis suggests many different methods to code, there is a general agreement among scholars that coding is a discovery process that requires an open mind.[1] With that in mind, I surveyed and studied various coding methods. Some researchers make coding look simpler,[2] others make it seem more complicated,[3] and still others

1. O'Reilly, *Ethnographic Methods*; Merriam and Tisdell, *Qualitative Research*; Gibbs, *Analyzing Qualitative Data*; Miles et al., *Qualitative Data Analysis*, 2020; Humble and Radina, *Moving beyond "Themes Emerged"*; Court, *Qualitative Research*; Miles et al., *Qualitative Data Analysis*, 2014; Saldaña, *Coding Manual*, 2013; Saldaña, *Thinking Qualitatively*; Saldaña, *Coding Manual*, 2016; Emerson et al., *Writing Ethnographic Fieldnotes*; Charmaz, *Constructing Grounded Theory*; Bazeley and Jackson, *Data Analysis with NVivo*; Jackson and Bazeley, *Data Analysis with NVivo*.

2. E.g., O'Reilly, *Ethnographic Methods*; Merriam and Tisdell, *Qualitative Research*.

3. E.g., Saldaña, *Coding Manual*, 2016; Charmaz, *Constructing Grounded Theory*; Miles et al., *Qualitative Data Analysis*, 2014.

somewhere in between.[4] In the end, a decision had to be made on how to go about coding a vast amount of data. I sensed that my data was percolating with insights and meanings that were begging me to uncover and put into a new language that would express the ideas underneath. It was exciting and terrifying at the same time. Saldaña's work was very helpful in working through this challenge.[5] It was instructive about various coding methods and which ones were to be employed in this study. Many pages of my researcher memos indicate that I struggled to establish a specific coding plan. It was due to my lack of experience, uncertainty, a loose research design, an abstract conceptual framework, and a mountain of data.

According to Saldaña, one of the common mistakes made by qualitative researchers is to code a bulk of data in descriptive codes that only show the content of what the interviewees discussed.[6] It would be difficult to make meaning out of people's lived experiences when coded data only provide basic descriptions. To avoid this mistake and take the analysis in this study from a basic descriptive level to a more conceptual level, I needed to establish a systematic coding strategy early in the formal analysis stage.

Some of the questions I asked myself as I tried to begin coding were as follows:

- Where do I start coding first? Which interview or which fieldnote?

- What do I do with all these different types of data - interview transcripts (individual, couple, and group), fieldnotes, select newsletters, intercultural training materials, and websites?

- How do I code these different types of data? Same or different?

- What specific coding methods should I use?

These questions helped me narrow down my focus in the analytic process and coming up with an actionable coding plan.

INITIAL CODING STRATEGY

I decided that it would be wise to code an interview or two, along with a couple of fieldnotes, just to test out my coding methods and see what happened. It was something that could be done with relative ease, and perhaps even enjoyable. Thus, at the beginning of coding, I took a small bite approach to the task of analyzing the massive data. I started with interview

4. E.g., Court, *Qualitative Research*; Gibbs, *Analyzing Qualitative Data*.
5. Saldaña, *Coding Manual*, 2016.
6. Saldaña, *Coding Manual*, 2016, 76–78.

transcripts of individual interviews with Thomas and Mikyung, and a married couple interview with Joseph and Rachel.

I decided that the transcript of the interview with Thomas was an excellent choice to begin my coding exploration because his interview was concise, to the point, and conscientious. The interview transcript of Mikyung, his wife, was a natural choice for the next transcript to be coded. They had lived in three major cities in NAC and then moved to a smaller town. They had been a part of three different, both large and small teams. Even between the two, they were multicultural as Thomas was a Northern European and Mikyung an Asian. They had adapted well to NAC. Overall, they were capable ICWs in NAC who were significant contributors to their teams. Also, they were interviewed separately one-on-one, so they provided me with two separate transcripts from two separate individual interviews, which would give me two similar but different views.

The next transcript I chose was the interview with Joseph and Rachel. They were a married couple who were interviewed together. They were another example of ICWs who adapted to the local culture and language well; they were dynamic team leaders with a clear vision. Both couples had lived in NAC longer than ten years, which would have given them plenty of experiences in the local setting as well as their MCT. Along with these interview transcripts, I also coded fieldnotes. Whenever a thought occurred while coding these documents, I recorded it in a memo.

In these first coding activities, I mainly used three specific coding methods called In Vivo, Process (or Action), and Initial (or Open) Coding methods.[7] In Vivo Coding is a method that takes a word or phrase, or even a short sentence from the qualitative data to form a code.[8] Process or Action Coding refers to a coding method that uses gerunds (-ing words) to show actions and processes of individuals.[9] Initial Coding, also referred to as open coding, indicates "an initiating procedural step in harmony with first cycle coding processes."[10] This way of coding stays close to the data and remains exploratory, while all the initial codes are considered only provisional.[11] These three coding methods are grounded theory methods.[12] Al-

---

7. Saldaña, *Coding Manual*, 2016.

8. Saldaña, *Coding Manual*, 2016, 105–10.

9. Charmaz, et al., "Evolving Grounded Theory"; Saldaña, *Coding Manual*, 2016, 110–15.

10. Saldaña, *Coding Manual*, 2016, 115.

11. Charmaz, *Constructing Grounded Theory*, 116–18.

12. Saldaña, *Coding Manual*, 2016.

though grounded theorists advocate for line-by-line coding, I did not code line-by-line because of the large amount of data.

Using the Process Coding method for interview transcript for Thomas forced me to think of action and process in what he shared. It led me to ask, "What is Thomas doing here?" before deciding which word or phrase to use for a code. It was quite helpful in thinking of ways to describe and conceptualize what might be happening. In Vivo Coding captured meaningful moments in the lives of the participants in the language they used. These codes helped me think about what was happening and what might be the reason for them.

CODING DECISIONS AFTER FIVE DOCUMENTS

As coding progressed, I used Process Coding as the primary method and In Vivo the secondary. I also included a few Descriptive Coding and Versus Coding that contrasted two opposite attitudes or emotions.[13] After coding the first five documents, I reviewed the codes generated so far and the coding methods I used. Using a mixture of these methods to code the first five documents, I accumulated over 260 codes. The number of codes was too many already, and I wondered whether to combine them into fewer codes now or continue with this way of coding a bit longer. In the end, I decided to keep going by coding two more interview transcripts before making any adjustments to these codes.

For coding a fourth interview transcript, I "lumped" entire paragraphs or at least large portions of them into codes.[14] Rather than creating new codes, I tried to code them to existing codes as much as possible. For some segments of texts, I did "splitter coding" by choosing a word or phrase rather than sentences or a paragraph for a single code. Some texts could not be coded by Process Coding—they could not be put into verbs but needed to be done in Descriptive Coding with nouns or adjectives. I applied Process Coding to as many codes as possible, producing codes in gerunds that expressed the participant's actions.

Meanwhile, I continued to reflect on these coding sessions and recorded my thoughts and feelings in researcher memos. Some of the exemplar memos I wrote recorded my emotions as a researcher, personal reflections on the analytic process, and new ideas about how to analyze the data. One of these memos is the following:

---

13. See Saldaña, *Coding Manual.*

14. Saldaña, *Coding Manual,* 2016, 23–25.

Memo 2019-04-03 RQs, Coding, and Analytic Focus

I continue to struggle with coding and analysis. It's too ambiguous and uncertain. At times I don't feel like I'm discovering
anything new or anything worthwhile. However, I know things
can be different once I follow through with the entire analytical
process. I am not sure how long it will take. I can only afford the
next 3-4 weeks to complete the coding. Meanwhile, I continue
to oscillate on my RQs. I already formulated Revision 3.2. This is
not good. They need to be settled; otherwise, the entire analysis
can be shaken. These are the worries I have. On the other hand,
there are positive signs as follows:

1. The open, loose stance in my research design has influenced
   the entire research process, from developing a research focus
   and research questions, interview style and questions, types
   of data gathered, and even the coding process. It is impossible
   to be narrowly focused when the research was highly exploratory in both theory and context and thus was designed to be
   more open, more fluid, and more flexible.

2. I am suffering from it now during the analytical process. But
   in due time, I would think that I will see the benefit of this
   research design. What if I had used a tighter, more closed
   design? Without hardly any prior empirical studies using this
   kind of conceptual framework and applying it to a particular
   context that is intersecting many cultures? It is perhaps the
   only way to study it. Any tight and prior set up can ruin the
   study for data gathered can be faulty and superficial.

3. I focused on hybridizing processes that these workers experienced. But I had to ask questions that probed their lived
   experiences rather than their analysis of the complex experience. I am the one who has to do the heavy analytical lift-
   ing, not my participants. Besides, asking highly conceptual
   questions can easily lead to partial results. I think I did right
   by collecting stories, narratives, events, and lived experiences
   rather than their conceptual thinking that do not have the
   background of my research.

4. The RQ Version 3.2 addresses fundamental questions that
   require high-level conceptual analysis of data. I am seeking
   to learn how cultural processes of hybridization occur at a
   micro, individual level.

5. I need to be more confident about this whole process. I haven't done this in vain. I need to code away and consolidate and develop categories. Cultural differences, cultural diversity, and cultural change. Cultural homelessness. These are important items of interest to this research. I must analyze how they are experienced by my participants and find their meanings.

SUMMARY OF THE CODING PROCESS

In the initial coding phase, I coded five interview transcripts and a few field-notes. I used various coding methods described by Johnny Saldaña, namely, Initial Coding, Eclectic Coding, Descriptive Coding, Concept Coding, Process Coding, and In Vivo Coding methods.[15] I also used Simultaneous Coding and Versus Coding for a few different text segments.

This initial coding phase generated more than 420 codes. It was too many. In this coding phase, I tried to stay close to the data in coding and to produce codes that were more descriptive than analytical on purpose. It was an exploring phase where various ideas needed to be expressed and considered before consolidating them into more conceptual and analytical codes or categories.

Codes and groups of codes underwent continual revision through the next coding phases until the entire dataset was coded. Then codes were further refined; groups of codes were reviewed before being turned into categories. I consolidated many of these codes to form about 130 codes in a three-level hierarchy that were directly related to my select findings and analyses. The hierarchical structure of codes reflected my initial analysis; the structure represented the analysis, and the higher-level codes showed more meanings than the lower level codes. The structure included codes that went beyond descriptive toward a more conceptual level of analysis.

Now, these categories and codes became loose building blocks for further analyses of comparing the data between different cases, looking at patterns, and interacting further with existing literature. Later, a decision was made to develop three chapters in this book from these categories and one additional chapter for interpretation and synthesis that brought the content of the previous three chapters together in more advanced analysis. Even at this stage, I was still considering whether to combine and shuffle some of these categories around to present the findings. In this way, data analysis was on-going and never-ending throughout this research process.

15. Saldaña, *Coding Manual*, 2016.

APPLYING DRAMATURGICAL CODING

The Dramaturgical Coding method was used to code various stories and examples told by the participants. I found it to be an effective way to generate an understanding of social situations with tension or conflict reported by the participants.[16] This method of analyzing social life uses the image of a theatre as a metaphor to examine people's actions and to explain the reasons behind them.[17] Saldaña writes, "Dramaturgical Coding attunes the researcher to the qualities, perspectives, and drives of the participant. It also provides a deep understanding of how humans in social action, reaction, and interaction interpret and manage conflict."[18] Charmaz concurs that this way of looking at social life makes its normally invisible aspects more visible to the researcher.[19]

Dramaturgical analysis owes, at least in part, some of its key ideas to Erving Goffman's concepts.[20] Goffman saw two basic parts to individuals in their social conduct: "the individual as character performed" and "the individual as performer."[21] As theatrical performers, humans create impressions on the audience by playing their parts; as characters in a drama, people play out certain character attributes that they appear to possess.[22] It is a way to understand what goes on in the minds of people in their social interactions. Dramaturgical Coding derives its methods from this staging aspect of social life.

I applied this coding method to seventeen participant stories that were infused with tension and conflict. I would read through text and code segments that corresponded to the six dramaturgical categories—objective, conflict, tactic, attitude, emotion, and subtext. Once this was completed, I assigned each code generated to one of these six categories. I reordered the codes in a progression that would rearrange the story in a way that drew out elements of the story that were not as obvious or visible. Based on the progression of this newly ordered story, I wrote a memo, using the codes and their corresponding six categories, that interpreted the story in a new light, unfolding as a social drama. The following is an example of how the memo was written:

16. See Saldaña, *The Coding Manual*, 2016, 145–50; Charmaz, *Constructing Grounded Theory*, 273–77; Miles et al., *Qualitative Data Analysis*, 2020, 68–69.

17. Charmaz, *Constructing Grounded Theory*, 273.

18. Saldaña, *Coding Manual*, 2016, 146.

19. Charmaz, *Constructing Grounded Theory*, 274.

20. Saldaña, *Coding Manual*, 2016; Charmaz, *Constructing Grounded Theory*.

21. Goffman, *Presentation of Self*, 253.

22. Goffman, *Presentation of Self*, 17.

Memo 2019-09-11 Dramaturgical Coding-William #2 Identity

SUB: needing a belonging > CON: not having a clear identity > SUB: comparing with his wife > EMO: stressful, feel alone, hard > OBJ: finding own place > ATT: dissatisfaction with 'not really doing anything' > OBJ: finding a role > TAC: obtaining a professional credential; moving city

William came with an MCT, newly married to his wife, who had been a part of the team for a while now. Although he was a part of the team and that would have fulfilled his need for belonging, there was still something missing in his initial year or two in the country as the head of a household. Others on the team were ahead of him in terms of language skills. He lacked a clear professional identity in the local context. His wife, on the other hand, was well-established in her work and ministry since she had already spent several years in the country. All these contributed to his stress and a sense of isolation as he felt that he was alone.

He needed to figure out a way to get established locally without too much pressure. His dissatisfaction with the lack of a role and identity grew over time, and he had to do something about it. In the end, an opportunity emerged to get a professional credential. A job opportunity gave him a new professional identity and a chance to practice the training he just received. As he and his wife were pursuing their dream of serving in a more remote area within NAC, they sought a new location of service. They found an opportunity in a small city with an international non-profit. They ended up moving to another city, which gave them a fresh new start in this new city with their identity as a professional and NGO worker.

William's struggle with identity was more pronounced than other workers whom I interviewed. Identity is dialogically constructed in the context. As a European and a married man, William entered this North African context without a clear profession or role. He had to reconstitute his identity over time to function well in the context. The process of developing his local identity was stressful, demotivating, and humiliating for him. Still, in the end, his perseverance and opportunities that he seized paid off, and he is now very well-established as a respectable professional and is serving in a significant missional role in the region. It shows negotiating social relations in NAC requires a prolonged period of assessing oneself, local people's view of oneself, and persevering through to develop a clearer and more acceptable identity.

Bibliography

Abu-Lughod, Lila. *Do Muslim Women Need Saving?* Cambridge, MA: Harvard University Press, 2013.

———. "The Objects of Soap Opera: Egyptian Television and the Cultural Politics of Modernity." In *Worlds Apart: Modernity Through the Prism of the Local*, edited by Daniel Miller, 190–210. London: Routledge, 1995.

———. "Writing Against Culture." In *Recapturing Anthropology: Working in the Present*, edited by Richard G. Fox, 137–62. Santa Fe, NM: School of American Research Press, 1991.

Adeney, Miriam. "Why Cultures Matter." *International Journal of Frontier Missiology* 32 (2015) 93–97.

Agar, Michael. "Culture: Can You Take It Anywhere?" *International Journal of Qualitative Methods* 5 (2006) 1–16.

———. *Language Shock: Understanding the Culture of Conversation.* New York: William Morrow and Company, 1994.

Agar, Michael H. *Culture: How to Make It Work in a World of Hybrids.* Lanham, MD: Rowman & Littlefield, 2019.

Ahmad, Aijaz. *In Theory: Classes, Nations, Literatures.* London: Verso, 1992.

———. "The Politics of Literary Postcoloniality." *Race and Class* 36 (1995) 1–20.

Anderson, Benedict. *Imagined Communities: Reflections on the Origin and Spread of Nationalism.* 2nd ed. London: Verso, 1991.

Ang, Ien. "Beyond Chinese Groupism: Chinese Australians between Assimilation, Multiculturalism and Diaspora." *Ethnic and Racial Studies* 37 (2014) 1184–96.

———. "Identity Blues." In *Without Guarantees: In Honour of Stuart Hall*, edited by Paul Gilroy et al., 1–13. London: Verso, 2000.

———. "Inhabiting the Diasporic Habitus: On Stuart Hall's Familiar Stranger: A Life Between Two Islands." *Identities* 25 (2018) 1–6.

———. *On Not Speaking Chinese: Living Between Asia and the West.* London: Routledge, 2001.

———. "Together-In-Difference: Beyond Diaspora, Into Hybridity." *Asian Studies Review* 27 (2003) 141–54.

Appadurai, Arjun. "Globalization and the Research Imagination." *International Social Science Journal* 51 (1999) 229.

———. *Modernity at Large: Cultural Dimensions of Globalization.* Minneapolis: University of Minnesota Press, 1996.

———. "Putting Hierarchy in Its Place." *Cultural Anthropology* 3 (1988) 36–49.

Archer, Margaret S. *Making Our Way through the World: Human Reflexivity and Social Mobility.* Cambridge: Cambridge University Press, 2007.

Arnett, Jeffrey Jensen. "The Psychology of Globalization." *American Psychologist* 57 (2002) 774–83.

Asad, Talal, ed. *Anthropology and the Colonial Encounter.* London: Ithaca, 1973.

Austin, Clyde N., and John Beyer. "Missionary Repatriation: An Introduction to the Literature." *International Bulletin of Missionary Research* 8 (1984) 68–70.

Axford, Barrie. *Theories of Globalization.* Cambridge: Polity, 2013.

Baker, Dwight P., and Robert J. Priest, eds. *The Missionary Family.* Pasadena, CA: William Carey Library, 2014.

Bakhtin, M. M. *The Dialogic Imagination: Four Essays.* Edited by Michael Holquist. Translated by Caryl Emerson and Michael Holquist. University of Texas Press Slavic Series 1. Austin: University of Texas Press, 1981.

Bauman, Zygmunt. "From Pilgrim to Tourist—or a Short History of Identity." In *Questions of Cultural Identity*, edited by Stuart Hall and Paul Du Gay, 18–36. London: Sage, 1996.

Baumann, Gerd. *Contesting Culture: Discourses of Identity in Multi-Ethnic London.* Cambridge: Cambridge University Press, 1996.

———. "Dominant and Demotic Discourses of Culture: Their Relevance to Multi-Ethnic Alliances." In *Debating Cultural Hybridity: Multi-Cultural Identities and the Politics of Anti-Racism*, edited by Pnina Werbner and Tariq Modood, 209–25. London: Zed, 1997.

———. *The Multicultural Riddle: Rethinking National, Ethnic and Religious Identities.* New York: Routledge, 1999.

Bazeley, Patricia, and Kristi Jackson, eds. *Qualitative Data Analysis with NVivo.* 2nd ed. London: SAGE, 2013.

Benet-Martínez, Verónica, and Ying-yi Hong, eds. *The Oxford Handbook of Multicultural Identity.* Oxford Library of Psychology. Oxford: Oxford University Press, 2014.

Berger, Peter L. *The Sacred Canopy: Elements of a Sociological Theory of Religion.* Garden City, NY: Doubleday, 1967.

Berry, John W. "Acculturation." In *Handbook of Socialization: Theory and Research*, edited by Joan E. Grusec and Paul D. Hastings, 543–58. New York: Guilford, 2007.

Bhabha, Homi K. "Cultural Diversity and Cultural Differences." In *The Post-Colonial Studies Reader*, edited by Bill Ashcroft et al., 155–57. London: Routledge, 2006.

———. "Culture's In-Between." In *Questions of Cultural Identity*, edited by Stuart Hall and Paul Du Gay, 53–60. London: Sage, 1996.

———. "Foreword." In *Debating Cultural Hybridity: Multi-Cultural Identities and the Politics of Anti-Racism*, edited by Pnina Werbner and Tariq Modood, ix–xiii. London: Zed, 2015.

———. "In Between Cultures." *NPQ: New Perspectives Quarterly* 30 (2013) 107–9.

———. *The Location of Culture.* Routledge Classics edition. London: Routledge, 1994.

———. "Unpacking My Library . . . Again." In *The Post-Colonial Question: Common Skies, Divided Horizons*, edited by Iain Chambers and Lidia Curti, 199–211. London: Routledge, 1996.

Bloomberg, Linda D., and Marie F. Volpe. *Completing Your Qualitative Dissertation: A Road Map From Beginning to End.* 3rd ed. Thousand Oaks, CA: SAGE, 2016.

Bloomberg, Linda Dale, and Marie F. Volpe. *Completing Your Qualitative Dissertation: A Road Map From Beginning to End.* 4th ed. Thousand Oaks, CA: SAGE, 2019.

Bonhoeffer, Dietrich. *Life Together: A Discussion of Christian Fellowship.* Translated by John W. Doberstein. New York: Harper and Row, 1954.

Bosch, David J. *Transforming Mission: Paradigm Shifts in Theology of Mission.* Maryknoll, NY: Orbis, 1991.

Bourdieu, Pierre. *Distinction: A Social Critique of the Judgement of Taste.* Translated by Richard Nice. Cambridge, MA: Harvard University Press, 1984.

———. *In Other Words: Essays Toward a Reflexive Sociology.* Translated by Matthew Adamson. Stanford: Stanford University Press, 1990.

———. *The Logic of Practice.* Translated by Richard Nice. Stanford: Stanford University Press, 1990.

———. *Outline of a Theory of Practice.* Translated by Richard Nice. Cambridge: Cambridge University Press, 1977.

Brewer, Paul, and Sunil Venaik. "The Ecological Fallacy in National Culture Research." *Organization Studies* 35 (2014) 1063–86.

———. "Globe Practices and Values: A Case of Diminishing Marginal Utility?" *Journal of International Business Studies* 41 (2010) 1316–24.

———. "Individualism—Collectivism in Hofstede and GLOBE." *Journal of International Business Studies* 42 (2011) 436–45.

———. "On the Misuse of National Culture Dimensions." *International Marketing Review* 29 (2012) 673–83.

Brewster, E. Thomas, and Elizabeth S. Brewster. *Language Acquisition Made Practical: Field Methods for Language Learners.* Pasadena, CA: Lingua, 1976.

Brinkmann, Svend. "Doing Without Data." *Qualitative Inquiry* 20 (2014) 720–25.

Brinkmann, Svend, and Steinar Kvale. *InterViews: Learning the Craft of Qualitative Research Interviewing.* 3rd ed. Los Angeles: SAGE, 2015.

Brubaker, Rogers. "Categories of Analysis and Categories of Practice: A Note on the Study of Muslims in European Countries of Immigration." *Ethnic and Racial Studies* 36 (2013) 1–8.

———. "The 'Diaspora' Diaspora." *Ethnic and Racial Studies* 28 (2005) 1–19.

———. "Ethnicity without Groups." *European Journal of Sociology* 43 (2002) 163–89.

———. *Ethnicity without Groups.* Cambridge, MA: Harvard University Press, 2004.

———. "Social Theory as Habitus." In *Bourdieu: Critical Perspectives*, edited by Craig Calhoun et al., 212–34. Chicago: The University of Chicago Press, 1993.

Brubaker, Rogers, and Frederick Cooper. "Beyond 'Identity.'" *Theory and Society* 29 (2000) 1–47.

Burke, Peter. *Cultural Hybridity.* Cambridge: Polity, 2009.

Burrows, William R. "Theological Ideals, Cross-Cultural Realities: Syncretism and Hybridity in Christian Culture Crossings." In *Traditional Ritual as Christian Worship: Dangerous Syncretism or Necessary Hybridity?*, edited by R. Daniel Shaw and William R. Burrows, 20–38. American Society of Missiology Series 56. Maryknoll, NY: Orbis, 2018.

Buruma, Ian, and Avishai Margalit. *Occidentalism: The West in the Eyes of Its Enemies.* New York: Penguin, 2004.

Charmaz, Kathy. *Constructing Grounded Theory.* 2nd ed. Thousand Oaks, CA: SAGE, 2014.

Charmaz, Kathy, et al. "Evolving Grounded Theory and Social Justice Inquiry." In *The SAGE Handbook of Qualitative Research*, edited by Norman K. Denzin and Yvonna S. Lincoln, 411–43. Thousand Oaks, CA: SAGE, 2018.

Chiu, Chi-Yue, and Ying-yi Hong. *Social Psychology of Culture*. New York: Psychology, 2006.

Cho, Yong Joong, and David Greenlee. "Avoiding Pitfalls on Multi-Cultural Mission Teams." *International Journal of Frontier Missions* 12 (1995) 179–83.

Christofferson, Ethan J. *Negotiating Identity: Exploring Tensions Between Being Hakka and Being Christian in Northwestern Taiwan*. American Society of Missiology Monograph Series 13. Eugene, OR: Pickwick, 2012.

Clifford, James. *The Predicament of Culture: Twentieth-Century Ethnography, Literature, and Art*. Cambridge, MA: Harvard University Press, 1988.

Clifford, James, and George E. Marcus, eds. *Writing Culture: The Poetics and Politics of Ethnography*. Berkeley: University of California Press, 1986.

Court, Deborah. *Qualitative Research and Intercultural Understanding: Conducting Qualitative Research in Multicultural Settings*. Abingdon, UK: Routledge, 2018.

Deleuze, Gilles, and Félix Guattari. *Anti-Oedipus: Capitalism and Schizophrenia*. Translated by Robert Hurley, Mark Seem, and Helen R. Lane. New York: Viking, 1977.

Derrida, Jacques. *Dissemination*. Translated by Barbara Johnson. Chicago: The University of Chicago Press, 1981.

———. *Margins of Philosophy*. Translated by Alan Bass. Chicago: The University of Chicago Press, 1982.

———. *Of Grammatology*. Translated by Gayatri Chakravorty Spivak. Baltimore, MD: Johns Hopkins University Press, 1976.

———. *Writing and Difference*. Translated by Alan Bass. Chicago: The University of Chicago Press, 1978.

Dickie, Virginia A. "Data Analysis in Qualitative Research: A Plea for Sharing the Magic and the Effort." *American Journal of Occupational Therapy* 57 (2003) 49–56.

Dirlik, Arif. "The Postcolonial Aura: Third World Criticism in the Age of Global Capitalism." *Critical Inquiry* 20 (1994) 328–56.

"Edward Said." In *Wikipedia*, February 21, 2021. https://en.wikipedia.org/w/index.php?title=Edward_Said&oldid=1008155477.

Emerson, Robert M., et al. *Writing Ethnographic Fieldnotes*. 2nd ed. Chicago: The University of Chicago Press, 2011.

Escobar, Samuel. "Evangelical Missiology: Peering into the Future at the Turn of the Century." In *Global Missiology for the 21st Century*, edited by William D. Taylor, 101–22. Grand Rapids: Baker Academic, 2000.

Ewing, Katherine Pratt. "Between Cinema and Social Work: Diasporic Turkish Women and the (Dis)Pleasures of Hybridity." *Cultural Anthropology* 21 (2006) 265–94.

Fanon, Frantz. *Black Skin, White Masks*. Translated by Charles Lam Markmann. New York: Grove, 1967.

———. *The Wretched of the Earth*. New York: Grove, 1963.

Farah, Warrick. "Motus Dei: Disciple-Making Movements and the Mission of God." *Global Missiology English* 2 (23, 2020). http://ojs.globalmissiology.org/index.php/english/article/view/2309.

Featherstone, Mike. *Undoing Culture: Globalization, Postmodernism and Identity*. Thousand Oaks, CA: SAGE, 1995.

Fellows, Richard, and Anita M. M. Liu. "Use and Misuse of the Concept of Culture." *Construction Management and Economics* 31 (2013) 401–22.

Flanders, Christopher L. *About Face: Rethinking Face for 21st-Century Mission*. Eugene, OR: Pickwick, 2011.

Flick, Uwe. *Managing Quality in Qualitative Research*. 2nd ed. Thousand Oaks, CA: SAGE, 2018.

Foucault, Michel. *The Archaeology of Knowledge*. Translated by A. M. Sheridan. London: Tavistock, 1972.

———. *Language, Counter-Memory, Practice: Selected Essays and Interviews*. Edited by Donald F. Bouchard. Translated by Donald F. Bouchard and Sherry Simon. Ithaca, NY: Cornell University Press, 1977.

———. *Madness and Civilization: A History of Insanity in the Age of Reason*. Translated by Richard Howard. New York: Pantheon, 1965.

———. *The Order of Things: An Archaeology of the Human Sciences*. New York: Pantheon, 1971.

———. *Power/Knowledge: Selected Interviews and Other Writings, 1972–1977*. Edited by Colin Gordon. Brighton, UK: Harvester, 1980.

Fox, Richard G., ed. *Recapturing Anthropology: Working in the Present*. Santa Fe, NM: School of American Research Press, 1991.

Friedman, Jonathan. "Global Crises, the Struggle for Cultural Identity and Intellectual Porkbarreling: Cosmopolitans Versus Locals, Ethnics and Nationals in an Era of De-Hegemonisation." In *Debating Cultural Hybridity: Multi-Cultural Identities and the Politics of Anti-Racism*, edited by Pnina Werbner and Tariq Modood, 70–89. London: Zed, 1997.

———. "The Hybridization of Roots and the Abhorrence of the Bush." In *Spaces of Culture: City, Nation, World*, edited by Mike Featherstone and Scott Lash, 230–56. Theory, Culture & Society. London: SAGE, 1999.

García Canclini, Néstor. *Consumers and Citizens: Globalization and Multicultural Conflicts*. Translated by George Yúdice. Minneapolis: University of Minnesota Press, 2001.

———. *Hybrid Cultures: Strategies for Entering and Leaving Modernity*. Translated by Christopher L. Chiappari and Silvia L. López. Minneapolis: University of Minnesota Press, 1995.

———. "Introduction: Hybrid Cultures in Globalized Times." In *Hybrid Cultures: Strategies for Entering and Leaving Modernity*, translated by Bruce Campbell, xxiii–xlvi. Minneapolis: University of Minnesota Press, 2005.

———. "The State of War and the State of Hybridisation." In *Without Guarantees: In Honour of Stuart Hall*, edited by Paul Gilroy et al., translated by Kristin Pesola, 38–52. London: Verso, 2000.

Geertz, Clifford. *The Interpretation of Cultures*. New York: Basic, 1973.

George, Sam. "Diaspora: A Hidden Link to 'from Everywhere to Everywhere' Missiology." *Missiology* 39 (J2011) 45–56.

Gibbs, Graham R. *Analyzing Qualitative Data*. 2nd ed. The SAGE Qualitative Research Kit. London: SAGE, 2018.

Gilroy, Paul. "Route Work: The Black Atlantic and the Politics of Exile." In *The Post-Colonial Question: Common Skies, Divided Horizons*, edited by Iain Chambers and Lidia Curti, 17–29. London: Routledge, 1996.

Goffman, Erving. *The Presentation of Self in Everyday Life*. New York: Anchor, 1959.

Green, Julie A. "Cultural Theory Training for Multicultural Teams: A 'Clumsy' Solution for a 'Wicked Problem.'" PhD diss., Fuller Theological Seminary, 2013.

Grusec, Joan E., and Paul D. Hastings, eds. *Handbook of Socialization: Theory and Research*. New York: Guilford, 2007.

Gupta, Akhil, and James Ferguson. "Beyond 'Culture': Space, Identity, and the Politics of Difference." In *The Anthropology of Globalization: A Reader*, edited by Jonathan Xavier Inda and Renato Rosaldo, 65–80. Blackwell Readers in Anthropology 1. Malden, MA: Blackwell, 2002.

Hafez, Sherine, and Susan Slyomovics, eds. *Anthropology of the Middle East and North Africa: Into the New Millennium*. Bloomington: Indiana University Press, 2013.

Hall, Stuart. "Conclusion: The Multi-Cultural Question." In *Un/Settled Multiculturalisms: Diasporas, Entanglements, Transruptions*, edited by Barnor Hesse, 209–41. London: Zed, 2000.

———. "Cultural Identity and Diaspora." In *Identity: Community, Culture, Difference*, edited by Jonathan Rutherford, 222–37. London: Lawrence & Wishart, 1990.

———. *Familiar Stranger: A Life Between Two Islands*. Edited by Bill Schwarz. Durham, NC: Duke University Press, 2017.

———. "New Ethnicities." In *"Race", Culture, and Difference*, edited by James Donald and Ali Rattansi, 252–59. London: SAGE, 1992.

———. "When Was 'the Post-Colonial'? Thinking at the Limit." In *The Post-Colonial Question: Common Skies, Divided Horizons*, edited by Iain Chambers and Lidia Curti, 242–60. London: Routledge, 1996.

Hammersley, Martyn, and Paul Atkinson. *Ethnography: Principles in Practice*. 3rd ed. London: Routledge, 2007.

Hanciles, Jehu. *Beyond Christendom: Globalization, African Migration, and the Transformation of the West*. Maryknoll, NY: Orbis, 2008.

———. "Migration and Mission: Some Implications for the Twenty-First-Century Church." *International Bulletin of Missionary Research* 27 (2003) 146–53.

Hannerz, Ulf. *Cultural Complexity: Studies in the Social Organization of Meaning*. New York: Columbia University Press, 1992.

———. *Transnational Connections: Culture, People, Places*. London: Routledge, 1996.

Hermans, Hubert J. M., and Harry J. G. Kempen. "Moving Cultures: The Perilous Problems of Cultural Dichotomies in a Globalizing Society." *American Psychologist* 53 (1998) 1111–20.

Hibbert, Evelyn, and Richard Hibbert. *Leading Multicultural Teams*. Pasadena, CA: William Carey Library, 2014.

Hibbert, Evelyn, and Richard Yates Hibbert. "Managing Conflict in a Multicultural Team." *Evangelical Missions Quarterly* 53 (2017) 1–8.

Hiebert, Paul G. *Anthropological Insights for Missionaries*. Grand Rapids: Baker, 1985.

———. *Anthropological Reflections on Missiological Issues*. Grand Rapids: Baker Academic, 1994.

———. "An Evaluation of Church Growth." *International Journal of Frontier Missiology* 33 (2016) 77–81.

———. *The Gospel in Human Contexts: Anthropological Explorations for Contemporary Missions*. Grand Rapids: Baker Academic, 2009.

———. "The Missionary as Mediator of Global Theologizing." In *Globalizing Theology*, edited by Craig Ott and Harold A. Netland, 288–308. Grand Rapids: Baker Academic, 2006.

Hine, Cathy. "Negotiating from the Margins: Women's Voices (Re)Imagining Islam." In *Dynamics of Muslim Worlds: Regional, Theological, and Missiological Perspectives*, edited by Evelyne A. Reisacher, 113–34. Downers Grove, IL: IVP Academic, 2017.

Hoersting, Raquel C., and Sharon Rae Jenkins. "No Place to Call Home: Cultural Homelessness, Self-Esteem and Cross-Cultural Identities." *International Journal of Intercultural Relations* 35 (2011) 17–30.

Hofstede, Geert. *Culture's Consequences: Comparing Values, Behaviors, Institutions and Organizations Across Nations*. 2nd ed. Thousand Oaks, CA: SAGE, 2003.

Hofstede, Geert, et al. *Cultures and Organizations: Software of the Mind: Intercultural Cooperation and Its Importance for Survival*. 3rd ed. New York: McGraw-Hill, 2010.

Hollinger, David A. *Protestants Abroad: How Missionaries Tried to Change the World but Changed America*. Princeton: Princeton University Press, 2017.

Holmes-Eber, Paula. *Daughters of Tunis: Women, Family, and Networks in a Muslim City*. Boulder, CO: Westview, 2003.

"Homi K. Bhabha." *Wikipedia*, January 19, 2021. https://en.wikipedia.org/w/index.php?title=Homi_K._Bhabha&oldid=1001312057.

Hong, EunSun Sunny. "A Grounded Theory of Leadership and Followership in Multicultural Teams in SIL." PhD diss., Biola University, 2014.

House, Robert J., et al., eds. *Culture, Leadership, and Organizations: The GLOBE Study of 62 Societies*. Thousand Oaks, CA: SAGE, 2004.

Howell, Brian M. *Christianity in the Local Context: Southern Baptists in the Philippines*. New York: Palgrave Macmillan, 2008.

———. "Globalization, Ethnicity, and Cultural Authenticity: Implications for Theological Education." *Christian Scholar's Review* 35 (2006) 303–21.

———. "Multiculturalism, Immigration and the North American Church: Rethinking Contextualization." *Missiology* 39 (2011) 79–85.

Howell, Brian M., and Edwin Zehner, eds. *Power and Identity in the Global Church: Six Contemporary Cases*. Pasadena, CA: William Carey Library, 2009.

Hsu, Danny. "Searching for Meaning in a Hybrid and Fractured World: Contemporary Chinese Cultural Identity and Its Implications for Missiology." *Missiology* 45 (2017) 103–15.

Huddart, David. *Homi K. Bhabha*. London: Routledge, 2006.

Humble, Áine M., and M. Elise Radina, eds. *How Qualitative Data Analysis Happens: Moving beyond "Themes Emerged."* New York: Routledge, 2019.

Huntington, Samuel P. *The Clash of Civilizations and the Remaking of World Order*. New York: Touchstone, 1997.

Hutnyk, John. "Adorno at Womad: South Asian Crossovers and the Limits of Hybridity-Talk." In *Debating Cultural Hybridity: Multi-Cultural Identities and the Politics of Anti-Racism*, edited by Pnina Werbner and Tariq Modood, 106–36. London: Zed, 1997.

———. "Hybridity." *Ethnic and Racial Studies* 28 (2005) 79–102.

———. "Hybridity Saves?" *Amerasia Journal* 25 (1999/2000) 39–58.

"Ien Ang." *Wikipedia*, May 4, 2020. https://en.wikipedia.org/w/index.php?title=Ien_Ang&oldid=954750070.

Inda, Jonathan Xavier, and Renato Rosaldo. "Tracking Global Flows." In *The Anthropology of Globalization: A Reader*, edited by Jonathan Xavier Inda and Renato Rosaldo, 2nd ed., 3–46. Blackwell Readers in Anthropology 1. Malden, MA: Blackwell, 2008.

Izenberg, Gerald. *Identity: The Necessity of a Modern Idea*. Philadelphia: University of Pennsylvania Press, 2016.

Jackson, Alecia Y., and Lisa A. Mazzei. "Thinking With Theory: A New Analytic for Qualitative Inquiry." In *The SAGE Handbook of Qualitative Research*, edited by Norman K. Denzin and Yvonna S. Lincoln, 717–37. Thousand Oaks, CA: SAGE, 2018.

————. *Thinking with Theory in Qualitative Research*. Abingdon, UK: Routledge, 2012.

Jackson, Kristi, and Pat Bazeley. *Qualitative Data Analysis with NVivo*. 3rd ed. Thousand Oaks, CA: SAGE, 2019.

"Jan Nederveen Pieterse." *Wikipedia*, October 8, 2020. https://en.wikipedia.org/w/index.php?title=Jan_Nederveen_Pieterse&oldid=982438145.

Jenkins, Philip. *The Next Christendom: The Coming of Global Christianity*. 3rd ed. New York: Oxford University Press, 2011.

Joh, Wonhee Anne. *Heart of the Cross: A Postcolonial Christology*. Louisville, KY: Westminster John Knox, 2006.

Johnson, Todd M., et al. "Christianity 2018: More African Christians and Counting Martyrs." *International Bulletin of Mission Research* 42 (2018) 20–28.

Kakutani, Michiko. "'The Satanic Verses': What Rushdie Wrote." *The New York Times*, February 23, 1989. https://www.nytimes.com/1989/02/23/books/the-satanic-verses-what-rushdie-wrote.html.

Keller, Catherine, et al., eds. *Postcolonial Theologies: Divinity and Empire*. St. Louis, MO: Chalice, 2004.

Kim, Jonathan Y. "Perceptions of Working Relationships Among Multicultural Team Members in International Mission Agencies: A Languacultural Analysis." PhD diss., Trinity International University, 2013.

Kompridis, Nikolas. "Normativizing Hybridity/Neutralizing Culture." *Political Theory* 33 (2005) 318–43.

Kraidy, Marwan M. "Hybridity in Cultural Globalization." *Communication Theory* 12 (2002) 316–39.

————. *Hybridity, or the Cultural Logic of Globalization*. Philadelphia: Temple University Press, 2005.

Kuper, Adam. *Culture: The Anthropologists' Account*. Cambridge, MA: Harvard University Press, 1999.

Laroussi, Farid. *Postcolonial Counterpoint: Orientalism, France, and the Maghreb*. Toronto: University of Toronto Press, 2016.

Lave, Jean, and Etienne Wenger. *Situated Learning: Legitimate Peripheral Participation*. Cambridge: Cambridge University Press, 1991.

Lee, Michael Hakmin. "Interdisciplinary Reflections on the Resilience of Racial Constructs." *Missiology* 44 (2016) 194–206.

Lee, Min-dong Paul, Winnie Fung, and Joey Fung. "Doing Incarnational Business as Mission: A Case Study in India." *Evangelical Missions Quarterly* 52 (2016) 118–27.

Lee, Peter T. "Reimagining 'Culture' in Intercultural Missionary Training." Paper presented at the annual meeting of Association of Professors of Mission, Notre Dame, IN, June 14, 2019.

Lee, Peter T., and Godfrey Harold. "Potential or Threat?: Adopting Cultural Hybridity as a Concept for Diaspora Missiology." *The South African Baptist Journal of Theology* 28 (2019) 2–14.

Lee, Peter T., and James Sung-Hwan Park. "Beyond People Group Thinking: A Critical Reevaluation of Unreached People Groups." *Missiology* 46 (2018) 212–25.

Lee, Peter Taehoon. "Toward a Third Space of Cultures: Hybridity and Multiethnic Leadership in Christian Mission." In *A Hybrid World: Diaspora, Hybridity, and Missio Dei*, edited by Sadiri Joy Tira and Juliet Lee Uytanlet, 217–31. Littleton, CO: William Carey, 2020.

Leung, Angela K.-y, et al., eds. *Cultural Processes: A Social Psychological Perspective.* Culture and Psychology. New York: Cambridge University Press, 2011.

Lewellen, Ted C. *The Anthropology of Globalization: Cultural Anthropology Enters the 21st Century.* Westport, CT: Bergin & Garvey, 2002.

Liu, Shuang. *Identity, Hybridity and Cultural Home: Chinese Migrants and Diaspora in Multicultural Societies.* London: Rowman & Littlefield, 2015.

Locke, Lawrence F., et al. *Proposals That Work.* 6th ed. SAGE, 2014.

Mallon, Colleen Mary. *Traditioning Disciples: The Contributions of Cultural Anthropology to Ecclesial Identity.* American Society of Missiology Monograph Series 8. Eugene, OR: Wipf & Stock, 2010.

Mann, Steve. *The Research Interview: Reflective Practice and Reflexivity in Research Processes.* New York: Palgrave Macmillan, 2016.

Marcus, George E. *Ethnography through Thick and Thin.* Princeton: Princeton University Press, 1998.

Marcus, George E., and Michael M. J. Fischer. *Anthropology as Cultural Critique: An Experimental Moment in the Human Sciences.* Chicago: University of Chicago Press, 1986.

Maxwell, Joseph A. *Qualitative Research Design: An Interactive Approach.* 3rd ed. Applied Social Research Methods Series 41. Thousand Oaks, CA: SAGE, 2013.

McConnell, Douglas. *Cultural Insights for Christian Leaders: New Directions for Organizations Serving God's Mission.* Mission in Global Community. Baker Academic, 2018.

McDougall, James, and Judith Scheele, eds. *Saharan Frontiers: Space and Mobility in Northwest Africa.* Bloomington: Indiana University Press, 2012.

McSweeney, Brendan. "Cultural Diversity within Nations." In *Remaking Management: Between Global and Local*, edited by Chris Smith et al., 61–89. Cambridge: Cambridge University Press, 2008.

———. "Dynamic Diversity: Variety and Variation Within Countries." *Organization Studies* 30 (2009) 933–57.

———. "Fashion Founded on a Flaw: The Ecological Mono-Deterministic Fallacy of Hofstede, GLOBE, and Followers." *International Marketing Review* 30 (2013) 483–504.

———. "Globe, Hofstede, Huntington, Trompenaars: Common Foundations, Common Flaws." In *Transculturalism and Business in the BRIC States: A Handbook*, edited by Yvette Sánchez and Claudia Franziska Brühwiler. New York: Routledge, 2016.

———. "Hall, Hofstede, Huntington, Trompenaars, GLOBE: Common Foundations, Common Flaws." In *Transculturalism and Business in the BRIC States: A Handbook*, edited by Yvette Sánchez and Claudia Franziska Brühwiler, 13–58. Abingdon, UK: Routledge, 2016.

———. "Hofstede's Model of National Cultural Differences and Their Consequences: A Triumph of Faith—a Failure of Analysis." *Human Relations* 55 (2002) 89–118.

McSweeney, Brendan, et al. "Claiming Too Much, Delivering Too Little: Testing Some of Hofstede's Generalisations." *Irish Journal of Management* 35 (2016) 34–57.

Melucci, Alberto. "Identity and Difference in a Globalised World." In *Debating Cultural Hybridity: Multi-Cultural Identities and the Politics of Anti-Racism*, edited by Pnina Werbner and Tariq Modood, 58–69. London: Zed, 1997.

Memmi, Albert. *The Colonizer and the Colonized*. Translated by Howard Greenfeld. Expanded ed. Boston: Orion, 1965.

Mernissi, Fatima. *The Veil And The Male Elite: A Feminist Interpretation Of Women's Rights In Islam*. Translated by Mary Jo Lakeland. Reading, MA: Addison-Wesley, 1991.

Merriam, Sharan B., and Elizabeth J. Tisdell. *Qualitative Research: A Guide to Design and Implementation*. 4th ed. San Francisco: Jossey-Bass, 2016.

Messner, Wolfgang. "The Misconstruction of Hofstede's Uncertainty Avoidance Dimension: The Fallacy of Ecological Operation without Construct Validity at the Individual Level." *Journal of Global Marketing* 29 (2016) 298–313.

Midgley, David F., et al. "Diversity and Unity of the Global Mosaic: Reimagining National Culture in the 21st Century." *INSEAD Working Papers Collection* no. 3 (January 13, 2019) 1–60.

Miles, Matthew B., et al. *Qualitative Data Analysis: A Methods Sourcebook*. 3rd ed. Thousand Oaks, CA: SAGE, 2014.

———. *Qualitative Data Analysis: A Methods Sourcebook*. 4th ed. Thousand Oaks, CA: SAGE, 2020.

"Mimicry, n." In *OED Online*. Oxford University Press. http://www.oed.com/view/Entry/118659.

Moore-Gilbert, Bart. *Postcolonial Theory: Contexts, Practices, Politics*. London: Verso, 1997.

Moreau, A. Scott, et al. *Effective Intercultural Communication: A Christian Perspective*. Grand Rapids: Baker Academic, 2014.

Moreau, A. Scott, et al. *Introducing World Missions: A Biblical, Historical, and Practical Survey*. 2nd ed. Grand Rapids: Baker Academic, 2015.

Moreau, A. Scott, and Beth Snodderly, eds. *Reflecting God's Glory Together: Diversity in Evangelical Mission*. Pasadena, CA: William Carey Library, 2011.

Nathan, Ganesh. "A Non-Essentialist Model of Culture: Implications of Identity, Agency and Structure Within Multinational/Multicultural Organizations." *International Journal of Cross Cultural Management* 15 (2015) 101–24.

Navarrete, Veronica, and Sharon Rae Jenkins. "Cultural Homelessness, Multiminority Status, Ethnic Identity Development, and Self Esteem." *International Journal of Intercultural Relations* 35 (2011) 791–804.

Nederveen Pieterse, Jan. "Globalisation as Hybridisation." *International Sociology* 9 (1994) 161–84.

———. *Globalization and Culture: Global Mélange*. 3rd ed. Lanham, MD: Rowman & Littlefield, 2015.

———. *Globalization and Culture: Global Mélange*. 4th ed. Lanham, MD: Rowman & Littlefield, 2020.

———. "Hybridity, So What?: The Anti-Hybridity Backlash and the Riddles of Recognition." *Theory, Culture and Society* 18 (2001) 219.

———. *Multipolar Globalization: Emerging Economies and Development*. New York: Routledge, 2018.

Nehrbass, Kenneth. *God's Image and Global Cultures: Integrating Faith and Culture in the Twenty-First Century*. Eugene, OR: Cascade, 2016.

Newcomb, Rachel. *Everyday Life in Global Morocco*. Bloomington: Indiana University Press, 2017.

Noble, Greg. "'It Is Home but It Is Not Home': Habitus, Field and the Migrant." *Journal of Sociology* 49 (2013) 341–56.

Oberg, Kalervo. "Cultural Shock: Adjustment to New Cultural Environments." *Practical Anthropology* 7 (1960) 177–82.

O'Donnell, Kelly, ed. *Doing Member Care Well: Perspectives and Practices From Around the World*. Pasadena, CA: William Carey Library, 2013.

———. *Global Member Care: The Pearls and Perils of Good Practice*. Vol. 1. 2 vols. Pasadena, CA: William Carey Library, 2011.

O'Donnell, Kelly, and Michèle Lewis O'Donnell, eds. *Global Member Care: Crossing Sectors for Serving Humanity*. Vol. 2. 2 vols. Pasadena, CA: William Carey Library, 2013.

Ohnuki-Tierney, Emiko. "Always Discontinuous/Continuous, and 'Hybrid' by Its Very Nature: The Culture Concept Historicized." *Ethnohistory* 52 (2005) 179–95.

O'Reilly, Karen. *Ethnographic Methods*. 2nd ed. Oxon, UK: Routledge, 2012.

Ortner, Sherry B. *Anthropology and Social Theory: Culture, Power, and the Acting Subject*. Durham, NC: Duke University Press, 2006.

———, ed. *The Fate of "Culture": Geertz and Beyond*. Berkeley: University of California Press, 1999.

Ott, Craig. "Globalization and Contextualization: Reframing the Task of Contextualization in the Twenty-First Century." *Missiology* 43 (2015) 43–58.

Papastergiadis, Nikos. "Tracing Hybridity in Theory." In *Debating Cultural Hybridity: Multi-Cultural Identities and the Politics of Anti-Racism*, edited by Pnina Werbner and Tariq Modood, 257–81. London: Zed, 1997.

Parker, David. "The Chinese Takeaway and the Diasporic Habitus: Space, Time, and Power Geometries." In *Un/Settled Multiculturalisms: Diasporas, Entanglements, Transruptions*, edited by Barnor Hesse, 73–95. London: Zed, 2000.

Patton, Michael Quinn. *Qualitative Research and Evaluation Methods: Integrating Theory and Practice*. 4th ed. Thousand Oaks, CA: SAGE, 2015.

Pierson, Paul E. *The Dynamics of Christian Mission: History Through a Missiological Perspective*. Pasadena, CA: William Carey International University Press, 2009.

Plueddemann, James E. *Leading Across Cultures: Effective Ministry and Mission in the Global Church*. Downers Grove, IL: IVP Academic, 2009.

———. *Teaching Across Cultures: Contextualizing Education for Global Mission*. Downers Grove, IL: IVP Academic, 2018.

Plummer, Jo, and Mats Tunehag. "A Growing Global Movement: Business as Mission." *Evangelical Missions Quarterly* 56 (2020) 32–34.

Pocock, Michael, et al. *Changing Face of World Missions: Engaging Contemporary Issues and Trends*. Encountering Mission. Grand Rapids, MI: Baker Academic, 2005.

Pollock, David C., et al. *Third Culture Kids: Growing up Among Worlds*. 3rd ed. Boston: Nicholas Brealey, 2017.

Prabhu, Anjali. *Hybridity: Limits, Transformations, Prospects*. Albany: State University of New York Press, 2007.

Pratt, Mary Louise. *Imperial Eyes: Travel Writing and Transculturation*. 2nd ed. New York: Routledge, 2008.

Reisacher, Evelyne A., ed. *Dynamics of Muslim Worlds: Regional, Theological, and Missiological Perspectives*. Downers Grove, IL: IVP Academic, 2017.

Robert, Dana L. *Christian Mission: How Christianity Became a World Religion*. Chichester, UK: Wiley-Blackwell, 2009.

Roembke, Lianne. *Building Credible Multicultural Teams*. Pasadena, CA: William Carey Library, 2000.

Rushdie, Salman. *The Satanic Verses*. New York: Viking, 1989.

Rutherford, Jonathan. "The Third Space: Interview with Homi Bhabha." In *Identity: Community, Culture, Difference*, edited by Jonathan Rutherford, 207–21. London: Lawrence & Wishart, 1990.

Rynkiewich, Michael A. "The Challenge of Teaching Mission in an Increasingly Mobile and Complex World." *International Bulletin of Mission Research* 44 (2020) 335–49.

———. "Corporate Metaphors and Strategic Thinking: 'The 10/40 Window' in the American Evangelical Worldview." *Missiology* 35 (2007) 217–41.

———. "'Do Not Remember the Former Things.'" *International Bulletin of Mission Research* 40 (2016) 308–17.

———. "Do We Need a Postmodern Anthropology for Mission in a Postcolonial World?" *Mission Studies: Journal of the International Association for Mission Studies* 28 (2011) 151–69.

———. "Mission in 'the Present Time': What About the People in Diaspora?" *International Journal of Frontier Missiology* 30 (2013) 103–14.

———. "Person in Mission: Social Theory and Sociality in Melanesia." *Missiology* 31 (2003) 155–68.

———. *Soul, Self, and Society: A Postmodern Anthropology for Mission in a Postcolonial World*. Eugene, OR: Cascade, 2011.

———. "The World in My Parish: Rethinking the Standard Missiological Model." *Missiology* 30 (2002) 301–21.

Said, Edward W. *Culture and Imperialism*. New York: Alfred A. Knopf, 1993.

———. *Orientalism*. New York: Vintage, 1979.

———. *Out of Place: A Memoir*. New York: Vintage, 1999.

Saldaña, Johnny. *The Coding Manual for Qualitative Researchers*. 2nd ed. Thousand Oaks, CA: SAGE, 2013.

———. *The Coding Manual for Qualitative Researchers*. 3rd ed. Thousand Oaks, CA: SAGE, 2016.

———. *Thinking Qualitatively: Methods of Mind*. Thousand Oaks, CA: SAGE, 2015.

Saldaña, Johnny, and Matt Omasta. *Qualitative Research: Analyzing Life*. Thousand Oaks, CA: SAGE, 2018.

Sam, David L., and John W. Berry, eds. *The Cambridge Handbook of Acculturation Psychology*. 2nd ed. Cambridge: Cambridge University Press, 2016.

Samson, Jane. *Race and Redemption: British Missionaries Encounter Pacific Peoples, 1797–1920*. Grand Rapids, MI: Eerdmans, 2017.

Sanneh, Lamin. *Translating the Message: The Missionary Impact on Culture*. 2nd ed. Maryknoll, NY: Orbis, 2009.

Sayer, Andrew. "Reflexivity and the Habitus." In *Conversations About Reflexivity*, edited by Margaret S. Archer, 108–22. Abingdon, UK: Routledge, 2010.

Scheele, Judith. *Village Matters: Knowledge, Politics and Community in Kabylia, Algeria*. Woodbridge, UK: James Currey, 2009.

Schreiter, Robert. "Cosmopolitanism, Hybrid Identities, and Religion." *Exchange* 40 (2011) 19–34.

Schreiter, Robert J. *The New Catholicity: Theology Between the Global and the Local.* Maryknoll: Orbis, 1997.

Shaw, R. Daniel. "Beyond Syncretism: A Dynamic Approach to Hybridity." *International Bulletin of Mission Research* 42 (2018) 6–19.

Shaw, R. Daniel, and William R. Burrows, eds. *Traditional Ritual as Christian Worship: Dangerous Syncretism or Necessary Hybridity?* American Society of Missiology Series 56. Maryknoll, NY: Orbis, 2018.

Shweder, Richard A. "Moral Maps, 'First World' Conceits, and the New Evangelists." In *Culture Matters: How Values Shape Human Progress,* edited by Lawrence E. Harrison and Samuel P. Huntington, 158–76. New York: Basic, 2000.

Silzer, Sheryl Takagi. *Biblical Multicultural Teams.* Pasadena, CA: William Carey International University Press, 2011.

Spivak, Gayatri Chakravorty. "Can the Subaltern Speak?" In *Marxism and the Interpretation of Culture,* edited by Cary Nelson and Lawrence Grossberg, 271–313. Urbana: University of Illinois Press, 1988.

Spradley, James P. *The Ethnographic Interview.* Long Grove, IL: Waveland, 1979.

Stake, Robert E. *The Art of Case Study Research.* Thousand Oaks, CA: SAGE, 1995.

Stockhammer, Philipp W. "Questioning Hybridity." In *Conceptualizing Cultural Hybridization: A Transdisciplinary Approach,* edited by Philipp Wolfgang Stockhammer, 1–3. Transcultural Research—Heidelberg Studies on Asia and Europe in a Global Context. Heidelberg, Germany: Springer, 2012.

"Stuart Hall (Cultural Theorist)." *Wikipedia,* January 30, 2021. https://en.wikipedia.org/w/index.php?title=Stuart_Hall_(cultural_theorist)&oldid=1003792592.

Sylvain, Renée. "Disorderly Development: Globalization and the Idea of 'Culture' in the Kalahari." *American Ethnologist* 32 (2005) 354–70.

Thomson, Greg. "The Growing Participator Approach (GPA) A Brief State of the Art and Some Practical Illustrations." *Growing Participator Approach* (blog), January 16, 2013. https://growingparticipatorapproach.wordpress.com/the-growing-participator-approach-gpa-a-brief-state-of-the-art-and-some-practical-illustrations/.

Tiénou, Tite. "Reflections on Michael A. Rynkiewich's 'Do Not Remember the Former Things.'" *International Bulletin of Mission Research* 40 (2016) 318–24.

Tira, Sadiri Joy, and Tetsunao Yamamori, eds. *Scattered and Gathered: A Global Compendium of Diaspora Missiology.* Eugene, OR: Wipf & Stock, 2016.

Touburg, Giorgio. "National Habitus: An Antidote to the Resilience of Hofstede's 'National Culture'?" *Journal of Organizational Change Management* 29 (2016) 81–92.

Trompenaars, Fons, and Charles Hampden-Turner. *Riding the Waves of Culture: Understanding Diversity in Global Business.* 3rd ed. New York: McGraw-Hill, 2012.

Trouillot, Michel-Rolph. "Adieu, Culture: A New Duty Arises." In *Anthropology Beyond Culture,* edited by Richard G. Fox and Barbara J. King. Oxford: Berg, 2002.

Tung, Rosalie L., and Alain Verbeke. "Beyond Hofstede and GLOBE: Improving the Quality of Cross-Cultural Research." *Journal of International Business Studies* 41 (2010) 1259–74.

Tylor, Edward Burnett. *Primitive Culture: Researches into the Development of Mythology, Philosophy, Religion, Language, Art and Custom.* 2nd ed. Vol. 1. Mineola, NY: Dover, 1873.

Useem, Ruth Hill, and Richard D. Downie. "Third-Culture Kids." *Today's Education* 65 (1976) 103–5.

Uytanlet, Juliet Lee. *The Hybrid Tsinoys: Challenges of Hybridity and Homogeneity as Sociocultural Constructs among the Chinese in the Philippines.* American Society of Missiology Monograph Series 28. Eugene, OR: Pickwick, 2016.

van der Veer, Peter. "'The Enigma of Arrival': Hybridity and Authenticity in the Global Space." In *Debating Cultural Hybridity: Multi-Cultural Identities and the Politics of Anti-Racism,* edited by Pnina Werbner and Tariq Modood, 90–105. London: Zed, 1997.

Venaik, Sunil, and Paul Brewer. "The Common Threads of National Cultures." *Australasian Marketing Journal (AMJ)* 23 (2015) 75–85.

———. "Critical Issues in the Hofstede and GLOBE National Culture Models." *International Marketing Review* 30 (2013) 469–82.

———. "National Culture Dimensions: The Perpetuation of Cultural Ignorance." *Management Learning* 47 (2016) 563–89.

Venn, Couze. "Narrating the Postcolonial." In *Spaces of Culture: City, Nation, World,* edited by Mike Featherstone and Scott Lash, 257–81. Theory, Culture & Society. London: SAGE, 1999.

Vivero, Veronica Navarrete, and Sharon Rae Jenkins. "Existential Hazards of the Multicultural Individual: Defining and Understanding 'Cultural Homelessness.'" *Cultural Diversity and Ethnic Minority Psychology* 5 (1999) 6–26.

Walls, Andrew F. *Crossing Cultural Frontiers: Studies in the History of World Christianity.* Maryknoll, NY: Orbis, 2017.

———. "The Gospel as Prisoner and Liberator of Culture." In *The Missionary Movement in Christian History: Studies in the Transmission of Faith,* 3–15. Maryknoll, New York: Orbis, 1996.

———. "Mission and Migration: The Diaspora Factor in Christian History." *Journal of African Christian Thought* 5 (2002) 3–11.

———. *The Missionary Movement in Christian History: Studies in the Transmission of Faith.* Maryknoll, NY: Orbis, 1996.

Wan, Enoch, ed. *Diaspora Missiology: Theory, Methodology, and Practice.* 2nd ed. Portland, OR: Institue of Diaspora Studies-U.S., 2014.

Wang, Bingyu, and Francis L. Collins. "Becoming Cosmopolitan? Hybridity and Intercultural Encounters Amongst 1.5 Generation Chinese Migrants in New Zealand." *Ethnic and Racial Studies* 39 (2016) 2777–95.

Weiss, Robert S. *Learning from Strangers: The Art and Method of Qualitative Interview Studies.* New York: Free, 1995.

Wenger, Etienne. *Communities of Practice: Learning, Meaning, And Identity.* Cambridge: Cambridge University Press, 1998.

Werbner, Pnina. "Essentialising Essentialism, Essentialising Silence: Ambivalence and Multiplicity in the Constructions of Racism and Ethnicity." In *Debating Cultural Hybridity: Multi-Cultural Identities and the Politics of Anti-Racism,* edited by Pnina Werbner and Tariq Modood, 226–54. London: Zed, 1997.

————. "Introduction: The Dialectics of Cultural Hybridity." In *Debating Cultural Hybridity: Multi-Cultural Identities and the Politics of Anti-Racism*, edited by Pnina Werbner and Tariq Modood, 1–26. London: Zed, 1997.

————. "The Limits of Cultural Hybridity: On Ritual Monsters, Poetic Licence and Contested Postcolonial Purifications." *Journal of the Royal Anthropological Institute* 7 (2001) 133.

Werbner, Pnina, and Tariq Modood, eds. *Debating Cultural Hybridity: Multi-Cultural Identities and the Politics of Anti-Racism*. London: Zed, 1997.

Wicker, Hans-Rudolf. "From Complex Culture to Cultural Complexity." In *Debating Cultural Hybridity: Multi-Cultural Identities and the Politics of Anti-Racism*, edited by Pnina Werbner and Tariq Modood, 29–45. London: Zed, 1997.

Willis, Michael. *Politics and Power in the Maghreb: Algeria, Tunisia and Morocco from Independence to the Arab Spring*. New York: Oxford University Press, 2014.

Wise, Amanda. "Sensuous Multiculturalism: Emotional Landscapes of Inter-Ethnic Living in Australian Suburbia." *Journal of Ethnic and Migration Studies* 36 (2010) 917–37.

Wuthnow, Robert, and Stephen Offutt. "Transnational Religious Connections." *Sociology of Religion* 69 (2008) 209–32.

Yin, Robert K. *Qualitative Research from Start to Finish*. 2nd ed. New York: Guilford, 2016.

Yip, George. "The Contour of a Post-Postmodern Missiology." *Missiology* 42 (2014) 399–411.

Young, Robert J. C. *Colonial Desire: Hybridity in Theory, Culture, and Race*. London: Routledge, 1995.

Yúdice, George. "Translator's Introduction: From Hybridity to Policy: For a Purposeful Cultural Studies." In *Consumers and Citizens: Globalization and Multicultural Conflicts*, by Néstor García Canclini, ix–xxxviii. Minneapolis: University Of Minnesota Press, 2001.

Zurlo, Gina A., et al. "Christianity 2019: What's Missing? A Call for Further Research." *International Bulletin of Mission Research* 43 (2019) 92–102.

Author Index

Abu-Lughod, Lila, 15, 18, 32, 40, 52, 53, 54, 61, 78, 221, 240
Adeney, Miriam, 45
Agar, Michael, 32, 141, 199–200, 221
Ahmad, Aijaz, 32, 35
Amselle, Jean-Loup, x
Anderson, Benedict, 18
Ang, Ien, xi, 9, 10, 13, 19, 20, 21–22, 23, 24, 35, 40, 70, 209, 213, 221, 273
Appadurai, Arjun, 8, 15, 42, 43, 221
Archer, Margaret S., 173
Arnett, Jeffrey Jensen, 232
Asad, Talal, 15
Atkinson, Paul, 48, 73
Austin, Clyde N., 189
Axford, Barrie, 13, 19, 28, 36, 37

Baker, Dwight P., 6
Bakhtin, M. M., 23, 25, 217
Bauman, Zygmunt, 212, 222
Baumann, Gerd, 15, 19, 159, 221–24, 225, 226, 228, 233, 235
Bayart, Jean-François, x
Bazeley, Patricia, 67, 276
Benet-Martínez, Verónica, 232
Berger, Peter L., 54
Berry, John W., 232, 275
Beyer, John, 189
Bhabha, Homi K., 13, 14, 15–16, 20, 22–24, 25–28, 32, 35, 37, 39, 40, 41, 42, 201, 204–5, 217, 273
Bloomberg, Linda D., 11, 74
Bonhoeffer, Dietrich, 132
Bosch, David J., 241

Bourdieu, Pierre, xi, 103, 170, 210–11, 216, 234
Brewer, Paul, 7, 8, 224
Brewster, E. Thomas, 79
Brewster, Elizabeth S., 79
Brinkmann, Svend, 66, 67
Brubaker, Rogers, 19, 32, 211, 234
Burke, Peter, 13, 15, 28, 35, 37
Burrows, William R., 45, 241
Buruma, Ian, 8

Charmaz, Kathy, 67, 68, 69, 276, 278, 282
Chiu, Chi-Yue, 232
Cho, Yong Joong, 7
Christofferson, Ethan J., 45
Clifford, James, 15
Collins, Francis L., 40
Cooper, Frederick, 32
Court, Deborah, 4, 5, 67, 74, 276, 277

Deleuze, Gilles, 14
Derrida, Jacques, 14, 204
Dickie, Virginia A., 62
Dirlik, Arif, 15, 32, 36
Downie, Richard D., 238

Emerson, Robert M., 48, 67, 276
Escobar, Samuel, 231
Ewing, Katherine Pratt, 40

Fanon, Frantz, 16
Farah, Warrick, 119
Featherstone, Mike, 15
Fellows, Richard, 7

Subject Index